Edited by Virgil W. Dea__

John Brown to Bob Dole

Movers and
Shakers in
Kansas
History

University Press of Kansas

Published by the University Press of Kansas (Lawrence, Kansas 66045),
which was organized by the Kansas Board of Regents and is operated
and funded by Emporia State University, Fort Hays State University,
Kansas State University, Pittsburg State University,
the University of Kansas, and Wichita State University

Library of Congress Cataloging-in-Publication Data

John Brown to Bob Dole : movers and shakers in Kansas history / edited
    by Virgil W. Dean.
      p.   cm.
    Includes bibliographical references and index.
    ISBN 978-0-7006-1429-5 (cloth : alk. paper)
    ISBN 978-0-7006-1723-4 (pbk. : alk. paper)
    1. Kansas—Biography. 2. Kansas—History.   I. Dean, Virgil W.
  F680.J64 2006
    978.1—dc22   2005022808

British Library Cataloguing-in-Publication Data is available.

Printed in the United States of America

10 9 8 7 6 5 4 3 2 1

The paper used in this publication is recycled and contains 30 percent
postconsumer waste. It is acid free and meets the minimum
requirements of the American National Standard for Permanence of
Paper for Printed Library Materials Z39.48-1992.

To my parents,

Adell W. (1926–2004) and Nelda "Margie" Dean,

Kansans who made the difference in my life

Contents

Preface

Few scholars today would agree with Thomas Carlyle's assertion that "History is the essence of innumerable biographies," or with Ralph Waldo Emerson, who opined, "There is properly no history; only biography." And we certainly would reject out of hand the former's belief that "the history of the world is but the biography of great men." For good reason, the "Great Man" approach to historical interpretation fell from grace long ago; nevertheless, most would agree that biography is a legitimate tool for studying the past, and the reading public continues to devour biographical tomes about famous women and men, be they politicians, explorers, military leaders, artists, entertainers, or celebrities of other sorts. Thus, we hope a collection of original biographical essays focusing on the lives and times of "representative" Kansans who made a difference will find a receptive audience and enhance our understanding of the state's history.

Interestingly, that history (and biography), because of the unusual and momentous circumstances of Kansas' birth, always has been of no little controversy and of great interest to its people. Although many of its early chroniclers were partisans and their stories far too celebratory, we nevertheless can appreciate their enthusiasm for our state's history and hope for a rekindling of some of that traditional fascination with a unique past as we approach the 2011 sesquicentennial of Kansas' birth as a state.

Kansas historiography is *not* littered with many great biographical studies, but Kansas history is indeed unique, significant, and full of fascinating biographies—interesting and important individuals who made a difference and whose life stories can tell us much about our past. Thus, *John Brown to Bob Dole: Movers and Shakers in Kansas History* explores a century and a half of Kansas history through the lives of its people—representative characters associated with the incidents and issues of the past that molded the character of Kansas and Kansans, women and men who arguably effected change in their respective arenas.

To stave off some critics, perhaps it should be said that this is not a book just about famous or interesting Kansans. And it is not a "celebration" of prominent women and men who have called Kansas home. It is a study of some of the many Kansans who have "made a difference" in both positive and negative ways. The selections were carefully and thoughtfully made, but anyone with more than a superficial knowledge of Kansas history, including the editor, could put together another list or two of twenty-seven Kansans equally deserving of such attention.

Thanks are due many individuals, I am sure. First among them, however, must be Fred Woodward for approaching me in mid-2002 with an idea—suggested to him by Senator Sam Brownback—for a collection of new biographical essays on notable Kansans whose lives helped color the character of our state. Second, as always, a big thank-you is due to my wife, Jan Dean, whose love and patience with me and my history habit are seemingly limitless. Because of the nature of this project, my greatest gratitude is owed to the twenty-six contributors—many of whom I am privileged to count among my personal friends as well as professional colleagues—who made it all possible.

John Brown
to Bob Dole

Introduction: Kansas History, Kansas Biography

Virgil W. Dean

"If it were possible to obliterate the history of Kansas there would be little found within its boundaries to make it distinguished among the states of this Union," wrote Edwin C. Manning, president of the Kansas State Historical Society, in 1911. "Other states have higher mountains, deeper rivers, broader lakes, more extensive forests, richer minerals, as fertile soil, as salubrious a clime, larger cities, more lofty spires and greater universities. What, then is there that at the mention of the name of Kansas spurs the youth, quickens the blood, inspires the muses and thrills the patriot? It is the spirit of its history."[1]

A decade before, another president and a longtime secretary of the society, William E. Connelley, opened his laudatory biography of James Henry Lane with an emphasis on the individual's impact on his state's unique history. "The high order of Kansas society is the result of the great intelligence and the exalted genius of the founders of the State," wrote Connelley. The history of Kansas was "an inspiration" to its citizens in large part because "this State was born of a struggle for liberty and freedom. So fierce were the fires kindled here in these causes that they purified the nation. It is only necessary for us to be well informed in the history of our State to make us love her, to make us devoted to her, to make us patriotic. The history of Kansas is full of men who will grow in stature as long as man loves liberty." Connelley's prose is purple and his interpretation far too simplistic, but few would challenge his view that "great men [and women] leave the impress of their genius upon the institutions they help to found" and that "to rightly understand the institutions of our State, it is necessary that we should have some knowledge of the [women and] men who builded it."[2]

The history of Kansas, of course, commenced several thousand years before Connelley and Manning's patriots arrived on the scene.[3] But the history of the territory and state, and of those men and women who sought to shape it in their own image, began in the mid-nineteenth century. For the last one hundred and fifty–plus years, these Kansans have made a difference for good, and sometimes for ill, in their diverse areas of endeavor, and their biographies can tell us a great deal about our collective history.

Some of these notable Kansans can be classified as "agitators," individuals who excited public opinion and moved their fellow citizens to action in response to real and perceived political, social, and economic problems. In part, at least, this is so because of the state's identification with several "radical" reform movements, from abolitionism to Populism to civil rights. Kansas agitators such as John Brown, James H. Lane, William H. Russell, Mary E. Lease, Kate Richards O'Hare, Gerald B. Winrod, Esther Brown, and Vern Miller shook up the status quo and in some cases brought about significant change.

Not surprisingly, Kansas also has hosted its share of people who might more appropriately be classified as "motivators." These individuals were more traditional in their approach than the "agitators," but they were no less significant and often had a more permanent impact. Thus, all Americans and especially all Kansans can look to Clarina I. H. Nichols, Mary "Mother" Bickerdyke, Charles M. Sheldon, William Allen White, Alfred M. Landon, Walter A. Huxman, Dwight D. Eisenhower, and more recently Bob Dole for examples of leadership or as galvanizers of social and political change. In short, through persistence, example, and the persuasiveness of their ideas, these individuals emerged as leaders and perhaps shapers of national and state opinion.

Finally, Kansas can lay claim to a good number of real "innovators," people who effected change through the introduction of new ideas or methods of doing everything from growing and grinding wheat to protecting the public's health. In this regard, contributing authors have examined the ways in which their particular Kansas innovator's accomplishment has changed the face and character of Kansas and the nation. Joseph McCoy, Theodore C. Henry, Frederick H. Harvey, Bernhard Warkentin, Samuel J. Crumbine, Emanuel and Marcet Haldeman-Julius, Ray Hugh Garvey, John Steuart Curry, Gordon Parks, and Wes Jackson are just a few of the Kansans who deserve the "innovator" epithet and warrant our attention.

Although many have focused on the "founders," each of the five chronological eras covered in this volume—Bleeding Kansas and the Civil War, 1854–1865; the postwar period of settlement (or resettlement) and development, 1865–1890; the age of reform, 1890–1920; reaction, depression, and war, 1920–1945; and Kansans and Kansas since World War II—featured many Kansans who made a difference. Each contained its agitators, motivators, and innovators.

Before the first of our five historical eras, Kansas was "unorganized" territory—the home of numerous indigenous peoples, Plains tribes and less nomadic Indians such as the Kansas, Pawnees, and Osages. As part of "Indian Country," this land was shared after 1830 with about twenty different tribes from east of the Mississippi River who had been resettled west of Missouri under the federal government's Indian removal policy. It was promised for "as long as the grass grew and water ran," but in 1853 and 1854 the government commenced the negotiation of another removal, and with the ever-increasing desire for further westward expansion, the U.S. Congress passed the Kansas-Nebraska Bill on May 26, 1854. Immediately, the "Kansas Question" became the focus of an emotionally charged national debate, and, in the territory soon called "Bleeding Kansas," the two sides—proslavery and antislavery settlers—squared off in a sometimes violent contest.[4]

The Kansas-Nebraska Act provided that territorial settlers themselves, not the U.S. Congress, decide the slave question—"popular sovereignty." As a result, partisans on both sides of the Mason-Dixon Line focused on Kansas and the question as to whether it would be slave or free. In the beginning, at least, many appeared to believe that Nebraska would enter the Union as a free state and Kansas as a slave state. Because the neighboring state of Missouri was a slave state, this seemed like the natural outcome. But reopening the "settled" question of slavery in the territories was more than the growing antislavery forces in the North could tolerate, and they began to organize to contest the area.

As many scholars have demonstrated over the years, "the struggle that ensued in Kansas Territory was, above all, a contest to control land," but to really control land and capital one must also be in a position to influence the political process. Missourians with an immediate stake in the outcome, such as the entrepreneur and slaveholder William H. Russell, quickly poured across their border with Kansas. David Rice Atchison, Missouri's senior senator from Platte City, and the brothers John H. and Benjamin F. Stringfellow "urged their people to resist the abolitionist plot to surround their state with free territory" and helped establish the proslavery town of Atchison. Russell and his friends did the same for Leavenworth, staking claims to land inside and outside the city, establishing a significant financial infrastructure, and working to control the political structures to protect their investment.[5]

But, as these Missourians soon learned, geographic proximity was no guarantee for the long term. In addition to "free soilers" from their own and other nearby states who wanted to seek their fortune in the newly opened territories, the New England Emigrant Aid Company and other groups formed throughout the North and Northeast to promote and support free-state settlement. The first organized band of New Englanders arrived in the territory in July 1854 and soon founded the city of Lawrence, forever marking it as the focal point of abolitionist activity. Among the first to settle in Lawrence and the vicinity were Charles and Sarah Robinson, Samuel C. Pomeroy, and Clarina I. H. Nichols, who arrived with the fourth Emigrant Aid party in October.

They were followed in 1855 by many others, with wide-ranging views on the major issues of the day. Best known among the ultra-abolitionists was John Brown, who followed his sons to Kansas in the fall, beginning his brief but momentous Kansas sojourn on their claim southwest of Osawatomie. Another was James H. Lane, a Democratic politician from Indiana who soon staked his future on the free-state movement and became one of its most dynamic if controversial leaders. Lane's appeal and popularity among a large segment of the Kansas people can be explained in part by the fact that he was "one of them." As Lane told a large crowd in Wisconsin in June 1856, he was always "surprised to find that a great many people suppose that Kansas is settled mostly from New England, and thence abolitionists. The fact was that Kansas was mostly settled by western men . . . conservative people," not abolitionists.[6]

As Nicole Etcheson demonstrated, however, Bleeding Kansas radicalized Lane and his fellow Westerners, and they turned the tide for the free-state cause. By the summer of 1858 they had won control of the territorial legislature at the polls and defeated the infamous, proslavery Lecompton Constitution. When delegates met at Wyandotte in July 1859 to draft the territory's fourth and final constitution, the slavery issue was all but decided. They adopted a free-state instrument, which, thanks in large part to Clarina Nichols, contained important rights for the women of Kansas, and the electorate ratified it later that year. Kansas subsequently joined the Union as the thirty-fourth state on January 29, 1861, amidst the dissolution of that Union during the secession crisis that preceded the nation's tragic Civil War.[7]

As Kansas' great but tragic first decade came to a close, many looked forward with great anticipation. Kansans longed for the end of the Civil War for many reasons, not the least of which was their desire to get on with the full-time business of building a state. These endeavors, of course, had not come to a standstill with the shots at Fort Sumter four years before, and much business activity and promotion was carried on during the hostilities. The Kansas State Agricultural Society, for example, was founded in 1862 "to promote [settlement and] the improvement of Agriculture, and its kindred arts, throughout the State," and the society's official journal, *The Kansas Farmer,* commenced publication on May 1, 1863. "When this unholy rebellion is crushed," predicted the *State Record,* "a tide of immigration must set into Kansas. No other new state offers better inducements. It is sure to come. Then will grow up a free, industrious, frugal State—a State that we trust will always be true to the principles of Freedom, for which in its infancy it has suffered so much." Despite the fact that certain brutes had murdered "some of the best and bravest of our citizens," said Governor Thomas Carney in January 1864, "in all else, abundance enriched the producer and all the industrial class."[8]

Such optimism carried Kansans into their era of settlement and development. Kansas was the place to be, and the place to go. Kansans were interested in economic development, and Kansas proved itself quite tolerant of the foreign born and even, at times, African Americans, who came to the state before, during, and after the war. American Indians were the exception, of course, and they were forced to move aside once again to make way for Euro-American resettlement of yet another agricultural frontier.

The dynamic growth and expansion that marked this period can be measured in several ways. A look at population statistics shows that from an enumerated population of 107,206 in 1860, the Kansas figure climbed to one million in 1880 and nearly a million and a half (1,428,000) in 1890. Most were native born and had come to Kansas from another Union state, and many were veterans, as we learn in Bruce Kahler's essay on Mary Bickerdyke and the veteran community that venerated her. However, the state's foreign-born population, most of whom hailed from the British Isles or Germany, was substantial. European immigrants, as a percentage of the population (13.3), peaked in 1870, but they continued to come, including significant numbers from southern and eastern Europe around the turn of the twentieth century. African Americans made up 4 percent of the population by the 1880s.

Fueling much of this growth was the nation's premier nineteenth-century industry—the railroad, also the greatest promoter and facilitator of Western settlement. In January 1864 just two railroads had commenced construction in Kansas, and only fifty miles of the Kansas Pacific's initial line had been completed. Within five years of the war's end, however, the line had reached the Kansas-Colorado border and the state had about one thousand miles of track, with much more under construction. Thanks to the federal government's generous subsidy (the Pacific Railroad Act of 1862), Kansas' two major carriers held vast tracts of land that they wished to sell to industrious farmers and entrepreneurs in order to cover the cost of construction and to guarantee future profits from the shipment of passengers and freight.

In one way or another, the "iron horse" was largely responsible for the presence in Kansas of such representative "developers" as Joseph G. McCoy, the visionary cattle trader who for all practical purposes brought the cattle-trailing industry and the "cowboy" to Kansas; T. C. Henry, promoter of large-scale wheat production on the fertile plains of central Kansas; the Mennonite miller Bernhard Warkentin, whose innovations, perhaps, did more to make Kansas the "wheat state" than those of any other individual; and, of course, the innovative restaurateur Frederick Harvey, who made travel to and through Kansas much less tiresome.

The "long drives" from Texas made the Kansas towns of Abilene, Newton, Ellsworth, Wichita, and Dodge City famous. From these towns the cattle were shipped east by rail. This colorful interlude lasted only about twenty years, but the end of the trail-driving era did not mean the death of the industry. It did change dramatically, however, and in the process became one of the state's most significant. High-quality, homegrown livestock became increasingly important; thousands of head of cattle fattened on the bluestem grasses of the

Flint Hills; and by 1881 Kansas City, Kansas, had emerged as a major cattle- and hog-marketing center, second only to Chicago, with a multimillion-dollar meatpacking industry.[9]

Also closely linked to railroads, and of course to agriculture, is perhaps Kansas' most significant—if little heralded—industry: milling. Gristmills were established early on, and as agriculture, especially wheat farming, flourished, milling and grain storage made Kansas a milling state. By the mid-1880s flour and feed milling had become the state's leading industry, and grain storage fa- cilities dotted the Kansas landscape, becoming a symbol of the state's abun- dance and economic vitality. (In the twentieth century, as Craig Miner demon- strates in his essay in Part 4, R. H. Garvey and his elevators took the grain storage industry to a new level.) During the 1880s an even greater "revolution" transformed the industry. Hard winter wheat, especially Turkey Red, became the small grain of choice on the Kansas plains, and milling technology adapted to the change. Kansas City became the state's major milling center by 1900, but over 350 mills of various capacities continued to operate throughout the state, and at least a dozen smaller cities could claim to be significant mill towns well into the twentieth century.[10]

But all was not well during this period of rapid growth. Mark Twain used a prominent Kansas politician, Senator Samuel Pomeroy, as the model for the corrupt Senator Dilworthy in *The Gilded Age,* and segments of the state's population were not happy with their plight. Kansas became a breeding ground for numerous reform and third-party movements, and some thought Kansans were just prone to agitate for change and for legislating good behavior. A successful prohibition movement resulted in a constitutional ban on the manufacture and sale of intoxicating liquors, and throughout this era the women's suffrage movement gradually gained more and more parity for women at the Kansas polls.[11]

The nineteenth-century reform movement most closely identified with Kansas and the state's predominantly rural population, however, was Popu- lism. During this age of industrialization, Kansas farmers, like those elsewhere in the West and the South, could see only a growing inequality in a system that seemed to favor industry over agriculture as it never had before. Many of these Kansas farmers turned first to the National Farmers' Alliance and Industrial Union (Farmers' Alliance), with its gospel of monetary reform and coopera- tives, and then supported the movement's broader agenda when it entered the political arena in 1890. Reformers such as William A. "Old Whiskers" Peffer,

Jeremiah "Sockless Jerry" Simpson, "Little" Annie Diggs, and, of course, Mary E. Lease carried the People's Party banner and articulated the grievances of their farm constituents. These Kansas firebrands accepted the proposition that it was necessary to "establish popular control over the commercial and industrial system to insure a political democracy." For them, Populism was a cry for "political justice" and not just "a redress of economic grievances," and they often "complained more of the arbitrary and unrestricted power of the railroads and their potential for oppression than of excessive tolls in themselves." In the tradition of all good third-party movements, they also introduced and popularized a far-reaching reform agenda that would in many respects come to fruition after the turn of the century.[12]

William Allen White, who contributed to the demise of the Populists and the success of conservative Republicanism over the young, progressive Democrat/Populist from Nebraska, William Jennings Bryan, with the editorial "What's the Matter with Kansas?" apologized just a few years later for much of what he had written and came to support much of the Populist agenda. White admitted that he was never really able to figure the Populists out. The best the Republicans could do, he wrote, "was to yell 'Socialism' at the Populists and predict a recurrence of the French Revolution."[13]

Populists failed to accomplish any "revolutionary" reforms, but they did attract state and national attention to key issues, and Populist legislation made life somewhat better for the laborer. Such laws helped farmers through stockyard regulation and by providing for the inspection, grading, weighing, and handling of grain. Populist legislatures created the bank commissioner's office and adopted the Australian (secret) ballot. And under the leadership of progressive reformers after the turn of the century, many of the goals first raised by Populists were accomplished.

Unlike Populism, progressivism was not synonymous with a political party. In fact, with the exception of 1912, there was no progressive party, and "progressives" could be found in large numbers in both major parties and various third-party movements—the term included everything from managerial reform on the right to democratic socialism on the extreme left, and it has been argued that "progressivism was not a movement in any meaningful sense." "There was no single progressive constituency, no agreed-upon agenda, and no unifying organization or leadership. . . . The term progressivism refers not to a single movement but to a widespread, many-sided effort after 1900 to build a better society in the United States."[14]

In Kansas the usual approach is to view the progressive movement through the activities of the "Insurgent" Republicans, or "Boss Busters"—William Allen White, Joseph L. Bristow, Henry J. Allen, and Walter R. Stubbs, among others. Devoted disciples of Theodore Roosevelt and his brand of progressivism for the first dozen or more years of the twentieth century, these relatively young Kansas politicos made a difference in their state and nation. They helped create an environment conducive to change in many areas, and as a result Kansas women finally achieved equal suffrage, workers gained better conditions on the job and a measure of security, and electoral reforms increased the opportunity for voter participation. Kansas progressivism also included the pioneering public health efforts of Dr. Samuel J. Crumbine, secretary of the State Board of Health; the social gospel activities of the Rev. Charles M. Sheldon; and even the socialist agitations of Kate Richards O'Hare and the "radicals" of Girard, Kansas' *Appeal to Reason* (included in an impressive lineup of editors and contributors was Emanuel Haldeman-Julius, who, with his wife, Marcet, subsequently brought classic literature and new social commentary to the masses through the Little Blue Book series).

Unfortunately, the reform impulse in Kansas seems often to have included a moralistic undercurrent that on occasion justified legal or extralegal actions to force conformity—prohibition and anticigarette laws are the most obvious examples—and create a climate of intolerance. "Red Kate" O'Hare, a mother of four, was convicted and imprisoned under provisions of the Espionage Act during the "Great War" for not supporting the war effort; most Kansans, "progressive" and otherwise, supported President Woodrow Wilson's drive for "100 percent Americanism," which spilled over into the 1920s and seemingly justified a more conservative, less tolerant society.[15]

That decade was marked by positive and negative developments. Intolerance, exemplified by an active and politically powerful Ku Klux Klan, and labor strife, especially among southeast Kansas coal miners (Governor Allen's Industrial Court remedy was heralded as a nationally significant progressive measure by some and as a reactionary, promanagement measure by others), were characteristic. Farmers, who for the most part had enjoyed an unprecedented period of prosperity during the 1910s, suffered the most in an economic recession/depression that came in the wake of World War I. It hit farmers especially hard because they had expanded their production to meet wartime demand and incurred considerable debt to do so. In part because of these circumstances, farmers were again energized to use their organizations and receptive politicians, such as Kansas senator Arthur Capper, to get the government to do something to address their "problem."

But, although the decade's "prosperity" certainly did not reach everyone, many enjoyed the fruits of the mass-production, mass-consumption economy. Living conditions improved in rural areas too. There were naysayers, of course: Arthur Capper, editor and publisher of the *Topeka Daily Capital,* for one, warned his readers in 1914 what happened when "the success of the nation" became inseparably linked to "Prosperity," which had come to mean "big transactions, growth on every hand, increase of capital and facilities in all directions . . . in short, that the most rapid development was what prosperity signified, and therefore the fulfillment of the idea of American life." In other words, if growth is good, more growth is better. In 1925 Capper's newspaper lamented the fact that "the small business man is gradually giving way before the corporation, the chain stores, the mail order 'octopus' and so on."[16]

As the Depression decade opened, Kansans were, at the very least, apprehensive, so they elected a Democratic governor, Harry H. Woodring. Two years later they even voted for a Democrat, Franklin Delano Roosevelt, for president (despite the fact that a native Kansan, Vice President Charles Curtis, was running for reelection on the Hoover ticket). Even more disconcerting to the traditional leadership was the substantial vote cast for Dr. John R. Brinkley of Milford. The "good doctor," who became famous during the 1920s for his goat-gland operations and as a pioneer broadcaster, effectively used his Milford radio station, KFKB, during his 1930 write-in campaign for governor. His populist message during this time of severe depression was obviously attractive to many voters, and Brinkley again sought the governorship in 1932, finishing in third place with 244,607 votes, only 34,000 votes behind the winner, Republican Alfred M. Landon. Statewide voter discontent during the 1930s also was reflected in support for Wichita's anti-Semitic preacher and publisher, Gerald B. Winrod, and nationally for such characters and vague programs as Father Charles E. Coughlin's National Union for Social Justice, Dr. Francis E. Townsend's Old Age Revolving Pension scheme, and Senator Huey P. Long's Share-the-Wealth movement. Although they reelected Landon in 1934, Kansas voters elected two Democratic members to the U.S. House of Representatives in 1932—one, Kathryn O'Loughlin McCarthy of Hays, was the first woman elected to Congress from Kansas—and one Democratic U.S. senator, George McGill. They chose another Democratic governor, Walter A. Huxman, a New Dealer from Hutchinson, in 1936, the same year that they endorsed a second term for FDR instead of supporting the national candidacy of their own governor.[17]

The Kansas experience, of course, was little different than that of the other forty-seven states. Like the rest of the country, Kansans were still suffering the effects of the Great Depression when war contracts and demand began to stimulate the economy about 1940, doing what government relief programs could not.

Kansans, like most Midwesterners, tended to be more isolationist in their attitudes toward foreign affairs than some other Americans. But when war came to America on December 7, 1941, most enthusiastically joined the crusade against worldwide fascism and totalitarianism. Some Kansas editors and other individuals, however, openly opposed U.S. involvement in this second World War, as they had the first, and retained their strident antiwar positions. A few became increasingly anti-Semitic, anti-Roosevelt, and critical of the war effort. Kansas has the dubious distinction of having had three such opponents of the war indicted for treason and included as defendants in the "mass sedition" trial of 1942–1944 (*U.S. v. Winrod*, July 1942)—Wichita editors Gerald B. Winrod and Elmer J. Garner and the latter's son, James F. Garner. The federal government's zealous pursuit and prosecution of homegrown fascists before and especially after U.S. entry into the war gave rise to the so-called Brown Scare, which in turn fostered an environment conducive to the Red Scare of the late 1940s and the 1950s.[18]

For the most part, however, Kansans who experienced the war on the home front bought bonds, participated in civil defense activities, organized scrap drives, tolerated shortages and rationing, worked in war-related industries, and provided many other forms of support. Although some local production was good only for the duration of the war, industrial expansion laid the foundation for a truly mixed Kansas economy. Wichita's aircraft industry (especially Boeing, Beech, and Cessna), which was significant before the war, continued to prosper after, benefiting greatly from the war boom and demands of the Cold War to follow. Other companies also thrived: Coleman Company "had over $1 million in defense contracts in 1941, and through the war provided ammunition chests, shell casings, fuses, and, most memorably to many servicemen, the famous Coleman portable stoves."[19]

Kansas was, according to Craig Miner, more "like the nation" in the years following World War II.[20] But an interesting cast of Kansas characters, such as Esther Brown, Dwight D. Eisenhower, Gordon Parks, Vern Miller, Bob Dole, and Wes Jackson, to name just a few, have made a difference on the national and state levels.

Kansas in 1949, according to the journalist and author Kenneth S. Davis, expressed "on the popular level a burgeoning internationalism," but Davis and others also thought Kansans had grown complacent and too conservative. Milton Eisenhower, the younger brother of the general who would soon be president, wrote, "It would have occurred to no one to call Kansas complacent or commonplace in the years from 1860 to about 1915. On the contrary, Kansas was known as among the most progressive of all States, high-minded, quick to react to needs, a leader in a dozen forms of social legislation." But during the intervening decades, "a complacency strange to Kansas tended to smother honest criticism and discourage creative genius. Kansas lost its distinction as a social barometer for the nation, an exciting idea, a prophecy; she became simply one of the midland States." Davis agreed, writing in 1954 that the Kansas he knew had "not been distinctive for its intellectual leadership and political progressivism. On the contrary, a smug conservatism has generally prevailed in our ruling circles. . . . The typical Kansas politician has long ceased to be a brave, colorful fellow who coins vivid phrases, makes symbolic gestures around which social movements can cohere and so exercise personal leadership."[21]

Fifty years later another native Kansan, the author and historian Thomas Frank, wrote a similar lament in yet another "What's the Matter with Kansas?" Frank described a "Great Backlash," which, "like a French Revolution in reverse . . . pushes the spectrum of the acceptable to the right, to the right, farther to the right." He proceeded to examine this late-twentieth-century phenomenon "by focusing on a place where the political shift has been dramatic: my home state of Kansas, a reliable hotbed of leftist reform movements a hundred years ago that today ranks among the nation's most eager audiences for bearers of backlash buncombe."[22]

But the intervening half-century was not without significance for Kansas and Kansans. Nationally, perhaps the most historic developments were in the area of civil rights, and some of these battles were fought in Kansas. There were "no Jim Crow laws in the state of Kansas," observed the editor of the *Plaindealer,* Kansas City's fine African American newspaper, "but throughout the Republican dominated state under a Republican Governor, the 'Jim Crow rule' supplants the 'Jim Crow Law.'" In 1950 the nationally known Kansas author Nelson Antrim Crawford called attention to the state's "weak civil rights law" that a rather complacent legislature did not seem inclined to strengthen: "Negroes and Mexicans are excluded from many theatres and most restaurants and hotels, and a good many towns operate segregated elementary schools." Ironically, Topeka, the capital of "Free Kansas," took center stage in the landmark *Brown v. Board of Education* case, which overturned the "separate-but-equal" doctrine and launched the modern civil rights movement.[23] Most Kansans, perhaps, were reluctant to recognize the existence of this problem and slow to accept the need to change the status quo. Others, such as Walter Huxman, Esther Brown, and Gordon Parks, did what they could to call attention to inequities in the state and nation and to remedy the situation.

Another Kansan, Dwight D. Eisenhower, everyone's favorite wartime hero, presided over this transition decade as president of the United States. America in the 1950s witnessed the rise of a new and very different movement for civil rights that emphasized direct action over litigation, and Ike did not always support this movement with the vigor some would have liked. The decade also saw the institutionalization of America's Cold War containment policy. Appropriately, Eisenhower launched his political career while in his hometown of Abilene to lay the cornerstone for the Eisenhower Museum on June 6, 1952. After announcing his intention to seek the Republican presidential nomination, Ike waged an aggressive campaign, and at the polls an adoring electorate gave him a landslide victory over Democrat Adlai E. Stevenson II. Four years later President Eisenhower was reelected by an even larger margin, again over Stevenson.

The thousands of returning veterans who came home to Kansas soon after General Eisenhower's triumphant postwar visit—veterans such as Robert J. Dole of Russell—helped repeal the state's almost seventy-year-old prohibition amendment and launch a new era. They changed the face of Kansas, and the nation, by taking advantage of the GI Bill and attending colleges and trade schools in record numbers—many would not even have considered higher education an option before the war.

The World War II generation led a very different Kansas, socially and economically, than the one its members had experienced in their youth. The state's economy was now genuinely diverse, even though agriculture was still a large and important part of the mix. Changes in the nature of agriculture and industry meant new problems and issues related to such things as water, land use, and conservation. The preservation of the tall-grass prairie ecosystem was of prime concern to many throughout the era. Beginning in the late 1950s, Kansans confronted this issue, with some arguing for the sanctity of private property and agricultural stewardship and others insisting that the only way to protect this fragile ecosystem was through the creation of a national tall-grass prairie park.

Agriculture underwent change of revolutionary proportions just before the dawn of this new era. Kansas agriculture had been in the early stages of a demographic transformation and in the midst of a "technological revolution" prior to World War II, and the state's aging U.S. senator, Arthur Capper, worried about the viability of the "family farm," which "should not be a speculative enterprise. It should not be a one-crop or a one-project business. The activities on it should be diversified for the safety of the family unit which operates it." In Capper's America, this kind of agriculture was much preferred over large commercial enterprises. Despite Capper's entreaties and the lamentations of many others about the loss of a way of life, the agricultural landscape changed dramatically, especially during the last half of the twentieth century. Indeed, once the yeoman became a commercial producer, farming became less and less a way of life and more and more a business. During most of the twentieth century a predominant trend in American agriculture was toward fewer but larger farms. About 1910 Kansas had 178,000 farms averaging 288 acres each; by midcentury it had 135,000 averaging 374 acres. This trend accelerated thereafter so that by the mid-1990s Kansas had 65,000 farms averaging 730 acres each. In "wheat country" the average is more than 1,000 acres, and in Thomas County—focal point of Ray Garvey's farming enterprise—one of the state's leading producers of winter wheat, the average farm size is 1,285 acres. These immense production plants are owned and operated by families, corporations, and family corporations. Increasingly since World War II, absentee landlords, often called "sidewalk" or "suitcase" farmers, depending on how far from the farm they live, have run them. In the fall of 1999 Secretary of Agriculture Dan Glickman, a former Kansas congressman, worried that America would soon have just two kinds of farmers: "megaproducers" and "hobby farmers."[24]

Corporation or large-scale farming was certainly not invented in the post–World War II era, but it has become more dominant than ever before. The issues involving the establishment of huge corporate hog farms and dairy operations have split Kansas communities. For some it is simply an issue of economics. For others, such as Wes Jackson, quality of life issues and sustainability take precedence.

Federal census data in 1950 revealed that Kansas was no longer a "rural" state, as more than half of all Kansans then lived in an urban area. In 1960 the enumerated population exceeded two million, and in the 1990s the population topped 2.5 million. But despite relatively steady population growth over its nearly century and a half of statehood, Kansas has some twenty-first-century population-related issues to face—rural depopulation and aging, gentrification and sprawl, for example. As in the past, Kansas needs a crop of leaders (twenty-first-century agitators, motivators, and innovators) to take up these new challenges. Unfortunately, this commodity seems in short supply at present, and the concerns expressed by Ken Davis and Milton Eisenhower over fifty years ago ring even more true at present.

Whether politician, social activist, artist, or entrepreneur, how did the individual Kansans examined in this volume, and how will those who elicit this kind of attention in the future, impact their world and change our perception of the state and its people? Individuals do make a difference in the history of a state or nation. The objective of this collection of selected biographies is to explore the lives of notable Kansans who affected the state's history and exemplify some of those issues and characteristics that make the Sunflower State worthy of popular and scholarly attention—the agitators, motivators, and innovators who made Kansas *Kansas*. "Biography is, of the various kinds of narrative writing," wrote Samuel Johnson, "that which is most eagerly read and most easily applied to the purposes of life." Thus, by examining the lives of representative Kansans—their blemishes as well as their many admirable traits and accomplishments—we can expect (or at least hope) to turn a new generation on to "the spirit" of Kansas history and provide all with a better understanding of ourselves as a people: Kansans, Americans, and citizens of the world.

PART ONE

BLEEDING KANSAS AND THE

CIVIL WAR, 1854–1865

No history can ever be written which will be satisfactory to those who took part in those early struggles. It was a time of intense excitement, and those who passed through those scenes retain vivid impressions of them. Any description will seem tame compared with the graphic picture they have in mind.

Then it is impossible to do justice to all the actors engaged. The movement that saved Kansas was of the people, rather than of the leaders. There were leaders, but they were leaders chiefly because they went before. They did not create the movement, nor the sentiment out of which it grew. The people moved towards Kansas of their own impulse. . . . They were moved by individual conviction and a common impulse. Men and women who have never been heard of displayed a spirit of self sacrifice and heroism as worthy of remembrance as anything history records of the noted names. No history can do honor to all who deserve it.

It is becoming quite common to under-rate the heroism that saved Kansas for freedom. The cold blooded historian goes mousing among old letters and he finds that these early heroes were men and women, of like frailties with ourselves. But the glory of heroism is not that angels come down to mingle in the affairs of men, but that common men and women, when the occasion demands, can rise to such sublime heights to heroism and self sacrifice.

It becomes the people of Kansas to appreciate her own history and the men who laid the first foundations.

—*Rev. Richard Cordley,* A History of Lawrence, *1895*

John Brown of Osawatomie

Jonathan Earle

Numerous American localities stake a claim to John Brown. Torrington, Connecticut, proudly proclaims itself Brown's birthplace. He is buried at the foot of one of the most spectacular mountains in New York's Adirondack range, in the town of North Elba, a multiracial enclave that Brown considered home. The Brown family also spent many years in Hudson, Ohio, and rural Pennsylvania. And, of course, sleepy Harpers Ferry, West Virginia, played host to Brown's famous raid, one of the most spectacular and significant ever conducted on American soil.

Brown spent relatively few of his fifty-nine years in Kansas, most of it in two stretches from October 1855 to October 1856 and from May 1858 to February 1859. But the connection between Kansas and "Old Osawatomie Brown" is indelible. It was in Kansas that Brown shook off the tethers of his "old" life of failed business ventures and family melodrama and metamorphosed into the abolitionist warrior-prophet who has ever since maintained a tenacious hold on the nation's imagination. When he arrived at his sons' claims on North Middle

John Brown (May 9, 1800–December 2, 1859), whose hatred for and resolve to strike a blow against the national sin of slavery seems reflected in this 1857 tintype, arrived in Kansas Territory in the fall of 1855 and quickly made his presence felt, with his willingness to resort to violence to further his abolitionist objectives. Courtesy of the Kansas State Historical Society.

Creek in eastern Kansas near Osawatomie, he was a nobody: a failed businessman and absentee husband. The John Brown who left Kansas Territory in 1859 was a man wholly transformed: a fugitive from justice, a guerrilla leader, a military hero, a tactician, and an antislavery man of action. He used this heroic and, to some, titillating reputation to raise money in the East and put in place his plan to invade the South, capture a federal arsenal, and arm the region's slaves for large-scale insurrection. Despite the plan's ultimate failure, Brown's Harpers Ferry raid did more than any other event during that turbulent decade to drive a wedge between North and South and bring on the Civil War. In fact, after Harpers Ferry and Brown's trial, conviction, and hanging the war became inevitable as partisans on each side painted drastically different pictures of the events and the man behind them. More than any other person connected with territorial Kansas, John Brown played a central role in the most significant movement of the age: the crusade against slavery that led to our nation's bloodiest conflict.

Of course, many Kansans (then and now) did not want the image of a fiery-eyed warrior associated with their state. Ambivalence is perhaps the most accurate way to describe the way Kansans since 1855 have felt about the abolitionist. Certainly he was (and remains) the best-known territorial resident: when Kansans were asked, just before the turn of the twentieth century, to offer up two subjects for statues in the U.S. Capitol rotunda, Brown easily won a straw poll. Yet during his own time Brown's participation in the Pottawatomie massacre convinced many territorial residents on both sides of the slavery issue that he was dangerous and unstable. A generation later even the editors of the *Weekly Journal* in Lawrence—once one of the pro-Brown towns of Bleeding Kansas—wanted John Brown's Kansas connections to disappear. "The charitable thing to say of Brown is that he was a lunatic," wrote the editors in May 1900, the centennial of the abolitionist's birth. "He was a disturber even in the east, a dead beat, a swindler. . . . His hands were bloody, and his nature was that of a wolf. His desire was to kill and to slay. . . . It is time to remove the halo from the head of John Brown, and sell it to the junk man."[1]

Brown remained just as controversial thirty-nine years later, when the muralist John Steuart Curry made a bearded, wild-eyed, and righteous-looking Brown the center of his *Tragic Prelude,* painted for the east corridor of the state capitol in Topeka. Reproduced to great acclaim in *Life* magazine in 1939, Curry's Brown quickly assumed an iconic status. But Kansans wary of being known for the state's wild weather, freaks, and fanaticism chafed at the image. "John Brown was just a crazy old coot," according to one state senator. "He was nothing but a rascal, a thief, and a murderer . . . whose memory should not be perpetuated." Stung by the criticism, Curry left the mural project unfinished and refused to sign his name to his east-corridor masterpiece. It appeared that Kansas itself did not wish to remember one of its most prominent sons.[2]

Brown's reputation has, of course, risen and fallen with the times, although it is important to mention that his standing has always remained heroic among the nation's African Americans. He is routinely invoked as a precursor of causes across the political spectrum: the civil rights movement; the movement to outlaw abortion; and even the militia movement that gave rise to the American terrorist Timothy McVeigh, who considered Brown a hero. How Brown became such a significant and multifaceted force—a Kansan who made a difference—is the subject of this essay.

John Brown was born on May 9, 1800, in Torrington, Connecticut, in a spare, shutterless farmhouse. Although his ancestors had been among the first settlers in New England and both his father and grandfather had fought in the Revolutionary War, Brown was born into precarious circumstances. After two centuries of white settlement, land in southern New England had been divided and subdivided so many times that even eldest sons could often expect to inherit little. This so-called man-land crisis fueled the peopling of upstate New York, the growth of cities, and westward migration. Brown's father, Owen, a tanner, decided to move his family to Ohio's Western Reserve, hoping to gain possession of land to pass on to his children.

Religiously, Owen Brown resembled a seventeenth-century Puritan more than the deist—some would say atheist—President Thomas Jefferson, who won election in the year of John Brown's birth. Owen Brown taught his children to fear his austere, Calvinist God; he also taught that slavery, which was enjoying a major resurgence in the Southern states after the invention of the laborsaving cotton gin, was a "great sin." Just as slavery was exploding into the fertile bottomlands of the old Southwest, the young John Brown had his first personal encounter with the institution and its brutality. During the War of 1812, Owen Brown won a contract to provide beef to the American forces near Detroit. Brown entrusted his twelve-year-old son with the job of gathering the cattle and driving them over one hundred miles to the army's outposts in Michigan. John Brown recalled lodging after one of these drives with a landlord who owned a "very active, inteligent [sic], and good feeling" slave close to his own age. That night the man beat the boy with an iron shovel while the adolescent Brown watched in horror. He later wrote that the beating transformed him into "a most *determined Abolitionist*" from that point forward, leading him to declare an "*Eternal war*" on slavery.[3]

John Brown followed his father into the tanner's trade and married a pious woman named Dianthe Lusk in 1820. The couple began their married life in the midst of a period of intense religious revival that historians call the Second Great Awakening. Americans everywhere were reeling from wave after wave of social and cultural change as territorial expansion, a market revolution, and the spread of plantation slavery uprooted people and shattered old social patterns. One reaction people had to this rapid change was to flock to evangelical revivals—meetings designed to produce religious conversions, led by preachers who were trained to that task—in which they revived and remade American religious life. But Brown had little use for the loving and forgiving God who began to appear in the sermons of some of the more liberal Second Great Awakening preachers. His God remained one of wrath and justice.

Brown raised six children by Dianthe (a seventh died at birth), according to one biographer, with "a rod in one hand and the Bible in the other." His attention to discipline made a powerful impression on his children. On one occasion, after punishing his son John Jr. with lashes from a "nicely-prepared blue-beech switch," he handed the whip to his son, stripped off his shirt, and ordered the boy to beat him as well, "until he received the balance" of his son's punishment. When the boy struck him, he demanded harder and harder blows until John Jr. drew blood. Only later did John Brown Jr. conclude that his father was offering him a "practical illustration" of his belief that the innocent must also suffer for the collective guilt of sinful humankind.[4]

Dianthe Brown died in childbirth in 1832 in New Richmond Township, Pennsylvania, where the Browns had moved in 1826. Less than a year later the thirty-three-year-old Brown married Mary Ann Day, the sixteen-year-old daughter of a local blacksmith. Mary gave birth to thirteen children during her marriage to John Brown, beginning with Sarah in 1834.

During Brown's tumultuous and sad time in New Richmond, he must have been aware of dramatic changes that forever shook the antislavery movement in the United States. Organized opposition to slavery during the 1810s and 1820s was essentially limited to isolated groups of free blacks, Quakers, and the American Colonization Society, founded in 1816 to bring about the gradual, voluntary (and compensated) emancipation of slaves and their "repatriation" to West Africa. In 1829 David Walker, a free black Boston merchant, published *Appeal in Four Articles,* which called for a violent overthrow of slavery and excoriated the colonization movement. Distributed throughout the Atlantic seaboard, the *Appeal* helped unite African Americans in a movement for the immediate abolition of slavery. Walker's publication also reached white activists such as William Lloyd Garrison, a professional reformer and product of the evangelical reform culture spawned by the Second Great Awakening. On January 1, 1831, Garrison published the first issue of his newspaper the *Liberator,* in which he thundered that slavery was a national sin and demanded immediate emancipation. "I am in earnest," he wrote. "I will not equivocate—I will not excuse—I will not retreat a single inch—AND I WILL BE HEARD!"[5]

Seven months after Garrison's clarion call, a black lay preacher in Southampton County, Virginia, named Nat Turner led the largest slave insurrection in U.S. history, killing fifty-five white men, women, and children in a spree that lasted three days. Turner's rebellion ignited an explosion of fear among Southern slaveholders, who engaged in a retaliatory rampage of their own: as many as 120 African Americans, including many innocent victims, lost their lives as a result of the revolt. Slaveholders squarely laid the blame for Turner's revolt at the feet of abolitionists such as Walker and Garrison, although Garrison had never called for the violent overthrow of slavery. It is important to note, however, that at that time white abolitionists such as Garrison; Arthur and Lewis Tappan; Theodore Dwight Weld; and John Brown's father, Owen, occupied the political fringes in antebellum America. Their antislavery activities incurred violent and often murderous reactions not just in Southern states but also in Northern cities such as Rochester, New York, and Philadelphia. Weld was called the "most mobbed man in America," and Garrison was dragged by a rope through the streets of Boston by one antiabolitionist mob. After 1833, when the Tappans and Garrison joined forces to found the American Antislavery Society to coordinate petition drives, speaking tours, sermons, newspapers, and tracts, immediatist abolitionism (which demanded the immediate, unconditional end of all slavery in the United States) constituted the most intense and important moral crusade in the nation's history.

With the abolitionist movement on the rise, Brown decided to become more involved. In the fall of 1834 he became convinced that God was about to bring the South's slaves "out of the house of bondage." Brown urged his neighbors in New Richmond to prepare to receive streams of runaways in their homes, a prospect that no doubt antagonized even his antislavery acquaintances. Brown also planned to take a more personal role in the struggle by adopting an African American boy to "give him a good English education . . . and above all, try to teach him the fear of God," and by opening a school for blacks. He urged his brother Frederick, then living in Hudson, to convince some "first-rate abolitionist families" in Ohio to move to New Richmond and help finance the ambitious project. "I do honestly believe," he wrote, "that our united exertions alone might soon, with the good hand of our God upon us, effect it all."[6]

Brown's scheme for a black schoolhouse in Pennsylvania, while visionary, was hardly practical, given his finances. During Dianthe's illness Brown had let his tanning business slide, and he had increasing difficulty in providing for his rapidly growing family. By the spring of 1835 he was bankrupt, and he walked away from his property in Pennsylvania to return to Ohio's Western Reserve. There he tried his hand at land speculation, traded cattle and sheep, and opened another tannery. Each of these business ventures failed, and a growing number of unhappy investors brought lawsuits against their former partner, an occurrence that became a pattern in the business life of John Brown.

Brown's conversion to radical abolitionism came in the aftermath of the brutal murder of the antislavery editor Elijah Lovejoy at the hands of a mob in Alton, Illinois, in November 1837. At an Ohio prayer meeting John Brown suddenly stood up and raised his right hand. There, before a roomful of witnesses, he pledged to devote the remainder of his life to the eradication of slavery.[7] Yet, unlike the vast majority of abolitionists, who banded together in societies, sewing circles, petition drives, or prayer groups, John Brown went his own antislavery way. Perhaps this isolation was due to his lack of skills as a team player and listener, but Brown was becoming well known for berating fellow reformers for religious "errors" and supposed moral inconsistencies. His radical ideas about racial equality also set him apart from mainstream abolitionists, only a minority of whom shared his views. In 1838, for example, Brown dropped a "bomb shell" on his fellow congregants at the Congregational Church by escorting visiting African Americans to sit with him in the family pew. A year later church elders expelled the Browns, technically for being absent without reporting their whereabouts. After this incident Brown never again attended regular church services.

In 1844, again on the verge of bankruptcy, Brown entered into a partnership with a wealthy Akron businessman named Simon Perkins. Within two years he had convinced Perkins to join him in (and finance) an ambitious venture to buy wool from shepherds across the Northeast, grade it, and transport it to Springfield, Massachusetts, in order to command higher prices from New England buyers. After relocating to Springfield, Brown met and befriended several of the town's black citizens, many of whom were runaways from the South. He subscribed to the *Liberator* and the black abolitionist Frederick Douglass's *North Star*. In November 1847 Douglass took time out from a lecture tour to answer Brown's invitation to discuss "urgent business" at his spare Springfield home. Douglass recalled that after sharing a meal, Brown announced that he had a "plan" to liberate the nation's slaves and unfolded a weathered map of the United States on the table. Running a finger up and down the Allegheny Mountains, Brown said that God had placed them there "for emancipation of the negro race." He then explained his idea for an advance force to camp in the mountains, moving up and down the chain while liberating and arming the South's slaves—a plan Brown called the "Subterranean passway." Douglass expressed doubt that Brown could evade the Southerners who would inevitably come after him and seemed unwilling to abandon the notion of convincing slaveholders to willingly free their slaves. But Brown held firm to his contention that slaveholders would never give up their property without the use of force, and Douglass conceded that his plan "had much to commend it." Douglass later wrote a letter to the *North Star* announcing his interview with Brown, who "though a white gentleman, is in sympathy, a black man, and as deeply interested in our cause, as though his own soul had been pierced with the iron of slavery."[8]

Brown put his plans to rest for the next several years, most of which he spent farming and spiriting fugitives to Canada from his farm in remote upstate New York. But the lives of John Brown and his family changed forever with the introduction of the Kansas-Nebraska Act in January 1854. The brainchild of Senator Stephen A. Douglas of Illinois, the bill sought to organize territory in the Louisiana Purchase north of present-day Oklahoma to pave the way for a transcontinental railroad linking the gold fields in California to Chicago and the East. Such organization was viewed by many Americans as long overdue: white settlers had for some time been encroaching on Indian lands in the fertile river valleys west of Missouri. But each addition of new territory to the United States inevitably inflamed the controversy over whether the lands would allow slavery or remain free soil, with each struggle seemingly more dangerous to the Union than the last.

Just four years earlier the Compromise of 1850 had attempted to satisfy both Southerners and Northerners on contentious issues such as the status of land seized from Mexico and the slave trade in the District of Columbia. But the compromise's central feature, a new fugitive slave law, tilted toward the South by placing the federal government squarely on the side of slaveholders. Moreover, slavery had supposedly been excluded forever from the entire Louisiana Purchase north of 36°30' by the 1820 Missouri Compromise, and many Northerners were dismayed that Douglas's Nebraska bill put the territory of Nebraska and Kansas back in play. But Douglas was not finished; with an eye on the 1856 Democratic presidential nomination, he rushed to make his bill even more palatable to the South. He divided the new territory in two, with Nebraska encompassing the modern states of Nebraska, the Dakotas, and Montana, and Kansas encompassing the state's current boundaries and some of what would eventually become Colorado.

To Northerners such as the Browns, the meaning of this legislative sleight of hand was clear: Kansas was to be marked out for slavery while Nebraska would remain free. Douglas himself, a believer in "popular sovereignty"—letting a territory's settlers decide for or against slavery—famously claimed to "care not" whether the settlers in the new territories voted for or against slavery as long as "the tide of immigration and civilization" was permitted to roll onward.[9]

But thousands of Americans—including John Brown and his family—did care. When it became clear that Southerners had the votes in Congress to pass the Kansas-Nebraska Act, the New York Whig William Seward stood up on the floor of the Senate and told his Southern colleagues: "Since there is no escaping your challenge, I accept it in behalf of the cause of freedom. We will engage in competition for the virgin soil of Kansas, and God give victory to the side which is stronger in numbers as it is in right." The race for Kansas was on, and the Brown family was in the thick of it from the very beginning. It was a defining moment for them and the nation.[10]

In the weeks after the passage of the Kansas-Nebraska Act on May 26, 1854, Missouri residents used their proximity to outpace free-state emigration to the new territory of Kansas. But as the year wore on, settlers from the North first equaled and then surpassed the numbers of those from the South. It was during that summer that John Brown's son John Brown Jr. decided to emigrate and stake a claim in Kansas—to become a farmer there as well as a soldier on the front lines of the battle against slavery. Brown's sons Jason, Owen, Frederick, and Salmon agreed to join their elder brother, as did Samuel Adair, the husband of John Brown's half-sister Florilla. At first the elder Brown declined to join the party, writing his son that he felt "committed to operate in another part of the field." He added that if he "were not so committed, I would be on my way this fall."[11] By May 1855, however, Brown had changed his mind. He had received a long letter from John Jr. asking for help procuring weapons for the fight against proslavery settlers and "border ruffians." "The friends of freedom are not one fourth of them half armed, and as to Military Organization among them it no where exists in this territory," the son wrote. The letter struck exactly the right chord for the abolitionist who had intermittently planned to confront the "Slave Power" with violence, if necessary; John Brown left for Kansas soon after, leaving Mary and a new baby—Ellen, his twentieth—in North Elba. He also left behind numerous lawsuits and business entanglements in Ohio, Massachusetts, and Great Britain for a new life as a full-time soldier in the war against slavery—a life that would stretch from his departure for Kansas to his descent from the gallows in Virginia four years later.[12]

The old man was shocked at what he found when he arrived in October 1855 at the rude southeastern Franklin County settlement his sons had named Brown's Station. Most of the family were debilitated with fever, "shivering over their little fires, all exposed to the dreadful cutting winds."[13] Brown and his son-in-law quickly sprang into action, building structures, bringing in the meager harvest of beans and squash, and chopping wood for the coming Kansas winter. The elder Brown's arrival almost certainly saved the family's Western experiment from immediate disaster.

Despite the continuing hardships of frontier life, antislavery politics was a constant factor for the Browns, even during the difficult months of late 1855. During the previous March proslavery Missourians had illegally crossed the state line in droves to elect a proslavery territorial legislature labeled "bogus" by the emerging free-state majority. Then the legislature convened in July and passed a draconian legal code that essentially outlawed antislavery action, thought, and speech. The territorial code stipulated that only proslavery men would be allowed to hold office and serve on juries and outlined severe punishments for speaking out against slavery, helping runaway slaves escape, and possessing books about slave rebellion or fomenting insurrection. To combat the "bogus" legislature, free-state settlers including John Brown Jr. met in a separate convention to create an alternative constitution for Kansas.

Almost immediately after the elder Brown's arrival in late 1855 the residents of Brown's Station received word that a free-state settler had been murdered by a proslavery Virginian after a dispute. This emboldened citizens in the antislavery town of Lawrence, thirty miles north of Brown's Station, to hold a protest meeting where they agreed to take up arms. The proslavery county sheriff and governor, informed that an armed force in Lawrence was in "open rebellion" against the laws of the territory, mobilized the militia and invited back the "border ruffians" who had fraudulently swung the election the previous spring. A large and rowdy mob began to gather on the banks of the Wakarusa River south of Lawrence, spoiling for a fight.

Armed to the teeth, the Browns arrived on December 7. Once they reached the Free State Hotel, the fortresslike headquarters of the Lawrence free staters, the elder Brown was quickly commissioned as a captain in the First Brigade of Kansas Volunteers and given command of a small company (mostly consisting of his own sons) called the Liberty Guards. The guards saw little action that day because the governor was able to broker a deal whereby the increasingly intoxicated Missourians massing outside town would retreat and the free-state leaders would announce that they had no intention of resisting the laws of the territory. Violence in Lawrence was, for the moment, averted.

The Kansas winter briefly quelled the tensions of the previous fall. But the coming of spring brought the most violent period of Bleeding Kansas, beginning with the "sack of Lawrence" on May 21, 1856. Word of the impending assault, led by Sheriff Samuel Jones under the authority of a warrant issued by a proslave grand jury, on the "free state fortress" reached Brown too late; by the time his Liberty Guards reached the vicinity Jones's posse had leveled the Free State Hotel with a barrage of artillery shells, burned and looted several other homes and businesses, and destroyed two free-state newspapers, tossing their printing presses into the river.

Brown was thirsty to avenge the sack of Lawrence, but he also may have received news on the morning of May 24 about a vicious attack on Senator Charles Sumner by Congressman Preston Brooks in the U.S. Senate. Brooks had beaten Sumner unconscious with a heavy cane on the afternoon of May 22 in reaction to a speech the Massachusetts senator had delivered about Kansas that included personal attacks on Brooks's uncle, a senator from South Carolina. Years later Brown's son Salmon recalled that a messenger had brought the news and that Brown and Salmon's brothers had gone "crazy—*crazy*. It seemed to be the finishing, decisive touch." Whereas Sumner's Kansas speech had been tinged with self-righteousness and insult, Brown's more exactly matched that of his Southern foes. "We must fight fire with fire," Brown said, according to one of his followers. "Something must be done to show these barbarians that we, too, have rights."[14]

Leading four of his sons and three others to a proslavery settlement at nearby Pottawatomie Creek that same night, Brown's men dragged five settlers from their cabins and split open their heads with broadswords. The choice of weapons was no accident: Brown told one son that he wanted to sweep down on the sinners with the force of an avenging angel. Controversy surrounds the killings that came to be known as the Pottawatomie massacre, much of it stemming from the fact that John Brown never formally confessed to his role in the murders.[15] The dead men owned no slaves, nor had they participated in the assault on Lawrence. Most observers could agree on two facts, however: the murders made John Brown a legend and a household name—in the North as well as the South—and they guaranteed that Kansas would continue to "bleed" profusely in 1856.

Brown's act of horrific violence gave voice to the rage and despair many free-state Kansans experienced during the fifteen months after the election that created the "bogus" legislature. Coming so soon after the sack of Lawrence, the murders helped spur formerly peaceful settlers to act with force, even as their political leaders called for calm and negotiation. "Violence breeds violence," wrote James Hanway, who was shocked at the murders but continued to support Brown and condemn the proslavery party. "They advocate assassination and now that 5 persons have been murdered on their side perhaps they will learn that such hellish sentiments when carried into effect, will work equally to the destruction of pro-slavery men."[16]

This new feeling of defiance and opposition led many free-state settlers—most of whom condemned the Pottawatomie murders—nevertheless to gather their weapons and take to the brush for out-and-out battle with the proslavery side. Leading the way was John Brown, whose legend was growing fast. He was now an outlaw, with a price on his head and federal troops, vigilantes, and crowds of Missourians in constant pursuit. Brown's guerrilla band initially hid out near Ottawa Creek and was the subject of a colorful description by the Scottish-born journalist James Redpath: "A dozen horses were tied, all ready saddled for a ride for life, or a hunt after Southern invaders. A dozen rifles and sabers were stacked around the trees . . . and two fine-looking youths were standing, leaning on their arms, on guard near by." Brown "stood near the fire, with his shirt-sleeves rolled up, and a large piece of pork in his hand. . . . He was poorly clad, and his toes protruded from his boots."[17] Leading the pursuit of Brown and his men was Henry Clay Pate, a Missouri border ruffian who had been deputized as a U.S. marshal and commanded a band of twenty-eight men. While camping at Black Jack, just off the Santa Fe trail five miles east of Prairie City (modern-day Baldwin), Pate was surprised by Brown's party at dawn on June 2, 1856. After two hours of pitched battle among the tall oak trees, creekbeds, and wagon ruts, Pate surrendered, only to find that he had capitulated to a mere handful of ragtag antislavery fighters. John Brown later called this action "the first regular battle fought between Free-State and Pro-Slavery men in Kansas"; more importantly for historians of the Civil War era, it was the first recorded battle between two organized military forces on opposite sides of the slavery question. There would, of course, be many more in the decade to come.

Black Jack and the ensuing Battle of Osawatomie on August 30, 1856, sealed John Brown's fame as a fearsome guerrilla fighter. General John W. Reid and 250 men set out to destroy the free-state town of Osawatomie, with the intent of capturing or killing the outlaw Brown. Brown's son Frederick was the first person killed in the battle, which rapidly disintegrated into a prolonged shoot-out along the Marais des Cygnes River. Brown's men were eventually forced to retreat, and the old man watched the town burn. He told his son Jason that "God sees it. I have only a short time to live—only one death to die, and I will die fighting this cause. There will be no more peace in this land until slavery is done for. I will give them something else to do than to extend slave territory. I will carry the war into Africa." Brown meant that he would next attack slavery where slavery already existed: in the South itself.[18]

Recent scholarship suggests that fifty people died from the convulsions of violence that historians call "Bleeding Kansas."[19] Not until President Franklin Pierce sent a new territorial governor and 1,300 federal troops to Kansas in September did the violence subside. Brown, ill with dysentery and pursued by scores of bounty hunters and federal marshals, slipped out of Kansas and headed east via Nebraska. He promised his wife, Mary, that he would return to the territory "if the troubles continue and my health will admit." The territory's troubles, of course, did continue—but Brown and his band of guerrillas had struck a decisive blow that, in retrospect, turned territorial politics on its head: hundreds of free-state settlers, many sent by the New England Emigrant Aid Company, continued to pour into the territory. Demographic reality quickly trumped electoral fraud, and the free staters began to assert more control in the territory. Meanwhile, John Brown had other plans for his war against slavery.[20]

Brown spent the first ten months of 1857 raising money for his crusade. It was during this time that he also began updating his plan to attack slavery in the South by means of a "Subterranean passway" in the Appalachian Mountains. He began to focus his plans on the federal arsenal at Harpers Ferry, Virginia (now West Virginia)—a quiet town without a significant military guard. John Brown returned to Kansas briefly in November 1857 and recruited his first volunteers for the assault before making his way to Iowa for training. Six months later Brown returned to Kansas after the Marais des Cygnes massacre claimed the lives of five free staters, using the alias Shubel Morgan and for the first time sporting a stunning white beard that reminded those who saw him of pictures of Old Testament prophets. In December 1858 Brown led a daring raid into Missouri to rescue eleven slaves and spent the next month spiriting them along the Underground Railroad in Kansas. After a final battle on January 31, 1859, John Brown left the territory for the last time, heading to Canada with the fugitives before setting out for Maryland to prepare his raid on Harpers Ferry.

Brown's plan was to capture the arsenal and use the weapons to free and arm slaves along the Appalachian mountain chain from Virginia to Northern Alabama. He hoped that a heavily armed and mobile force of ex-slaves would trigger a larger uprising among other enslaved and free blacks, quickly leading to a civil war and the destruction of slavery. After dark on October 16, 1859, Brown led twenty-one men—five black and sixteen white—across the river into the town of Harpers Ferry. Although they occupied the sleeping town without resistance, the slave revolt Brown hoped to inspire never materialized. Instead, local citizens, militiamen, and U.S. troops under the command of Bvt. Col. Robert E. Lee trapped the raiders inside an old fire-engine house and on October 18 stormed the building. Brown surrendered after ten of his men (including two of his sons) were killed.

The raid was over just thirty-six hours after it had begun, and Brown and six of his followers were hastily convicted and sentenced to hang after a sensational trial in Charles Town, Virginia. Yet Brown's fearless and dignified conduct during the proceedings and later on the gallows added to his mythic status in the North. Some even spoke of Brown as a martyr: Henry David Thoreau called him an "angel of light," and Ralph Waldo Emerson said "he has made the gallows as glorious as the cross." Later, during the Civil War that Brown's actions in Kansas and Virginia had done so much to hasten, Union soldiers sang that John Brown's body "lies a-mouldering in the grave/ his truth is marching on."

Simply put, it was his time in Kansas Territory that made a dedicated but little-known abolitionist into the complex, mythic, and immortal figure whose "truth is marching on." Brown's decision to abandon the usual abolitionist tactics of petitions, lectures, and moral suasion in favor of intimidation, terror, and guerrilla warfare ensured that slavery's end would not come without significant bloodshed. He used the lawlessness and remoteness of Kansas Territory to put his new, violent plans into place and build a reputation as a new kind of antislavery warrior. It is a complicated legacy with which Kansans continue to struggle. But there can be no doubt that John Brown of Osawatomie played a central, even paramount, role in ensuring that the Union remained inviolable and that slavery was forever destroyed in the United States.

James H. Lane: Radical Conservative,

Conservative Radical

Nicole Etcheson

Men are also representative; first, of things, and secondly, of ideas.
—Ralph Waldo Emerson, 1850

What did James H. Lane represent? We expect biographies of leading historical figures to show us what they stood for, but Jim Lane's chameleonlike blending into shifting political backgrounds challenges the biographer's ability to categorize. He began his career as a Democrat who supported the Kansas-Nebraska Act, which removed the prohibition against slavery in the northern part of the Louisiana Purchase and replaced it with popular sovereignty, the doctrine that the settlers themselves would decide whether to have slavery. But Lane quickly moved to leadership of the free-state movement, which opposed the territorial legislature because it had been elected by voters from Missouri, not Kansas Territory. Most famously, Lane was the man

James H. Lane (June 22, 1814–July 11, 1866), "the Grim Chieftain," cultivated the unkempt, near-crazed persona reflected in this 1861 image. Perhaps the Free State Party's most pugnacious and controversial leader, Lane finished his political career as one of the state's first two U.S. senators. Courtesy of the Kansas State Historical Society.

who, upon migrating to Kansas, declared that he would as soon buy a black slave as a mule. But within a decade Lane had become an advocate of black rights, recruiting black troops into the Union Army and allying himself with the Radical Republicans in Congress. Such apparently extreme swings prompted a Kansas settler to observe that Lane was "troubled with about as little principle as any man in the Territory."[1]

Despite Lane's shifts in political position, his life reveals important trends in United States and Kansas history. He was a product of a frontier fraught with sectional tensions and occasional violence. Historian William Connelley called him "the leader of this Western spirit." He was a Jacksonian American whose sloppy demeanor and demagogic politics reflected an age in which the common man ruled. During Lane's lifetime, political rights for white men were the overriding political creed, and for this creed he fought in Bleeding Kansas. His racism, too, reflected the majority values of his society. But like Kansas and the rest of the country, Lane came to recognize the need for expanded black rights. In the best biography of Lane, Wendell Holmes Stephenson sought to "explain Lane's transition from Indiana conservatism to Kansas radicalism."[2] But there was no such clear-cut transition. Rather, in his early career, Lane was a conservative who opposed what he saw as the extremism of abolitionism and racial egalitarianism. Bleeding Kansas persuaded him to accept a wider measure of black rights and forced him into defiance of the Democratic Party and administration. In that sense he became a radical, but never so radical as the Radical Republicans with whom he was occasionally allied in his later career.

Born June 22, 1814—either in Lawrenceburg, Indiana, or Boone County, Kentucky—Lane was a child of the Midwestern frontier. While his father, Amos, was of Scots-Irish descent, his mother's family hailed from Connecticut. Lane would exploit this geographic ambiguity for political effect. As a congressman from Indiana he claimed the Hoosier state, but at the Topeka constitutional convention in Kansas he called himself a Kentuckian. In a typical Lane straddle, he once wrote that he was "born on the bank of the Ohio river" but failed to specify which bank.

Jim Lane's father was an attorney and a politician. Having served in the Indiana legislature and in Congress as a Jacksonian Democrat, Amos Lane was known for his "remarkable oratorical ability," a gift his son would inherit. Jim Lane, however, would try business before turning to other pursuits. With his brother-in-law, he had a pork-packing enterprise in Lawrenceburg for several years. Given later accounts of Lane's erratic handling of money, it is hard to imagine that this venture could have been a success. In any case, Lane moved on to more adventurous pursuits. In fact, violent adventures would become an integral part of his life story.[3]

When the war with Mexico broke out, Lane organized a company from Dearborn, Indiana. The volunteers elected him an officer. During the Battle of Buena Vista a crisis occurred for the U.S. forces when another Indiana regiment mistakenly retreated, opening a hole in the U.S. line that the Mexican forces quickly exploited. Along with Mississippi troops, Lane's regiment, the Third Indiana, was brought up to close the gap and save the army. A decade later in Kansas, Lane's supporters continued to celebrate the battle and Lane's role in it. After Lane's regiment returned home, Lane raised another and sailed again for Mexico. By this time, however, the war was over.

Lane's association with violence was not confined to the field of battle. He became involved in affairs of honor with a fellow officer during the U.S.-Mexican War, an Indiana politician while he was lieutenant governor, and a

Kansas territorial governor's private secretary. In his most famous near affray, Lane challenged Senator Stephen A. Douglas. Lane had brought a memorial from the free-state Topeka movement to Washington. In the Senate, Douglas denounced it as a forgery, all the signatures being in the same handwriting. Lane explained that the signatures had been copied over from the original but felt sufficiently insulted to make the challenge. When Douglas claimed his privilege as a member of Congress to ignore the challenge, Lane deferred magnanimously to that privilege while calling it a coward's way out.[4]

Lane did not always invoke the code of honor. When a dispute arose over a land claim and the ownership of a well, Lane killed his neighbor and fellow free stater, Gaius Jenkins, with whom the Lanes refused to share the well. On the day of Jenkins's death, Lane had turned two members of the Jenkins household away from his property. When Jenkins himself broke down the fence that Lane had built to keep him out, Lane shot him. Lane later claimed it was an act of self-defense. Defense witnesses supported that claim, and Lane was acquitted.[5]

Kansas Territory had long offered Lane the opportunity to exercise the military skills he had learned in the U.S.-Mexican War. Free-state leaders named Lane a brigadier general and authorized him to command forces defending Lawrence during the Wakarusa War of 1855. As the free staters erected fortifications, Lane drilled an estimated 600 to 800 men. The following summer, during the events of Bleeding Kansas, Lane was one of the few free-state leaders to escape arrest.

Lane used his freedom to organize a route through Iowa and Nebraska, permitting emigrants to avoid the more perilous Missouri River route that exposed them to harassment by proslavery forces. There was much concern among territorial officials about "Lane's Army of the North," which was expected to invade the territory with hundreds of armed men. But having promised not to challenge the federal troops, Lane arrived back in Kansas with only a small party and entered Lawrence alone. Not long after his return, Lane joined the guerrilla fighting. On the night of August 12, 1856, Lane's force besieged a proslavery fort at Franklin. After several hours Lane's men backed a wagon filled with hay up against the proslavery blockhouse and set the hay on fire. The proslavery men fled, whereupon Lane's force of less than 100 took a six-pound cannon and arms. Three days later the free staters attacked a proslavery fort on Washington Creek, burning the fort after its defenders fled. Lane's force also attacked proslavery troops at the small settlement of Hickory Point on September 13. Failing to "blot . . . out" the enemy that day, Lane retreated. That night he learned that the territorial governor was sending troops. The next day another free-state leader renewed the attack, but Lane stayed away.[6]

Even after the guerrilla war had ended, the free staters turned to Lane's military expertise. A Topeka convention in 1857 authorized Lane to protect voting. Lane issued "general orders" to organize military companies and to requisition arms. In late 1857, when free staters finally gained control of the territorial legislature, Lane was elected major general of the territorial militia. That winter he led an expedition into southern Kansas, where proslavery and free-state forces were in conflict.

The national Civil War gave Lane an opportunity to reprise his military role, and he received an appointment as brigadier general of volunteers. His command, the Kansas Brigade, went on incursions into Missouri and saw action at Dry Wood Creek and Morristown. Most famously, on September 23, Lane's men burned Osceola. Lane claimed that, because the enemy took refuge in the town, he had to shell it, "and in doing so the place was burned to ashes." He claimed that fifteen to twenty of the enemy had been killed and wounded. Lane justified the raid, which would fester in the memory of Missourians for generations afterward, by arguing that Osceola "was the depot of the traitors for Southwestern Missouri."[7]

Lane's men became notorious for their depredations against Missouri civilians. Maj. Gen. Henry W. Halleck, who generally deplored the actions of Lane and other Kansas commanders, lamented, "I receive almost daily complaints of outrages committed by these men in the name of the United States, and the evidence is so conclusive as to leave no doubt of their correctness." Lane, in fact, became so notorious that to "huzza for James H. Lane" became an incendiary act in Missouri. Lane had hoped to lead an expedition into Arkansas and Indian Territory, but when he found that the War Department would insist that he be subordinate to another commander, he abandoned the plan.[8]

It was as a civilian, then, that Lane survived Quantrill's raid on Lawrence, Kansas. Lane escaped out a back window into a cornfield when the Confederate guerrillas attacked the town in August 1863. Despite his ignominious flight, he was soon rallying men to pursue the raiders. After Quantrill's raid Lane capitalized on Kansans' desire for retaliation. He pressured an anguished Gen. Thomas Ewing to punish the border counties of Missouri and urged, as one observer described it, the "indiscriminate murder of all border

Missourians." Gen. John M. Schofield was forced to intervene to prevent Lane from leading an invasion of Missouri.[9]

A year later Lane was prominent during Price's raid into Missouri. In the fall of 1864 Kansas was threatened with invasion by a Confederate force under General Sterling Price. As Kansans mobilized to repel this threat, both Kansas senators, Lane and Samuel C. Pomeroy, joined Maj. Gen. Samuel R. Curtis as volunteer aides-de-camp. Lane spent two weeks with Curtis's forces and, along with others, "displayed much coolness and gallantry under the fire of the enemy."[10] Lane's well-publicized performance during Price's raid helped secure his reelection to the Senate. Price's raid was Lane's last military venture. The military leader was, however, only one of Lane's personas.

As a product of the Jacksonian age, Lane well represented the period. His personal style immediately identified him as a "common man." Many commented on Lane's slovenly appearance. "On the street he is not noticeable above a woodchopper or a tall lean hog drover," a Kansas man observed. During the guerrilla fighting of 1856 free staters attempted to disguise Lane in order to prevent his capture by U.S. troops. Samuel Walker recalled, "So we tried nitrate of silver on his face, but it would not change him; and then we tried putting old clothes on him; but the worse clothes we put on, the more like Jim Lane he looked."[11]

Lane's personal life was stormy and revealing of the male dominance accepted by nineteenth-century society. Some critics claimed that he switched to the free-state side only because the proslavery-dominated territorial legislature refused to grant him a divorce, although there is no documentary evidence to support or disprove that assertion. Lane had married Mary E. Baldridge in 1841, and the couple had four children. After moving to Kansas Mary Lane returned to Indiana and petitioned for divorce in 1856 on the grounds that Lane had abandoned her and three of their children. George W. Brown claimed that Lane had "shamefully abused" his wife, causing her to flee in her nightclothes. Rumors circulated that Lane had liaisons with other women. But despite his abuse and womanizing, Mary Lane reconciled with her husband and remarried him.[12] Her motives are unknown, but one can surmise that she succumbed to her husband's considerable charisma as well as to the grim realities of life without a male supporter.

Lane was not, however, a reliable breadwinner. His defenders said he looked impoverished because he cared nothing for money. He might ask a merchant to cash a draft of several hundred dollars, saying that he had money in an Eastern bank but needed the funds immediately. When it transpired that the funds did not exist, Lane would declare that there had been a mistake but would nonetheless fail to repay the merchant. On several separate occasions critics charged Lane with personally profiting from scrip issued by the Topeka government's executive committee and funds intended for the relief of Kansas settlers.[13]

Temperance may have been Jim Lane's only personal virtue. It was said that he never drank. In 1857 Lane joined the Methodist church on probation, saying that he intended to honor his dying mother's wish that he become a church member. By 1859 he had "professed conversion" and been accepted into the church. Although some scoffed, others thought him sincere. John Speer, Lane's newspaperman ally, said that "occasionally he exhorted in church meetings" and revivals.[14]

Lane's personal style—his ragged clothes, his ability to charm, and his advocacy of Christianity—were part of a style of democratic politics that he perfected. Lane's political career began in Indiana immediately after his return from the U.S.-Mexican War. In 1845 he was nominated for a seat in the state legislature but was not elected. However, he was elected lieutenant governor in 1848 and to Congress in 1852. The role he played there was not particularly distinguished. He concerned himself with measures important to Westerners, such as a homestead bill. A Democrat, Lane voted for the Kansas-Nebraska Act. He did not run for reelection, claiming that he was in poor health. His biographer thought he had already decided to move to Kansas Territory, but it is also true that the bill was unpopular in the North, including Indiana, for opening the territory to the possibility of slavery.

Newly arrived in Kansas, Lane chaired a Democratic convention in June 1855 in Lawrence. He hinted that he was close to Senator Douglas and President Pierce and privy to their wishes. When his efforts to organize the Democrats in Kansas failed, Lane joined the free-state cause. Claiming that he had been deceived into believing that the people of Kansas would indeed "have the right to form their own institutions," Lane switched sides when he saw "the ballot-boxes were desecrated—the bogus Legislature was elected by armed mobs." He begged, "God forgive me for so enormous and dreadful a political sin—I voted for the bill," meaning the Kansas-Nebraska Act.[15]

Lane worked hard for the free-state cause. He wrote the platform for the Big Springs meeting, one of the early assemblies that launched the free-state movement. He presided over many committees and conventions, including the Topeka convention, which formally organized the movement, and the free-state executive committee that called elections and oversaw results. He, often along with Charles Robinson, drafted letters to public officials pleading the free-state case. And he campaigned extensively against the proslavery Lecompton Constitution. In that campaign, Speer remembered, "On one day [Lane] rode ten miles to speak at eight o'clock in the morning, and thirty more to speak at 3 o'clock in the afternoon, and still twenty more to speak at 7 o'clock at night." He presided briefly over the short-lived Minneola constitutional convention before it moved to Leavenworth.[16]

Territorial Governor John Geary wrote that most settlers, whether free-state or proslavery, were peaceful men, but a few agitators caused a great deal of trouble. In Geary's opinion Lane was one such troublemaker. One free stater asserted, "Lane is a demagogue and very popular with western men, that don't know him, well posted in the art of schullduggery." Given these often scathing assessments, how did Lane flourish in Kansas politics? Part of his ability as a politician—or, as his critics saw it, a demagogue—lay in his oratorical skill. An observer described a Lane speech as "flaming." Upon his death both of the senators who eulogized him commented on his speaking abilities. Senator Pomeroy noted Lane's "impassioned eloquence . . . he swayed multitudes who would hang upon his lips with breathless emotion, while they regarded his voice as little less than the breath of omnipotence."[17]

Lane's political appeal also lay in his willingness to share the experience of the common man. One free stater reported, during the guerrilla fighting of 1856, "If there is little to eat every one has as much as he, and after halting for the night he stations his sentry prepares every thing possible and then for his rest spreads a blanket or skin on the ground sits down and leans his head on his knees to sleep for a while. . . . And thus he goes week after week with no thought of pay no honor abroad."[18] It is doubtful that Lane gave no thought to rewards for his work, but his style was that of the democratic leader.

The culmination of Lane's political ambitions was a seat in the U.S. Senate. He was believed to be maneuvering for one in 1856 and 1858, when it seemed that Kansas might become a state. Finally, in 1861, Kansas did become a state and Lane one of its senators. The backroom deals and legislative maneuvering involved in securing his seat were complex but successful. His appointment to the army, however, would have seemed to necessitate his resigning from the Senate. On that assumption, Governor Charles Robinson appointed a replacement to fill Lane's supposedly empty seat. In the dispute that followed, Lane claimed never to have accepted the brigadier generalship. The Senate voted to let him keep his seat. In effect, Lane found a way to eat his cake and have it too. He kept his Senate seat yet continued to act as commander of "Lane's Brigade." In the fall of 1862 the War Department gave Lane the authority to recruit troops in Kansas. This action undercut Robinson's authority, but the governor's protests proved unavailing. In fact, some credited Lane with controlling the military district through compliant puppets such as Gen. James G. Blunt.[19]

President Abraham Lincoln allowed Lane this unusual political influence. Some have attributed Lincoln's favoritism to the two men's similarities: both were self-made men from the Midwestern frontier. When Lane raised a company of Kansas men to protect the president's mansion during the opening days of the war, they were called the Frontier Guards. Craig Miner argued persuasively that Lane was a useful political ally when other Kansas politicians, notably Robinson, did not support the president.[20]

Lane's political success was attributable not just to his extraordinary abilities but also to a political philosophy typical of the Jacksonian era: fealty to the rights of white men. Lane used the rhetoric of fundamental American principles to justify the free-state cause. In an October 1855 speech at Franklin, Lane compared the free-state resistance to the territorial government to the patriots' resistance to British tyranny. Lane's proclamation calling for the election of delegates to the Topeka constitutional convention was a ringing, Jeffersonian invocation of the abuses the free soilers had suffered. Lane detailed the desecration of the ballot box, the denial of the right of suffrage, and the attacks on free speech that impelled the free soilers toward forming their own state.[21]

But Lane initially envisioned these rights as only for whites. During the summer of 1856, when a black man tried to join Lane's guerrilla force, Lane ordered him returned to his master, saying, "We were not fighting to free black men but to free white men." Not until he saw how hard the slave power fought to preserve itself in Kansas did Lane realize its perniciousness. But this was an antislavery argument rooted not in moral outrage at black bondage but in the threat such bondage posed to the rights of whites.

Lane was comfortable with slavery. He claimed to have had a black mammy when he was an infant and boasted in 1857 that he and his father had often helped Kentuckians recover fugitive slaves in Indiana. While Lane was an Indiana congressman, he avowed, "I am no advocate of slavery." But as a conservative, Union-loving man, "I have gone as far, and will go as far . . . to maintain the constitutional rights of gentlemen representing slave States . . . as any man." In addition to Lane's famous remark that he would as soon buy a slave as a mule, Sam Wood recalled that Lane once said he would favor slavery in Kansas if the territory were suitable for hemp and tobacco.[22]

Lane not only accepted slavery but also shared the racism that underlay much of U.S. society. When Lane tried to rally opposition to the proslavery territorial government, he called members of that government "nigger worshippers." He pointed to the code of laws the proslavery territorial legislature had written, which provided harsher penalties for crimes against slave property than for crimes against whites. He observed that the legislature had passed laws providing the death penalty for kidnapping a "stinking, dirty, thieving nigger" but only fines and jail time for kidnapping a white person. "Who loves blacks more?" Lane asked, the proslavery legislature or the so-called Black Republicans, oft derided for their concern with black rights? Among free staters Lane proposed a law excluding free blacks from Kansas. Such laws were typical of Midwestern states such as Indiana in which residents did not want to compete with black laborers, slave or free.[23]

Although Lane was a professed conservative on racial issues, Bleeding Kansas radicalized him. In a major speech made while a senator, he said that it was during the Kansas civil war that "we learned the colored possessed the qualities of the soldier." During the Civil War he spoke against an amendment to forbid the military from interfering with slavery. Detailing the experience of Bleeding Kansas, Lane dwelt on ballot fraud, described violence against free staters in lurid terms, and detailed the prostitution of the Constitution and the army to the uses of the slave oligarchy. He concluded that the slave owners "have forced upon us this struggle, and I, for one, am willing that it shall be followed to its logical conclusion." Lane asserted "that the institution of slavery will not survive . . . the march of the Union armies, and I thank God that it is so."[24] However, Lane did not detail the crimes against the slaves as justification for abolition, but rather the crimes against white men. Such views were typical Lane: radical results based on conservative principles.

Because of his association during the Civil War with some of the most radical advances in black rights, Lane has been seen as more radical than he in fact was. Although he disclaimed any desire for the Kansas Brigade "of interfering in anywise with the institution of slavery," he did not want his men to "become negro thieves, nor shall they be prostituted into negro catchers. The institution of slavery must take care of itself." In other words, he would not encourage slaves to run away, but he would not aid masters to recover them. Lane also believed in the disloyalty of slave masters and that the loss of their property was therefore just. "Confiscation of slaves and other property which can be made useful to the Army should follow treason as the thunder peal follows the lightning flash." To the dismay of Missourians, Lane generally equated slaveowning with anti-Union sentiment. Lane even delegated his chaplain, H. D. Fisher, to escort runaway Missouri slaves to safety in Kansas, a far cry from his refusal to free blacks during the guerrilla fighting in 1856.[25]

More importantly, Lane was among the first in the country to enlist black troops in the Union army. Lane continued organizing black troops despite protests from the War Department. He even appointed a black officer, albeit without permission from the War Department. Lane's troops, who fought an 1862 skirmish in Bates County, Missouri, are credited as the first black troops to see combat. Nonetheless, they were not officially mustered into the army until January 1863, after other Union black regiments.[26]

In his advocacy of black troops, Lane did not necessarily endorse equality. In a speech at Cooper Union, he said, "I would like to see every traitor who has to die, die by the hand of his own slave." Not only did Lane see arming slaves as a way to punish their secessionist masters, he saw enlisting blacks as a way to share the dangers being suffered by white troops. "A Negro could stop a bullet as well as a white man," according to Lane.[27]

Like Lincoln during the Civil War, Lane favored colonization as a solution to the nation's racial divisions. He voted in favor of colonizing free blacks from the District of Columbia and even introduced a bill to set aside part of Texas as a home for blacks. He hoped to see "these two races separated, an ocean rolling between; that—South America—the Elysium of the colored man; this the Elysium of the white." Lane also feared that if the freedmen remained near their former masters, Southern whites would attempt to oppress them. Since Lane doubted that the United States would give blacks "social and political equality," it was better for them to have their own country.[28] Although this was undoubtedly less than a racially egalitarian view of the potential for black rights, Lane was nonetheless prescient in his predictions.

However tainted with racism his motives may have been, again and again Lane voted on bills and amendments in a way that advanced black rights. He voted in favor of allowing witnesses "of color" to testify in certain cases; for an amendment that "colored troops" be counted toward a state's quota; for repealing the Fugitive Slave Act; against amending the Thirteenth Amendment to exclude blacks from citizenship; against discriminating in pay against black troops; and against railroad segregation in the District of Columbia. As with his advocacy of black troops, he often supported the radical position for conservative reasons. During a senatorial debate Lane dismissed fears that once free, African Americans would intermarry with whites. "There is not a white lady in Kansas who requires the eloquence of a Senator or a legal enactment to control her choice as to a husband." This was not because intermarriage was acceptable but because "the ladies of Kansas . . . are intelligent, refined, proud of their blood and race, and will select husbands therefrom."[29]

Lane's opinions on black suffrage were similarly equivocal. He objected to provisions in the proposed Fourteenth Amendment that withheld representation in Congress if suffrage was denied. Lane demurred that Kansas might want to limit black suffrage only to educated blacks but would suffer loss of representation for that restriction. While Lane seemed willing to accept some black suffrage, he stoutly maintained that there should be a "qualification," such as education, for black voting, a condition he doubtless would have found unacceptable if required of white men.

Lane may have adroitly managed the politics of the Civil War period, but he displayed less skill during Reconstruction. Perhaps because he had derived benefits from his relationship with President Lincoln, he allied himself with President Andrew Johnson. Lane presented the credentials of the Arkansas senators elected under presidential reconstruction policies and introduced a resolution for Arkansas' readmission. Lane argued that Johnson was merely carrying out Lincoln's intentions for reconstruction and that congressional plans for reconstruction were too extreme for most Northern states to accept. Lane spoke movingly of the danger to the Republican Party of a split between its executive and legislative wings. He wished to "harmonize" the party.

Harmony was impossible. Although Lane had voted for the Civil Rights Bill of 1866, he was not prepared to defy Johnson's veto of that bill. Radical Republicans were enraged by the veto, and Lane tried unsuccessfully to persuade them that the veto was Johnson's "constitutional right" and was "merely . . . a vote to reconsider." Having broken with the Radical Republicans on this issue, Lane found himself unpopular in Kansas. When he returned home in the summer he found Kansans angry about his support for Johnson. At the same time, reports surfaced that Lane had profited from Indian contracts. Lane dismissed the "imputation" of wrongdoing contained in newspapers as "a baseless calumny." Nonetheless, it bothered him to be "received with cold and clammy indifference. . . . No crowds escorted him to his home. Old friends rather avoided him."[30]

Those who did not avoid Lane noted wild swings in his emotions that they attributed to illness or insanity. Although psychological diagnosis of historical figures is fraught with controversy and difficulty, it seems possible that Lane had always been either bipolar or psychopathic. Observers and historians noted Lane's unusual energy, which Connelley called "boundless, limitless." Connelley also remarked on Lane's "strong, potent, overpowering" personal magnetism. Observing that Lane was a "genius" but pointing to "the wavy line separating genius from insanity," Connelley concluded, "I think there is no doubt that Lane was at times of unbalanced mind." In 1856 Lane threatened suicide when thwarted by free-state leaders. Abelard Guthrie, frustrated at Senator Lane's failure to attend to business that he had promised Guthrie he would take care of, wrote, "I often think he is insane, or his extraordinary moral obliquity at least often produces effects so nearly like it that one is in doubt as to the true origin of his aberation [sic] of mind." Lane's erratic behavior and wild swings of temperament, as well as his suicidal urges, indicate a bipolar personality. His personal magnetism and "moral obliquity," his "sublime" ability to lie, may indicate the charming but emotionally superficial psychopathic personality.[31]

On July 1, 1866, while riding with two other men, Lane got out to open a gate. He drew a revolver, bade his companions farewell, and shot himself through the roof of the mouth. He lingered for ten days, unconscious, before dying on July 11. It was a violent and dramatic end to an often violent and dramatic life.

William H. Russell: Proslavery Partisan and

Western Entrepreneur

Rita G. Napier

William H. Russell was a charismatic man who developed a financial network that served as the basis for a huge "empire on wheels." Because his freighters pushed into areas not yet settled by white Americans, Russell operated in the context of newly developing economic opportunities. Not only did Russell and his partners, Alexander Majors and William B. Waddell, build the greatest transportation empire in the West, but Russell also grabbed opportunities in the newly opened areas to become a builder of businesses and institutions. He was a risk-taker who borrowed heavily to fund freighting and who speculated, sometimes illegally, in western lands and in townsites. Although Russell retained a gold-plated reputation for integrity that was the essential foundation for securing Eastern credit to fund military outfitting, he also gambled in his entrepreneurial quests. The Pony Express, for example, was a romantic venture that gave Russell, Majors and Waddell great visibility

William H. Russell (January 31, 1812–April 1,1872), often remembered as a Western freighter and as a founder of the famous but short-lived Pony Express, also was an early proslavery agitator and leader who helped "cleanse" Leavenworth of his free-state adversaries. Courtesy of the Kansas State Historical Society.

but lost money from the start and helped destroy Russell financially. He was "an aristocrat by nature" who never performed physical labor and preferred fine living with "clean linen, dainty food and a comfortable bed." At home Russell used slave labor and fought to transplant slavery to Kansas when he moved his headquarters there in 1855. He was impetuous and volatile, but he dealt in grand ideas and grand schemes that worked brilliantly for a time.[1]

Although Russell, Majors and Waddell was "the largest and most influential freighting firm on the western frontier," Russell's role has never been fully chronicled. The impact of freighting operations in infusing capital, defining routes, purchasing supplies locally, and creating jobs has gone largely unrecognized in territorial Kansas history, so state histories have not acknowledged him as a major land speculator or as an active and effective proslavery leader. William H. Russell is a significant figure whose role as a Western entrepreneur, as well as the engineer of much of the Bleeding Kansas–era violence in Leavenworth, demands explication.[2]

Born in Vermont on January 31, 1812, William Hepburn Russell thoroughly absorbed Southern values and behaviors in Lexington, Missouri, where he spent his teen years. He aspired to great wealth, but he began his commercial capitalist career as a store clerk. Working for the Aull brothers, Missouri's frontier chain-store operators, Russell daily experienced both the Santa Fe trade (the profitable exchanges between various businesses in the United States, including many in Missouri, and Santa Fe, still a part of Mexico, that utilized the Santa Fe trail) and fur-trade businesses. He learned their operations in detail and soon entered the same business himself.[3]

The Western freighting business that Russell and associates came to dominate emerged with William Becknell, who first recognized in 1821 that Santa Fe, under Mexican rule, was open for business after a long period of U.S. exclusion. Between 1821 and the 1840s the Santa Fe trade flourished, and traders successfully extended capitalism into the Southwest. Trade routes tied East and West in permanent bonds guarded by the army and ratified by the war with Mexico. Subsequently, military protection increased because Native Americans, resentful of the wagon trains and the accompanying environmental degradation of their lands, attacked and plundered the trains when possible.[4]

The military was slow to accept private rather than army freighters, but during the Mexican War the quartermaster's failure to supply goods in a timely fashion convinced the army to bid out contracts. The period of 1844 to 1850 saw tremendous growth in private freighting of military supplies, which promised to reduce costs. Before long, however, both the army and the various freight companies grew dissatisfied with the system of annually renewed contracts. In 1855 the army decided to ship all supplies with one freighter, but the excessive outfitting costs meant no single freighter could provide the service. This dilemma called forth a new freighting firm: Russell, Majors and Waddell. Each of the men had experience in outfitting and freighting, and each offered significant strengths. Russell provided easy access to credit through his financial network. William Waddell had years of experience in both outfitting and freighting and had diverse financial interests. Alexander Majors, himself a freighter, knew the business thoroughly and had some wagons and oxen on hand. Each partner, wrote authors Raymond and Mary Settle, was a "highly respected businessman in his community."[5]

These three men formed a partnership in December 1854 and became the sole freighter for the army for the next two years. With Waddell supervising from Lexington, Missouri, the company moved its headquarters to Leavenworth, Kansas Territory, and began to organize this massive operation. Majors undertook the practical work; he hired the teamsters, loaded the trains, and oversaw road operations. Russell, the moneyman, traveled to New York and Washington to negotiate contracts and secure financing. Fortunately, his reputation and those of his partners were so sound, and the government contract so secure, that Russell was able to borrow $500,000 to initiate the project. Freighting proved successful in 1855 and 1856. The company made $150,000 each year, and it appeared that future government contracts were imminent.[6]

Buoyed by this success, Russell energetically diversified his interests in the town of Leavenworth and established a financial infrastructure there at an early date. He was among the first men who brought capitalist thinking to the territory and built institutions and organizations to put it into action. Russell used his imagination and ingenuity to develop other opportunities in the new town. First the partners organized a "Cash Store," or general merchandise outfit, under the ownership of Majors, Russell & Co., which supplied a wide assortment of groceries and sundries to new settlers. In addition, wrote the Settles, "Early in 1855 they erected a large building to house a store and offices of the freighting firm." They also built a blacksmith shop, a wagon-repair shop, extensive corrals, a lumberyard, a meat-packing plant, and a sawmill. In addition Russell focused on local financial services. He traveled to Washington, D.C., and arranged with Luther Smoot of Suter, Lea & Company to open a bank in Leavenworth, making it appear, falsely, that Suter and Lea were involved. Russell joined with others to organize the Leavenworth Fire and Marine Insurance Company and became involved in railroad promotion. All these activities helped develop the new town and make money for the partners. Theirs was a diverse and profitable set of investments.[7]

The partners were also major speculators who invested heavily in town and rural lands and helped form the market in land in and around Leavenworth. Land speculation characterized much of westward expansion, but the extent of Russell's activity in eastern Kansas was unusual. The methods used to obtain the land included the filing of illegal claims and the threat of violence, approaches that were often considered "business as usual" in the West.[8]

Leavenworth's location adjacent to the fort, its central position at the eastern entrance to the territory, and the existing roads and trails that ran westward all indicated strong potential for development. Land rose in value quickly over initial low prices, and Russell, Majors and Waddell's decision to locate the freighting firm's headquarters in Leavenworth significantly accelerated town development. Lot values in the town rose as well, and local promoters were ecstatic. The partners participated in this early rise by purchasing fifty-three town lots for offices and other freighting activities.[9]

Such land speculation was a tricky business. An increase in land value was certain because the government price was so low: preempted land sold for only $1.25 per acre. Since the value of adjoining land in settled areas already was substantially higher than the government price, land newly opened to resettlement could be expected to increase in price. But the land on which the squatter city of Leavenworth sat—part of the Delaware Trust Lands—posed a particular problem. Under the 1854 treaty made with the Delaware Indians, it was no longer open to resettlement. To help the tribe secure more money for its land, the commissioner of Indian Affairs had written the treaty requiring that it be sold at auction to the highest bidder only after its value had increased. Nevertheless, the town company set up its squatter city. Since the company held no title, all its investors could sell was a promise to turn over title when or if they obtained it. In the meantime, their occupation remained illegal. Russell, who admittedly had considerable clout in Washington, counted on the town company's ability to change government policy over time. But it was still a risky investment.[10]

Between 1854 and 1857 Russell made yet another speculative venture in Delaware lands. He asked his employees—wagon masters, teamsters, and clerical help—to take up their own illegal claims. These workers registered

160-acre farm claims, the amount ordinarily available for preemption, in their own names, then turned these claims over to Russell and his partners when they obtained title. It is unclear whether they received a fee for the favor, but by this ruse Russell, Majors and Waddell staked a claim to 5,120 acres of Delaware land.[11]

During this time tensions in Leavenworth mounted, and rumors of violence proliferated. Interested buyers made open threats to prevent competitive bidding, and perhaps one-third of the free-state population was run out of town by Russell, among others; he apparently was willing to use whatever means were necessary to control the city government.

The territory's slavery contest grew heated in 1855 and erupted into violence in 1856. Both sides urged their partisans to immigrate to Kansas Territory, and Russell vigorously backed the proslavery side. As a slaveholder and major Kansas landowner, he had good reason for fighting to establish the institution in the territory, but before bringing his slaves into Kansas, he needed assurance that territorial laws would protect them as his property. To strengthen his cause, Russell joined with David R. Atchison in an association to make Kansas a slave state. Russell served as treasurer, and together they issued an "Appeal to the South," urging Southerners to send both emigrants and money for the cause. In the fall of 1855, when proslavery partisans formed a "Law and Order" Party, Russell joined it.[12]

The clearest evidence of his active participation in the conflict came in 1856, the year of "civil war" in Kansas. On August 31 and September 1 proslavery forces in Leavenworth rounded up a large number of free staters, forced them down to the levee and onto steamboats, and told them not to return. Prominent citizens were forced to leave for "personal safety." Proslavery advocates stole or destroyed their property and, in at least one case, burned a store belonging to a free-state activist. They murdered William Phillips, a lawyer who had vociferously opposed the proslavery forces, and shot and maimed his brother. Throughout these incidents, William H. Russell was not a quiet bystander. Government officials later took testimony, mostly from businessmen and professionals, of this attempt to cleanse Leavenworth of the free-state settlers. Their words made clear that Russell was a major leader issuing orders to proslavery forces. When Captain Fred Emery's group murdered Phillips and began to burn his house, "Before all the furniture had been got out of Phillips's house, William H. Russell rode up to the company; he was riding on a mule," explained John J. Luce. "He countermanded the order to burn the building, consequently no further attempt was made to burn it." Russell apparently also issued the order to sack free-state stores and homes and to store the plunder gained from such raids in Josiah B. McAfee's church. The obvious subservience of the proslavery forces to Russell shows him to have been a major proslavery leader in Leavenworth in 1856.[13]

In December the town company gave free rein to Russell; Sackfield Maclin, an officer at the fort; and Clinton Cockrill, a wealthy Missourian with heavy investment in the townsite, to negotiate a solution to the land problem. The territorial governor, John W. Geary, was asked to join them in the hope that he could help prevent the expected violence. Finally Norman Eddy, who supervised the sale of Delaware lands, agreed to accompany Russell to Washington to broker a solution. Because of his connections, Russell succeeded in obtaining the entire site for the town company for $24,000, or about a third of its appraised value.[14] Thus, several key values were imprinted in the town's culture: Indians did not deserve a fair deal; federal officials could and should be manipulated to achieve self-serving ends; and powerful, wealthy men had distinct advantages even on the frontier.

But, as history has shown repeatedly, no commanding presence rules forever. For Russell, Majors and Waddell, 1857 proved a business nightmare and the beginning of the partners' eventual failure. The company still held a sizable government contract, the outfitting of which cost the firm about $500,000. In May 48 trains set out using 645 wagons carrying 3,870,797 pounds of supplies. The wagons were pulled by 7,740 oxen and driven by about 700 teamsters and their assistants. If all went as it had in 1855 and 1856, 1857 held promise of being another profitable year. But the beginning of the Mormon War changed everything.[15]

When President James Buchanan decided to move against the Mormons, who had set up an independent society in Utah that potentially blocked future attempts to unify the West, the quartermaster at Fort Leavenworth told Russell that his company would have to transport 2.5 million pounds of supplies to Salt Lake City. This army request exceeded the terms of the partners' contract. Furthermore, it was too late in the season to send the additional supplies. In addition, since no contract had been drawn up for this additional run, Russell and his company would have to "rely" on Congress for reimbursement after the job was done. Russell said they could not accommodate the request; the commanding officer said he would "not accept their refusal."

Unfortunately, the company had no money to initiate the run. It stood heavily in debt for the trains dispatched earlier that season, so failure on this run could mean the company's ruin. Still, refusal to cooperate might mean exclusion from future government freighting contracts, the major business on which the partners relied.[16]

The war went badly for the freighting company. Col. Carlos A. Waite, the officer in charge in Utah, refused to protect the trains. The Mormons attacked the wagons, burned grass the oxen needed, and destroyed army provisions. Since the trains had departed late in the year, oxen died of starvation and exposure. Russell, Majors and Waddell managed to deliver 2,264,013 pounds of cargo, which meant the government owed them $323,201.05, but the company also began to prepare a claim for enormous losses.[17]

In January 1858 Russell, Majors and Waddell negotiated an army contract to freight more supplies the 1,200 miles to Utah and a second contract to freight army supplies to New Mexico. However, the army's funds were depleted, and the War Department could not even pay for the successful freighting in 1857. The company also had lost $319,020.45 on the late trains sent out. The War Department owed Russell's company $642,242.45. Since the company operated on credit, Russell needed these funds to continue operations in 1858. "The fact is that Russell, Majors and Waddell, having enjoyed an unbroken period of prosperity since 1855, was not only financially embarrassed, but its credit was seriously impaired," concluded Raymond and Mary Settle. Russell tried to work his magic again by dealing directly with Secretary of War John B. Floyd. Since his company's credit was already in the red, Russell asked if he could write drafts, or "acceptances," on the War Department against the earnings of the firm in transporting military supplies in 1858. According to the Settles, business houses commonly used this procedure to raise money. In this situation acceptances would be used to guarantee payment until the War Department paid the company and it could pay the bills. Floyd agreed to issue acceptances. "No fraud was intended," but the plan was questionable, and this new credit pushed the company further into debt. Then, instead of passing a bill to make up the War Department's Mormon War deficiency, Congress ordered an investigation of the contracts, in which both the "Mormon difficulty" and the integrity of Russell, Majors and Waddell were ferociously attacked. The firm's reputation was soiled. Although in 1858 the government paid some of the $2,425,378.35 it owed Russell, Majors and Waddell, the partners tried to extricate themselves from their existing 1859 contract. Again, Secretary Floyd refused to grant their request.[18]

Nevertheless, the company, with Russell still developing new schemes, continued to expand. Although recognizing the danger, he impetuously set the company on an imaginative but disastrous course. He organized the Pony Express in April 1860 and efficiently operated it for eighteen months. It was a spectacular enterprise, but it lost the ailing company even more money.[19]

In the eight months from December 1859 to August 1860, $967,006.01 in debts came due. The situation spiraled to a financial crisis in 1860. Clearly, if the partners had had the capital to purchase all the supplies, animals, and equipment the army needed each year, they would have remained successful. But $500,000 was a huge sum at the time, and no freighter then operating had such resources. Because of Russell's connections to financiers and the three men's reputation for integrity, they could borrow the necessary sum each year. But success depended on a tight payment schedule from the War Department. Russell had expected government requisitions to arrive as usual in early spring, but in 1860 the requisition came in July, and so he borrowed money that had to be repaid in June and July. When bills came due and Russell had no government payments in hand, he became desperate. He approached a clerk at the Department of the Interior—Godard Bailey, a man related to Secretary Floyd's wife. Bailey agreed to help Russell by providing state securities to bypass the current crisis, but he required that the bonds be returned. Russell managed to secure enough for the bonds to pay bills just coming due.

To stay afloat Russell had to borrow still more money, but a large repayment was coming due in August. With the threat of civil war looming, the nation's economy weakened sharply. Bondholders pressured Russell to protect them, and Bailey revealed to Russell for the first time that he had borrowed the bonds from the Indian Trust Fund. Russell and Bailey, realizing the severity of the situation, unwisely decided to use more bonds. Russell surely understood at this point his complicity in embezzlement. Unfortunately, the money from these bonds failed to resolve the problem. He could not pay the company's debts, nor could he retrieve the bonds and return them to Bailey.[20]

Bailey finally bolted and wrote a full confession of his misdeeds to the secretary of war. President Buchanan issued arrest warrants for both Bailey and Russell. Russell was still in New York City, frantically trying to rectify the situation, when he was apprehended and taken to Washington, D.C. The affair became embroiled in partisan politics. Russell testified before the select committee of the House of Representatives and, when brought to trial, argued that he could not be prosecuted because of his previous testimony. After another technical objection the indictments against him were quashed. The money provided to Russell and his partners, including the charges upon the War Department, was almost entirely lost. The government never paid Russell, Majors and Waddell for the company's losses in the Mormon War. All three partners lost their money and their reputations. Although Russell tried to salvage something from his empire, his options were limited. He then tried to recoup his wealth in the gold fields of Colorado. Ultimately, Russell was reduced to selling his home in New York, and in 1868 he applied for bankruptcy. The debts listed totaled $2,498,630.85.[21]

William H. Russell epitomized the West as we are coming to understand it. He embraced westward expansion and the opportunity it represented as one culture displaced others and transplanted its own institutions. As an enthusiastic entrepreneur, Russell seized upon a broad range of opportunities, sometimes going beyond his company's abilities, but some of these projects spawned important institutions and economic activities. Others, such as the Pony Express, lost money. The efficient, high-quality transportation the company provided extended and supported U.S. power in the West, and Russell's efforts produced new stores, banks, insurance companies, a hotel, and stations that became towns along trails. In the end, heavy borrowing and the catastrophe of 1857 bankrupted the company. The government's failure to reimburse it sealed the fate of Russell and the company.

Russell often desired opportunity at the expense of others. Using illegal methods, he seized some of the best rural lands of eastern Kansas that ordinary settlers might have secured. The methods he used stripped wealth from the Delaware tribe, a group that had already been victimized by the program of Indian removal, and he plied his influence in Washington to obtain legal title to the Leavenworth townsite situated on Delaware trust lands.

The firm's failure and the bond fraud has dimmed Russell's place in history, but he was a giant figure who made enormous contributions to Kansas and Western history. Russell never returned to the West but spent his last years in New York "alone and forgotten." His family brought him back to Missouri when he fell ill in 1872, and he died there the same year.

Clarina Irene Howard Nichols: "A Large-Hearted, Brave, Faithful Woman"

Kristen Tegtmeier Oertel

In the *History of Woman Suffrage,* a monumental account of women's struggle for the right to vote, the editors Susan B. Anthony, Elizabeth Cady Stanton, and Joslyn Gage remember Kansas prominently as "historic ground where Liberty fought her first victorious battles with Slavery . . . and the first State where the battle for woman's enfranchisement was waged." The famous suffragettes noted that Kansas women "worked with indomitable energy and perseverance" to secure voting rights in the state, and they venerated one woman in particular. They claimed, "To Clarina Howard Nichols the women of Kansas are indebted for many civil rights. . . . She is a large-hearted, brave, faithful woman, and her life speaks for itself."[1]

Nichols's remarkable life could speak for itself, but curiously, only a few scholars have written about her, and, ironically, she has been dubbed the "forgotten feminist of Kansas." Why has Nichols—who is largely responsible for

Clarina I. H. Nichols (January 25, 1810–January 11, 1885), a nationally known Vermont women's rights activist before moving to Kansas Territory with the fourth New England Emigrant Aid party in the fall of 1854, continued that struggle after her arrival and labored "to subsist [her] two sons in the Free State army of Kansas." Courtesy of the Kansas State Historical Society.

Kansas being the first state in the country to allow women to vote in school board elections—been forgotten? The answer, in part, lies in Nichols's clever rhetorical strategy and in her embodiment of a traditional feminine identity. In her analysis of Nichols's early speeches, Karlyn Kohrs Campbell argued that Nichols "used a feminized rhetorical role in a highly aggressive way. Under the strategic window dressing of femininity came a thundering denunciation of male treatment of women." Nichols was foremost a devoted wife and mother, but she used these positions as launching pads for scathing critiques of the way wives and mothers were regarded in the eyes of the law. She developed a nonconfrontational style that often incorporated humor, but her congeniality and wit did not weaken her resolute arguments for social and political change. At times she cited natural rights philosophy as justification for an expansion of human rights in America, and she often used her thorough knowledge of legal and political texts to support her claims. But fundamentally she used her status as a devoted Christian and mother, often capitalizing on the conventional aspects of her lifestyle to lobby for extremely unconventional political rights. Thus, Nichols was a motivator, but she was not an agitator, and because of her skillful and practical activism, Kansas entered the Union in 1861 with a state constitution that guaranteed women more civil rights than any other state in the nation at the time.[2]

Although Nichols's story began in Vermont and ended in California, her most remarkable strides in the fight for women's rights took place in Kansas, where she lived from 1854 to 1871. Born Clarina Irene Howard in West Townshend, Vermont, on January 25, 1810, she was raised and educated in Vermont until her marriage to Justin Carpenter in 1830. While married to Carpenter, Nichols gave birth to a daughter and two sons but soon became estranged from her abusive husband and divorced him in 1843. Later that year she married George W. Nichols, editor and publisher of the *Windham County Democrat,* a paper she "secretly" ran as her husband became increasingly ill. She did not publicly acknowledge her management of the paper until 1850, claiming that she had to prove her worth as an editor before revealing her gender. In a letter to Susan B. Anthony, Nichols explained the philosophy behind her anonymity:

> I have labored for years (6) under my husband's hat, laying the foundations, creating step by step the sentiment thro the various channels of my knowledge, before I came out in my own name to give to my sex a personal offering. My

husband wished me to do so before; but I wished to make sure that I had secured the confidence of men in my ability to conduct their political paper; before I threw myself on their support in the matter of legal & social reforms. I
feel that men compel us to prove our equal intellect in order to [achieve] the
full influence of our moral & social organization.[3]

By editing the *Democrat,* Nichols engaged the public in a way that was indica-
tive of her overall activist strategy; she gained the trust of her readers and
argued the merits of her causes before aligning them with the politically
charged term "Woman's Rights."

Nichols used the *Democrat* as a vehicle to advocate improvements in
women's inferior social status, and soon Vermont women enjoyed their "first
breath of a legal civil existence." In 1847 Vermont passed a law that gave
women the right to bequeath property; in 1849 and 1850 the state passed legislation that further enhanced women's property rights and enabled them to
insure their husbands' lives. Because of her public activism on the part of
women in Vermont, Nichols was invited to speak in New Hampshire and Massachusetts on women's suffrage and on temperance, another reform movement that she fervently embraced.

Nichols's activism in the East ignited with her speech at the National
Woman's Rights Convention at Worcester, Massachusetts, in October 1851. Her
speech, "On the Responsibilities of Woman," marked her as an effective yet
"womanly speaker"; in it she persuasively argued that women could fulfill their
responsibilities as wives and mothers only if they were given expanded civil
rights. It was through her involvement in these women's rights conventions during the early 1850s that she met Susan B. Anthony, and it is clear that Nichols
motivated and encouraged Anthony in her early pursuit of women's rights. Ten
years younger than Nichols, Anthony had only recently joined the suffrage
movement after lobbying in favor of temperance and being discouraged by the
movement's male-dominated leadership. Nichols wrote to Anthony in April
1852 and predicted her legendary dedication to the suffrage movement: "It is
most invigorating to watch the development of a woman in the work for humanity: first, anxious for the cause and depressed with a sense of her own inability;
next, partial success of timid efforts creating a hope; next a faith; and then the
fruition of complete self-devotion. Such will be your history."[4]

Like Anthony, Nichols exhibited "complete self-devotion" to the cause of
women's rights, but she soon expanded her political activism in the mid-1850s

to include abolitionism, which partly inspired her migration to Kansas Territory. Nichols moved to Kansas in October 1854 after the Kansas-Nebraska Act had reopened the territory north of the Missouri Compromise line to the possibility of slavery and galvanized abolitionists and free soilers throughout the country. She viewed Kansas as a place ripe for social change, hoping that both abolitionism and women's rights would take root in the nascent and growing free-state communities. She described her fellow pioneers as "people whose character and whose destiny are to turn the scales of westering power for the *right,* for the *true.*" In addition to embracing the antislavery cause, she noted that many Kansas pioneers seemed inclined to support the expansion of women's rights. Writing from Lawrence in November 1854, Nichols remarked that she was among like-minded friends in the free-state community: "The *women* are 'strong-minded.' And by the way, 'strong-mindedness' will be no objection to a woman, among the pioneers to Kanzas."[5]

"Strong-minded" women such as Nichols supported women's rights and opposed slavery in the territory, and Nichols frequently knitted these dual concerns together. She temporarily left Kansas after her husband's sad and untimely death in August 1855, but she continued to publicize and support the free-state cause while in Vermont settling her husband's estate. She wrote letters to the Kansas free-state papers and used this medium to continue her advocacy of women's rights in the territory. In one such letter, Nichols praised the free-state women for their unselfish and courageous behavior in the sectional conflict there: "[Kansas's] 'strong minded' women will be content to run bullets, transfer ammunition, and inspire their husbands and sons with hope, faith and courage, until public offices of honor and trust are redolent of domestic peace and quiet before they ask a share in their responsibilities. Yes, woman, self-denying now as in the past, is forgetting herself and her wrongs in the great national wrong that threatens to deprive the manhood of the nation of the right and the power to protect the altars and the hearths consecrated to God and humanity." Nichols lauded Kansas women's contributions to the fight against slavery but soon asked her readers how women should be rewarded for their efforts, inquiring, "What new pledges of humanity shall eternal justice win from the Legislators of Kansas?" and wondered, "What new rounds will Kansas add to the ladder of Freedom?" Nichols encouraged the territory's leaders to expand women's property rights, especially for widows, and urged Kansas to distinguish itself among the states as a champion for humanity. She closed her editorial with a plea to Kansas legislators: "I ask you not to do by woman as she has been done by in the legislation of other States. . . . I entreat you to legislate for the mothers, legislate for your wives as you legislate for yourselves. Make them your companions, your equals in legal rights, that in case you die first, your children may still nestle in a mother's arms, be restrained by the loving authority of a mother, and never fail for a protector by reason of the legal inability of their most disinterested parent and friend."[6]

Nichols appealed to her male readers' sense of duty to their children in an effort to gain increased legal rights for women, a nonthreatening method that would eventually prove successful. Indeed, Nichols's nonconfrontational style was paramount to her success. Evidence of this philosophy abounded in her letters as she approached her male readers with humor, respect, and measured intelligence. For example, she noted that married women were often referred to in the legal community as "legally dead" or "dead in law" but quipped that these "dead women [had] been resuscitated in hopeful numbers" by recent laws that granted them property rights. Furthermore, she assured her readers that "in laying bare the injustice which the legislation of the past has perpetrated upon woman, I do not charge malicious nor intentional wrong upon man." Nichols believed that intelligent men were not guilty of "premeditated injustice" against women, but she did not excuse men's ignorance of women's legal rights.

Nichols repeatedly demonstrated her broad knowledge of the legal statutes regarding women and revealed the inconsistencies and contradictions embedded within the logic (or illogic) of the codes. She found it ironic that single women had the legal right to own real property, although they rarely had any opportunity to obtain it, whereas married women and widows, who were more likely to amass property, had no legal right to retain it. According to Nichols, "at the very period when every right of the individual woman is made of tenfold more value by reason of her greatly multiplied needs and responsibilities, in the new relations consequent upon marriage," a woman lost the very rights that could facilitate her ability to fulfill her wifely duties, mainly her childbearing and rearing responsibilities.[7] Again Nichols referred to society's traditional beliefs in women's roles in the private sphere to plead for expanded legal rights in the public sphere.

Nichols's activism was amplified in the spring of 1856 when proslavery forces sacked the antislavery town of Lawrence and Massachusetts senator Charles Sumner was attacked on the Senate floor by South Carolina representative Preston Brooks. She wrote, "The late news from Kansas and the horrible outrage on Senator Sumner in Congress, have roused me from the stupor of my grief, and I feel an intense desire to be up and doing. Ah, what can I do? Talk? 'Lend me your ears.'"8 And talk she did; Nichols embarked upon a public speaking tour designed to raise money and support for the free-state settlers in Kansas. Armed with reports of the "Sack of Lawrence" and the caning of Sumner, Nichols traveled throughout the country to garner support for Kansas settlers.

During the summer and fall Nichols presented roughly fifty Kansas lectures in Vermont, New Hampshire, Massachusetts, Connecticut, Pennsylvania, and New York. Horace Greeley, editor-in-chief of the New York *Tribune,* and Thaddeus Hyatt, a philanthropist and abolitionist, conscripted her to lecture for the Kansas National Aid Committee. Nichols wrote to Hyatt and reported that she could not find "a house that would hold (standing) all the people who came to hear me on Kansas. The people are *awake.*" Nichols suggested to Hyatt that he also employ Susan B. Anthony to lecture and gather money for the free-state movement. She wrote that Anthony had "the executive ability and the experience admirably adapted to the work. . . . She has a brother in the Free State army in Kansas and if I take the post you propose I would solicit her as my *right hand* woman."9 Nichols enlisted Anthony, and they both spread the word about the political tyranny in Kansas, even though their lectures likely disturbed many audience members' beliefs about the proper separation of women and politics.

Nichols deflected much of the criticism about her public speaking by couching her activism within the realm of her motherly duties. This method was more than just a rhetorical tool for Nichols because her son, Aurelius Carpenter, had fought with John Brown in the battle of Black Jack in June 1856 and had suffered a bullet wound; she felt compelled to raise financial and emotional support for the Kansas cause that had embroiled her entire family. She solicited assistance from the women of New York and appealed to their sense of motherly responsibility: "Are you mothers? Let me speak to you for the mothers of Kansas. I am one of them. My sons are among the sufferers and the defenders of that ill-fated Territory; their blood has baptized the soil which they yet live to weep over, to love, and to defend. I ask of you, mothers of New York, but a tithe of the sacrifices and devotion of the mothers of Kansas. . . . Can you withhold from them the bread that shall win to you the blessing of those ready to perish?"10 Nichols also addressed the New York women as wives and sisters, seeking sympathy for the husbands and brothers who had sacrificed their Eastern comforts and even their lives for a free Kansas. Her dramatic and romantic style elicited a strong response from her Eastern "sisters," and Nichols and her converts raised hundreds of dollars for free-state settlers. In fact, by 1860 the New York Ladies Kansas Relief Society had transported $707.65 worth of clothing and goods to the territory.[11]

Nichols viewed firsthand the benefits of her speaking tour in the East after her return to Kansas in the spring of 1857. She moved her family to the new town of Quindaro, where she joined the staff of the radical free-state newspaper, the *Chindowan*. She reported in the paper that the "Friends of the East . . . did so much to soften the privations of these pioneers." She commented that much of the tea she drank in fellow settlers' homes was "charity tea" and that the diverse fashions in the territory were evidence of "charity garments." Nichols was grateful for the assistance of her Eastern sisters, but she also noted that the Kansas settlers had gained strength and heartiness from the adversity they had experienced during the winter of 1856–1857.[12]

As the slavery issue appeared resolved with the election of the free-state territorial legislature in 1857 and the defeat of the proslavery Lecompton Constitution, Nichols returned her political activism to women's rights. She was asked by the Moneka Woman's Rights Association of Linn County, founded in 1858 by ardent abolitionists John and Susan Wattles, to serve as its official messenger to the state constitutional convention in 1859, and she accepted without hesitation. With her knitting in hand, she took a permanent seat "beside the chaplain," where she quietly and persistently lobbied for women's suffrage and property rights. After introducing himself to the sole female delegate at the convention, territorial Governor Samuel Medary asked Nichols, "You would not have women go down into the muddy pool of politics?" Nichols skillfully replied, "Governor, I admit that you know best how muddy that pool is, but you remember the Bethesda of old; how the angel had to go in and trouble the waters before the sick could be healed. So I would have the angels trouble this muddy pool that it may be well with the people; for you know, Governor Medary, that this people is very sick."[13]

Nichols was eventually invited to address the entire constitutional body, and her words persuaded many of the delegates of the necessity of imparting certain political rights to women. She reported on the success of her first address to Susan Wattles and claimed, "The reception of my plea was hearty and spontaneously sympathized." Two convention attendees from Nebraska praised Nichols's eloquence and promised their support for several of her resolutions.

The men noted her nonconfrontational yet persuasive style: "Although not prepared fully to endorse all your views; still we are free to acknowledge that if all advocates of 'Woman's Rights' were discreet and womanly in their arguments as you—much might be done for suffering humanity. We earnestly desire to see the laws amended that a woman shall be able to control her children, her earnings and her property." Nichols addressed the convention again a week later, after a group of citizens petitioned the convention, and asked to use its hall for her lecture. The convention delegates unanimously agreed; she spoke to an "overflowing house," and the delegates issued a resolution thanking Nichols for her "eloquent and highly *convincing* lecture."[14]

In part because of her successful elocution and the numerous petitions Nichols's supporters submitted, the Kansas constitution included unprecedented provisions for women's civil rights. Although Nichols failed in her ultimate goal to secure unconditional suffrage, she reveled in the smaller victories that granted women the right to vote in school board elections, expanded their property rights, and provided the right to custody of their children in cases of divorce. Charles Robinson, the first state governor of Kansas, wrote of Nichols that it was "to her influence we [owe] all that is liberal to woman in our constitution & laws."[15]

But Nichols did not cease in her efforts to secure full suffrage for Kansas women after 1861. She believed it imprudent to push for women's rights during the Civil War, and she encouraged her colleagues to quiet their voices. During the war Nichols moved to Washington, D.C., and worked for the Quartermaster's Department before assuming a position as matron for a home run by the National Association for the Relief of Destitute Colored Women and Children. But as soon as the war concluded she began pressing the Kansas legislature and governor for complete enfranchisement, and she canvassed throughout the state in 1867 during the impartial suffrage campaign. This complicated referendum suffered from its members' reluctance to fully support both women's and Negro suffrage, but Nichols appears to have endorsed both causes from the beginning. As early as 1859 Susan Wattles wrote to Nichols that she "sympathize[d] with you perfectly in the sentiments you express about laboring for the colored people. I wish the Republican party were more thoroughly Anti-Slavery." In 1867 Nichols argued in favor of impartial suffrage in the *Vermont Phoenix:* "For very shame, the voters of Kansas should ratify the amendments striking out the words *white* and *male* from the constitution. . . . The present government of Kansas is 'bogus' to the women and blacks of the state."[16]

While Nichols theoretically embraced the idea of enfranchising both blacks and women, she acknowledged the utility of pursuing one goal at a time. In May 1859 she conceded that it would be extremely difficult to get both measures passed simultaneously. In a letter to Susan Wattles, she reluctantly declared, "In reference to any allusion in our petition to the enfranchisement of the colored—I am forced to the conclusion that it would mar our effort and do no good to them. I am persuaded that the enfranchisement of woman involves their enfranchisement and the sooner we get our hands into the ballot box the sooner will their freedom come."[17] Nichols believed that once women received the vote, they would wield their newfound political power to help enfranchise blacks. Thus, her desire to pursue women's suffrage first appears to be motivated not by racism, unlike some of her colleagues in the national movement, but instead by her sense of practicality. She truly felt that the most efficient and effective method of achieving the vote for both women and blacks would be to work on the objectives one at a time.

Unfortunately, many of her colleagues in Kansas and elsewhere disagreed with Nichols's egalitarian philosophy. While campaigning in Kansas in 1867 Susan B. Anthony and Elizabeth Cady Stanton eventually allied themselves with the virulent racist Democrat George Francis Train, a man who embraced women's suffrage but attacked the notion of enfranchising African Americans as ludicrous. In contrast, an invitation to Nichols in 1859 to speak in favor of women's suffrage at a rally in Westport, Missouri, was revoked when knowledge of her "antislavery antecedents" preceded her visit across the border.[18] Although discouraged by such occurrences, Nichols persisted in her pursuit of impartial suffrage.

History reminds us that Nichols's path toward political equality for women and blacks led to a dead end in Kansas, as both measures to amend the state constitution failed in 1867. There is no evidence in her surviving papers that Nichols's spirit wavered in the midst of these defeats. She published extensively in the late 1860s and early 1870s and maintained her optimism in the fight for full suffrage rights. In 1869 she published the essay "The Bible Position of Woman," in which she skillfully analyzed Bible passages, particularly those in the Book of Genesis, and interpreted them in ways that cast women as equal helpmates to men. She believed, "All that really stands in the way of woman's political equality now, is the waning belief that the Bible is opposed to it," so she made every effort to change the public's perception about scripture.[19]

After 1870 her failing health prevented her from giving public lectures, but she increasingly relied on her pen to wage war against antisuffragists. Writing to Susan B. Anthony in 1870, Nichols lamented her declining health but took solace in her ability to support her younger peers in the cause for women's rights: "I sometimes cry out at being hedged in by circumstances, from joining the triumphant march of womanhood. I seem almost to have dropped out by the way, unable to keep up, but bearing in my hand the cup of water, it may be, from the wayside spring, to refresh the swifter of foot. But O how I watch and pray! I do all I can with my pen."[20]

Nichols carried her powerful pen to California when her poor health and her family's tenuous financial situation compelled their move from Kansas in 1871. Although she kept moving west, Nichols maintained her ties with her Eastern sisters and sustained her involvement in the suffrage movement until her death in 1885. Writing repeatedly to the *Woman's Journal,* a weekly suffragist periodical published in Boston, Nichols articulated familiar themes about the subjugation of women in America. After publishing "The Bible Position of Woman," she frequently blamed Christian theology as the root source of the belief in women's inferiority. In an 1877 letter to the *Journal,* Nichols argued, "From the beginning, our pulpits, more especially those of the Orthodox sects, have taught and fostered a despotic relation of the sexes. Man to rule; Woman to be ruled. . . . In all but the name and power to sell—a relation the counterpart of Negro slavery, and defended from the same theological platform."[21] Many clergymen were appalled by her accusations and responded by attacking her character. Nichols countered these attacks with her characteristic wit and logic, and neither her "strong-mindedness" nor her faith weakened in her old age.

Clarina Nichols never ceased her advocacy for women's rights, indeed, for human rights, during her lifetime. As her ailing health declined and she approached her death, she did so with the knowledge that her cause would be taken up by a new generation of suffragettes. In a written address to the Worcester Woman's Suffrage Convention in 1880, Nichols noted, "The leaders in the Suffrage movement may all die—[but] two to one will spring from the ranks to bear aloft the glorious banner of a free womanhood." In her brief remembrances, begun in 1880 during her "invalid hours," Nichols reflected upon her life and its significance. She lamented her failure to keep a diary and remarked that it could have been "a legacy of instructive and entertaining experiences."[22] Had she written down a record of these experiences, perhaps historians and scholars would not so easily have forgotten her. Her contributions to abolitionism and to expanding women's rights in Kansas and throughout the country should secure this "large-hearted, brave, faithful woman" a venerated place in the history of the state and the nation.

PART TWO

SETTLEMENT AND

DEVELOPMENT, 1865–1890

The country here is just beautiful here, and by the way, we have the best claim around here. . . . I think we surely have a good farm. Sam spaded where the sod had been taken off for the house & the ground worked up almost like an ash heap. I think I will like Kansas. [April 12, 1885]

Well, I think Kansas is certainly the home for the poor man. I believe in a few years we will know what it is to have a good home, plenty around us & something for a rainy day. (I feel it in my bones that way.) [June 27, 1885]

—*Flora Moorman Heston, Clark County, 1885*

Joseph G. McCoy and the Creation of

the Mythic American West

Jim Hoy

Joseph Geiting McCoy, one of eleven children of David and Mary Kilpatrick McCoy, was born in Sangamon County near Springfield, Illinois, on December 21, 1837. He died in Kansas City, Missouri, on October 19, 1915, and is buried in Maple Grove Cemetery in Wichita, Kansas, where he lies next to his wife, who died four years before he did.[1]

A glance at Joseph McCoy's life suggests nothing out of the ordinary. Like many aspiring young men of his time, he heeded Horace Greeley's advice and was drawn to the West. There, again like many others, McCoy tried his hand at a number of ventures in the hope of making his fortune. Ultimately, none of his ambitious enterprises in real estate, business, or politics succeeded in making him rich or famous, yet his legacy is arguably as great as that of any other Kansan. Although McCoy's may not be a household name, he is in large part responsible for creating the conditions that led to the creation of America's

Joseph G. McCoy (December 21, 1837–October 19, 1915), a young, enterprising Illinois cattle dealer who moved to Abilene in 1867, about the time this clean-shaven image of him was made, changed the face of the country's cattle industry, essentially creating the conditions that gave rise to America's dominant myth—the Wild West of the Great American Cowboy. Courtesy of the Kansas State Historical Society.

dominant myth—the Wild West of the Great American Cowboy. Without McCoy and the "long drive" he helped to create, this great American icon might never have come into existence, and certainly not in its current recognizable and symbolic form.

After completing his formal education, which included a year at Knox College, McCoy, who had been reared on a farm, started out as a farmer-stockman breeding and selling mules in rural Illinois. His entrepreneurial and adventurous spirit surfaced early when, in 1861, he sold at a good profit a stockcar-load of his mules in Kentucky, a project that required transport on five different railroad lines. Apparently the success of this venture buoyed both his confidence and his wallet sufficiently that upon his return he married a neighbor girl, Sarah Epler. For the next several years McCoy worked on his own, raising sheep for wool and buying, fattening, and selling cattle, hogs, and sheep. He also continued to deal in mules and shipped livestock to markets both near (Chicago and Cairo, Illinois) and far (New Orleans and New York). He became a successful stockman and livestock feeder.

Over the course of his life McCoy engaged in many other occupations. He was at one time or another a real estate investor and developer, a businessman, a livestock commission-firm owner, a grocer, a storekeeper, a fence dealer, a livestock inspector, a politician, and a writer. As an author he is important for having written the only contemporary account of the great cattle-drive era that followed the Civil War. Two of his jobs could be described in modern terms: consultant and public relations agent. As the latter he was hired in 1872 to promote the city (or, more accurately at that time, the town) of Wichita to prospective cattle shippers. As a consultant he worked for several different agencies. He was hired by the U.S. Census Bureau, for instance, to determine the number of range cattle in the southwestern plains for the years 1880 and 1881 and to estimate the number of Texas cattle that were driven to Kansas in 1866 and in 1880. He was hired in 1881 to help the Cherokee Nation collect fees and taxes on cattle being grazed on tribal lands. Officials in Newton hired McCoy to design and build that town's stockyards when the Santa Fe Railroad extended its tracks there in 1871. Undoubtedly the most unusual job undertaken by McCoy was his brief stint, in 1893, as a U.S. Treasury agent assigned to the Oregon-Washington region to intercept smuggled shipments of opium from China.[2]

Of all his activities and business ventures, the one that had the greatest effect on McCoy's life and legacy occurred early in 1867 when he entered the cattle-fattening business in Illinois with two of his older brothers, William and James. This partnership would lead him to Kansas and to Abilene later the same year. Illinois, at the time, was the second-largest producer of beef cattle in the nation. The largest was Texas, and it was the importation of Texas range cattle into Illinois feedlots that brought McCoy into prominence in his own lifetime and into legend in ours.

At the end of the Civil War cattle were so numerous in Texas as to be essentially worthless. As McCoy humorously noted, the number of cattle he owned determined the measure of a Texan's poverty at this time: the bigger the herd, the poorer the rancher. With the demand for beef rising rapidly in the eastern states, however, the value of these numerous Texas steers could be multiplied ten- to twentyfold in Chicago. Both Texas ranchers and entrepreneurs from elsewhere realized the economic potential of this situation.

Getting the cattle to the East in market-ready condition, however, presented a number of obstacles. To fatten the cattle, owners had to get them to the Midwest. Farmers there raised corn in abundance, and the tall grasses of the prairie states were renowned for putting flesh on steers quickly and economically. In the first years after the war no railroads extended from the Midwest into Texas, and although a few cattle were transported by boat up the

Mississippi, it was not an efficient means of moving the huge numbers involved. The most effective way of getting cattle to the Midwest was driving them overland, as had been done before the Civil War. By trailing them slowly through the lush prairie grasslands along the Shawnee Trail, which led through eastern Indian Territory to the railroads in central Missouri, or through eastern Kansas and on to Iowa and Illinois, steers could actually gain weight as they made their way north. In 1866, however, as in the 1850s, opposition arose from local farmers because of Texas fever, a serious disease carried by Texas longhorns that killed northern cattle.[3]

In the first year following the war the great majority of longhorns followed the Shawnee Trail to Sedalia, Missouri. The Texas drovers, however, were no match for the irate Missouri farmers, who formed vigilance committees and actively, indeed violently, resisted the passage of Texas cattle through their lands. Drovers were threatened with guns, beaten, and horsewhipped to such an extent that the days of driving cattle through Missouri and eastern Kansas were essentially over. This was where Joseph McCoy's vision and foresight changed the course of history and inspired the birth of one of our nation's greatest folk heroes: the American cowboy.

The year 1867 was pivotal for McCoy. That year, as part of the brothers' cattle-feeding operation, he bought some Texas cattle from fellow Illinoisan W. W. Sugg, from whom he learned of the great numbers of cheap cattle in Texas and the great difficulties Missouri and Kansas farmers caused for the drovers who attempted to deliver them from Texas to Illinois. Within six months McCoy had solved that problem by locating, building, and opening an outlet for Texas cattle in Kansas. McCoy did not found the town of Abilene, but he put it on the map. Nor did he ever, so far as is known, visit Dodge City, but without him that town would never have become a major part of the legend of the American West.

McCoy is credited as having been the first to conceive the idea of locating an outlet for Texas cattle at or near the western edge of the Texas fever deadline, or boundary of the quarantined area, in Kansas. His first plan was to establish a port on the Arkansas River, near Fort Smith, from which longhorns could be shipped up the Mississippi to Cairo, Illinois, then hauled by train to upstate farms and feed yards. He decided, however, after visiting with businessmen in Kansas City, to explore the possibility of a railroad-shipping center in Kansas, a decision that was solidified after a chance meeting with Texas cattleman J. J. Myers in June at the Hale House hotel in Junction City. McCoy told Myers about his scheme of establishing a shipping point for cattle along the Kansas Pacific Railway. The Texan gave McCoy immediate validation, assuring him that whoever provided the facilities so described not only would have all the business he could handle but would prove "a benefactor to the entire Texan live stock interest. . . . There are moments in ones existence when a decision, or a purpose arrived at, shapes future actions and events— even changes the whole tenor of ones life and labor," McCoy wrote. "Such was the effect of the two brief hours spent in conversation by the Texan drover and the Illinoisan."[4]

A provision of a Kansas law passed in late February 1867 allowed an exception for Texas cattle to cross the quarantine line in order to be driven to some point on the Union Pacific Railroad, Eastern Division (soon the Kansas Pacific), west of "the first guide meridian west from the sixth principal meridian." McCoy, having extracted from skeptical and reluctant railroad officials permission to build shipping facilities and a promise of $5 for each carload of cattle shipped, set out to find a good location. Attempts to locate his pens in Junction City, Solomon, and Salina met discouragement of one sort or another, but when McCoy arrived at Abilene, a village with, as he noted, a mere dozen crude log buildings, one two-room store, and one saloon, he had his site: "Abilene was selected because the country was entirely unsettled, well watered, excellent grass, and nearly the entire area of country was adapted to holding cattle. And it was the farthest point east at which a good depot for cattle business could have been made." Technically, this site may not have met the legal requirements of the recently passed Kansas law, but with Governor Samuel Crawford's backing McCoy moved his plan forward without hesitation.[5]

Construction of the stockyards began on the first of July, and within two months pens capable of holding 3,000 head of cattle had been built, as had an office and a barn. A set of scales for weighing cattle was installed, and the Drovers Cottage, a hotel for cattlemen, was nearing completion. On September 5 twenty carloads of cattle left Abilene for Chicago, the first of some 35,000 head that would be shipped over the next two months.

Word spread quickly among Texans that Abilene provided a reliable outlet for their cattle with no farmers to get in the way. Not that homesteaders had not settled in Dickinson County, and not that they were not initially opposed to the proposed influx of disease-bearing Texas longhorns. McCoy, learning that they had formed an organization to stop the drives, proposed a meeting with the settlers to which he took several Texas cattle owners. Although McCoy extolled the potential economic benefits to the farmers, who would have a high-demand market for their products and access to inexpensive cattle to which they could feed their hay and cornstalks, the Texans were "bartering with the Kansans for butter, eggs, potatoes, onions, oats, [and] corn" and paying more than the asking price. In addition, the cattlemen pledged a bond that would pay settlers for trampled crops or local cattle that died from Texas fever. McCoy's economic arguments won over the leader of the opposing farmers, who proclaimed his conversion: "Gentlemen, if I can make any money out of this cattle trade, I am not afraid of 'Spanish fever [Texas fever];' but if I can't make any money out of this cattle trade, then I am d—d afraid of 'Spanish fever.'"[6] Thus, McCoy's grand scheme of providing a marketing and shipping venue for Texas cattle in the central plains was successfully launched only half a year after it was first conceived. A similar scheme, hatched by the Kansas Live Stock Company in Topeka on February 27, only one day after the Kansas legislature legalized, with restrictions, the driving of Texas cattle to Kansas, came to naught. Only Joseph G. McCoy had the drive, the persuasiveness, and the resources to bring a plan for locating a facility for Texas cattle west of Topeka to fruition—and in a remarkably short time.

Abilene thrived, thanks to McCoy. With the backing of his partnership with his brothers, McCoy had bought 250 acres of land when he first came to Abilene, on some of which he built his Great Western Stockyard and some of which he held as a real estate investment. McCoy also built the Drovers Cottage, a three-story hotel with a hundred rooms, a restaurant, a bar, and a billiard room that opened for business in 1868. This impressive structure was a good investment, for it soon became a popular gathering place for drovers, shippers, feeders, and traders—many working cowboys were actually more attracted to the Alamo or the Bull's Head saloons. McCoy contracted with James and Lou Gore to manage the hotel. Mrs. Gore was an especially fortunate choice as proprietor, for she proved to be very popular with the Texans. She was, in McCoy's words, a "Florence Nightingale" to tired and sick drovers. A year later McCoy, strapped financially, sold the hotel. When the cattle trade moved west to Ellsworth in 1872, the Drovers Cottage followed, riding the rails to its new location.[7]

McCoy's relationship with the Kansas Pacific Railway Company was contentious. By his own account he found railroad officials prone to break contracts. If indeed the railroad had paid McCoy Brothers the amount originally agreed upon, then the cattle shipped from Abilene would have made the partners rich. In addition to the 35,000 shipped in 1867, McCoy stated that 75,000 passed through Abilene the following year; 150,000 the year after that; 300,000 in 1870; and 600,000 in 1871, Abilene's last year as a cowtown. Not all these cattle were actually shipped by rail, for many of them came to Abilene and were sold there, then driven overland to ranches in Wyoming and Montana or to Indian reservations in the Dakotas. Nevertheless, enough departed on the Kansas Pacific that the railroad, faced with what must have seemed an exorbitant sum, reneged on its obligation, leading McCoy to pursue legal action. Although he eventually won in court after a two-year battle, the expense of the effort, combined with an unprofitable purchase of 900 cattle, forced him into bankruptcy in 1870. Not only did he have to sell the Drovers Cottage and his real estate holdings, but he also lost the Great Western Stockyard. It was a financial blow from which neither he nor his brothers ever fully recovered.[8] Needless to say, McCoy's comments on the railroad and its officers were negative, although often tinged with wry and sometimes biting humor, if not complete bile. He noted, for instance, that in his initial meeting with Kansas Pacific officials, his plan was called wild and chimerical. He stated that a railroad official later attempted to bribe him and that the company backed out on its commitment to help pay damages to Dickinson County farmers who had suffered legitimate losses. The railroad, McCoy alleged, was lukewarm toward his plan from the first and nearly delayed the initial shipments in 1867 by not building until the last minute the sidetrack and switch it had promised.

McCoy was especially irritated with the railroad when it attempted to divert business from Abilene by building its own stockyards at Brookville. His irritation grew when, in the two years following the end of shipping at Abilene, the railroad spent significant sums of money in promoting the shipping business, something it had never done at Abilene. Considering his difficulties with the Kansas Pacific, McCoy can perhaps be forgiven for not noting the company's positive 1868 report to stockholders recognizing the value of the cattle trade.[9] One positive result of McCoy's financial struggles with the railroad was that the need for money caused him to start writing the journalistic articles that formed the basis for his book, which, as noted before, is the only firsthand contemporary account of the cowtown era. McCoy's prose is clear, informative, and entertaining. Referring to himself as "the Illinoisan," he not only described his own efforts to establish a cattle market at Abilene but added greatly to our understanding of all aspects of the cattle business during the initial years of the great drives: supply, demand, banking, meat-packing plants, commission houses, wintering cattle, feeding cattle, lobbying legislatures, Texas fever, cattle drives, and valuable profiles of many cattlemen from Texas and other states. McCoy also provided some of the first descriptions of the cowboy that have become part of the myth. Twentieth-century Hollywood may have invented the face-off on Texas Street and the fast draw, but the innate character of the cowboy hero of popular culture was well described by McCoy:

> fond of a practical joke, always pleased with a good story, and not offended if it was of an immoral character; universal tipplers, but seldom drunkards . . . always chivalrously courteous to a modest lady; possessing a strong, innate sense of right and wrong, a quick, impulsive temper, great lovers of a horse and always good riders and good horsemen; always free to spend their money lavishly for such objects or purposes as best please them; very quick to detect an injury or insult, and not slow to avenge it nor quick to forget it; always ready to help a comrade out of a scrape, full of life and fun; would illy brook rules of restraint, free and easy.

McCoy also wrote of the cowboy's activities once he hit town after months on the trail: first a trip to the barber; then a visit to the haberdasher for a new set of clothes, including a hat and boots with stars decorating the tops; all topped off by a night at the saloon, the theater, the card tables, the dance hall, and the bawdy house. Often these rowdy, drunken evenings, passed among the dregs of society (or, as McCoy termed them, "bad characters, both male and female; of the very worst class in the universe"), ended in gunfire with the cowboy "deal[ing] out death in unbroken doses to such as may be in range of his pistols."[10]

Such behavior, if allowed to continue unrestrained, would have been bad for the cattle business that McCoy was promoting. Drunken, potentially fatal disturbances in riotous saloons could be quelled only through "force and terror. No quiet turned man could or would care to take the office of marshal, which jeopardized his life; hence the necessity of employing a desperado, one who feared nothing, and would as soon shoot an offending subject as to look at him." These words were the closest allusion McCoy made to his most momentous decision (in terms of the creation of the mythic Wild West) as mayor of Abilene: hiring James Butler "Wild Bill" Hickok as marshal in April 1871. McCoy had been active in Abilene civic affairs from his arrival. He was named one of five trustees when the town was first incorporated in 1868 and was its first elected mayor, assuming office just a few days before Hickok's appointment. Hickok's reputation as a gunfighter preceded him and was in fact considered a major qualification for the position. Along with Wyatt Earp, Hickok is the most celebrated of the legendary lawmen of the Wild West, and a significant part of Wild Bill's legend was created in Abilene. In the nonfiction books written about him, as well as the many films, television shows, and fictional portrayals, Wild Bill Hickok is usually portrayed as the epitome of the colorful, steel-nerved, fast-drawing, straight-shooting Western lawman.[11]

Thus, many if not most of the elements at the heart of the Western myth were to be found in the Abilene that McCoy created or in the life and times about which he wrote: cattle roundups, trail drives, the rip-roaring nightlife of the cowtown, the fearless lawman, and above all the carefree cowboy. The era of open-range ranching and long trail drives that McCoy helped to usher in and bring to national attention would continue for only a couple of decades, drawing to a close in the late 1880s with the extension of railroads into the Southwest and the fencing of the open range, but Abilene's glory days ended after the shipping season of 1871. Competition from other shipping points (Ellsworth, Newton, and Wichita), along with an influx of settlers, were factors in its demise as a cowtown.

Ironically, one of the strongest voices for prohibiting the cattle trade came from a man who had initially supported McCoy's efforts to bring the trade to Abilene, a man whom McCoy, in fact, had encouraged to move from Illinois to Abilene. In 1868, a year after his arrival, T. C. Henry wrote the resolution that emanated from a meeting of businessmen and farmers, a resolution that emphatically welcomed Texas cattle to Dickinson County, quarantine law or not. Two years later, however, having invested in farmland with the intention of making the county a major wheat producer, Henry was advocating a herd law, and in 1872 he wrote a circular on behalf of the Farmers' Protective Association that called for a complete end to the cattle trade.[12]

This opposition largely caused the transformation of Abilene from one of the wildest cowtowns of the West into a quiet county seat in farming country. Joseph McCoy moved on to help other cattle towns, Newton and Wichita, then to various other jobs and homes before settling in Wichita. The idea that should have made him rich drove him instead to insolvency, thanks to the perfidy (as he saw it, anyway) of railroad executives. His extensive knowledge of cattle was not wasted, for much of his later employment involved that business in one way or another. But the world of cattlemen is a narrow one, all things considered, and his fame even within that world was relatively short-lived.

McCoy's lasting importance lies in the creation of the pervasive mythology of the American West: in the image of the roving cowboy who symbolizes freedom in a classless society where a person's worth is determined by character, not birth; in the image of the gun-wielding lawman wearing a white hat, the knight-errant of the prairies who takes on the forces of wrong despite all odds and always triumphs because right prevails. McCoy did not purposely set out to create these hero figures; that honor lights upon the Bill Codys and Wild Bill Hickoks and Wyatt Earps, men who consciously or otherwise created a larger-than-life image. It was McCoy, however, whose business plan for a new kind of cattle market created the conditions under which the American cowboy and his mystique flourished. After all, men had been working livestock from the backs of horses for centuries all over the world, as they had been in Texas since the late eighteenth century. But none of these herders or drovers became the prototype of the American cowboy; that image emerged in the massive trail drives, and those great trail drives went first to Joe McCoy's Abilene.

6

Theodore C. Henry: Frontier Booster and Nostalgic Old Settler

Thomas D. Isern

The canonization of T. C. Henry is palpable in the Kansas Room, upstairs in the Abilene Public Library, where relics of his life are exhibited. His goateed photograph is at the upper left of the collection of fifty hung in the "Founders of Abilene" group. Across the floor stands the most prominent artifact in the room. "This cherry wood over-mantel," the curious are informed, "was salvaged from the fine old Victorian home of T. C. Henry located at what is now Fourteenth and Buckeye. It was made in Pennsylvania especially for the Henry home." For the benefit of those ignorant of Henry's significance, the legend provides this summary statement: "T. C. Henry, 'Wheat King of Kansas,' was largely responsible for changing Abilene from a 'cow town' to a home town for farmers." A final injunction, printed in emphatic capitals, states: "READ: CONQUERING OUR GREAT AMERICAN PLAINS BY STUART HENRY."[1]

Theodore C. Henry (June 21, 1841–February 2, 1914), the self-proclaimed "Kansas wheat king" and a founder of winter-wheat culture on the plains, pioneered large-scale production in the 1870s, vigorously promoted the town of Abilene, and came to typify and synthesize two frontier types—the booster and the pioneer. Courtesy of the Kansas State Historical Society.

The biography of Theodore C. Henry is a maypole around which historical commentators have woven their layered images and interpretations. The first was T. C. himself, who made the *Transactions of the Kansas State Historical Society* the venue for two essays of remembrance notable for their admixture of disarming candor, wily narrative, and droll wit. In "The Story of a Fenceless Winter-Wheat Field," after recounting how he came to the plains, Henry established his claim to be the Kansas "Wheat King" and the founder of winter-wheat culture on the plains.[2]

When T. C.'s younger brother, Stuart Henry, assumed the mantle of old-settler historical authority, it fit poorly because of the large chip perched on his shoulder. He was angry about the portrayal of Abilene in *North of 36,* by Western novelist Emerson Hough, and devoted a lengthy appendix in *Conquering Our Great American Plains* to cataloging the other book's historical inaccuracies, conveniently forgetting that it was a work of fiction. Stuart Henry's true grievance was a matter not of fact but rather of omission: T. C. Henry was omitted from Hough's story of Abilene. Much of the rest of Stuart's book was devoted to a portrayal of T. C. Henry as a man of vision, an enlightened town leader who redeemed the "Great American Desert" by demonstrating and promoting winter-wheat culture to a skeptical public.[3]

Stuart Henry's inflated and moralistic claims were perfectly designed to provoke that irascible stickler, Kansas historian James C. Malin. Malin's masterly *Winter Wheat in the Golden Belt of Kansas* made T. C. Henry a focus of critical scrutiny—and specifically attacked Stuart Henry for irresponsible myth making. Malin dwelled upon that author's "secret five acres story" and demolished it. Stuart Henry asserted that in the fall of 1870 his brother planted five acres of winter wheat, doing so secretly so as not to be mocked by his neighbors, who insisted that winter wheat was no good for the region. The crop succeeded, but his fellow farmers and stockmen jeered T. C.; nevertheless, he persisted and thus saved the country from economic ruin. Among other things, Malin demonstrated that Henry was not alone in winter-wheat culture at the time and that the story was "contrary to all canons of reasonableness as well as to the historical facts." More generally, he adjudged T. C. Henry, a real estate dealer, as "most conspicuous . . . in advertising value if not in influence upon agriculture. . . . In these respects he is like so many who are noted as leaders only because of an ability to make themselves heard above the voices of others."[4]

As if all of this furnished too little grit for controversy, Robert R. Dykstra served up T. C. Henry as a frontier chameleon, a changeling who first helped Joseph McCoy usher in the Abilene cattle trade and then, espying the main chance along other lines of development, turned against McCoy and the drovers, ran to the arms of the farmers, and enriched himself in the real estate business. Dykstra's Henry was not full-bodied, but the visible parts were unattractive; Henry's leadership of Abilene affairs fell somewhere between statesmanship and charlatanism.[5]

Laying aside old feuds and focusing on T. C. Henry, it is possible not only to sketch his historical actions coherently but also to make sense of them—thanks in large part to recent historical scholarship. The historian David M. Wrobel, for example, described two important types of Western narrative: booster literature, which looks ahead hopefully, and pioneer reminiscence, which looks backward nostalgically.[6] The two types seem incompatible: Was it possible for one individual to be the author both of promotional tracts and of pioneer, reminiscent narratives? T. C. Henry was that individual. Frontier capitalist, dealmaker, political opportunist, blatant propagandist that he was, he nevertheless emerged in later years as an interpreter of pioneer experience. In both roles he exhibited remarkable intellectual, rhetorical, and personal talents.

Born to a prosperous farm family in Ontario County, New York, in 1841, T. C. Henry received a public school and academy education, after which he served for a few years as a high school principal. In 1865 he went south to Alabama, where he commenced cotton farming with hired labor. Southern whites would have called him a carpetbagger; Henry claimed to have been a humanitarian, building a free school for black children. Whatever his motives, his ventures were economically disastrous, and Henry departed for Illinois in October 1865. There he read law with Joseph McCoy's attorney. It appears that Henry followed McCoy to Abilene in late 1867, although it is unclear what the relationship was between the two at this point—their subsequent estrangement caused the two ordinarily loquacious men to be silent on the matter.[7]

Henry, who was joined in Abilene by his widowed mother and his brother, was an Abilene booster from his first arrival. After a few months writing promotional copy for a land dealer, he became a realtor himself, in partnership with James B. Shane. Dykstra explained that Shane had the agency for some 200,000 acres of Kansas Pacific Railway land. Shane ran the office for Shane & Henry in a frame building just north of the Henry residence; Henry was the salesman, and they also had a silent partner, lawyer S. A. Burroughs.[8]

Although prospering by sales of and personal investments in land, Henry, Shane, and Burroughs were not satisfied. Politics offered additional opportunities, not only by the usual direct profits deriving from personal involvement in government during the era but also because they could influence local affairs in directions that would prove generally favorable to the land business. Henry was wonderfully candid about this: "I soon caught on," he wrote. "Within two years I captured a county office [recorder of deeds]. . . . My two partners were both county officers, and all together, including some deputyships, we held about four-fifths of what there was of them in sight. Having successfully organized what the envious termed 'the court-house ring,' we gained a second term. Meanwhile I was steadily adding to my land holdings."[9]

During this time, Henry also entered public affairs as an advocate of the cattle trade, which had made a small start in 1867, then swelled in 1868—to the distress of some local farmers and stock-raisers, who suffered damage to their crops from transient herds and infection of their livestock with Texas fever. Dykstra chronicled Henry's part in a crucial April 1868 meeting convened in the open air at Humbarger's Ford of the Smoky Hill River, south of Abilene. Farmers attending expected to air their grievances—indeed, the announced purpose of the gathering was "taking action with reference to the enforcement of the Texas Cattle Law," or quarantine law. However, businessmen quickly elected a hotelkeeper from Solomon chairman and Henry secretary of the meeting. Despite some rancorous discussion, motions favoring the cattle trade were adopted and published.[10]

This declaration of a "permanent interest" in the Texas cattle trade notwithstanding, Henry soon moved, gradually and strategically, to put an end to it. During "the first two seasons no effort was made to control the disorder and suppress the brazen lawlessness of the rough element gathered here," he remembered. The Henrys claimed to have been morally offended by these developments, and perhaps they were. But the calculated manner in which T. C. abandoned his old friends, playing both sides and moving into the camp of his former enemies, argues for another explanation: Henry, a businessman and investor, kept his nose to the wind, sensed changes, and navigated them adeptly so as to further his own interests. Certainly his old friend McCoy, although never mentioning Henry by name, had T. C. and his cronies in mind when he wrote certain passages of his *Historic Sketches of the Cattle Trade:* "When the cattle trade at Abilene had withstood so much bitter and powerful opposition, and still continued to increase, every one conceded its success," McCoy wrote, no doubt recalling the events at Humbarger's Ford. Nevertheless, McCoy was terribly disappointed in 1871 when the cattle trade ended in Abilene, especially since "the trade was driven away by the schemes and concerted actions of a trio of office seekers."[11]

Following the cattle season of 1869, Henry and his allies got Abilene incorporated and sought effective law enforcement. Police work was a holding action, however; the more basic solution to Abilene's problems, as Henry saw it, was to turn the tide in favor of farming. On October 19, 1870, Henry addressed the Dickinson County Agricultural Society, imploring area farmers to forget their Eastern and Midwestern ways, lay aside their obsessions with corn and hogs, and adapt to the country. Henry encouraged wheat culture and insisted that deep plowing was the key to success. He was no advocate of cereal monoculture, however; he called for investment in Texas cattle, which could be upbred over time with improved sires; exploitation of native range, which offered an advantage over eastern states, where meadows had to be established; and the development of a mixed-farming economy. The most remarkable point came near the end, however. Fencing in a timber-poor land was a problem, Henry thought—"But I believe in this and in other respects we can devise an arrangement that is adapted to our situation and to our necessities, and that is a suitable herd law"—a law requiring stockmen to restrain (fence or herd) their beasts and keep them out of farmers' crops or be held liable for damages. Henry recommended this measure as a boon to agriculture, but he well knew it would be the death of the cattle-trailing enterprise. Within the year Henry and area farmers had carried the day—Texas drovers and their cattle were no longer welcome in Dickinson County.[12]

Resolving the issue of the cattle trade was part and parcel of a general transition in Henry's life through which he looked to a different sort of future for the country and for himself, a transition that was neither simple as to cause nor clear-cut as to direction. First he married—subsequent censuses list a wife, Ellen, and children George, Ross, and Lewis. By 1880 the family had two live-in servants, and about 1875 the Henrys moved into a new house he had built at the north end of Abilene; surrounded by outbuildings and trees, it stood impressively on a rise overlooking the town. An additional monument to Henry's success—a hotel called the Henry House—was constructed in 1875 and described a few years later in Andreas's *History of Kansas* as "the only brick hotel in town and a very fine building. . . . The building is three stories, and the upper floors are all used for hotel purposes."[13]

These were the years, from 1873 on, when Henry made his name as the Wheat King of Kansas and made the term "Golden Belt" a commonplace for the region. Although something of an innovator, Henry by no means invented or even pioneered winter-wheat culture (which at that time used soft winter wheats, hard red winter wheats not yet having come into currency) in Kansas. Malin credited Henry, however, as a master promoter who publicized and encouraged winter-wheat culture, among other agricultural reforms. Henry both sparked and profited from the agricultural boom in Dickinson County and along the Kansas Pacific Railway. In 1872 he had bought out Shane's interest in the real estate firm, Shane & Henry, and the following year he did the same to his main competitor, National Union Land Office, the firm of C. H. Lebold. Consolidating control over the land business, Henry faced bright prospects. The *First Biennial Report* of the State Board of Agriculture, published in 1877, depicted Dickinson County as ripe for development.[14]

In order to jump-start land sales, Henry commenced contract farming to break ground; demonstrate the feasibility and profitability of winter-wheat farming; make money on grain sales (of course); and, most importantly, attract public attention and buyers to the railroad and other lands he had for sale. Historians generally have relied on two sources for Henry's farming activities: his own account in the *Transactions of the Kansas State Historical Society*, 1905–1906, and the newspaper research done by Malin. These describe how in the fall of 1873 he contracted to break 500 acres of railroad land, resulting in a good crop in 1874, harvested with a header (a harvesting implement better suited for winter wheat than the binder) before the grasshopper invasion of that year and threshed with a steam engine and separator (quite an early use of such an outfit). Henry referred to this post–herd law initiative as his "fenceless" wheat field. In the following years he broke more and more ground, some of it acquired with partners, until he had 10,000 acres in cultivation, about half of that in his "main field" stretching between Abilene and Detroit. It was quite a sight, Henry recalled: "In those years the trainmen were instructed," presumably at Henry's instance, "to call out to the passengers, 'We are coming to Henry's wheat-field.' All this spread the story of my success."[15]

As Henry explained in 1904, experience convinced him that Kansas "from Fort Riley westward, was not a corn country, nor was it a spring wheat country . . . and being a large holder personally and also agent for the Union Pacific Railroad Company [formerly Kansas Pacific], which had large bodies of land grant lands for sale, it was a matter of some considerable concern to me as to what should be done." The fenceless winter-wheat field of 1873–1874 proved "a veritable oasis" in a depressed countryside. "There was much ridicule," explained Henry, "because the theory was then that fall wheat required a winter climate more severe than that of Kansas. That I proved was not the case." Henry did quite well through 1878, by which time he had nearly 15,000 acres in cultivation, but "1879 was a dry year—a very disastrous year. I think my farming operations caused me a loss of seventy-five or a hundred thousand dollars. Wheat and corn were almost a total failure."[16] Thereafter Henry steadily reduced his farming operations, and in 1883 he moved to Colorado, there to pursue other development ventures. The year before he had ceased touting wheat culture and instead endorsed stock-raising as the path to prosperity. On February 1, 1882, he addressed the Central Kansas Stock Breeders Association meeting in Manhattan: "Western Kansas [in which he included Dickinson County] is particularly adapted to stock growing. . . . The attempt to sustain a population there wholly or mainly by grain growing alone, must be conceded, I am sure, after ten years effort, to be unsuccessful." This statement obviously was grounded in personal loss, but astonishingly, considering his own history, Henry continued, "I can imagine no spectacle more painful to an old Kansan, than a family from the east just entering the state with a seat full of railroad literature, bound for a homestead. How clearly he foresees the experiences which will surely transform those bright, smiling, hopeful faces into a circle of sad, sobered, disheartened creatures. . . . The soil is fertile and the climate unobjectionable, but the rainfall is insufficient to sustain general farming."[17] Henry called for the preservation of native grasses; for repeal of the homestead, preemption, and timber-culture acts; for appraisal and sale of public lands for grazing use; but for keeping the herd law in place. He envisioned a country of improved stock and settled ranches, not open range. In essence, Henry now repudiated most of what he had said and written during the previous decade and a half.

Henry had spent the past few years disseminating just the sort of "railroad literature" he was denouncing in 1882. At the same time, notably, he had begun his migration from the rhetoric of the booster to that of the old settler. During the mid-1870s he wrote promotional tracts under the title *Henry's Advertiser*. Much of the content was typical booster verbiage—grand climate, plentiful rainfall, and no problems with grasshoppers!—but much was also historical. Henry recounted the struggle against slavery in territorial days and the struggle against drought in early settlement days—not exactly attractive images for home-seekers. The references made sense, however, in the light of a speech he gave at the Fourth of July celebration in Abilene in 1876. In this "Historical Address" Henry ranged back to territorial days and earlier, speaking of the "races of savages" and their "barbarous wars" that preceded white possession of the land. He speculated about which white explorers might first have glimpsed the future Dickinson County and alluded to the beginnings of settlement on Chapman Creek in the 1850s. He reviewed county and town organization, the day of the Texas cattle trade, and the influx of farmers. Already in 1876 Henry was speaking as an old settler, helping his fellows situate themselves in relation to the past and in the present situation.[18]

Such talk was no aberration for Henry. Previously neglected by historians but significant in consideration of Henry's pioneer voice was his October 1902 "Address to the Old Settlers Re-union at Enterprise, Kansas." By this time Henry was near the close of his second career as an irrigation and land developer in Colorado. In typical old-settler style he invoked memories of the "dauntless struggle" en route to the "magnificent fruition" now achieved. He recalled alighting from a train in Kansas in December 1867: "My stout young heart barely mastered the only homesickness I have ever felt. . . . The picture of that dreary landscape and the sense of my utter, remote isolation abide with me to this hour." He sketched Squire Barber, Doc Moon, Joe McCoy (Henry's only historical mention of his onetime friend), and enough other local-color characters in early Abilene to make "a treasure trove for an American Dickens!" Exhibiting the same wry self-deprecation he would use in his "Fenceless Winter Wheat," Henry poked fun at his own real estate puffery but held proudly to his "Wheat King of Kansas" title—for that was his moment of glory. The address then ranged over broad territory but near the end sounded a theme that can easily be read as a retrospective rationale for Henry's youthful machinations in Abilene: "If this Republic shall endure, the moral forces must animate and vitalize its being." His final paragraph was chock-full of old-pioneer sentiment: "It is entirely improbable that we shall ever all meet again," he wrote. "Already the majority of those of my day and generation have gone to the 'great beyond.'"[19]

T. C. Henry died on February 2, 1914, "virtually penniless from his long efforts at developing irrigation in Colorado," wrote James E. Sherow, but he was widely, if ambivalently, eulogized. At Henry's Abilene funeral, the local editor C. M. Harger invoked the title "Wheat King" and said, "Back in the '70s, T. C. Henry was one of the big men of Kansas. He was a man with a vision; his enthusiasm knew no bounds." Henry would have been pleased that, as Harger noted, "early day settlers from up and down the Smoky Hill journeyed to Abilene . . . to attend the funeral."[20]

Judged by popular standards of material values, or by historical standards that fix on the same, T. C. Henry was a failure in life. He was a failure twice (three times if you count his brief youthful fling with cotton culture in Alabama). He made himself a fortune and "a big man" in Abilene, but by over-reaching, he lost it all. By his own account he gambled on the Kansas environment and lost. Certainly other factors, such as the lax management endemic to such sprawling agricultural enterprises, were at work, but the point is that Henry lost his Kansas fortune because of his own excessive ambition. Similar things happened with Henry's Colorado ventures, and at his death there was no fortune, the ultimate measure of a frontier capitalist.

En route to business failure, Henry achieved notable, even historic, successes. He was a player in frontier Abilene—with a supporting, sometimes visible role in establishing the Texas cattle trade and the lead, or at least a catalytic, role in curtailing and then ending that trade. Historians also have been impressed by Henry's willingness to address issues of environment and its limitations on human enterprise, the necessity of adaptation to subhumid conditions. Malin, for example, debunked exaggerations of Henry's contributions to wheat culture but credited him as an effective promoter. Henry was an individual who sensed and adapted to circumstances, but historians have not given him sufficient credit for going beyond adaptation, for shaping his circumstances. He engineered local development along lines conducive to his evolving vision. He assessed, he envisioned, he intrigued, and he acted. He was a person of agency—including agency for his own ultimate economic demise.

Considered another way, T. C. Henry was no failure. Sometime in the mid-1870s he began to consider, and attempt to fix, his place in history. This is where the ideas of David Wrobel are particularly useful. Henry, even at the height of his career as a frontier booster, an enterprise of which he was a master, waxed reflective over themes and narratives in regional history. He saw the potential of these themes and narratives not only to help sell land but also to make him, and other "old" settlers, a place in remembrance. Historians give Henry mixed reviews, but the point is that they write about him. This historical attention comes as the direct result of T. C.'s, and his brother Stuart's, assiduous attention to the Henry legacy. T. C.'s early historical treatises may have been long neglected, but his sketches in the *Transactions of the Kansas State Historical Society* were influential in shaping his historical image. At times, indeed, in reading Malin's treatments of Henry's life, it is an open question whether Malin is employing Henry to illustrate his own interpretations of regional history or Henry is providing those interpretations to the historian. Stuart's *Conquering Our American Plains* is a flawed work, based on imperfect memories, and a biased work, but it also is influential. In its chapters the essential theme of Dykstra's *Cattle Towns* is discernable. Again, it appears that the memoirist inspired the scholarly historian. T. C. Henry a failure? Certainly not, by the standards of historical memory.

As the philosopher of history John Lewis Gaddis has said so effectively in *The Landscape of History,* in the practice of history there is no such thing as an independent variable.[21] Nothing ever happens because of a single cause; every cause interacts with others in ways peculiar to historical circumstances; historians achieve their best understandings when they account not only for the direct relationship of causes to the subject under consideration but also for the interaction of causes with one another. T. C. Henry stands as an object lesson. There is no reason to think that he was a unique person, and if he were, it would only diminish his significance. Rather, Henry is a salient and instructive figure because he typified the frontier types—booster and pioneer—and synthesized them so adroitly.

Frederick H. Harvey and the Revolution in

Nineteenth-Century Food Service

H. Roger Grant

Following the Civil War, Kansas became home to a remarkable entrepreneur. The fame of Frederick Henry Harvey came from achieving a simple objective: setting the standard for quality meals and accommodations in the American West. In the 1870s this "Civilizer of the West" realized that eating facilities along the trunk-rail lines of the trans-Mississippi West did not meet the needs of the traveling public. Food was commonly bad, often cold and of poor quality, and good hygiene was seldom followed in preparing or serving it. Moreover, meals were limited in variety and served in a sloppy fashion, often too slowly to permit patrons to reboard their waiting trains on time. Harvey had several earlier careers before entering the railway dining and accommodation business and making his name synonymous with excellence in the field. In time "Harvey food" and the "Harvey House" were not only a haven for rail travelers and residents in the West but institutions that had no parallel in the nation.[1]

Frederick H. Harvey (June 27, 1835–February 9, 1901), considered by some the Englishman who "civilized the West," founded a chain of restaurants along the route of the Santa Fe railroad in the late 1870s that set a new standard for cleanliness, service, and food quality. Courtesy of the Kansas State Historical Society.

Arguably, Harvey represented a type of contemporary businessperson. In a logical fashion he responded in practical ways to food challenges of his era. The observation made by Ralph Waldo Emerson that "an institution is the lengthened shadow of one man" holds merit. If this insightful American philosopher had lived in Kansas in the latter part of the nineteenth century, he might have had Harvey Houses in mind as the institution and Fred Harvey as the man.

Unfortunately, not much information is available about the early life of Fred Harvey. He was born in London, England, on June 27, 1835. It appears that his father, an Englishman, was named Charles and that his mother, Helen Manning Harvey, was of Scottish descent. The young Harvey was baptized into the Anglican faith and may have become an ardent churchgoer. By 1850 Harvey, like thousands of his countrymen, had decided that the best opportunities could be found in the New World and not in merry old England. His future would be in a limitless America.

Harvey, still in his early teens, arrived in the United States and settled in New York City. Being an Englishman probably was not a hindrance in finding employment in America's largest city; Harvey surely did not feel the sting of the ubiquitous "Irish Need Not Apply" signs. Yet he started his American work career at a point on the employment ladder hardly higher than the most discriminated-against foreigner. Harvey willingly accepted manual labor; after all, he had little education and little money. His first job was that of a $2-a-week busboy and dishwasher in a small Manhattan café, where he began to acquire knowledge about the restaurant business. In time Harvey would validate what became the popular Horatio Alger "rags-to-riches" story, achieving wealth and fame by dint of hard work, determination, pluck, and luck.[2]

For reasons not known, Fred Harvey decided not to remain in New York, and he set out for the hinterlands. Rather than traveling to a popular Midwestern destination, for example, Pittsburgh, Cincinnati, or Chicago, he chose New Orleans, probably taking advantage of cheap water transport that flourished between New York and the Crescent City. But after working in the dining facilities of local hotels, the seemingly rootless Harvey decided to relocate elsewhere. Surely a contributing factor in his decision was the generally unhealthy environment of this Mississippi River entrepôt, highlighted by a massive outbreak of yellow fever that killed over 5,000 residents early in the 1850s. Harvey contracted this frequently fatal disease, but he regained his health.[3]

The next stop for the young Harvey was St. Louis, a city that enjoyed convenient and inexpensive steamboat connections with New Orleans. Although St. Louis was a smoky place, in part because of seasonal temperature inversions, its reputation for health was far better than that of the communities of the lower Mississippi River valley. Moreover, St. Louis was a booming city and seemed destined to become the greatest emporium of the region: "[Located] on the mighty Mississippi, below the mouth of the vast extended Missouri, draining a country of unrivaled productiveness . . . capable of sustaining a population as dense as almost any region of the globe," enthused a resident in the mid-1850s. "While just above enters the Illinois, draining the very heart of that most productive State—while to the north . . . the states of Iowa and Wisconsin—the northern part of Illinois and Minnesota, each of them destined to sustain millions . . . of agriculturalists and mechanics, will always have their natural markets at St. Louis." This was a sensible destination for Harvey, indeed, for any ambitious individual wanting a better life.[4]

Abandoning his earlier pursuits in New York City and New Orleans, the slim, vigorous Harvey worked as a merchant-tailor and jeweler. Why he pursued these trades is a mystery; still, he had not abandoned a career in food service. His employments in St. Louis allowed him to accumulate capital that in 1859 he invested in a restaurant, which probably had always been his long-range business strategy. As was common, Harvey did not go it alone; rather, he entered a partnership that allowed him to better leverage his money and theoretically to reduce his risks.

The St. Louis interlude was mostly good for Harvey. His eating establishment initially flourished, he became a naturalized citizen, and he married "pretty" Barbara Sarah (Sally) Mattas in 1859. The outbreak of the Civil War in April 1861 changed his business world, and unfortunately for the worse. It was not so much a matter of wartime inflation, food shortages, or local strife but rather the defalcation of his business partner. Apparently this individual, an ardent Southern sympathizer (Harvey loyally backed the Union), took flight with the restaurant funds, planning to use the money to support the Confederacy. This bizarre course of events forced the enterprise into liquidation.[5]

Harvey was undaunted by his bad luck. He briefly found work with the Missouri River Packet Line Company, a steamboat concern that plied the Missouri River between St. Louis and Omaha, Nebraska. It was likely a bout of typhoid fever that caused Harvey to seek employment elsewhere. His next recorded job was that of a distributing clerk for the U.S. Post Office in St. Joseph, Missouri, a gateway community to the trans-Missouri West. St. Joseph was not only a busy port on the Missouri River, but it recently had become the western terminus of the Hannibal & St. Joseph Railroad (H&StJ), which provided a direct railroad link with Chicago, the emerging railroad mecca of America. St. Joseph also remained a starting point for wagon travel on the Oregon and California Trails.[6]

While with the post office in St. Joseph, Harvey got his first intimate exposure to the burgeoning railroad industry. It was at this time that the H&StJ revolutionized an essential aspect of American commerce; in July 1862 the railroad placed into regular service the nation's first railway post office (RPO) car, allowing the sorting of mail while in transit on the line between Quincy, Illinois, and St. Joseph. This imaginative approach to handling intercity mail had been the brainchild of William A. Davis, St. Joseph's assistant postmaster and the man who had hired Harvey for the postal position. Soon Harvey became one of the first two on-board RPO employees who traveled the H&StJ.

Conceivably Harvey could have had a long and economically secure job with the post office, either in a traditional office role or with the Railway Mail Service. Instead he decided to "go railroadin'." Many a young mid-nineteenth-century man opted for a career in the nation's premier big business. At first Harvey worked for the H&StJ as a freight solicitor and shortly thereafter joined the North Missouri Railroad (NMR) as its general western agent. The NMR appeared poised for true economic greatness, but Harvey did not wait for that day; instead he added another railroad to his professional résumé. This true "boomer" joined the Chicago, Burlington & Quincy Railroad (CB&Q), parent company of the H&StJ. His official employer, at least initially, was a wholly owned subsidiary, the Kansas City, St. Joseph & Council Bluffs Railroad. Ultimately Harvey and his family, which now included two sons and three daughters (two infant sons earlier had died of scarlet fever), made their home in Leavenworth, Kansas. Here Harvey served as a commercial freight agent for the ever-expanding and financially robust Burlington Route system.[7]

A classic workaholic, Harvey became involved in more than railroad business. He acquired ranchlands in Kansas and invested in a recently opened hotel in Ellsworth, a community situated on the main stem of the Kansas Pacific Railway (later Union Pacific System), 225 miles west of Kansas City. About 1870 he also dabbled in still another line of work, commercial journalism. Harvey did not become a reporter or copy editor but an advertising solicitor. Successfully meeting people and winning their support were Harvey's skills. His employer was Col. Daniel R. Anthony, a Leavenworth newspaper publisher. At the time of Harvey's death, Anthony remarked, "Fred Harvey was the best newspaper advertising solicitor I ever knew." He added, "He solicited eastern business for the [Leavenworth] Conservative for a number of years while engaged in the railroad business, and he was very successful. I paid Mr. Harvey $3,000 one year for the eastern business he secured. We had an arrangement whereby he was to secure at least $12,000 a year from the East, and always did so, and often much more." Harvey "was a splendid solicitor and made a success of everything," Anthony concluded.[8]

By the 1870s Fred Harvey, this Englishman of "slight build, nervous, [and] quick action," had become known as a person whom everyone could trust. He fully subscribed to the belief that a man's word must be his bond. Years later a Topeka judge, W. C. Hook, opined, "I have never known a man who maintained a higher or more honorable standard of conduct than Fred Harvey. In the contemplation of any business act or venture, whether affecting the wealthy or the poor, his first thought always was, is it equitable?" Judge Hook explained, "It is easy to learn the principles of equity and honesty in the abstract, and it is also easy to apply them in the administration of the affairs of others, but it is most difficult to achieve and merit the reputation which Mr. Harvey possessed of forever keeping them in view as the guiding and unvarying rules of one's own conduct. To all who knew him intimately his life stands as an example; it is worthy of emulation."[9]

As a maturing adult Fred Harvey, this adopted son of Kansas, became distinguished for his willingness to work and his integrity as a businessperson. In no way did he resemble those unpopular and much-discussed "wheeler-dealers" of Gilded Age America. He was hardly a character from a Mark Twain novel. Wearing his different business hats meant nearly constant journeys by train, and he learned much from his travels. Since dining cars were relatively rare, intended for first-class passengers, long-distance coach passengers either brought along their own "eats," bought food items from trackside or on-board venders, or ate in depot lunchrooms or the occasional depot hotel.

The latter two options could be either wonderful or terrible, mostly the latter. Complaints abounded. These generally negative feelings about food associated with rail travel found their way into the popular travel guides of the day. One publication, designed for passengers in the West, appeared in 1869 and contended that "railroad restaurants are chiefly kept by very avaricious and inhospitable persons who demand fifty cents for admission into their rooms, but manage, either by not opening their doors for several minutes after the train arrives, or by a deficiency of attendants, to deprive their customers of a fair opportunity of receiving or appropriating a fair compensation for their money in the form of viands." Continued the writer, "Frequently, too, the food is filthy bread badly baked and unwholesome; the tea and coffee cold, or so bitter and black that they are far from furnishing an agreeable repast."[10]

Realizing a need and sensing an opportunity, Harvey responded. About 1875, at age forty, he teamed up with J. P. Rice, an area entrepreneur, to obtain control of an existing eating-house at Wallace, Kansas, situated in the western part of the state on the Kansas Pacific Railway. This loose partnership of Harvey and Rice also became involved in another eating-house located even farther west at Hugo, Colorado. But differences soon developed between the two restaurateurs, probably over the issue of quality control, and Harvey abandoned his contact with the Kansas Pacific. Fortunately, unlike the business affair in St. Louis more than a decade earlier, Harvey did not lose financially when his relationship with Rice collapsed.[11]

Harvey did not abandon his vision for trackside eateries that offered good food in clean, pleasant surroundings. Instead he suggested to the Burlington Route, his employer, that he be allowed to establish a series of restaurants along its lines. His suggestion fell on deaf ears. Understandably, Harvey next considered the Atchison, Topeka & Santa Fe Railroad (Santa Fe). After all, this was an expanding railroad rapidly developing a regional network of lines whose operations were based near his home. Moreover, as a minor official of the Burlington, Harvey knew white-collar personnel on the Santa Fe, just as he did on other area carriers. Early in 1876 his knowledge of railroad personnel led him to Charles Morse, the Santa Fe superintendent in Topeka. Morse liked what Harvey proposed and took his request to Thomas Nickerson, the Santa Fe president. The men agreed that Harvey be allowed to experiment with food improvements on the property and turned the Topeka lunch counter over to him. There was no signed contract; these men trusted one another. At this point a unique, long-lasting symbiotic relationship began between Harvey and the Santa Fe.[12]

What proved to be a superb business success began in modest surroundings. A brochure, distributed by the Santa Fe in the mid-1920s, made much of the humble inception: "It is not easy to visualize the start of it all. . . . The beginning was indeed primitive—a small space partitioned off in the shed-like station at Topeka, Kansas, when the State and the town and the railroad were young. But into that little room the world of travel at once began to make daily pilgrimages." Crowed the writer, "The word had been passed down the line that at Topeka station you could get something different to eat—sandwiches that were of recent date, succulent chicken and steaks, ham and eggs that made you want a second helping, fresh country butter, the choicest of maple syrup on the most delicious of wheat cakes, pies home baked, coffee made just right and steaming hot." There was more to be enjoyed at the Topeka eatery: "The lunchroom itself was kept clean, the napery spotless, the silver and glass polished. The meal was served by attractive waitresses."[13]

Even though the financially cautious Harvey would not sever his employment with the Burlington Route until 1882, he unquestionably devoted much of his extra energy to his various business activities. Being a practical entrepreneur, Harvey hired a trusted acquaintance from Leavenworth to manage the lunchroom operation. Yet, as would be his style, he kept the Topeka facility under his watchful eye. The sensation at Topeka quickly prompted Harvey to push ahead with similar operations along the line. Indeed, one historian of the Santa Fe contended, "The counter's success frightened the management of the Santa Fe, which feared that all passengers would detrain at Topeka and find the food so good they would travel no farther and leave the Kansas plains empty of settlers!"[14]

Following the Topeka eatery was the operation at Florence in Marion County, an important Santa Fe station slightly more than 100 miles "down line" from the capital city. In late 1877, encouraged by railroad officials, Harvey acquired an existing hotel at Florence known as the Clifton House, located in an attractive wooded area southeast of the depot. He then sold the property to the Santa Fe, and on January 1, 1878, he contracted with the railroad to provide eating and hotel facilities. The Harvey House network had begun.

The new Florence hotel was an immediate success. "Everybody takes breakfast and supper there," observed the *Florence Herald,* "and he gets a square meal all the time." Not only did Harvey continue his commitment to quality food and service, but some contemporaries may have thought that he splurged to make the Clifton House a showplace and the model for his future operations. To manage his evolving business, Harvey hired William Phillips, head chef of the prestigious Palmer House in Chicago, to take charge. Soon Phillips, who received an impressive $5,000 annual salary, made the Clifton House the pride of Florence. No wonder the local newspaper gave the restaurant such high praise. Phillips, who made the hotel his temporary home, paid handsomely for the best locally produced foodstuffs, including $1.50 a dozen for prairie chickens; $.75 for a dozen quail; and higher-than-average rates for butter, eggs, and seasonal produce.[15]

As the Santa Fe pushed its track toward the Southwest, by 1880 reaching Albuquerque, New Mexico Territory, and five years later San Diego, California, so too did the operations of Fred Harvey expand. Later there would be a route to San Francisco Bay and Chicago and a plethora of branch and secondary lines throughout the Southern Plains and the Southwest. Stations such as Dodge City, Hutchinson, Lakin, and Newton, Kansas; La Junta and Trinidad, Colorado; Albuquerque, Gallup, Lamay, and Las Vegas, New Mexico Territory; Ash Fork, Kingman, Williams, and Winslow, Arizona Territory; and Barstow and Needles, California, had either lunchrooms, hotels, or both. Although these facilities were not as architecturally attractive as their twentieth-century replacements, the overall quality of the food and service was high. For example, when required because of local alkali-laden streams, water for coffee and tea was brought in by railroad tank car, "maintaining the standard."

Although Harvey hired an increasing number of employees, he remained a "hands-on" businessman. His life of travel did not end with the Harvey Houses; he continued to ride thousands of miles annually over the Santa Fe and other lines. Just as Ray Kroc of McDonald's fame made frequent inspections of his franchises, so too did Harvey go into the field, always vigilant as to matters of food and service quality. Harvey wanted to insure that his "sky-high standards" were never compromised. When once visiting a kitchen at an unidentified location, he heard a clamor in the dining room:

> "What caused all of the trouble?" Mr. Harvey asked the Steward.
> "Oh, that man is an out and out crank. No one can please him."
> "Of course he is a crank," agreed Harvey, "But we must please him. It is our business to please cranks, for anyone can please a gentleman."[16]

Time and time again, Harvey refused to compromise over any reduction in quality. Employees understood. If they did not, they found their tenure with the Harvey company terminated. And workers could not question Harvey's authority. "Fred Harvey was an autocrat, and from his decisions there was no appeal." Yet he also cared about loyal employees, offering job protection and a pension system.[17]

This attention to details helps to explain the success of Harvey in the food and accommodations business and why more Harvey Houses appeared. By the time of his death in 1901 his company operated forty-seven restaurants and fifteen hotels, and Harvey had struck a deal with the Santa Fe to manage its fleet of railway dining cars. Although Harvey remained attached to the Santa Fe, his firm developed ties with affiliated carriers, including the Frisco System (St. Louis–San Francisco Railway) that the Santa Fe had purchased in 1890.[18]

Part of the Harvey success story was his closeness with the Santa Fe. Arguably, if a satisfactory relationship had not persisted, Harvey might have stumbled or at least not achieved the wealth that he ultimately acquired. Benefits from the railroad involved not just the monopoly of services, buildings, and other physical commitments but also the preference in transportation. Remembered an acquaintance, "[Harvey] used to ask [the Santa Fe] for everything, he asked and kept on asking, and finally he got it." These rewards were considerable: "He paid no freight or express, no telegraph bills or traveling expenses. He even shipped his help around without paying for them. No wonder he could buy better food than anybody else and serve it cheaper. No local place could compete with him." Of course the Santa Fe, because of the Harvey connection, became a popular tourist and business route. "Fred Harvey has become a byword for all that is good in the way of railway meals, be it dining room or dining car, and consequently our [Santa Fe] little slogan, 'Fred Harvey Meals all the Way' has a world of meaning to it."[19]

The far-flung Harvey Houses required the considerable and constant movement of supplies and personnel. Food, dishes, linens, and an array of other items traveled from central points to individual lunchrooms, dining halls, and hotels. Then there were the full-time employees, including superintendents, managers, and auditors. Hardly surprisingly, Harvey opted for a railroad-style business organization. He knew the structure, and he correctly surmised that it suited his operations.[20]

Of all the Harvey workforce, the most famous were the "Harvey Girls." These usually young, attractive women wore plain black dresses with "Elsie collars" and black bows, black shoes and stockings, and heavily starched white aprons. Undeniably, they became living symbols of the enterprise. In a sense these hundreds of women were to the Harvey House what Ronald McDonald and Colonel Sanders became to McDonald's and Kentucky Fried Chicken. They were the "women who opened the West" and were immortalized by Hollywood in the 1945 Metro-Goldwyn-Mayer film *The Harvey Girls*. In his quest to establish quality service Harvey hit on the notion of hiring young, single women (between the ages of eighteen and thirty) to wait on tables and generally meet the public, supervised by a matron and manager. A typical Harvey House would have between fifteen and twenty-five Harvey Girls, with a woman who served as head waitress. These employees, who were always Euro-Americans (people of color, including Hispanics and Indians, worked as dishwashers, maids, and "pantry girls"), usually came from "back East" and received good salaries (and tips), board and room, opportunities for advancement, railroad passes, and a sense of belonging to the extended "Harvey family." Yet the turnover rate was relatively high, perhaps because of strict supervision, dormitory living, and the rule against marriage during the first year in service. Still, many "Harvey Girls" stayed for long periods and it was common for those who married to show their admiration by selecting "Fred Harvey" as the Christian names for their boy babies. One source estimated that at least 4,000 males received Harvey's name.[21]

The public loved "Meals by Fred Harvey" served by these "Harvey Girls." No one said it better than Elbert Hubbard, the guru of the American arts-and-crafts movement: "At Fred Harvey's you are always expected. The girls are ever in their best bib and tucker, spotlessly gowned, manicured, groomed, combed, dental-flossed—bright, intelligent girls—girls that are never fly, flip nor fresh, but who give you the attention that never obtrudes, but which is hearty and heartfelt."[22]

The Harvey approach to business made Fred Harvey a wealthy and seemingly happy man. While not in the financial league of an E. H. Harriman, a John D. Rockefeller, or a Frederick Weyerhauser, Harvey enjoyed the good life in Leavenworth. His home contained those objets d'art that appealed to him and his wife, including china purchased at Christie's auction house, fine English prints, and Italian marble and bronze statues. He continued to embrace his British heritage, maintaining a degree of cultural identity. For example, he requested that his main daily meal be served at noon, an afternoon "high tea" at 4, and tea again at 7. Harvey enjoyed business and pleasure trips to the British Isles.

Despite his successful career and attractive domestic surroundings, Harvey suffered from a variety of health problems. Apparently an intestinal disorder bothered him greatly and became cancerous. An operation in 1899 probably gave him a couple more years of life, and during these years he and Sally traveled widely, visiting France, Germany, and Italy, largely in search of a cure or at least physical relief.[23]

The Fred Harvey Company continued after Harvey's death in 1901. His sons Ford and Byron and a son-in-law continued the family business. For nearly two decades before their father's death, these men had worked in various roles for the firm. A smooth transition within the Harvey family avoided any disruptions in daily operations or delays in completing planned expansions. After 1901 the sons worked closely with the Santa Fe and extended the operations of the company, especially in the area of luxury resorts. Soon the Alvarado Hotel in Albuquerque, New Mexico; the El Tovar, the "crown jewel," on the south rim of the Grand Canyon in Arizona; and the El Ortiz in Lamy, New Mexico, drew thousands of satisfied patrons annually and further enhanced the name of Fred Harvey. In the process the Harvey experience heightened an interest in and appreciation of the cultures of the American Southwest. In a sense, Harvey and the Santa Fe introduced America to Americans. The death of the founder did not interrupt corporate activities, and for decades the Harvey family carried on the traditions established by this Englishman who "civilized the West." Only in the recent past did the business dissolve and the last Harvey House close.[24]

Bernhard Warkentin and the Making of the

Wheat State

Norman E. Saul

If anyone can take credit for Kansas becoming quickly and dramatically the wheat state, it is Bernhard Warkentin. He can also vie for first place among all the immigrants to the United States from the Russian empire—and there were many—in regard to economic and social impact. The successful introduction of Turkey Red wheat from Ukraine (or southern Russia) was a tremendous boon to the economy of the Great Plains. As one of the chief organizers of the Kansas Millers' Association, Warkentin led an industry that for many years was the most important in the region, transforming cowtowns into much more durable and stable milltowns. As a Russian Mennonite leader, he was instrumental in influencing hundreds of his coreligionists to settle in Kansas.

Bernhard Warkentin was born in the village of Altonau on the southwestern corner of the large Mennonite colony of Molochna on June 18, 1847. In

Bernhard Warkentin (June 18, 1847–April 1, 1908), who did more than any other individual to make Kansas the wheat and milling state, emigrated from Russia in the 1870s and convinced a large number of his fellow German-Russian Mennonites to follow. Courtesy of the Kansas State Historical Society.

the late eighteenth century Catherine the Great, inspired by French physiocratic beliefs that economic growth depended on the development of land resources, invited foreigners, mainly from German states, to settle in her empire's vacant borderlands and in new territories annexed from the Ottoman Empire. Saxons, Swabians, Hessians, Bavarians, and others welcomed the opportunity to escape devastating wars, having just experienced the Seven Years War (French and Indian); they accepted the offer of free land and exemption from recruitment and migrated to the Volga region, near Saratov, in the 1760s. They would become known as Volga Germans, and many of their descendants would later emigrate to Kansas, Nebraska, and other Western states.

The European Mennonites, followers of a strict Anabaptist leader, Menno Simons, came from two main backgrounds: the northern Netherlands (or West Friesland) or Switzerland. Many of the latter had moved into France, especially to the palatinate along the Rhine. Their main distinction from the larger Baptist congregations inspired by John Calvin was pacifism—rejection of any kind of violence or military service. To escape Dutch pressure to conform, a large group of the Friesian Mennonites migrated in the late seventeenth century to West Prussia, settling in an area near the port of Danzig (now Gdansk); they are often referred to as Danziger Mennonites. Facing conscription pressure from the military-minded Frederick the Great in the late eighteenth century, a substantial number accepted another invitation by the Russian empress to move to southern Russia, to Khortitsa on the Dnepr River below Kiev, and to Molochna ("milky"), after a river by that name, in what was then called New Russia. This territory had been annexed from the Ottoman Empire along with the Crimean Peninsula in 1783. The Molochna colony was located about fifty miles north of the port of Berdiansk on the Sea of Azov. A number of Mennonites of Swiss origin would migrate about the same time to establish settlements in Volhynia on the southwestern borderlands of the Russian Empire, now in Ukraine.[1]

Those who would emigrate to Kansas in the 1870s would come primarily from Molochna with smaller numbers from Volhynia and from Molochna daughter colonies in Crimea. Though many miles apart in Russia, they would settle on neighboring railroad land in Marion, Harvey, and McPherson Counties in 1873–1875. Most of the inhabitants of one village, Alexanderwohl, in the center of Molochna, and of a number of villages adjoining it, would make up the largest of the distinctive Mennonite settlements in Kansas. Their church, about fifteen miles north of Newton, is near Goessel, the only surviving town. The Crimean ("Krimmer") Mennonites founded villages just south of Hillsboro in Marion County, and the Swiss-Volhynians occupied lands to the west of the Molochna Mennonites around Moundridge and Hesston. The three groups are represented today by three colleges: Bethel College in North Newton (Molochna), Tabor College in Hillsboro (Crimean), and Hesston (Swiss). All came from Russia and, though German or Friesian speaking, were labeled "Rooshian" because of different characteristics from other German immigrants.[2]

The Mennonites in Russia prospered, at least in comparison to the rest of the agricultural population, most of which was restricted and oppressed by serfdom. They introduced merino sheep and led in other innovations that involved machinery, livestock, and grains. As in most societies, despite communal and egalitarian principles, stratification occurred. The Warkentin family belonged to the Russian Mennonite upper class, which included the remarkable scholar and leader Johann Cornies. Taking advantage of the location of Altonau on the Molochna River, Bernhard's father, Bernhard Aron Warkentin, besides owning a substantial farm, erected a mill that served a large portion of the colony. Some accounts credit him with introducing a variety of hard wheat from Crimea into Molochna in the 1860s. He certainly benefited from the growing demand for Russian wheat in mid-nineteenth-century Europe and the proximity of Altonau to the Sea of Azov port of Berdiansk. In other words, he was a leader of an emergence into a larger Russian economic sphere and was related to other prominent Mennonite families, such as the Wiebes and Corniesses.[3]

Causing a considerable stir in the Mennonite colonies in June 1871 was the news of a Russian edict, scheduled to take effect in 1874, that would remove special privileges from a variety of classes and ethnic groups with the liberal goal of equality in mind. For the Mennonites, losing their exemption from recruitment into the Russian military was a serious matter. The overcrowding of the original colonial settlements was another problem. Delegations presented their case in St. Petersburg to no avail, and talk of another historic trek to a new land was soon common. A well-known Russian general visited the colony to discourage emigration, which was probably a bad decision on the part of the central government. The news about the impending edict quickly spread through the Mennonite network. A Canadian land agent in Central Europe made a special trip to South Russia, while the American consul in Odessa became interested in the Mennonites' plight. Cornelius Jansen, a prominent Mennonite in Berdiansk, who also served as Prussian consul, consulted his British cohort about emigration to Canada. Disappointed with the result, he became an early and outspoken advocate for the solution of emigration to the United States. Alexanderwohl became the center for meetings of those wanting to leave, and one of its leaders, Dietrich Gaeddert, after conferring with Jansen, especially promoted the growing determination for emigration in 1872. He influenced two other leaders, Leonhard Suderman and Jacob Buller, in that direction.[4]

As a youth Bernhard Warkentin Jr. frequented his father's mill, delighting in the hustle and bustle of the machinery and of a prosperous business concern. He also attended gymnasium, or secondary school, in Halbstadt, the "capital" of Molochna, and business school in Odessa. With his close friend David Goerz, he saw the sights of the magnificent Russian capital, St. Petersburg, and traveled to Western Europe to visit Mennonite communities in the palatinate. By 1871, in his early twenties, he would have been quite aware of the implications of the proposed Russian law for him personally. Influenced by Jansen after having visited him in Berdiansk in April 1872, and sponsored by his father, Warkentin joined three other young Mennonites—Philipp Wiebe, Peter Dick, and Jacob Boehr—on an inspection tour of the United States in the spring of 1872. Their leader and guide was Boehr, a friend from the palatinate rather than Russia, who had better contacts in America. They arrived in New York in June, their first destination being Niagara Falls, true to their tourist agenda.[5]

After a visit with John Funk, editor of a major Mennonite newsletter, *Herold der Warheil*, in Elkhart, Indiana, the tourists journeyed to Chicago to see the aftermath of the great fire. Warkentin split off from the others in August to see Christian Krehbiel, a Mennonite elder from the palatinate, in Summerfield, Illinois, about thirty miles east of St. Louis. He commented to Goerz that the sheep were inferior to those in Russia and "the wheat not the best." With Dick that summer he toured Minnesota and went through Nebraska to Cheyenne, then to Denver, and returned to Summerfield by way of Kansas, stopping at the Brookville Hotel near Salina.[6]

Warkentin established his American base in the Krehbiel household. Naturally curious about American milling practices, he frequented the local mill, operated by Conrad Eisenmayer, who was experimenting with a new steel roller technology developed by Pillsbury in Minnesota. Welcomed into this Lutheran German immigrant family, Warkentin soon became enamored of Eisenmayer's daughter. He enrolled in a nearby Methodist school (McKendrie College in Lebanon, Illinois) to learn English but was soon caught up in the movement to North America of his Russian brethren, who had decided to send a delegation to investigate settlement possibilities. Warkentin guided some of these advance scouts from Molochna of 1873 to Manitoba, Texas, Kansas, and elsewhere. One can understand why, after a couple of severe winter weeks in Canada, Warkentin's own preference was for Texas. The delegates from Bergthal, influenced by Jacob Schantz, a Mennonite leader in Berlin (now Kitchener), Ontario, favored Canada because of a Canadian guarantee of exemption from military recruitment, and many of their constituents would eventually settle there.[7] Despite direct appeals, the U.S. Congress refused to consider a special exemption, referring the matter to the states for consideration, and several states complied with the Mennonites' requests, but those exemptions applied only to the National Guard. The majority of incoming Mennonites, nevertheless, saw Kansas and Nebraska as their best opportunities, considering climate, availability of water, and the excellent transportation arrangements provided by railroads.

In the meantime, Christian Krehbiel had determined in late 1873 to move with twenty-five families of his congregation to an area in Kansas just north of Halstead, a railroad center on the Santa Fe line. C. B. Schmidt, land agent of the railroad in Topeka, envisaging future sales to immigrants, provided good terms and sold Warkentin just under 200 acres at $6 an acre along the Little Arkansas River on the edge of Halstead, where Warkentin erected a water-powered grist mill with stone grinders three feet in diameter. In the meantime, he became a pioneer, along with Funk and Krehbiel, in organizing the Mennonite Board of Guardians to assist the emigration of brethren from Russia, and serving as its business manager. He and other American leaders would arrange contacts with railroad agents, meet the ships in New York, negotiate transportation inland, and arrange transit lodging in Elkhart and Summerfield. Warkentin personally campaigned for funds among the Old Order Mennonites near Lancaster, Pennsylvania, and obtained $2,000, despite their concern that these Russians were not true Mennonites. Thanks to Warkentin's own choice and the energetic pursuit of Mennonites by "partner" Schmidt, many of the new immigrants would choose Kansas over Canada or neighboring Nebraska. During the summer of 1874 Warkentin was constantly on the move between Kansas, Illinois, Indiana, and the East Coast to meet the incoming ships and arrange transportation for $15–20 for each adult as far as St. Louis.[8]

After that hectic year, which witnessed the occupation of much of three counties—Harvey, Marion, and McPherson—by "Rooshian" Mennonites, Warkentin deserved a rest. In July 1875 in Halstead he married Wilhelmina Eisenmayer, daughter of his miller friend of Summerfield. She was registered more familiarly as "Mina" on the wedding announcement and as "Millie" in the 1880 census, which also recorded two children, Edna and Carl. Warkentin's father came from Russia for the event, accompanied by Schmidt, who had gone there to recruit more immigrants.[9] The Eisenmayer family, though not Mennonite, also decided to relocate from Illinois to Halstead and in 1876 engineered the move of the water-powered mill to larger quarters along the railroad and its transition to steam power. Both Warkentin's father and father-in-law were no doubt instrumental in financing what would become a major base in Halstead of commercial wheat-flour processing in America. Needless to say, the business prospered under the Warkentin/Eisenmayer management. The Warkentin house in Halstead, built in 1883, survives as testament to that success.

But Halstead had its limitations as much of the business in the region gravitated toward Newton, the seat of Harvey County. In 1886 Warkentin and Eisenmayer purchased the Monarch Steam Mill in Newton, which dated to 1877, and quickly renovated it to accommodate new steel roller machinery. The Halstead and Newton mills combined placed them in the forefront of a burgeoning industry for the state, though they would certainly have competition from others in McPherson and Hutchinson, and especially from Christian

Hoffman in Enterprise, a town near Abilene similar in size to Halstead. These new millers did not look back, enlarging and expanding their capacity in the years that followed.[10]

The major innovation of the Kansas flour mills during the decade of 1884–1894 was the replacement of the large millstones, like those used in Warkentin's original mill in Halstead, by smaller cylindrical steel rollers enclosed in wooden boxes. A good surviving example is the Smoky Hill Roller Mills and Museum in Lindsborg. Warkentin may have first witnessed the beginnings of this milling transition in Illinois. By 1884 the Halstead Mills were experimenting with a double set of Allis corrugated rolls, a similar set of smooth rollers, and a single set of Stevens rolls. A coal-fired steam engine powered an output of 225 barrels of flour a day, one of the largest in Kansas at that time. By 1891 the Halstead enterprise had expanded to 400 barrels a day and twelve double sets of rollers. By 1896 the Newton Milling and Elevator Company had renewed its "Monarch" label and expanded to thirteen sets of steel rollers that produced 400 barrels of flour a day. In other words, the two mills in Halstead and Newton were about equal in expansion and output. In 1900 Warkentin purchased a flour mill in Blackwell, Oklahoma, to take advantage of the rapid development of the Cherokee Strip.[11] His mills were now shipping many carloads of flour a week to American urban bakeries and abroad.

Prominent as probably the largest employer in the county, Warkentin also became involved with banking and insurance companies in Newton. He was a major benefactor and promoter of Bethel College when it was established in North Newton. Although he converted to Presbyterianism, Warkentin remained on the college's board of trustees as treasurer for many years. In 1886–1887 he built a new home near the mill in Newton that survives today with most of its original furnishings and kitchen equipment as a museum open to the public.[12]

Warkentin's greatest contribution came from renewing his Russian connections with his father and other relatives who remained there, and with the variety of wheat that he remembered. Turkey Red (*krasnaya turetskaya*) was so labeled by Russians because of its color and its origin in the Ottoman Turkish Crimea in the eighteenth century, though it may have come there from the Kosovo region of the Balkans by way of Albanian tax collectors (some linguistic references indicate an Albanian origin). This wheat that he knew, or something very similar, first came to Kansas in 1873 in the baggage of Mennonites from the Crimea and was probably planted at Gnadenau, near Hillsboro, that year in small plots.[13] Flour from this wheat could not be produced in quantity at that time because the millstones, then prevailing, were inadequate for grinding hard grains. It was a laborious process, especially in sifting the grit (from the stones) from the flour. It was possible, however, to mill the Turkey Red wheat for home consumption at the wind-powered mill at Gnadenau (recently reconstructed as a working model at the Adobe House Museum in Hillsboro).

Testing of a large number of wheat samples was occurring in the late nineteenth century by agricultural colleges and Department of Agriculture experimental farms. Warkentin emphasized the importance of this particular variety from Russia and made certain that it was included in the tests. He first imported substantial quantities of what would soon be broadly known as Turkey Red about 1886. He helped organize and was the first president of the Kansas Millers' Association in 1888 to promote a concentration on that wheat so mills could economize by processing only one variety.[14] Turkey Red flour, though sold under many labels, was high in gluten and protein, much in demand for crusty bread and rolls in Europe and among the large number of new immigrants from Eastern and Southern Europe in U.S. cities. It came to dominate the growing emphasis on wheat cultivation in Kansas by the turn of the century and through World War I and the 1920s. By that time three Newton mills, led by Warkentin's, were processing four million bushels of wheat into a million barrels of flour each year.[15]

In 1896 Warkentin formed an alliance with famed cereal specialist Mark Carleton of the U.S. Department of Agriculture. Educated at the Kansas Agricultural College in Manhattan, Carleton knew the region well, understanding its Russian Mennonite heritage and Warkentin's introduction of Turkey Red. Carleton made his first trip to Russia in 1897. Although perhaps best known for his discovery of durum wheat and its introduction into the United States around 1900, he also worked closely with Warkentin to find the best selections of Turkey Red. Warkentin, having turned part of his Halstead farm into a U.S. Department of Agriculture experimental station, instructed Carleton in 1900 to buy 20,000 bushels of Turkey Red in Crimea, specifying the places to find it.[16]

By this time the Warkentins were seasoned world travelers. On April 1, 1908, during a tour of the Holy Land with his wife and a few friends, Warkentin suffered a tragic accident that brought a premature end to his life and career. A young Turk in a neighboring compartment was showing off a revolver to his companions when it went off. The bullet penetrated the partition into the next compartment to mortally wound Warkentin, who died a few hours later in a Beirut hospital. His body was taken back to Newton, accompanied by his widow and his old Russian friend David Goerz. His son Carl and son-in-law, Maurice Alden, inherited the milling operation and expanded it in 1919 to include the Midland Flour Milling and grain terminus in Kansas City. The Warkentin milling operation would succumb, like many others, to the consolidation mania that followed World War II.[17]

The memory of Bernhard Warkentin is preserved in the Newton house, now a museum, where his widow lived for many more years; in the Monarch mill that was saved from demolition in the 1990s to become the site of the Old Mill Restaurant; in Bethel College in North Newton; and in his papers that are preserved there. His real legacies are the waving fields of golden grain that parade across the Kansas landscape every year in June—and those towering Kansas cathedrals along the railroads.

PART THREE

THE AGE OF REFORM, 1880–1925

Kansas is the Mother Shipton, the Madame Thebes, the Witch of Endor and the low barometer of the nation. When anything is going to happen in this country, it happens first in Kansas. Abolitionism, prohibition, Populism, the Bull Moose, the exit of the roller towel, the appearance of bank guarantee, the blue sky law, the adjudication of industrial differences—these things came popping out of Kansas like bats out of hell. Sooner or later other states take up these things, and then Kansas goes on breeding other troubles. Why, no one seems to know.
—*William Allen White, "Two Famous Questions," 1922*

The best they [Republicans] could do was to yell "Socialism" at the Populists and predict a recurrence of the French Revolution. The charge against the Populists that they were Socialist had more basis in fact than we Republicans understood; for, after all, Populism stemmed back to the creed of the Grangers and the Greenbackers, who were led by the old Abolitionists, those who proclaimed the rights of men. . . . They were trying to establish economic as well as political equality, to help the underdog, to cut down some of the privileges that wealth carried by reason of its size and inherent power. It was all Karl Marx, highly diluted; and the Republicans, who did not realize how true their indictment was, continued to cry "Socialism" at the top of their lungs without really believing it. . . .

I think, looking back nearly forty years to those days when Roosevelt and La Follette and a thousand little Roosevelts and La Follettes in state houses and legislatures, in city halls and country towns, were cleaning those dirty economic and political stables of the ancient giants who followed the Civil War, we were part of a world movement. . . . we were trying to establish all over the civilized world more equitable human relations. We were trying to distribute the economic surplus of the machine age. . . .

The under dog bothered us all. . . . We believed faithfully that if we could only change the environment of the under dog, give him a decent kennel, wholesome food, regular baths, properly directed exercise, cure his mange and abolish his fleas, and put him in the blue-ribbon class, all would be well. We reformers who unconsciously were sucking at the pabulum of the old Greenbackers and Grangers and Populists were intent upon making wholesome dog biscuits for the under dog. We did not know that we were merely treating the symptoms. . . . Our sympathies were responding excitedly to a sense of injustice that had become a part of the new glittering, gaudy machine age.

—Autobiography of William Allen White, *1946*

Mary Ann "Mother" Bickerdyke:

A Gilded Age Icon

Bruce R. Kahler

During the 1880s and 1890s Kansas was known by many of its citizens as the "Soldier State." They were proud that territorial Kansas had witnessed the first stirrings of the Civil War and that the new state of Kansas had sacrificed so much for the Union. Now, after the conflict, Kansans cited statistics to show that their state had become the favored destination of veterans from throughout the loyal North. Governor John A. Martin, himself a Union veteran, declared in 1885 that every regiment in the army and every important battle in the Civil War were represented by "old soldiers" presently living in Kansas.[1]

These old soldiers, along with their families and friends, built a large and prominent veterans' community. The network of organizations and institutions they created and the distinctive culture that they developed touched the daily lives of most Kansans in the Gilded Age. As in other Northern

Mary Ann "Mother" Bickerdyke (July 19, 1817–November 8, 1901) loved and risked all for her "boys in blue" while serving as a Civil War nurse, and the veterans' community of Kansas, the "Soldier State," in turn spared no effort to commemorate her selfless sacrifice on their behalf. Courtesy of the Kansas State Historical Society.

states, the Grand Army of the Republic (GAR) was the largest organization of veterans. Its political and social activities were complemented by those of an auxiliary group, the Women's Relief Corps (WRC). The veterans' community erected over one hundred soldier monuments in public squares and cemeteries throughout the state, wrote and published war memoirs, and supported several newspapers, most notably the *Western Veteran* in Topeka. Perhaps its most visible and enduring achievement was the establishment of institutions such as the State Soldiers' Home at Fort Dodge, the western branch of the National Soldiers' Home in Leavenworth, and a Soldiers' Orphans' Home in Atchison.[2]

Ostensibly, the purpose of this community and its culture was to keep alive the memory of the Civil War. But on closer examination we can see that the veterans' organizations had a more particular goal in mind. The Soldier State was united by a profound sense of obligation to the Union soldiers and a determination to acknowledge what it owed them. Veterans were proud of their service and collective accomplishment. The crucible of war had transformed them into comrades who for the rest of their lives shared a deeply felt appreciation for each other, and they expected to be honored by all Union-loving Americans. If there was a touchstone for the GAR and the WRC, it was best expressed on that huge banner hanging on the Capitol in Washington, D.C., during the grand review of Union troops in May 1865: "The Only National

Debt We Can Never Pay Is the Debt We Owe to the Victorious Union Soldiers." Two decades later, as most veterans moved into their forties, Northerners felt a growing sense of urgency about paying that debt.[3]

Although the debt owed these veterans could never be fully repaid, Kansans had to try, or admit moral failure. The veterans' community devoted itself, therefore, to the virtue of gratitude. It would demonstrate how thankful it was by mourning the soldiers who had never returned from camp or battlefield, by caring for injured or diseased veterans, and by celebrating the efforts of all men and women who had helped destroy slavery and preserve the Union. To the extent that the Soldier State publicly promoted virtuous behavior, it contributed to the liberal mood emerging in Kansas during the 1880s. Like other reform movements, the veterans' community sought to improve society through the active intervention of government. The humanitarian impulse behind military pensions and veterans' homes could be realized only with government support. The benevolent spirit of the WRC led to its close association with the legislative campaigns of both the prohibition and women's suffrage movements.[4]

The most celebrated individual in the Soldier State was, ironically, not a soldier but a nurse. Mary Ann Ball Bickerdyke was the best-known Union army nurse in the western theater of the Civil War. Bickerdyke, born July 19, 1817, grew up and married in Ohio and then moved to Illinois. When war arrived in 1861 she was a widow with two sons and was practicing "botanic" medicine in the town of Galesburg. She began her career as a nurse by supervising the distribution of locally raised food and medical supplies at an army camp in Cairo, nearly four hundred miles to the south.[5]

Bickerdyke was a true comrade who had risked her own life while saving the lives of others on the front lines. Her love for the "boys in blue" was unquestioned, and she continued for many years after the war to do whatever she could on their behalf. But because she was nearly seventy when she moved to Kansas and was increasingly hampered by the inevitable effects of advanced age, her primary significance for the veterans' community was not as an activist but as the chief recipient of its commemorative efforts. The old soldiers idolized her and seized the opportunity of these last years of her long and storied life to make her the center of attention. They invited her to reunions, agitated for her pension, wrote her biography, named a home and hospital after her, publicly celebrated her eightieth birthday, and mourned her death. Each of these demonstrations of gratitude was a major event in the life of the Soldier State. Bickerdyke had become an icon in Gilded Age Kansas, a heroic figure upon whom the veterans could lavish their rich resources of appreciation.

Throughout the year of 1887 the town of Bunker Hill, Kansas, was nearly beside itself with anticipation. In February James R. Bickerdyke, principal of the local schools, informed the town newspaper that his famous mother was thinking about moving from San Francisco to live with him during her declining years. Over the next several months Mary Bickerdyke visited twice on her way to and from Kentucky, where her stepdaughter was dying. Late in November there was still some doubt as to whether this woman whose name was "familiar to almost every household in the Union and revered by all who know her" would remain in Kansas. The GAR and WRC organized a warm and enthusiastic reception ceremony for her, and a week later the paper was pleased to announce that Mary Bickerdyke was making a new home with her son.

Mary Bickerdyke's deep and enduring devotion to the soldiers was legendary, and thus she was known affectionately as "Mother Bickerdyke." During the war she was a field agent for the Northwestern Sanitary Commission, following the troops to such killing grounds as Shiloh, Vicksburg, and Atlanta. She foraged for supplies, prepared the men's meals, laundered their clothes and bedding, tended to their wounds, and provided them with moral support. After the war, while operating a railroad hotel and dining hall in Salina, Kansas, Bickerdyke arranged for the money and transportation needed to facilitate the migration of three hundred Illinois veterans and their families to the region. By the early 1880s she had become a pension agent and traveled the country documenting veterans' claims for government benefits. Although Bickerdyke's reputation for benevolence was also founded upon her work with the poor in Chicago, New York, and San Francisco, Northerners always knew her best as the "soldier's friend."[6]

Now in her seventies and living in Kansas, Bickerdyke continued to plead the veterans' cause and to nurse some of the old soldiers back to health. For example, Thomas Bolton, suffering from the ravaging effects of tuberculosis, "felt an irrepressible desire to be with Mother Bickerdyke." She agreed to take the frail invalid into her home and then hired a day and a night nurse to tend to his medical needs. In the meantime, she solicited the aid of U.S. Senator Preston B. Plumb in getting a pension for Bolton, corresponded with the veteran's GAR post about his financial affairs, and wrote comforting letters to his sister. More than a month after the old soldier's death Bickerdyke was still arranging through the mail for the legal disposition of his personal effects and a suitable guardian for his young daughter. Gratitude expressed both privately and publicly was Bickerdyke's sole reward. Bolton's own "deep, affectionate gratitude" for all that Bickerdyke had done was, according to the local newspaper, "characteristic of the true soldier." This was later borne out by a public statement from Bolton's fellow veterans in California: "It is, surely, a matter of pleasing satisfaction to the comrades of George H. Thomas Post to know that the last hours of their former fellow-member were soothed by the loving ministrations of good Mother Bickerdyke, whom we all hold in such reverence."[7]

Expressions of thanks such as these might strike us at first as mere courtesies, but add them to the many other heartfelt efforts, both large and small, to commemorate Mother Bickerdyke and we can see a highly significant phenomenon within the veterans' community. One obvious way for the veterans to express their gratitude was to invite Bickerdyke to their reunions as a guest of honor. Within six months of her move to Bunker Hill, the newspaper reported, "she has more invitations to meet with the old soldiers than she can accept." It was well known, however, that she enjoyed these events and "could not stand the temptation of meeting once more 'the boys in blue.'"[8]

The adulation that Bickerdyke received at these gatherings was a matter of considerable comment in the veterans' community. In 1890 O. H. Coulter, editor of the *Western Veteran,* observed that "at every reunion and encampment her advent is a signal for the heartiest outburst of enthusiasm." Five years later when she was introduced at the departmental encampment of the Kansas GAR a reporter noted that "all their distinguished visitors were for a time forgotten, and the audience struggled to shake her hand." State commander Theodosius Botkin asserted in 1897 that the old nurse's name was sacred to every Union veteran and had only to be mentioned at one of their meetings to evoke an exuberant "God, bless Mother Bickerdyke."[9]

No one has better described the effect that Bickerdyke's iconic status had on the veterans than Mary A. Livermore, former codirector of the Northwestern Sanitary Commission. In her best-selling memoir *My Story of the War,* Livermore recalled that Bickerdyke had been invited to come from San Francisco to attend the 1887 annual GAR reunion in Topeka. Arriving a bit late, she entered the rear of the convention hall just moments after the meeting had begun.

In an instant there was a joyful confusion in the neighborhood of the door, a rush, a subdued shout, a repressed cheer. The presiding officer called for order, and rapped vigorously with his gavel. . . . "Mother Bickerdyke is here!" shouted a chorus of voices in explanation, which announcement put an end to all thoughts of business, and brought every man to his feet, and sent a ringing cheer through the hall. All pressed towards the motherly woman, known by all soldiers in the West, many thousands of whom are indebted to her for care, nursing, tenderness, and help, in the direst hours of their lives. Gray-haired and gray-bearded men took her in their arms and kissed her. Others wept over her. Men on crutches and men with empty coat-sleeves stood outside the surging crowd, with shining eyes, waiting their turn to greet their benefactress.

Hugging, kissing, cheering, and weeping: Livermore captured marvelously the aging veterans' "irrepressible desire" to show their gratitude to Mother Bickerdyke. "It seemed," she said, "impossible for the men to pay her sufficient honor."[10]

Few things disturbed the old soldier community more than the possibility that Mother Bickerdyke might not receive the gratitude she deserved. This feeling explains why the issue of her government pension generated such anger. Friends had been imploring Congress for years to reward Bickerdyke with a regular income. The GAR considered levying an annual tax on its members to provide her with financial assistance.[11]

Mary Livermore was at last able to induce her congressman to introduce a special bill on Bickerdyke's behalf. With helpful testimony from Generals U. S. Grant, William T. Sherman, and John A. Logan, as well as a resolution from the national convention of the WRC, Bickerdyke was voted a $25 monthly pension on May 9, 1886. Livermore was pleased for her old associate yet still regarded the sum as a "niggardly and tardy recognition of her heroic services." That same year in San Francisco, where Bickerdyke was living at the time, Margaret B. Davis wrote the first book-length biography of "the woman who Battled for 'the Boys in Blue.'" "For years," Davis claimed, "[Bickerdyke's] heroic labors received no recognition from a Government that has been liberal in rewarding its soldiers." Davis's volume, therefore, was being published "specially for her benefit" and made ready for sale when the city hosted the national GAR encampment.[12]

Kansans who followed the controversy agreed with Livermore and Davis. Considering Bickerdyke's unparalleled contribution to the Union cause, the pension seemed too little and too late. Speaking in favor of Bickerdyke's claim for a pension at the 1884 national encampment of the GAR, Louise H. Brown, president of the Kansas WRC, stated that no army nurse was "more deserving the grateful recognition of her country." The editor of the *Kansas Knight and Soldier* added that if Bickerdyke "does not deserve recognition by Congress and by every comrade in the land, no one does." The *Topeka Daily Capital* bitterly denounced Congress for failing that year to pass Bickerdyke's pension while she was reduced to a "scanty living" in San Francisco. When the House of Representatives later passed the bill in her favor the *Capital* thought it long overdue since "no soldier wounded on the battlefield has a stronger claim on the gratitude of the nation than has this grand old lady."[13]

The most outspoken critic of the scantiness of Bickerdyke's pension was James Jones, editor of the *Russell Record*. The Bickerdykes had moved to Russell early in 1890. The town's weekly paper paid close attention to James Bickerdyke, who was now county superintendent of schools, and to his mother, Russell's most famous citizen. Jones was alive to any hint of ingratitude toward Mother Bickerdyke and was especially incensed by her small pension. "When we reflect how promptly congress grants pensions of $4000 to the widows of generals who in most cases are not in need and personally have done nothing to deserve it, the pittance granted to this noble woman, after so many years' delay is almost contemptible." He scoffed at small tokens of esteem, such as the easy chair and bouquet of flowers given to Bickerdyke at a Salina reunion, calling them "sentimental exhibitions." What she needed and deserved was money. Jones proposed that the GAR boys lobby the state's congressional representatives for a $2,400 yearly pension—eight times what Bickerdyke was then receiving.[14]

In the summer of 1895 the *Salina Republican* proudly announced that, as a consequence of her son's appointment to the faculty of Kansas Wesleyan University, Mother Bickerdyke would be returning to the town where she had lived nearly thirty years before. Jones was outraged at this blow to Russell's prestige. Certainly it was sad that James Bickerdyke, the best superintendent the county had ever had, would be going away. A far greater loss, however, was the truly "historic character" who would follow him. If it were not for the small size of her pension, Jones surmised, Mother Bickerdyke would choose to remain in Russell. But since she was dependent upon her son for a living, she felt compelled to leave with him. Jones treated the disappointing turn of events as if it were a punishment for the town's failure to fully acknowledge Mother Bickerdyke's value. He imagined a time when her biographer would point to the fact that "the people of Russell appreciated her so little that she was compelled to leave the town to hunt a grave." Had Bickerdyke spent her last days in Russell it would have been an "everlasting honor" and a "source of pride" to erect a monument to commemorate her deeds. But now that would not happen. "It is," said Jones, "a painful subject to dwell upon."[15]

James Jones would have been pleased to learn that there was a like-minded biographer already compiling information about Mother Bickerdyke's life. Julia A. Chase would not, as Jones had feared, charge the citizens of Russell, Kansas, with ingratitude, but she did share his concern about the inadequacy of Bickerdyke's federal pension. "What has the government done for this woman who served it so long and so well?" Chase asked after detailing in ten chapters her subject's spotless character and innumerable contributions to the nation. Her answer was that Congress had disgraced itself by waiting twenty years after the war to approve her pension and then by cutting in half the originally proposed amount. The amended figure was justified on the grounds that it was what other army nurses had received, but clearly Chase believed that Bickerdyke was exceptional and should have gotten much more. Years after the publication of her biography Chase scornfully referred to the twenty-five dollar pension as "not the wages of an office boy."[16]

President of the Kansas WRC in 1896, Chase hoped her authorized and "authentic" account of the old nurse might help the organization raise money for Bickerdyke, as Margaret Davis's earlier volume had intended. Although everyone involved, including Mother Bickerdyke, knew the book's moneymaking potential was limited, Chase believed it was a worthy demonstration of gratitude. Its writing and publishing, said Chase after Bickerdyke's death, were examples of how the GAR and WRC had "honored themselves in trying to honor her." This stood in stark contrast to Bickerdyke's meager federal pension and the paltry recognition extended by the state—a resolution of thanks for her assistance during the grasshopper invasion of 1874 and a portrait hanging at the Kansas State Historical Society.[17]

Chase's biography of Mother Bickerdyke reads like a longer, more formal version of the pension claims that the old nurse compiled for her veterans. Derivative and eclectic, like Bickerdyke's collection of supportive testimonies, *Mary A. Bickerdyke* makes no claim of originality or pretense of objectivity. It was pure hagiography. Chase assumed that a convincing portrait, one that would evoke its readers' gratitude for Mother Bickerdyke, had to be idealized, even worshipful.

The WRC seized yet another opportunity to pay tribute to the old nurse when, in December 1896, a few months after the publication of the biography, it agreed to take control of the GAR Reunion Grounds in Ellsworth. Fifteen cottages, a dining hall, and a visually striking hemispheric auditorium that seated five thousand people had been constructed on 160 acres of land a half mile outside of the town. The grounds were to be the permanent western site of the GAR departmental reunion, but Ellsworth's still rather remote location thwarted this plan after only two reunions, and the GAR boys were anxious to be rid of their white elephant. When a member of the WRC in Ellsworth suggested that the property might serve well as a home and hospital for disabled wives and widows of Union veterans, the state leadership enthusiastically proceeded with plans for its transformation.[18]

Outgoing WRC president Chase headed up the project. She was appointed president of the new institution's board of managers and given the power both to formulate a scheme for remodeling the facilities and to lobby the Kansas legislature for the required funds. First, however, Chase exercised the authority of her position and renamed the institution: the Mother Bickerdyke Home and Hospital. Chase later recalled how her friend's "eyes filled with happy tears when I told her what we had done, and she said: 'That is a million times better than a monument a mile high.'" It is quite possible that Chase also wielded her influence to ensure that Bickerdyke might live her last days at the home established in her name. She informed the local newspaper that admission to the home and hospital would be open only to "destitute wives, widows, mothers, sisters, and orphans of Union soldiers and sailors." By these terms Bickerdyke was ineligible for admission, but the list in the constitution, a document that Chase certainly had a major hand in writing, made one significant addition: "Army nurses who have the required proof of service." Mother Bickerdyke never did become a permanent resident at the Ellsworth home, but a room was reserved for her use during her frequent visits.[19]

The renovated facilities were dedicated on October 6, 1897. Mother Bickerdyke was there to witness the hanging of her portrait in the entrance space. Chase spoke about Bickerdyke's heroic career in the war and the help and encouragement received from WRC members. Despite its initial enthusiasm for the project, however, the WRC had to relinquish control of the home and hospital to the state just four years later. It would maintain its identity as a women's institution but be incorporated into the Kansas State Soldiers' Home.[20]

Of the many meetings held by the board of managers to prepare for the opening of the home and hospital, surely the most memorable was at Bunker Hill on July 19, 1897. Only a year after moving to Salina the Bickerdykes returned to the village where they had resided in the late 1880s. Now the veterans' community was planning a grand celebration of Mother Bickerdyke's eightieth birthday at her home and throughout the state. At the state house in Topeka Theodosius Botkin issued "General Order No. 4" of his term as Department Commander of the Kansas GAR. "Our grateful country delights to honor those who have stood forth in the hours of peril and defended her on the field and forum," he began. Not only soldiers and officers but many "angels of mercy" deserved such honors. Indeed, many surviving veterans were "a living proof of the debt which gratitude owes to these Queens of the REPUBLIC, THE ARMY NURSES!" It was only fitting, Botkin concluded, that Kansans show Bickerdyke, "while living, the affection with which we hold her, and the tribute we shall pay to her memory as the Queen of the Grand Army of the Republic, when her life's sands shall have finally run out."[21]

Botkin's outline of the procedures for executing his order was a perfect illustration of the GAR's bureaucratic mentality. Local posts were to formally adopt expressions of high regard and esteem for Mother Bickerdyke; send them to Topeka, where they would be bound together for presentation at the ceremony; and then establish a committee to arrange a campfire on July 19. The campfire would consist of short talks about the army nurses. All citizens would be invited to "enter into the spirit of the occasion reverently but with enthusiasm." Finally, a concise report about the program, including a list of participants, had to be submitted to headquarters, where it would be "carefully filed away for future reference." O. H. Coulter of the *Western Veteran* recognized that someone unfamiliar with the GAR might question the sincerity of gratitude expressed within such a rigid structure. "It was not, however, so much in compliance with these orders that the day was so elaborately and generally observed," he asserted, "but from a spontaneous desire on the part of the comrades to pay tribute and respect to this grand and heroic woman who did so much for them on battle-field, in camp, and in hospital."[22]

Coulter was the key speaker at a Bickerdyke celebration in Sterling. An estimated ten thousand people attended the daylong picnic and campfire, located in a large grove. The main event in Bunker Hill was a more modest affair, perhaps out of consideration for Mother Bickerdyke's weak stamina. She and another former army nurse, Mrs. A. G. Weed from Russell, were seated in a carriage pulled by sixty or more veterans from the Bickerdyke house to a large tent nearby. An afternoon of speeches and music followed. Botkin presented Bickerdyke with a silver water service, and she was given a wreath made of evergreens from her husband's grave in Galesburg, Illinois. Around the campfire that evening the old soldiers told their war stories once again.[23]

"Instead of celebrating her 80th birthday with banners and brass bands would it not have been better to have invested the amount in making her few remaining days comfortable?" James Jones persisted in his belief that Mother Bickerdyke was owed a better, more practical, form of gratitude. The poor woman had to borrow money when she was "obliged to leave Russell" and move to Salina, he argued. Chipping in to pay off her debt would be of more lasting benefit to her than the GAR event. Julia Chase was also unhappy. She thought Commander Botkin had recommended a permanent "Mother Bickerdyke Day" to be celebrated each July 19 and was disappointed when that did not come to pass. As for Mother Bickerdyke, the *Russell Journal* noted a look of sadness in her face during the ceremonies, but she later wrote to a cousin, "It was a royal day and long to be remembered, and it was so good of those old patients to show their gratitude so."[24]

Throughout her last four years of life Bickerdyke continued to write letters, receive visitors, and even help a few more veterans with their pension claims. But as her friend Florence Shaw Kellogg remarked, "she lived and worked more and more quietly with longer and more frequent resting spells between her hours of labor." The most notable event of these twilight years was a four-month trip in 1898 to visit friends and relatives in Ohio and Illinois. She was invited to the annual encampment of the Society of the Army of the Tennessee in Toledo, Ohio, where she was made an honorary member of the group and received its official badge.[25]

That badge was pinned on Bickerdyke's breast as she lay in state at her home on November 10, 1901. She had died two days earlier following a week during which she had fallen, been stricken with paralysis, and then gradually lost consciousness. The local veterans' groups organized a funeral service at the assembly hall of the Bunker Hill schoolhouse. Two GAR representatives then accompanied the body to Galesburg, where there was a second funeral and burial next to her husband and an infant daughter.[26]

James Jones was moved by Bickerdyke's funeral to reflect upon how and why the veterans' community idolized her so. It was true that she had ministered to the needs of many people in her long life, not just the boys in blue. Her beneficiaries included the poor who lived in Chicago, New York, and San Francisco. But Jones thought it was vitally important to recognize that these slum dwellers never attempted "to publicly express their gratitude, while the soldiers exhausted every effort to honor her name and show the veneration in which she was held." The virtuous behavior of the old soldiers was undeniable: thousands of men who had never had personal contact with Mother Bickerdyke nevertheless loved her for helping their comrades and for her devotion to the Union cause. "Being the bravest," Jones argued, "soldiers are the most tender, affectionate and grateful class of men and never forget a benefactor, hence their unbounded gratitude to their great and devoted army nurse."[27]

Julia Chase discovered that James Bickerdyke was not of the same "class of men" as the veterans. His ungrateful behavior after the funerals aroused in her an indignation that seethed for years. Soon after learning of James's death in 1904 Chase vented to a friend: "You know what I did for him in his great bereavement—wrote his letters & looked after many, many things, Wouldn't you have expected he would give me some little remembrance of 'Mother'—a cane, a book for instance. Well, he never gave me even a rag although he knew some of her things she herself had promised me." Even more unjust, James reneged on a promise to publish and distribute a memorial volume of funeral addresses and testimonials from friends that he had asked Chase to prepare. "He never so much as thanked me or reimbursed a penny of the expense I incurred," she said.[28] Julia Chase had done more than anyone else to demonstrate gratitude to Mother Bickerdyke. It was a fact that ought to be acknowledged—with gratitude.

It is time we recognize that the Soldier State played a leading role in the drama that was Gilded Age Kansas. Tens of thousands of Civil War veterans and their supporters participated in a community that presented their fellow Kansans with a serious moral challenge: the acknowledgment of their debt to the men and women who had preserved the Union and the attempt to repay them by practicing the virtue of gratitude. When Mary Bickerdyke moved to the state she provided the veterans' community with a perfect opportunity to meet that dual challenge. She had been a "mother" for so long and so well that now, in her final years, it was imperative that her "boys" show how thankful they were in any way they could. Florence Kellogg, in her 1907 biography of Bickerdyke, said Kansans ought to be proud that they had not failed to honor the old nurse. "As she grew older and more feeble our tender care for her increased, and she lacked for nothing that a grateful people could give her."[29]

10

Mary Elizabeth Lease: Advocate for Political Reform

Rebecca Edwards

Was Mary Lease a Kansas mover and shaker? In considering that question, the first issue is not whether Lease was a mover and shaker but whether she was a Kansan. It would be unfair to discount her citizenship based on her nativity. In 1890, the year she rose to sudden fame as a so-called Kansas farmer's wife, only a third of her contemporaries had been born there. A majority of the state's residents had undertaken migrations like Lease's, at age twenty, when she left western Pennsylvania to become a schoolteacher at the Osage Catholic mission. But after moving to Kansas Lease did not stay. Twice, in 1874 and again in 1897, Lease left the state in the wake of economic catastrophes. The second time she went for good, settling in New York until her death in 1933. She spent, then, about fifteen years of her life in Kansas and sixty-eight years somewhere else.

Mary Elizabeth Lease (September 11, 1850– October 29, 1933), who signed this ca. 1892 photograph "fraternally," settled in Wichita, where she studied law, championed social and economic reform, and gained a reputation even among her detractors as a spirited and effective orator and lecturer for the Farmers' Alliance and then the Populist Party. Courtesy of the Kansas State Historical Society.

But American national mythology firmly associates Lease with Kansas. Home to many progressive thinkers and activists in the 1880s and 1890s, the state played a central role in shaping Lease's political sensibilities and provided routes to celebrity that would not have been available elsewhere. As a shrewd politician Lease cultivated state pride, giving a famous address called "Kansas and Kansans" in which she spoke of the hardships suffered by pioneers and especially farm women. She helped build a movement historians have characterized as a farmers' revolt, and although Populism was more complex than that, Lease became a symbol of the oppressed rural families of the Plains. To Easterners she was, as a Boston paper put it, "the real, veritable and only genuine Mary E. Lease of Kansas." After her death one of her old foes, editor William Allen White, wrote that "as a voice calling the people to action she has never had a superior in Kansas politics." He concluded, "In the history of Kansas . . . she will deserve a bright paragraph."[1]

Lease had other important identities in addition to being a Kansan. Arriving in northwestern Pennsylvania as Mary Clyens on September 11, 1850, she was the first American-born daughter of immigrants who had fled Ireland in the wake of the famine. Joseph and Mary Clyens had been quite prosperous by Irish standards, renting two hundred acres in County Monaghan and occupying the middle ground between powerful English landlords and peasants. The Clyenses apparently left Ireland because of Joseph's agitation for Irish independence. Young Mary, a devout Catholic for the first four decades of her life, sustained a strong Irish identity. In the 1880s she spoke and raised funds for the Irish National League, and later her People's Party speeches frequently denounced British imperialism. The Clyens family sought in America the republican rights they had lacked at home. Before they left Ireland Mary's parents named her elder brother Patrick Henry Clyens, in honor of the Scots-Irish American Revolutionary hero. Patrick H. Clyens answered his namesake's call for liberty or death. Joining one of the first Pennsylvania regiments formed after Fort Sumter's fall, Pat died in the battle of Fredericksburg on December 13, 1862. His grieving father, who enlisted as a substitute for a wealthy lumberman's son, followed him into the Union army. Captured at the Battle of the Wilderness, Joseph died at the infamous Andersonville Confederate prison camp in August 1864. His wife, who had buried two infants back in Ireland, was left with four children at home on the family's modest farm. Joe, age sixteen, did a man's work to support his widowed mother. The three American-born children, Mary, Evelyn, and Francis, were respectively fourteen, ten, and five when their father died.[2]

Mary grew up fiercely independent. She later recalled taking long walks in the woods to recite poetry and practice declamation, and she cited Emerson's essay "Self-Reliance" as one of her favorite texts. Mary and Evelyn, both avid students, received financial support from a family friend to attend Catholic school at St. Elizabeth's Academy, just across the state border in Allegany, New York. After graduation Mary taught in the area before her move to Kansas. She arrived in Osage Mission at a time when reaching it still required a twenty-five-mile wagon trip from the nearest rail station in Humboldt. Lease later described herself in those years as a "backward rosy girl" who taught at the mission school and then for a term in the nearby village of Austin. Lively, dark-haired Mary soon caught the eye of Osage Mission pharmacist Charles Lease, eleven years her senior. In retrospect they were not well matched. Mary was "wonderfully ambitious," as her husband later put it; she was also a Catholic and, having lost both brother and father to the Union cause, a Republican loyal to the party of Lincoln. Charles, a Democrat, had conspicuously failed to serve in the Union army and came from an Illinois family of religious agnostics. But the couple ignored such differences at the start of their romance. Mary, the daughter of a poor immigrant widow, married up into the native-born Protestant middle class. Her well-liked husband led the local Masonic lodge and owned his own business, the City Drug Store, which appeared to be one of the most prosperous firms in town.[3]

Appearances were deceiving. Only a few months after Charles and Mary's wedding in January 1873 a disastrous depression hit the country, reaching Kansas with a wave of bank closings and railroad bankruptcies. Charles Lease's store, it turned out, was overextended and Lease himself heavily in debt. In May 1874 the City Drug Store went under. The Leases—with Mary now four months pregnant—moved down the Missouri, Kansas, and Texas rail line to the cowtown of Denison, Texas, where they started over in poverty. The decade that followed was filled with haunting tragedies. While Charles clerked for a succession of local druggists Mary took in laundry to help make ends meet. The couple's first child, Charles, survived, but two children born in 1877 and 1878 died of fevers in infancy. Back in Pennsylvania Mary's mother died in 1875, after which her siblings Evelyn and "baby" Frank (now in his late teens) came to live with the Leases. Frank went to work as a railroad fireman. On December 13, 1879—sixteen years to the day after Patrick's death at Fredericksburg—the family lost Frank, who was crushed under the train wheels in an all-too-familiar example of what a local paper called "the Perils of the Rail."[4]

Mary developed her political consciousness largely in response to these tragedies. So terrible were her years in Denison that she almost never spoke of them later and rarely even acknowledged that she had lived in Texas. Instead she channeled her grief and anger into political action. But Lease first coped with her misfortunes through private faith and a passion for literature. She wrote poems of tribute to those she mourned, many expressing hopes for reunion in heaven. A few years later, after moving back to Kansas, she submitted these to newspapers and established her first public voice. In the meantime she found herself, like thousands of women in the 1880s, influenced by the charismatic Frances Willard, leader of the Woman's Christian Temperance Union (WCTU). Willard visited Denison in 1882 on one of her nationwide tours, and within a few months Mary Lease became an energetic officer of Denison's WCTU. The temperance cause spoke to many of Mary's needs. Willard eloquently addressed the suffering of women and children at the hands of men who drank up their paychecks, and she was among the first American women to denounce domestic violence. WCTU leaders asserted that wives and mothers had a duty to speak on political questions, in order to protect their families, and they even claimed that women should vote.

This was all too much for the men of Denison, Texas. Local WCTU leaders faced fierce criticism for stepping "beyond their sphere." But despite criticism Mary Lease—now the mother of three living children, two-year-old Louise and baby Grace as well as eight-year-old Charles—persisted in antiliquor work. This probably caused tension in the family as well as the community. Pharmacists such as Charles Lease were targets of temperance advocates because they dispensed alcoholic formulas (along with morphine and an array of other drugs readily prescribed for everything from rheumatism to infant colic). Back in Kansas the divisions would deepen. After the state enacted prohibition, druggists flouted the law by selling various "medical formulas" that turned out to be just whiskey and beer.[5]

The family's move back to Kansas in September 1883, when their finances had stabilized, apparently came at Charles's initiative. Mary later explained rather dryly that "Mr. Lease got an idea that we would do better on a farm, and we moved away out west, to Kingman County, and took up a claim. There I lived in the very midst of the desert, solitary, desolate, with no society save my children. . . . It was an awful life, dreary, monotonous, hard, bleak and uninspiring." The depth of Mary's unhappiness is particularly notable because her time in the "desert" lasted no more than a year. In July 1884 the couple bought lots in the town of Kingman, and within a few months they had traded these for property in the bustling city of Wichita. Charles again found work as a pharmacist, making Mary's career as a "Kansas farmer's wife" a short one indeed.[6]

Within weeks of moving to Wichita Mary had plunged into an array of social and intellectual activities. In addition to publishing poems and letters she was active in the ladies' auxiliary of the Catholic Church. She continued her temperance work in Wichita's dynamic WCTU chapter, edited the group's column in the local *New Republic,* and gave an address to a WCTU convention in January 1885 titled "A Plea for the Temperance Ballot." Two months later she spoke on "Ireland and Irishmen" to raise funds for the Irish independence movement. By fall she was touring nearby towns to give temperance speeches. Pausing during her final pregnancy, she gave birth in January 1886 to a son named Ben Hur, in honor of the idealistic Christian convert in Lew Wallace's novel. The name was almost certainly Mary's choice rather than Charles's. Her public work, some of it now remunerative, was driven in part by Charles's continuing bad luck and financial haplessness, which would end in the couple's bankruptcy. Evidence suggests that by the time Ben was a toddler—if not before his birth—the Leases were largely estranged.[7]

In 1886 Mary Lease, with restless energy, ran on the Prohibition Party ticket for county superintendent of schools and helped organize a suffrage convention while simultaneously founding Wichita's first female literary club. By 1888 she had become a district organizer for the Knights of Labor and advertised herself as a speaker on "any phase of the labor problem." All these varied initiatives were facets of a central quest: to find remedies for poverty, women's poverty in particular. The Knights of Labor sought to bring together men and women, skilled and unskilled workers into a great union that would raise the living standard of the working class. Domestic servants and housewives were invited to join. Meanwhile, temperance leaders such as Willard grappled with the difficult question of whether alcoholism caused poverty or vice versa. Lease, like thousands of her counterparts in the movement, conducted a great deal of relief work during the harsh winter months of each year, gathering clothes and blankets and providing hot meals to the homeless. Willard—following an intellectual trajectory similar to Lease's—soon declared herself a Christian Socialist. Asking questions about poverty led Lease, like many others, to study economic and political theory. She even read law and passed the Kansas bar. Like many other women she agitated for the ballot not as an abstract right but as a vehicle for enacting specific policies for economic and social reform.

Early in her public career Lease showed both an inclination and talent for electoral politics, and in the wake of a series of failed strikes, Kansas Knights of Labor leaders were in the forefront in advocating political action. In 1888—just when Lease joined the movement—they created the Union Labor Party and conducted a spirited campaign for state and local offices. Lease gave an address to the Union Labor convention that was said in party circles to have "made her famous." The ensuing campaign was not a success, partly because of a suspicious explosion in Coffeyville right before Election Day. The bombing echoed the Haymarket explosion in Chicago two years earlier, which had tarnished the entire labor movement's reputation even though the Knights had been entirely uninvolved. The Republican press, drawing parallels to Haymarket, instantly blamed the Coffeyville bomb on "radical agitators" in the Union Labor ranks, damaging the party's credibility. Considerable evidence points instead to a small group of Republican conspirators—suggesting that some in the party already saw third-party radicalism as a serious threat, two years before the People's Party arrived on the scene.[8]

Lease, then, came to politics through the Knights, and to Kansans she did not arise from nowhere in the 1890 People's Party campaign. Thousands had already heard her speak or had read reprints of her addresses, and in Union Labor ranks she was working with a group of like-minded reformers who would create part of the nucleus of the People's Party. A much larger group of disaffected Kansans was preparing to join them. By the late 1880s thousands of farmers were joining the Farmers' Alliance, a vehicle for protesting their increasingly desperate economic plight. While criticizing government policies, most Alliancemen sought at first to work within existing Republican and Democratic structures. In some states, such as Iowa, Democrats headed off the new movement by adopting some of its planks. Kansas Democrats did not, and the state's Republicans—who had held virtually untrammeled power since the Civil War, and whose interests were deeply intertwined with those of railroad corporations—proved a fat target. In 1890, amid the hand-wringing of Farmers' Alliance leaders in other states, Kansas Alliancemen, Knights, and Union Labor reformers boldly joined together and launched the People's Party. To the astonishment of the nation, Populists captured four-fifths of the open seats in the Kansas House and five of seven congressional seats. When the legislature convened to elect a U.S. senator, Populists had enough power to replace Republican John J. Ingalls with their own William A. Peffer, a long-time spokesman for farmers' needs.[9]

On what platform did the Kansas People's Party win such sweeping victories, and in response to what circumstances? The woes of farmers and working people lay in the results of a revolution in transportation and trade, initiated earlier in the century with the rise of railroads, steamships, and other fossil-fuel technologies. With interpenetration of markets and opening of new lands, world crop prices suffered a long and disastrous decline. (Some historians mark the entire era from 1873 to 1899 as one long global depression.) But reformers such as Lease perceived that Republican policies had shaped the ways in which technology had transformed the economy over a thirty-year period in which government had been anything but laissez-faire. At both state and federal levels Republicans had given massive subsidies in land, bonds, and loan guarantees to railroads. Kansas, which one business journal dubbed "the creature of the railway," offered dramatic examples of the public debt, land speculation, overbuilding, chaotic competition, and "pooling" among railroads that resulted.

In the meantime Congress had instituted an array of other policies that caused resentment in the West and South. High protective tariffs benefited manufacturers at the expense of wheat and cotton farmers (and by almost every measure the South fared far worse than the West). The Supreme Court struck down a number of regulatory laws (especially those to rein in the power of railroads) on the grounds that states could not interfere with the flow of capital and labor nationwide. The U.S. bank system, created during the war, sharply favored the industrial Northeast, and after adopting a looser monetary policy to fund the war Republicans placed the country on the gold standard in 1879, calling in greenbacks and sharply contracting the money supply, which contributed to deflation. In the postwar era vastly more money circulated in the Northeast, where capital in the national banks was concentrated, than in other parts of the country. The results were dramatic (and compounded on the Plains by an intense drought starting in 1889). Interest rates on New York City mortgages averaged less than 5 percent; in western Kansas they averaged 12 percent. Per capita wealth in Suffolk County, Massachusetts, averaged $1,564; in St. Helena Parish, Louisiana, it stood at $86. Though Republicans accused the People's Party of fomenting regional conflict, they themselves had, intentionally or not, shaped a postwar economy of sharp regional imbalances.[10]

The People's Party offered a comprehensive critique of this system, calling for a looser money supply, public ownership of railroad and telegraph lines, greater regulation of corporations, and a federal progressive income tax on the very rich to generate revenue and mitigate extremes of wealth and poverty. Mary Lease brought to the fight an extraordinary talent for presenting these ideas to ordinary people. A shrewd strategist, she understood that Union Labor workingmen and reformers were already converts to the cause; her job in 1890 was to reach thousands of farmers, well organized and politically educated in the Farmers' Alliance, who still hesitated over joining a new party. It was they who would have to provide the bulk of People's Party votes, and Lease identified herself fully with their cause. "I have talked with the wives of farmers, whose hearts were breaking with the load of hopeless debt," she wrote after the campaign. "I have shared their homes, partaken of their fare, wept with them in their sorrows."[11]

Involved in the People's Party from its inception, Lease plunged into a three-month round of stump speaking during the fall 1890 campaign. As news of her exploits grew, so did the crowds. Though Lease was one of a dozen well-known speakers working in the campaign, she was clearly in a class by herself. Breathless reports used adjectives such as "electrified" and "spellbound." "Men threw their hats in the air and shouted," reported a politician in Olathe. "Women wept and tried to restrain the men folks." "Mrs. Lease was almost a phenomenal factor," wrote another observer. "Others spoke," remembered an editor in Miami County, "but made no impression like Mrs. Lease." Wild with enthusiasm at the conclusion of one address, men at a county fair carried Lease away on their shoulders. North of Topeka she "started an unquenchable fire." Victor Murdock of the *Wichita Eagle,* watching a People's Party demonstration wend its way through a small town, remembered a fellow reporter turning and exclaiming, "This is no parade; this is a revolution." "The voice of Mary Elizabeth Lease," Murdock added, "more than any other factor in it, made it so."

Lease's voice moved even hearers who disagreed with her message. "The man or woman who did not halt in wonder at the sound of her voice," wrote one Republican, "had no music in his soul. I have heard no speaking voice in my time to equal hers, in man or woman. It was contralto, rich, even, mellow." Her tone, remembered, was "normally tranquil and authoritative, but it could be elastically responsive to the needs of humor and of scorn. She could command an audience of men with the ease of a queen with courtiers; she could stir their risibles if she desired, and she could halve an opponent with a single slashing sentence." She was "terse, cogent, epigrammatical. . . . She did not flatter the farmers. She did not cajole them. She did not sue for their favor. She lashed them for their political indolence." A speech by Lease, wrote another listener, was "a medley of hot winds and cold chills, Italian zephyrs and brickbats; a scrap from the Sermon on the Mount fluttering on the brink of Hades and blown back by a breath as soft as ever cooled an infant's fevered brow."[12]

The brickbats made certain Populists almost as nervous as the Republicans. Even Lease's friends called her "almost fierce" and expressed the occasional wish that she would choose more temperate language. But Lease's legend as an angry woman rests in part on the apocryphal story that she told farmers to "raise less corn and more hell." (A Republican editor pinned this on Lease after borrowing it from a tale by another Populist speaker, Ralph Beaumont, who claimed to be quoting a disgruntled Southern congressman.) Lease preferred, rather, to have audiences warmed up with lighthearted songs, and she peppered her remarks with joke after joke, many of them on herself. She contrasted America's future with Europe's dark past and painted vivid pictures of the possibilities for reform. She could switch quickly from a review of statistics to the stirring lines of a sentimental poem such as Thomas Hood's

"Song of the Shirt," which described the plight of the toiling poor. Again and again she presented her arguments as plain logic. In a favorite move, she scoffed at the idea that the U.S. Constitution barred the government from lending money to farmers. The government lent to bankers, she observed; it had *given* millions to the railroads, and every state bonded its whiskey dealers. If the government could lend money on corn juice, why not on corn?

The key issue, Lease asserted, was recapturing equitable, democratic control of three national assets that the Republicans had handed over to large corporations: land, the money supply, and the national transportation system. The culprits, respectively, were owners of vast tracts of Western land, bankers and bondholders, and railroad companies. Considering the vast natural wealth of the continent and the hard labor of farmers and workingmen, Lease argued that every American ought to be living comfortably. Instead wealth had accrued to a few. Congress had "allowed the whole vast system of interstate commerce to be dominated by corporate Vikings and associated plunderers." Yet Lease argued that capital was easier to fight than monarchy. In the United States, she often said, the remedy was through "the ballot and not the bullet." She always ended on a note of hope. "No more millionaires, and no more paupers," she promised; "no more gold kings, silver kings and oil kings, and no more little waifs of humanity starving for a crust of bread." The power of her oratory can be measured by the torrent of requests that descended on Winfield editor Henry Vincent, who supervised her campaign schedule. "There are plenty of good speakers to be had," Vincent told Kansans impatiently. "You cannot all have Mrs. Lease." By August he announced that her calendar was full: "Do not call for Mrs. Lease, more."[13]

In some ways the Populist victory that November represented Mary Lease's greatest triumph. After 1890 she went on to play a role in national party councils and speak all over the country, touring with Populist presidential candidate James B. Weaver in 1892. But from Lease's point of view the party was running into serious difficulties. In early 1893, against her strenuous protests, Populist legislators engaged in a tense standoff with Republicans for control of a closely divided House of Representatives. The resulting "legislative war" precipitated a virtual military occupation of the Capitol and ended in Republican triumph, in the process generating terrible publicity for the new party. Kansas Populists' unwillingness to heed Lease's advice highlighted a broader problem. Lease, while shrewdly refraining from public advocacy of temperance and women's suffrage in the 1890 campaign, hoped the national party would adopt these goals. She shared this dream with thousands of Knights and Alliance members—especially women—and left-leaning prohibitionists such as Frances Willard, who hoped to merge the two parties. Their efforts failed in 1892, and the parties went separate ways, partly because thousands of grassroots female activists were underrepresented in decision-making councils. Lease's effort to become the first female U.S. senator foundered in the same year. Despite a nationwide petition drive endorsing her candidacy, with such prominent signatories as Susan B. Anthony, male party leaders dismissed the idea. They appointed Lease, instead, to the more "feminine" post of superintendent of the State Board of Charities, where she oversaw the state mental hospital and orphan asylums.

Lease resented this marginalization. She believed, with considerable justification, that she had brought Kansas Populists to power in the first place, and she apparently decided to unmake her work. While still campaigning for the party at the national level Lease denounced Kansas leaders such as Governor Lorenzo Lewelling and accused state Populists of corruption and mismanagement. She simultaneously attacked state suffrage leaders who were staunch Republicans; as in many other states the suffrage question became entangled in bitter partisan struggles, and an 1894 referendum went down to defeat. As early as 1894 Lease may have secretly leagued with Republicans and taken cash in exchange for these attacks. Unmoored from the Populists, she began experimenting with an array of other projects. She toyed with the idea of moving to Arkansas or California. She addressed Jacob Coxey's army of the unemployed as they marched through Pennsylvania and spoke on four separate occasions at the World Columbian Exposition in Chicago. She helped found a Kansas women's progressive club and a national peace society. Having broken with the Catholic Church, she joined the Disciples of Christ and then declared herself a Spiritualist.[14]

In 1895, in the midst of seeking new spiritual and intellectual anchors, Lease published her only book, *The Problem of Civilization Solved*. In it she proposed that the United States colonize South America and clear rainforest land for tropical agriculture, providing a new frontier for poor farmers from all continents of the world. Lease envisioned migration on such an immense scale that the resulting labor shortage would raise wages in the United States. She also depicted the creation of racially hierarchical plantations where, for a generation at least, African and Asian laborers would serve under the "tutelage" of Anglo landowners. It was an ironic vision for a daughter and sister of the Union dead, who once described herself as a radical republican. "Surrounded by the charms of nature," she wrote of the tropics, "while the nightingale warbles her magic melody and the feathery palms toss their plumes in the soft breeze, . . . the tired and world-worn Caucasian may find a peaceful home."[15]

Lease seems to have made a modest income from her political campaigning (not to mention from Republican bribes, one of which was substantial enough that she felt compelled to explain it publicly as an inheritance from an Irish aunt). Nonetheless, she and Charles went bankrupt, and Lease unmoored herself from her marriage as well as from the Kansas People's Party. At the invitation of her Populist friend Ignatius Donnelly she made several trips to Minnesota, and in 1896 she campaigned extensively there (though privately without enthusiasm) on behalf of Democratic and Populist presidential nominee William Jennings Bryan. Lease also made repeated visits to friends in New York, including fellow Populist-turned-Socialist Eugene V. Debs and his family. After her daughter Louise graduated from Wichita High School in 1897, Mary and the children moved to New York permanently. She filed for divorce, disentangled her finances from Charles's, declared bankruptcy, and started over once again. (Her son Charles's appointment as a Customs House clerk—unquestionably a Republican payoff for his mother's work—provided the main income for several years before Charles died of a sudden illness in 1905, at age thirty-one.) Lease lived quietly for most of her remaining years, working as an educational lecturer and possibly practicing law. She toyed briefly with Debs's Socialist Party but returned to the Republicans after endorsing William McKinley in 1900. Her only campaign activities after this were a series of stump speeches for Theodore Roosevelt's presidential bid in 1912, when he ran on the Progressive Party ticket.[16]

Roosevelt, whom Lease admired, carried many reform-minded Republicans with him into the new party, which advocated greater regulation of corporations, a national minimum wage, a progressive federal income tax, reforms in monetary policy, and also women's suffrage. By the 1910s, in fact, many Kansas Republicans who had bitterly denounced Lease in the 1890s (including one-time Wichita reporter Vic Murdock, now a reform-minded congressman) advocated Progressive causes along with her, and a few, such as Emporia editor William Allen White, were honest enough to admit that they had been wrong about the Populist program. Lease herself asserted, "Rooseveltism spells Populism—Populism with a big P. Progressive Republicanism has adopted every one of the former Populist tenets." "In these later years," she told a New York reporter, "I have seen, with gratification, that my work in Kansas in the good old Populist days was not in vain. The Progressive party has adopted our platform, clause by clause, plank by plank." She cited in particular the direct election of U.S. senators, public ownership of utilities, and women's suffrage (though she could have noted, also, that the last of these had never made it into the national Populist platform, and that that fact had played a leading role in her break with the party).[17]

Some historians have described the People's Party as a sort of "last hurrah" among old-fashioned farmers who looked back fondly on America's agrarian past and struggled to assert their political leverage in an industrial world that was rapidly leaving them behind. Lease was right in seeing it more as a starting point for the triumph of Progressive reform and ultimately Franklin D. Roosevelt's New Deal. In her speeches Lease warned about the dangers of an activist government that used its powers on behalf of the already powerful—a theme Thomas Jefferson would have recognized as his own. But she and her fellow Populists proposed remedies that, like the economic and political revolution that provoked them, would have bewildered the founding fathers. "We believe," declared the Populists' famous Omaha platform of 1892, "that the powers of government—in other words, of the people—should be expanded . . . as rapidly and as far as the good sense of an intelligent people and the teachings of experience shall justify, to the end that oppression, injustice, and poverty shall eventually cease in the land." As Lease herself put it, speaking at a Georgia Chautauqua in the same year, the remedy for extremes of wealth and poverty must be found in creating "a government, according to our constitution, for the most good to the greatest number." That, she hoped, would "bring about the day when there will be no more millionaires and no more paupers; . . . when we shall no longer see Cain in the palace and Abel in the slums." Mary Lease helped bring a party to power in Kansas that inspired a landmark series of legislative and constitutional initiatives. Though the party itself died—partly through her own efforts to kill it—her work in Kansas indeed made a difference. Lease advanced the fortunes of an array of measures, ranging from women's voting rights to the federal income tax and federal bank-deposit insurance. More broadly, she carried forward the dream of a future when, in her words, "We shall have not a government of the people by capitalists, but a government of the people, by the people."[18]

Charles M. Sheldon: Pastor, Author, and

Passionate Social Reformer

Timothy Miller

What would Jesus do? That phrase, or its acronym, WWJD, appears on clothing, bracelets, and book covers and in a hundred other places wherever evangelical Protestants can be found. Although many who embrace the phrase undoubtedly know nothing of its origin, a few, at least, know that it was first popularized slightly over a century ago by a Kansas minister named Charles M. Sheldon, whose smash best-selling novel *In His Steps* still graces the shelves of religious bookstores around the world. The evangelicals who embrace the inspirational Dr. Sheldon regard him as one of their own. Few indeed know that Sheldon, although a thoroughly pious man, was a liberal, not evangelical, Protestant, and a lifelong social reformer. This essay intends to round out the rather narrow picture of Sheldon that many hold, for he was certainly among the front ranks of the movers and shakers who created the most interesting parts of the history of Kansas.

Charles M. Sheldon (February 26, 1857–February 24, 1946) accepted a pastorate at Topeka's Central Congregational Church in 1889, about the time this image was made; he championed the spread of the social gospel, advocated prohibition, and wrote the sensationally best-selling novel *In His Steps: "What Would Jesus Do?"* Courtesy of the Kansas State Historical Society.

Born in Wellsville, New York, on February 26, 1857, Charles Monroe Sheldon came of age during the social gospel era, a time in American religious history of a great deal of social reform activity. The social gospelers used the platforms of their churches and denominations to work for a wide variety of social reforms—helping redeem the teeming industrial cities, turning local churches into social service institutions, and striving to limit the influence of unregulated industrial capitalism, for example. Unlike some of his social gospel peers, Sheldon never became a partisan political agitator, but his commitment to social reform was as strong as anyone's. He was also a religious innovator who wanted to reform theology and church practice.[1]

Sheldon's creative ideas were the direct cause of his move to Kansas. After graduating from Andover Theological Seminary in 1886, he took a pastorate in Waterbury, Vermont. Although the reforms he sought to institute there seem mild today (he urged pallbearers to keep their hats on during a 20-below-zero graveside service, for example), his flinty Vermont congregation found him just a bit too daring, and before long he got restless. When the new Central Congregational Church in Topeka asked him to become its first pastor, he accepted immediately. The chief attraction of the job was that he had no predecessor and thus might have room to innovate more freely than he could in Vermont.

And so Charles Monroe Sheldon came to Kansas at the beginning of 1889. It soon became apparent that he was no ordinary preacher, content to declaim on Sundays and tend the flock through the week. Soon after his arrival he became what he called a "Christian sociologist," exploring the real-life situations of the people around him. Early in 1890, during an economic depression, he donned old clothes and spent a week looking for a job, any job—and in enduring rejection after rejection developed deep empathy for the down-and-out of society. Later that year he decided to spend a week immersed in the worlds of each of eight "classes of people," including college students, African Americans, and newspaper workers.[2]

His week living among black Topekans turned out to have a decisive influence on Sheldon's life and work. Just across the street from Central Congregational was a squalid neighborhood occupied by former slaves and their progeny who had left Tennessee after the end of Reconstruction in 1877 as a part of the Great Exodus movement and had settled in several places in the Midwest, several thousand of them in Topeka. There a bankrupt real estate development provided unusually cheap building lots, and thus "Tennesseetown" took shape. Destitute, the African Americans had built crude homes, but the residents found few jobs and struggled to survive. Sheldon saw, up close, the poverty they endured and the brutal discrimination they faced. Resolving to attack the situation, he began giving evening lectures on a variety of practical topics ranging from principles of electricity to money management.

Before long Sheldon concluded that Tennesseetown needed a goodly array of basic social services, and as a first step he made arrangements to open a kindergarten. Leasing what had been a dance hall and speakeasy in the middle of the settlement and putting his parishioners to work remodeling it, he developed a facility in which the first black kindergarten west of the Mississippi opened in April 1893. It was a smashing success, not only providing basic education to the children but also giving their mothers desperately needed day care. By the time it was absorbed into the Topeka public school system in 1910, hundreds of students had passed through its program. The most prominent of them, as things turned out, came to be Elisha Scott, whose education Sheldon continued to encourage. Scott, with financial support arranged by Sheldon, went to law school at Washburn University and became a Topeka attorney. His sons followed in his footsteps, taking many early civil rights cases; one of them, Charles Sheldon Scott, was a lead attorney for the plaintiffs in *Brown v. Board of Education* when that case was first heard in the U.S. District Court at Topeka in 1951.[3]

Once the kindergarten space had been secured, a group of Central Congregational Church's young people decided to open the facility in the evenings as a library and reading room. Although decorum among the young patrons proved to be a chronic problem, the library remained open for many years and, at a minimum, provided a more uplifting environment than any other public place in Tennesseetown. Further expansion came with the addition of sewing classes for Tennesseetown girls and basket-weaving classes for boys. Cultural events became part of the uplift program, with musical programs and other special presentations. Eventually free medical care from visiting physicians, free legal help from volunteer attorneys, and small interest-free loans were available to people in need.

With social services in place, Sheldon and his congregation turned to upgrading the substandard housing in which most of the residents of Tennesseetown lived. Early in 1898 they launched efforts to improve the homes and clean up the yards; soon a new organization called the Village Improvement Society was awarding prizes for home repair, gardening, and other such efforts. Although at first some residents were hesitant—worrying, for example, that a cleanup program might lead to their not being able to keep hogs, an important part of their winter food supply—the program fairly soon received wide acceptance. In due course many houses were painted, lawns were improved, and trash was removed from the alleys. Residents received prizes of money and merchandise, and the popular program went on for several years thereafter.

And so it went for some two decades. Tennesseetown became a relatively tidy, if modest, neighborhood. Its crime rate dropped. Cooperation between the African Americans and their Caucasian neighbors became the order of the day. Sheldon was a great hero to the whole neighborhood and was paid the ultimate compliment when one of the Tennesseetown men said to him, "Brother Sheldon, your face may be white, but your heart is just as black as mine!"[4]

Charles Sheldon was an innovator within Central Congregational Church just as much as he was in the larger Topeka community. It was an in-house innovation that led to the phenomenon that gave him lasting fame, his authorship of *In His Steps,* one of the best-selling books in publishing history.[5]

The story of *In His Steps* began with what Sheldon called "sermon stories," which he began reading to his congregation in 1891. In those days the church routinely had both morning and evening services on Sundays, and the evening service suffered from chronic low attendance. One could not accuse Sheldon's parishioners, and especially the college students, of lack of devotion; they turned out well for Sunday school, the morning service, and the Christian Endeavor meeting in the afternoon. Getting them back out to the edge of town in the evening, however, was not so easy. Sheldon concluded that the problem was that he was preaching two sermons in one day; as he said years later, "I told all I know in the morning, and besides why should I preach another sermon to people who did not live up to the first one?"[6] In 1891 he had the brainstorm of writing stories that would be read to the congregation in weekly chapters, ending each installment at some crucial juncture so that his audience would have to return to see how things turned out.

He began writing the first of the stories that summer and reading it in September. The project was an immediate sensation; the church was filled to overflowing by the third week, not only with Central's members but with members of other churches as well. Literary critics who have examined Sheldon's incredible success in the marketplace have typically panned the "sermon stories" as pedestrian and formulaic, but Sheldon connected well with the Protestant masses. In addition to his cliff-hanging chapter endings, Sheldon's straightforwardly written works contained love stories, idealistic and committed characters, and strong social reform themes. People loved them and devoured them. The Sunday-night experiment went on for decades, and all of the stories were published as novels. Although many other authors published social gospel novels, none reached the public as well as Sheldon did.

In His Steps, the seventh of the sermon stories, is set in a Midwestern city called Raymond. Its protagonist is Henry Maxwell, pastor of the fashionable First Church of Raymond. The plot-setting vignette is vivid: a tramp walks into a church and, interrupting the fashionable Sunday service, delivers an articulate jeremiad against Christians whose lives do not sufficiently reflect their professed creed. At the peak of his oratory the tramp collapses (and soon afterward dies), but his message has pierced the hearts of the faithful people of First Church. Maxwell and a large group of parishioners resolve to try to lead Christ-like lives by asking themselves, "What would Jesus do?" when confronting any kind of moral decision. The rest of the book follows the flock as they work out their new ideal, including several congregants who work to redeem lost souls in the Rectangle, Raymond's seediest neighborhood. The story ends in Chicago, with the stalwart band improving society and making converts despite all manner of adversities.

Sheldon began reading *In His Steps* on October 4, 1896. A month later it began to appear in print: a Chicago weekly magazine called the *Advance* had purchased serial rights to the tale and began publishing the serial installments. Reader response was positive, and Sheldon tried to peddle the book rights to at least two publishing houses. They turned him down, however, and so Sheldon returned to the Advance company, which duly published it. It sold very well.

As it happened, small magazines in those days often did not bother to copyright their contents, and so as a piece of intellectual property *In His Steps* was not protected. In 1899 other publishers learned that the successful inspirational novel was in the public domain. Soon the flood began—publishers by the dozens began putting out their own editions of the book, many with cover prices of five or ten cents. Only a handful of the publishers ever paid Sheldon anything; his exact receipts will never be known, but it is safe to say that they were trivial compared to the overall circulation of the novel.

The proliferation of the book was stunning. In 1899 and 1900 it turned up as a feature in many daily and weekly newspapers. Its popularity was even more sensational in Great Britain than in America; there copies were sold by the millions at prices as low as a penny. Meanwhile, several dozen editions of the book were published in over twenty-five languages, including Armenian, Telugu, and Esperanto. No one will ever know how many copies were printed or sold, but they almost certainly reached the tens of millions. And readership was even greater as the cheap little novel was passed from believer to believer.

The story was inevitably destined to go beyond the printed page. Sheldon collaborated with a Washburn College professor on a stage-play version of the story, and a radio drama received wide circulation. A lantern-slide rendition of the tale appeared in 1900. Later a movie came out, although it was not very faithful to the book, and finally a comic-book version received wide distribution.

Although the masses embraced "Sheldonism" enthusiastically, critical response to the book was decidedly less positive. Some focused on Sheldon's style, which they decried as flat and lifeless. Others found Sheldon's ideas less than stimulating, given that the books always ended in rewards for the virtuous and suffering for the wicked. But those criticisms had little visible impact on Sheldon, who, after all, was out to nudge the consciences of Christians, not to create memorable literature.[7]

Sheldon continued to read sermon stories at Central Congregational Church and to publish them as novels for years afterward, but no other book remotely approached the success of the phenomenal *In His Steps.* Occasionally one drew fairly wide notice; *Jesus Is Here!* for example, one of three sequels Sheldon wrote to *In His Steps,* depicted Jesus back on earth, a dynamic man in a business suit who spoke boldly for needed social reforms. Many of them followed the scenario of *In His Steps,* with a protagonist (in several cases a young minister), or a group of them, fighting entrenched social evil and redeeming the world. Sheldon also published over a dozen other books, several of them anthologies of short devotional tracts and essays, plus quite a few pamphlets and hundreds of articles. One work that had a fairly wide readership was *The Everyday Bible,* which anticipated later biblical digests and paraphrases by retelling the biblical story in abridged form in plain, easy-to-read language. Occasionally a Sheldon book is brought back into print; in 2004 that happened to *Howard Chase, Red Hill, Kansas.*[8] But the only book with staying power has been the original, continuously in print for over a century and recently available in seven editions, including one in Spanish, from six publishers. Sales are estimated to remain in the tens of thousands per year.

One of the vignettes in *In His Steps* (recapitulated in other Sheldon works) became the basis for another memorable episode in Sheldon's life, one in which he put his reformist impulses into practice. A key episode in the book involves a newspaper publisher who joined the group that decided to ask, "What would Jesus do?" at every moral fork in the road. The publisher stopped running degrading news and refused to accept advertisements for objectionable products such as tobacco and liquor as well as ads that were in some way misleading. The new policy led to a financial crisis for the paper, but after a young heiress came to the financial rescue of the enterprise it gradually caught on with an increasingly enlightened public and ultimately proved a great success. The theme was a favorite of Sheldon's; something along those lines appeared in *Richard Bruce,* the first sermon story, as well as in later ones. In April 1895 Sheldon preached a sermon that outlined what his ideal paper would look like—how it would have uplifting content in place of the rubbish that characterized the papers of the day. In fact, as Sheldon knew, several experiments along those lines had taken place in real life, but none of them (at least in the United States) had prospered.

Into that situation came Frederick O. Popenoe. In August 1899 the young entrepreneur purchased the *Topeka Daily Capital,* a local newspaper that had encountered financial problems. Needing to turn the business around and pay off the loans he had taken out, Popenoe rather impulsively, late in 1899, offered Sheldon the opportunity to edit the *Capital* for a week to show just how a Christian daily newspaper might look. The week of March 13, 1900, was "Sheldon Week" in Topeka, with the good pastor at the helm of the daily. But in the meantime the experiment had progressed far beyond the level of a local project. As soon as the deal had been sealed, Popenoe engaged publicists to promote circulation and sell advertising. Among other things, the national membership of Christian Endeavor, a huge interdenominational Protestant youth movement of the day, was offered an outstanding deal: sell a subscription to the Sheldon Edition for twenty-five cents for the week, and keep a dime for your local organization. A huge throng of young people sold subscriptions by the thousands.

As the plan heated up, it became clear that Sheldon week would overtax the *Capital*'s press, which could print only 120,000 eight-page papers per day. So Popenoe made arrangements for satellite printing plants—in Chicago, New York, and finally London—to take up the slack. In the end circulation of the *Capital*—which normally ran to about 11,000 copies per day—reached more than 360,000.

Sheldon was not overly enthusiastic about the rather crass commercialization of his beloved concept, but he stayed the course. On Monday morning he showed up at the *Capital* office to begin work on the Tuesday paper (there was no Monday paper in those days). The paper that emerged the next day was, to say the least, not conventional. It began with "A Morning Prayer and Resolve," and the lead story was "Starving India," which was not really news (the wire reports on which Sheldon based the story were some weeks old) but an appeal to readers to contribute funds for famine relief. The front page also featured a denunciation of war and a diatribe against the liquor industry as well as a paean to the success of prohibition. Inside was an account of a fatal tenement fire in Newark, followed by an editorial denunciation of slumlords whose greed contributed to human misery. Other pages had reports of temperance and antismoking rallies, notices of meetings of charitable organizations, and various feature articles. Finally, segregated from the news, came the advertisements, the largest of them being for the *Christian Herald,* a leading Protestant magazine of the day.

And so it went for the rest of the week. As Sheldon had promised earlier, reports of criminal activity were muted in tone and accompanied by editorial notes explaining how the misdeed might have been avoided. There was no news of boxing or other activity Sheldon opposed. By conventional standards there was not a lot of news in the Sheldon Edition, but conventional news was not what Sheldon was about. More to his taste was the work of the society editor, Jessie Garwood, who was assigned to spend the week finding out how much money was being wasted on worthless social events. Garwood concluded that it all came to $1,716, and Sheldon editorialized that it should have gone to Indian famine relief.

Advertising felt the Sheldonian blue pencil just as strongly as the news did. Ads for alcohol and tobacco were automatically out, of course. There were no ads for any theatrical productions, and advertising for books and magazines was accepted only after Sheldon had examined and approved the works in question. All ads from Kansas City merchants were rejected because they might have competed with their Topeka counterparts, and Sheldon favored protecting hometown businesses.

At the end of the week came no Sunday paper. Sheldon was opposed to the printing and delivery of newspapers on Sunday, so a special paper would be printed on Saturday evening. (In fact the press could not handle the immense job; at 11:30 Sheldon sent the crew home, instructing them to print the rest of the run on Monday morning.) In the weekend edition news dropped away altogether in favor of material suitable for family Sunday reading, including Bible passages.

The Sheldon Edition received a great deal of ridicule in the national press, but it did have an impact. Most immediately, the paper raised $100,000 (plus a good deal of grain from Kansas farmers) for Indian famine relief. Sheldon was given $5,000 from the project's considerable profits, and he gave it all to a variety of charities, including a public drinking fountain in downtown Topeka. The good Topeka pastor practiced the precept that advertising has to be honest long before it attracted a widespread following.[9]

In the wake of the Christian daily newspaper experiment and the ongoing sales of *In His Steps,* Sheldon commanded a national pulpit, and he used it to promote his favorite social-reform programs. At the beginning of the twentieth century one of the strongest reform movements in the country was the crusade to abolish alcoholic beverages. Sheldon had always been an ardent prohibitionist—the problem of alcohol, and the necessity of fighting it, was a prominent part of most of his novels—and he used his prominence to campaign tirelessly for the cause. No methods seemed too strong for the crusading pastor. Although most respectable prohibitionists separated themselves from the "hatchitation," or physical destruction of saloons, of Carry Nation, for example, Sheldon invited her to give a talk at his church and later in life wrote articles praising her, arguing that it is the passionate who make reform movements effective.[10] The peak of that activity came with his participation in the "Flying Squadron," a whistle-stop campaign of prohibitionist leaders who would roll into town, hold a rally, and use the proceeds of the offering to buy tickets to the next town. Traveling 65,000 miles, the squadron and similar efforts helped push prohibition to the success it achieved with the passage of the Eighteenth Amendment in 1918. So passionate was Sheldon for the prohibition cause that he even took the campaign overseas, to Great Britain, Australia, and New Zealand, although prohibition never gathered a following in any of those countries that was anything like that in the United States. The zeal he had for that cause never abated; after legal liquor returned to the United States in 1933, Sheldon continued to urge a return to prohibition. By then, however, he was advanced in years, and people generally regarded him as a warm and fuzzy old man rather than a critic to be heeded.

Although Sheldon's commitment to prohibition was intense and constant, he was passionate about many other popular crusades of his day as well. The last decades of the nineteenth century and the first of the twentieth were, after all, the heyday of the social gospel movement, which ultimately sought nothing less ambitious than the establishment of the kingdom of God on earth. Sheldon's advocacy for the down-and-out of society had begun early in his ministerial career with his work to improve the lives of the African Americans of Tennesseetown and his ongoing empathy with the poor. As time passed his goals broadened, embracing the major reform issues of the day. He joined with his fellow social gospelers in promoting the rights of labor and emphasizing the dignity and worth of manual labor, telling his parishioners that "It is better to earn one's bread by the sweat of one's brow than to try to make a living by making other folks sweat."[11] In an age in which child labor was widespread, Sheldon denounced that practice as "inexcusable." Female domestic workers were another focus of Sheldon's labor interest; he pressed for fair pay, decent living quarters, and respect for the women who kept many a household running.[12]

Topeka was not the largest of American cities, but that did not keep Sheldon from speaking out on the urban problems that were characteristically at the heart of social gospel concerns. One of his more distinctive proposals was for the creation of "missionary policemen," officers who would not just arrest criminals but seek to turn wrongdoers from bad actors into good Christians. Sheldon himself provided something of a model for his concept during the early years of his campaign against alcohol in Topeka. When men ended up in jail as a result of his shut-down-the-saloons campaign, he would supply them with good reading matter in jail, sometimes give them a bit of money, and see that their families were cared for. In Sheldon's fiction, when police officers distributed Bibles on their beats and established empathetic relations with the citizenry, crime plummeted and the whole country turned to this new type of policing.[13] Sheldon also campaigned for prison reform, contending that penitentiaries were seedbeds for crime. Ever desirous of experience, he spent two weeks in the Kansas State Penitentiary investigating complaints of cruel and inhumane conditions; his report to the governor is said to have led to some alleviation of the grim environment he encountered.[14]

One part of the social gospel program was the use of church buildings and facilities for purposes other than Sunday worship and religious education. In the 1880s and 1890s hundreds of churches across the nation began to offer wide arrays of social services in their existing buildings and in new ones built for the new programs. Among the most common services offered, generally without charge, were lending libraries and reading rooms, practical-skills classes (cooking, sewing), gymnasiums, and wholesome entertainment such as game nights. Some "institutional churches," as they were called, went much further, with public baths, ambitious night schools, loan funds, and medical clinics.[15] Sheldon was a wholehearted backer of such expanded use of church buildings, and Central Congregational Church was kept busy seven days a week. When Sheldon retired in 1919 his parishioners decided to build as his monument an extensive facility that would turn Central into a true institutional church. In 1924 the new structure was opened, and the Sheldon Community House, as it was called, has provided public social services ever since.

Sheldon's last great social crusade was for world peace. A lifelong pacifist, he was dismayed by the horrors of World War I and during the interwar years wrote and spoke out for peace incessantly. What would Jesus do? "I believe the first thing Christ would do would be to call the whole world to repentance for its militarism," wrote Sheldon in 1934. "War is the most wicked, wasteful, stupid, cowardly and unchristian activity of the human race."[16] In 1931 Sheldon oversaw the erection of ten roadside billboards promoting peace to motorists traveling between Topeka and Kansas City. The passion for peace remained with him to the end of his life.

Sheldon's reformist agenda included alterations within the churches as well as in society at large. He urged unity among all Protestants, and ultimately among all Christians, and eventually became convinced that fine points of doctrine were the basis of much of the scandalous division of Christianity. Thus, he championed "untheological Christianity," a religion of action rather than concepts. As he concluded, "It is, indeed, easier to give assent to the Westminster Confession than to love one's enemies. It is not so hard to believe in the inerrancy of the Scriptures as it is to practice the brotherhood of man."[17] He wanted to make funerals upbeat occasions stressing the joy of immortality and simplify the ceremonies to help roll back the high cost of dying. He was an early advocate of pastoral counseling and promoted what he called a "Protestant confessional." He loved the church to the core of his being and wanted to make it as good as it could possibly be.

Did Sheldon make a difference? Undoubtedly. The "WWJD" bracelets and other trinkets are the least of it. Where Christians (and all people of conviction) work for social justice, there does Sheldon's work survive.

William Allen White: The Voice of

Middle America

Sally F. Griffith

Journalists and biographers loved to tell the story of William Allen White's arrival in Emporia, Kansas. *Life* magazine told it this way in a profile honoring his seventieth birthday in 1938: "Every small-town boy who ever dreamed of becoming a newspaperman knows the story of how William Allen White, with 27 years behind him and $1.25 in his pocket, rode the Santa Fe into Emporia, Kan., one day in 1895, borrowed $3,000 and bought the *Emporia Gazette,* and next year wrote an editorial called 'What's the Matter with Kansas?' which made him nationally famous overnight."[1]

It is the archetypal American success story that reaches back to Benjamin Franklin's arrival in eighteenth-century Philadelphia with a Dutch dollar and a copper shilling in his pocket. White's had its own twist, for when he stepped off the twilight train from Kansas City, he encountered "a considerable crowd of idlers who in that day came to the station" to watch the trains come in. As

William Allen White (February 10, 1868–January 29, 1944), the "sage of Emporia" and voice of Middle America, depicted here in 1914 at his *Gazette* office desk, reveled and prospered in his role as a small-town editor in Emporia for nearly fifty years. Courtesy of the Kansas State Historical Society.

he recalled the moment in his *Autobiography:* "The announcement had been made that I had bought the *Gazette*. I was a fairly familiar figure on the streets of Emporia." He faced an important decision: "Should I lug my heavy baggage uptown to the boarding house . . . and establish a reputation as a frugal, thrifty young publisher, or should I establish my credit in the community by going in a hack? . . . I decided, as a credit-strengthening act, to take the hack. . . . I never regretted it. . . . A good front is rather to be chosen than great riches."[2]

William Allen White *was* an American archetype, yet as this story suggests he also lived in a particular place and time, one spanning a significant transformation in American history. Born February 10, 1868, in Emporia, then a village of five hundred, he grew to manhood in a world of small-scale agriculture and artisan production just when it was being overtaken by the economic and social effects of national railroads, mass industrial production, and large-scale organizations. These changes involved culture at least as much as material things. As historian John Higham noted, nineteenth-century America had been held together—to the extent that it did cohere—by a shared ideology: ideas, beliefs, and goals based on a generalized Protestantism and democratic nationalism.[3] In the later part of the century, more formal, technical forms of unity relying on legal procedures, bureaucratic systems, and professional expertise promised to deal more efficiently with the nation's problems. Advocates promised that such impersonal systems, ostensibly operating only by means of science and reason, would cope better with an increasingly complex society and avoid ethnic, racial, religious, and political conflicts arising from older forms of cohesion.

Yet, as the "culture wars" of the latter twentieth century showed, ideology has continued to play an important role in America. Over a long and active life as journalist, author, politician and pundit, White observed and helped shape the period in which ideological and technical approaches first competed for primacy. He consistently served as a mediator between the old and new, reflecting the compelling issues of the day while demonstrating a remarkable ability to continue to grow in the breadth of his sympathies and understanding.

The Emporia of White's birth was a village on the edge of the rapidly moving frontier of white settlement on the western Great Plains. Through his parents he inherited two competing strains of nineteenth-century ideology. His father, Allen White, was an Ohio-born physician and businessman who loved politics and boosting his community. A Jacksonian Democrat, he shunned religious emotionalism and pressed his son to study the great leaders of classical Greece and Rome. Mary Hatten White was in many ways her husband's antithesis. Born to Irish Catholic parents but later adopted by New England Congregationalists, Mary White was intensely religious and emotional. As a college student she had witnessed one of the Lincoln-Douglas debates and fallen "madly, platonically, but eternally" in love with Abraham Lincoln. Thereafter she was a staunch Republican. She loved to read aloud to their only surviving child from works by sentimental nineteenth-century novelists, especially Charles Dickens. White recalled his parents' marriage as often stormy, inspiring in him a longing for harmony but also an awareness that "there are two sides to everything" produced by "seeing both sides well presented by those you love."[4]

A few years after White's birth the family moved farther west to El Dorado, a newly founded town where they soon became leading citizens. White remembered an "Elysian childhood" in which village blended smoothly with the woods and prairies surrounding it, before the coming of the railroad changed everything: "In the boy's world, it meant that homemade sleds and little homemade wagons would pass; that the bows and arrows which boys made by seasoning hickory behind the stove and scraping and polishing them with glass, would as an art disappear forever out of the life of American boys."[5]

As he grew, young White readily absorbed the values and practices of his culture. He naturally followed in his father's footsteps as a little Democrat, braving a schoolyard beating for wearing a Tilden and Hendricks scarf in 1876. But Republicans dominated Kansas politics, and after Allen White died in 1882 his son gradually moved to his mother's party. After a year at the College of Emporia, White decided to learn a useful skill and took a job as an apprentice printer at the little Democratic weekly that his father had supported financially. Though he returned to college after a few months, he continued to be connected with journalism for the rest of his life, gradually progressing from printer and compositor to cub reporter, editorial writer, and eventually publisher and editor of his own paper. He learned about all aspects of the business and observed at first hand the close ties between journalism, politics, and economics—particularly where the powerful railroads were concerned. After transferring to the University of Kansas, for example, he worked for the Lawrence *Tribune,* which survived largely through the job printing it did for the Santa Fe railroad, and learned how to manipulate the county's Republican nominating convention. He left the university without his degree to manage the *El Dorado Republican,* published by a close family friend, Bent Murdock, who had just been elected to the state senate. As a matter of course, his job included helping Murdock control the local Republican Party organization with the help of gifts of alcohol and cigars provided by the railroads.[6]

Even as White was learning the ropes of the pragmatic world of business and politics, he aspired to a career in the genteel world of culture. He read widely in the literature of the day and dabbled at writing dialect poetry and fiction. In a time of fluid vocational categories, he saw around him men like E. W. Howe and Eugene Ware who were respected "men of letters" as well as successful journalists, lawyers, and politicians. White's first short story, "The Regeneration of Colonel Hucks," drew on his insider knowledge of politics. It was a sentimental tale of an old Civil War soldier who was attracted to the rising Populist revolt but returned in the end to the Grand Old Party. The story won White the favor of Republican leaders and in 1891 a job on the Kansas City *Journal,* then controlled by the Santa Fe railroad.

As an editorial writer and political reporter in Kansas City, he came to know the inner workings of state and regional politics at a time when the People's Party was challenging the established order. A year later he moved to the *Kansas City Star.* Owned by real estate developer William Rockhill Nelson, the *Star* represented a new kind of mass-circulation journalism that was emerging in large cities throughout the nation. Advertising revenues freed it from dependence on political patronage and the need to follow a party line in reporting: "Every man on the paper, from top to bottom . . . was convinced of his own absolute freedom," White recalled, "his right to express himself unhampered save by the truth as he saw it."[7] He also wrote poetry and fiction and joined the Western Artists and Authors Society, through which he met and fell in love with another aspiring writer, Sallie Lindsay; the two were married in 1893. They had two children, William Lindsay and Mary Katherine. But the attractions of city life soon began to pall for White, who longed for his own paper and the independent political role in Kansas politics that such ownership entailed. He achieved this dream in 1895 with the purchase of the *Emporia Gazette,* a down-at-the-heels paper with a daily circulation under five hundred, for $3,000, all borrowed from political and personal contacts.

Calling on his varied journalistic experience, White reshaped the *Gazette* to stress local news while remaining a Republican paper. In his first editorial he promised that "while the politics will be straight, it will not be obtrusive. . . . The main thing is to have this paper represent the average thought of the best people of Emporia and Lyon County in all their varied interests." To demonstrate his commitment to the community, he vowed that "the new editor hopes to live here until he is the old editor, until some of the visions which rise before him as he dreams shall have come true."[8] He filled the newspaper with items boosting local development, whether promoting civic improvements or urging residents to support local businesses. He imbued the *Gazette* with the values of boosterism, which combined hard-nosed qualities of efficiency and rationality with appeals to loyalty and community spirit.

His efforts to appeal to a broad section of the community by standing above "cliques, or gangs, or crowds" nearly ran aground during the hotly contested presidential election of 1896, when a blistering editorial attacking Populism, "What's the Matter with Kansas?" was picked up by the Republican organization and reprinted throughout the nation. Its effective use of earthy Kansas vernacular and the national notoriety it achieved helped White's literary career, boosting sales of his first book of short stories, *The Real Issue,* published by Way and Williams of Chicago later that fall. But his local reputation was tarnished by the editorial's vituperative treatment of the state's Populists—whom he claimed had hurt the economy by attacking the "money power." He later admitted that it had been a mistake: "It was written because I was mad, and I could not do it again, or anything like it."[9]

The editorial made White known as a spokesman for the Midwest. He was increasingly sought after to write for established national magazines such as the *Atlantic* and *Scribner's* and for the more popular mass-circulation magazines such as *McClure's* that began to play an important role in American culture from the 1890s onward. He attempted to use his new contacts and audience to promote Emporia's and Kansas' economic development. In succeeding years he worked tirelessly to build the *Gazette* into a flourishing enterprise that employed the latest printing technologies and attracted a growing share of advertising revenue. By 1906 he had acquired several new presses and automatic typesetting machines, and the paper's circulation expanded to over three thousand. This prosperity was not unique but illustrated the transformation of community journalism at the turn of the twentieth century, based principally on the rise of national advertising for mass-produced consumer goods.

At the same time White underwent a gradual "conversion" from conservative to reform Republicanism. The shift was partly inspired by friendships with men and women who became leading figures in the Progressive reform movement. Most prominent was Theodore Roosevelt, whom White met on a visit to Washington in 1897. Nearly fifty years later he recalled their meeting in a tone usually employed in describing first love: "I had never known such a man as he, and never shall again. He overcame me. . . . He poured into my heart such visions, such ideals, such hopes, such a new attitude toward life and patriotism and the meaning of things, as I had never dreamed men had. . . . After that I was his man."[10] Roosevelt's stirring appeals to chivalric ideals of sacrifice and patriotism offered White a vision of a new kind of politics, but it was several years before he achieved sufficient economic independence to allow him to break with the dominant factions in the Kansas Republican Party.

One of the central issues in the rise of Progressivism in Kansas was the power wielded by the railroads, the first nationwide corporations. Reformers moved to ban railroads' provision of free passes to their allies—among them journalists such as White. Years later he admitted that his conversion had been encouraged by "the changed attitude I saw in the eyes of my fellow passengers on the railroads when I flashed my passes."[11] The railroads themselves welcomed a certain degree of regulation in order to control ruinous competition that had led many into bankruptcy in the 1890s. Noting this drive toward formal regulatory systems, some historians have labeled the period as a "search for order."[12]

White and many of his allies, however, perceived the reform movement as principally an idealistic crusade, a struggle on behalf of "righteousness." Noting the convergence of this "quickening of ideology" with "a dazzling elaboration of technical systems," John Higham observed that during the first two decades of the twentieth century "it seemed that a modernized Americanism and a social gospel could be the moving spirit of a technical society."[13] In Emporia, too, White joined with like-minded middle-class men and women in a series of different causes, from ridding the community of a disreputable physician through appeals to a new medical licensing board to enforcing laws against alcohol, gambling, and prostitution to building a municipally owned electric plant, a state-owned refinery to counter the power of the Standard Oil trust, and a large YMCA facility to protect youths from the influence of motion pictures and pool halls. All of these campaigns involved ideological and technical appeals in varying degrees.

White's writing for national magazines was influential in shaping a general belief that all of the disparate movements of the day were in fact parts of one shared movement that reflected a single righteous spirit. Often drawing on his access to prominent politicians, he reported candidly on the "inside" story about particular scandals, but he framed them within interpretations stressing the "moral uplift" that was at work. In "The Golden Rule," for example, published in the *Atlantic* in 1905, White argued that disparate political conflicts were all evidence that "the American people during recent years have been growing in mental and moral vision, and in spiritual force." In 1909 he collected a series of essays expressing his progressive faith in *The Old Order Changeth: A View of American Democracy*. He characterized a host of issues throughout the country as manifestations of a conflict between democracy and capitalism produced by industrialization, but that was in the end "a struggle in every man's heart between the unselfish and the selfish instincts of his nature." Over the preceding decade Americans had become aware of many wrongs in their society, and their greater consciousness, had produced a groundswell of "public opinion." Although they often focused on material issues, White argued, and Roosevelt agreed, that this was "a practical world of spiritual things." White disagreed with fellow reformers who thought that conditions could be improved through "law or system of laws" alone.[14]

White's most influential writing was his popular fiction, which presented heartwarming allegories for his Progressive vision in the form of depictions of small-town life. *In Our Town* (1906) contained a series of sketches seen through the window of a small-town newspaper office. His most popular work to that point, it won much praise for its realistic yet affectionate portrayal of human foibles. "You have put in it not only the life of your town," wrote fellow writer and reformer Brand Whitlock, "but the life of my town, and of all American towns." White's first novel, *A Certain Rich Man,* was completed in 1912 after many years of work and was based on the New Testament parable of the prodigal son, which White later admitted was also "the story of my own inner life." Set against the backdrop of the evolution of a Kansas town from a rough frontier community to a modern city, it was peopled with a large cast of vividly realized small-town characters, many modeled after actual figures in White's childhood. The rich detail of midwestern life and often harshly realistic psychological portraiture prompted William Dean Howells to include White as part of a contemporary trend toward "psychologism." Yet unlike naturalist writers such as Theodore Dreiser, White showed that human beings were capable of redemption through their connection to righteous values. His protagonist, John Barclay, had risen from poverty to become wealthy, powerful, and corrupt but was restored by his mother's love and his small-town ties. Though now largely forgotten, the novel's ungainly mixture of Frank Norris and Charles Dickens was extremely popular, and a quarter of a million copies were ultimately sold.[15]

White's national writings spoke to the beliefs and longings of his largely middle-class readers. Many turn-of-the-century urbanites had grown up in the country or small towns and remained nostalgic for the intimacy of the small-scale communities they had left behind. White offered a vision of America that projected onto the national scene an idealized vision of a small town—one that often looked strangely like Emporia. In his handling, the small town embodied essential virtues such as morality, neighborliness, basic equality, and civic spirit. Progressivism moved these virtues to a higher plane.

Unlike most of his Progressive colleagues, White refused repeated offers to leave Emporia and the *Gazette* and write full-time for national magazines. By remaining as publisher and editor of the *Gazette*—delegating much of the day-to-day work to faithful staff—White was able to retain an independent base while gaining a growing reputation as a freelance writer. His newspaper also was useful in promoting Progressive causes in Emporia and Kansas and keeping in close touch with the pulse of public opinion. He reserved the right to compose editorial eulogies for Emporians from all walks of life who had contributed something to their community. Keeping one foot in the small town and the other in the urban world of the new national media enabled White to mediate between the two.

As the focus of Progressive energies shifted from the states to Washington, D.C., White became increasingly involved in national affairs. When conservatives within the Republican Party thwarted Roosevelt's bid for another presidential term in 1912, White threw himself into founding a new Progressive Party. Until it collapsed in 1914, White worked tirelessly as a national committeeman, devoting much of his time to planning strategy, raising funds, campaigning, and boosting the new party in his newspaper and magazine articles. He served with, though often distrusted, newcomers to the movement such as industrialist George W. Perkins who emphasized technical values of efficiency and scientific rationality. Under their influence, the technical and centralizing side of Progressivism came into greater prominence while harnessing the movement's moral intensity.

Although at first agreeing with efforts to keep the United States out of the general European war that began in 1914, White embraced national mobilization when President Woodrow Wilson finally brought America into the war in 1917. Increasingly convinced that the war effort could be a means of forging a higher form of community, he energetically promoted public participation. By the end he concluded that the war had "aroused our intellects to an appreciation of our shortcomings. . . . [Its] suffering and grief will reawaken the national consciousness, clarify our mental powers and restore our national vision." After a trip to Europe in the fall of 1917 as an observer for the Red Cross, he wrote *The Martial Adventures of Henry and Me,* a semifictionalized account of his travels that sought to translate the war into terms familiar to small-town Americans.

With the end of the war and the failure of the Versailles Conference to establish a viable peace, America entered a period of disillusionment with Wilsonian and Progressive idealism. Reacting to the repression of freedoms during the war and the notorious Red Scare afterward, a younger generation of intellectuals turned away from progressive reform to "liberalism," which focused on the assertion of individual rights. White continued to try to bridge the increasingly divergent small-town and urban worlds, defending the former against charges of intolerance and complacency while lamenting the fads and sensational "ballyhoo" of the latter. After the war his perspective was broadened by travel in Europe, Latin America, and Asia. Learning that the United States had been the most restrictive of freedom of the press and speech, he for the first time became an ardent advocate of liberal values of free expression.

White was out of step with new currents in literature, however. When his second novel, *In the Heart of a Fool,* was finally published in 1918 the *New Republic* attacked it as overly sentimental and propagandistic; he soon stopped writing fiction altogether. Nonetheless, he continued to defend the essential humanity of small-town civilization against its urban critics. He praised Dorothy Canfield's portrayal of small towns, over the more jaundiced views of Sinclair Lewis, for capturing the inner "truth" as well as the material "facts." But the single piece of White's writing that most effectively expressed the virtues of small-town life was not planned as such. It was an editorial tribute written in the depth of grief for his sixteen-year-old daughter, Mary, who was killed in a riding accident in 1921. As he had done countless times before in the *Gazette,* he distilled into a few simple images the essential virtues of a life. Innocent but irreverent, joyous but thirsting for justice, Mary had loved to give people rides in her "jitney bus" of a car, eagerly organized Christmas dinners at the county poorhouse, and lobbied relentlessly for a restroom for "colored girls" in her high school. After describing the details of her short but dignified funeral, the editorial concluded, "A rift in the clouds in a gray day threw a shaft of sunlight upon her coffin as her nervous, energetic little body sank to its last sleep. But the soul of her, the glowing, gorgeous, fervent soul of her, surely was flaming in eager joy upon some other dawn."[16]

Emporians, who had known Mary all her life, appreciated the editorial, but so did the rest of the nation, for whom she became a symbol of exuberant innocence that stood as a shining rebuke to the sordid and superficial culture of the Roaring Twenties. The editorial was immediately reprinted in newspapers and magazines throughout the country and was read on nationally broadcast radio programs. Literary critic Christopher Morley, including it in a volume of essays later that year, observed, "This is not the sort of thing one wishes to mar with clumsy comment." Over following decades it was reprinted in hundreds of anthologies and school readers. The Whites were comforted that the essay's popularity kept their daughter alive "in the hearts of her kind, high-school and college students," long after her death. "Probably if anything I have written in these long, happy years that I have been earning my living by writing," White commented in his *Autobiography,* "if anything survives more than a decade beyond my life's span, it will be the thousand words or so that I hammered out on my typewriter that bright May morning under the shadow and in the agony of Mary's death."[17]

After the collapse of the Progressive Party White had returned to the Republican fold and managed to regain significant power as a leader of the state's progressive faction. Subsequently, he remained within the party, even in the 1930s, when he supported many of Franklin Delano Roosevelt's New Deal programs. Twice in the 1920s he departed from politics as usual to champion unpopular liberal causes. In 1922 he clashed with his Kansas allies over the right to publicly support striking railroad workers. He explained his ideas in an editorial, "To an Anxious Friend," a classic statement of libertarian principles of the primacy of "free expression" over the law and even fears of violence: "This nation will survive, this state will prosper, the orderly business of life will go forward if only men can speak in whatever way given them to utter what their hearts hold," he assured his opponents. "Reason has never failed men. Only force and repression have made the wrecks in the world."[18] Reprinted throughout the country, the editorial was awarded the recently established Pulitzer Prize the following year.

In 1924 White ran for governor of Kansas as an Independent to protest the regular parties' failure to denounce the rising prominence of the Ku Klux Klan in the state. "I want to be governor to free Kansas from the disgrace of the Ku Klux Klan," he stated in announcing his candidacy. His goal was primarily to publicize a cause, and he made no effort to create a genuine political organization, but the national press nonetheless avidly followed his campaign. As he had once labeled Populists an unrepresentative "rag-tag" element, he now lambasted the Klan as a small, intolerant minority and ridiculed its proclivity for absurd titles, "the cyclopses, pterodactyls, Kleagles, wizards and willopus-wallopuses . . . parading in the Kansas cow pastures." Although the campaign endeared him to urban liberals, it was no more popular at home than had been his editorials against the Populists, and he failed to carry even his own county.

White's experiences after World War I launched him on a new career as world citizen, manifested through his reporting and editorials and participation in a wide range of organizations. He had never traveled abroad until he took his family on a much-anticipated European tour in 1909. He returned during and after the war and reported on the Versailles Peace Conference. These experiences sparked a new interest in international affairs that continued despite Congress's failure to ratify the League of Nations. "War is a disease of civilization from which no country is immune when it breaks out," he wrote in the *Gazette* in 1921. He reported on the Washington Naval Disarmament Conference in 1921 and the signing of the Kellogg-Briand Pact in 1928. He participated in a number of national committees devoted to promoting peace through international cooperation. He and Sallie traveled widely in the 1920s and 1930s, including a visit to the Soviet Union in 1933. He fought against Republican high-tariff policies and rightly predicted that the Smoot-Hawley tariff of 1930 would be disastrous for the world economy. He supported the candidacy of progressive Republican Herbert Hoover and in 1930 accepted his appointment to a commission to study the troubled conditions in Haiti, occupied by troops sent by President Calvin Coolidge. The commission's criticisms of U.S. intervention spurred a reassessment that produced the Good Neighbor policy. Pursued under both Hoover and Roosevelt, the new approach substantially improved relations between America and Latin America.[19]

White's interest in foreign policy put him at variance with much of the leadership of the Republican Party, which had rejected what he called "the Rooseveltian attitude" in favor of isolationism. From the early 1930s onward his editorials called attention to the threat posed by the rise of fascism and aggressive nationalism in Germany, Italy, and Japan. Though for a time he hoped that enforcing neutrality would protect the United States, by the later 1930s he realized that the nation could no longer stand aside in a conflict between democratic nations and the Axis powers. After war began in 1939, White agreed to lead a movement aimed at persuading the public of the necessity of assisting European democracies. His help had been enlisted because of his national reputation for intelligence and integrity. As Washington columnists Drew Pearson and Robert S. Allen put it, "Bill White is a significant and vital American leader because he is an enlightened, vibrant spokesman of the great farm belt of the nation, because he is an unrelenting foe of provincialism and because he keeps Main Street alert."[20]

White's shift toward involvement was accelerated by the role played by his son, William L. White, who covered the war in Europe for newspapers and radio. In May 1940 he launched the Committee to Defend America by Aiding the Allies, which was instrumental in winning acceptance of a program to arm

Great Britain. By this time Germany had invaded Norway and Denmark and begun to move toward Holland and Belgium, and, White asserted, "America began to see what kind of a war it was, the fanatical conquest of a pagan ideology which justified slavery, which exalted cruelty, which banished chivalry, scoffed at the equality of men, and was aimed straight at the dignity of the human spirit."[21]

White's leadership of the committee was the capstone of a long and distinguished career that won him not only the respect but the affection of Americans from many walks of life. His shrewd observations on politics and life in general had earned him the title "Sage of Emporia." He was admired by both urban and rural Americans for having chosen to stay in Emporia and remain his own boss, despite many lucrative offers from national periodicals. In an age of growing specialization, he successfully combined diverse roles as journalist, businessman, man of letters, politician, and world citizen. Many of his urban friends were often exasperated at his refusal to endorse Roosevelt's candidacies or to come over to the Democratic Party in the 1930s. What many did not understand was that, despite his broadening outlook and widening horizons, White continued to think of himself as a small-town newspaperman. He loved the sense of personal intimacy and diversity of roles that this identity entailed. He realized that New Deal programs were fulfilling many of Progressivism's fondest hopes but worried that the growth of government bureaucracy would eliminate the need for traditional values such as independence and responsibility. "Can government chain its dollars, harness them to the common good, and still retain free men and free institutions?" he asked editorially. His beliefs remained in many ways tied to the personal ideology of his boyhood and youth.

By the end of his life, White had become in some ways an archetype of himself, the Small Town Editor, as embodied in the character of the narrator in Thornton Wilder's Our Town. He had observed and displayed central dichotomies of American character: optimism and idealism combined with shrewd pragmatism. Although he met his share of defeat and disillusionment, he never succumbed to the bleak cynicism that is often the resort of disillusionment.

He also remained loyal to the small-town ideal. In his many books and magazine articles in the 1920s and 1930s, he elaborated upon this ideal, emphasizing his belief in cooperation and social responsibility along with respectability and personal independence. Perhaps most influential was his

Autobiography, left unfinished at his death in 1944 but prepared for publication by his wife and son. It became a best seller and received the Pulitzer Prize in 1946. Taken as a whole, White's writing helped to fashion what one historian has called an "emerging rhetoric of Middle America" that has continued to resonate in political discussions long after his name has been forgotten.[22]

Samuel J. Crumbine: Individualizing the Standard for Twentieth-Century Public Health

K. Allen Greiner

Samuel J. Crumbine, a Dodge City physician and secretary of the Kansas State Board of Health during the first two decades of the twentieth century, was an innovator and a public health pioneer. He developed programs to purify food and regulate drugs, expand reporting of vital statistics, ban the common drinking cup and roller towel, expand child welfare and hygiene, and control venereal disease. Crumbine's successful campaigns were aided by his familiarity with patent medicine sales and marketing techniques and a long-standing populist heritage within the state of Kansas. But his attention to individual consciousness-raising and behavior change was a far greater contribution than any of the specific disease-control methods he proposed.

Samuel J. Crumbine (September 17, 1862–July 12, 1954), the celebrated secretary of the State Board of Health, seen here in 1911 at his office desk in Topeka, started practicing medicine in cowtown Dodge City. Courtesy of the Kansas State Historical Society.

Born in Venango County, Pennsylvania, on September 17, 1862, Samuel Crumbine was raised largely by his grandparents. He worked as a pharmacist's apprentice under the tutelage of a physician/pharmacist before enrolling at the Cincinnati College of Medicine and Surgery. While working on a medical degree, Crumbine purchased a drugstore near Dodge City, Kansas, and during summer vacations and holiday breaks from medical school he ran his pharmacy, dispensing medical advice and a variety of nostrums in a state that at that time had no medical licensure laws. Using funds from his pharmaceutical enterprises, he completed his medical degree in 1889; married Katherine Zuercher; moved permanently to Kansas; and soon set up shop in Dodge City, where he maintained a busy solo practice as a country doctor.[1]

Crumbine came to public health during a time of much social and political change. In 1889 Kansas was hit with drought and economic depression that soon gave rise to a "farm revolt." Falling crop prices and numerous farm foreclosures increased interest and membership in the expanding Farmers' Alliance movement, which soon led to the creation of the People's Party. These Populists—former liberal Republicans, some Democrats, and third-party activists—tapped the emotions of angry and debt-ridden farmers and decried the corruption of Wall Street and government, focusing largely on the struggle between the rich and the poor. For much of the 1890s Populists held numerous elective positions in the Kansas state house and the U.S. Congress.

By 1899 things had begun to improve for the state financially, and Republicans regained their former ascendancy—in part because the party began responding to public pressures to deal with corrupt and inefficient systems. This was good news for Crumbine. A Dodge City friend had helped the new Republican governor with his successful campaign, and Crumbine was appointed to the State Board of Health through this connection.

In 1902 the board asked Crumbine to evaluate an outbreak of smallpox in Pratt, Kansas. Crumbine traveled to Pratt, a railroad community about eighty miles east of Dodge, where he found fifteen active cases of smallpox. Most of the unvaccinated people who had been exposed were railroad employees or citizens who did business directly with the company. Crumbine was fearful that standard quarantine procedures would bring the railroad to a standstill, so he instituted a modified quarantine system that allowed exposed cases to remain at work if these individuals agreed to be vaccinated and to check in weekly with the county health officer. Crumbine's policies were economically and politically motivated, but at the same time they respected individual freedoms; his approach ameliorated tensions between railroad businesses and the medical and public health officials involved. His work received statewide praise, and in 1904 Crumbine was named executive secretary of the Kansas State Board of Health.[2]

The Board of Health had been without effective leadership for at least four years before Crumbine accepted the post as secretary. The board had never had extensive authority or the budget necessary to enact policies and create services to influence the public's health. The position of secretary was part-time and paid a meager salary. Crumbine's correspondence during the period reflects his interest in assuring that his new position would provide the authority to reform public health and enforce neglected statutes.[3]

Secretary Crumbine determined that education held the key to success in public health. "After giving the matter considerable thought," wrote Crumbine, "I determined to go straight to the people, to undertake a program of health education to insure the people's support." His individualized approaches led to extensive use of slogans to promote awareness. Slogans were intended to translate science into the vernacular with a tone quite similar to that used by contemporary pharmaceutical and patent-medicine marketing campaigns. The new field of microbiology and laboratory-supported medical science, for Crumbine, was the authority that justified public health actions and necessitated educational campaigns. An effort to demonstrate that flies were disease vectors began almost immediately.[4]

This "swat the fly" campaign gained local and national support at a time when public health was just beginning to receive full-time funding from Midwestern and central plains state governments. Historians have described Crumbine's fly work as important for promoting cohesion between sanitary science and the germ theory of disease.[5] By popularizing a belief in ties between insects and bacteria, Crumbine advanced theories of disease causation that were acceptable to a society still struggling with concepts of contagion and infection. Crumbine's initial campaign had a unique impact on individuals and communities ready to help in public health crusades but needing some personalized or personified motivation. The housefly, which threatened every individual home, provided that personification.

Unlike insect-vector campaigns from 1898 to 1902 aimed at mosquitoes carrying malaria and yellow fever, housefly campaigns relied on a domestic emphasis that implicated filth, insects, and microbes. Swat-the-fly efforts were specific to American households, and they were important to the popular acceptance of the germ theory because they assigned some responsibility for fly control to household occupants.[6] Crumbine brought his public health programs to the level of individual behavior and, at least with this particular campaign, virtually ignored the broader disease ecology. He meshed a populist style with scientific rhetoric to garner significant popular interest, and although the fly was scapegoated as the "filthy" vector, and thus given the lion's share of blame, in this way individuals were enlisted in eradication efforts. "Swat the fly" was important because it was Crumbine's first educational endeavor, and it had virtually no broader social agenda.

To ensure the success of his educational campaign, Crumbine sought to organize a statewide network of county health officers by sending them letters with rules and regulations. Typically busy with full-time private medical practices, these local health officials had varying degrees of knowledge of State Board of Health policies and limited exposure to recent scientific discoveries on germ theory and disease transmission. Soon Crumbine devised a more effective plan to disseminate information throughout the state, targeting health officers and physicians. The plan was hatched with the publication of the *Bulletin of the Kansas State Board of Health* in July 1905. Originally the *Bulletin* was intended to contain simple reports of disease, births, and death rates along with facts about infections and germs. Crumbine decided that, in addition, he should use the *Bulletin* as a spirited educational tool. He was not shy about forsaking the disinterested, objective enthusiasm of science for a louder, more engaging voice. He used slogans and unusual layouts to grab the reader's attention.[7] His housefly campaign reflected his educational philosophy.

Crumbine wrote and distributed the *Bulletin* monthly. The August 1905 issue promoted fly control as a front-page item. Flies had been linked to the spread of disease initially by Victor Vaughan of the Marine Hospital Service (MHS) in 1898. This work, carried out in Southern military camps during the Spanish-American War, described flies landing on food in mess tents. Vaughn noted that the flies left behind a trail of visible white lime, which had been sprinkled into latrines as a disinfectant. Typhoid had been epidemic in these camps, and the visual proof was sufficient to implicate flies in the spread of that disease.

Rural Americans already viewed flies as an annoyance, but reports by Vaughn and others cast them as a threat to the public. Medical textbooks from the first two decades of the twentieth century often reprinted images of bacteria grown from fly tracks after flies had wandered across culture media.[8] These images reinforced the scientific opinion that germs were everywhere and the public must learn a new vigilance to avoid potential diseases. Crumbine used multiple methods to convey this message.

Crumbine's letters and correspondence reveal that the MHS was the reference he turned to repeatedly for information on infectious disease and its control. He sought counsel from the surgeon general of the MHS several times during his first year in office. As Board of Health secretary, he referred to MHS studies to justify recommendations to his county health officers.[9]

The August 1905 *Bulletin* contained a treatise on the role of flies in disease spread and on methods of control. Thereafter the *Bulletin* did not mention flies again until June 1906, when a reprinted item from the *Journal of the*

American Medical Association discussed them in connection with tuberculosis transmission. In the early years of the *Bulletin* Crumbine printed pieces describing the many routes of disease transmission. He described the American Mosquito Extermination Society in the August 1906 *Bulletin*. In the October 1906 edition he blamed ticks for disease transmission, and in November he cited pets as disease carriers and included a discussion of culturing typhoid bacteria from pet fur.[10] But over the period from 1905 to 1910, Crumbine most consistently returned to the housefly.

The June 1907 *Bulletin* opened with the following front-page poem.

Read the Labels.

Swat
The Fly
By Scattering
The Manure Pile.

The New Kansas Water
And Sewage Law is a Dinger![11]

This is the first appearance of the phrase "swat the fly" in the *Bulletin*. In his memoir Crumbine recounted the genesis of the slogan. He attended a baseball game that he described as inspirational and exciting. With the score tied and a runner on third with one out, fans yelled, "Sacrifice fly," "Swat that ball," and "For Pete's sake, swat it." Crumbine combined the ballpark shouts and came up with "Swat the fly." This popular admonishment was printed on the front of the board's widely distributed "fly bulletin"—small four-page fliers that were stuffed in every outgoing envelope sent by the Board of Health from 1907 through 1910.[12] The slogan's popularity shaped Crumbine's public health career in Kansas and eventually even his tenure as director of the American Child Health Association.

According to Crumbine, there was no such thing as a "fly-swatter" before the slogan. Crumbine attributed its invention to a Kansas schoolteacher, Frank Weir. Kansans were soon "swatting" flies on their kitchen counters and calling the occupation a public health victory. Crumbine included a self-written script of a summertime sidewalk scene in the *Bulletin*. The short play set the stage with flies on sidewalk market-stands and finished with acutely ill children and family members. He used his flair for the dramatic to bring public health to the attention of many Kansans.[13]

Fly-vector theories were well received by Kansans, many of whom were eager to volunteer in new crusades against germs. Familiarity with reform movements prepared citizens for the urgent message, and individuals now had the opportunity to take up fly-swatters and control the spread of disease by bringing down insects with the flick of a wrist. Unfortunately, Crumbine and the Board of Health did not prescribe decontamination of household surfaces or hands once flies were "swatted" and removed. Detailed attention to scientific facts was not as important as capturing the public's imagination; the primary objective was to sell public health doctrine even if the finished product was slightly adulterated. A reflexive use of the same marketing that had characterized the patent-medicine industry for decades became common among public health professionals.

Messages heavy on narrative and light on laboratory underpinnings became part of an evolving campaign. Newspapers adopted the military metaphors Crumbine had used to describe his campaign against flies. The popular press helped him change the way individuals responded to flies in their homes and elsewhere. This public health "war on flies" and the germs they carried was novel to Kansans in 1906. The fly became an understandable and acceptable target for citizens who were only vaguely familiar with the microscopic concepts of bacteria and filterable agents—that is, viruses.

By the second decade of the twentieth century, however, skeptics began to oppose all-out fly vilification. Charles V. Chapin, a Rhode Island public health official and national leader, was among the earliest to criticize the selective use of scientific studies and the exaggerated use of fly-control measures. He was certain that public health policy could be more effective addressing other issues and believed that the transmission of infections by the fly was an insignificant occurrence for the typical town or city. Chapin's views were predictive of future developments. In 1916 a Kansas health official attending a Rockefeller conference stated that he had finally accepted the theory that flies were innocent of poliomyelitis transmission. Entomologists, many of whom had been strong proponents of antifly campaigns, described reservations by the 1930s, saying, "The slogan 'Swat the fly' has been taken all too literally in some places."[14]

The early-twentieth-century emergence of a "private side of public health" opened other doors for Crumbine and his fellow public health leaders. As a result, they were soon addressing venereal disease and associated sexual behavior. Venereal disease, genital infections with gonorrhea, chlamydia, and syphilis, had become widely recognized as a military problem prior to the onset of

World War I. The impact of these afflictions on active troop numbers became a major concern for military officials keen on maximizing the effectiveness and "strength" of the fighting force. As the U.S. entry into the European war approached, military officials began to implement venereal disease controls geared toward keeping men "fit to fight."[15]

In early 1918 the Kansas State Board of Health, in an attempt to aid the military, began to enforce regulations for the reporting and quarantine of all venereal disease cases. Federal authorities in camp zones around Forts Riley and Leavenworth began examining and quarantining women suspected of venereal disease. The numbers of incarcerated grew so rapidly that the State Board of Health established the State Industrial Farm for Women at Lansing to hold the "giddy young warbrides" or "wayward girls, whose delinquencies could not be proved in court" until such time as they were deemed noninfectious. Local law enforcement or county health officials across the state arrested women for "vagrancy," "delinquency," or prostitution. Women could be held without trial if a physician's examination found them to be an "infectious risk."[16]

State and federal governments across the country granted early-twentieth-century medical, military, and public health professionals significant latitude to act against germs and citizens. There was popular support for institutional and state intervention to control the lives and actions of the infected. State boards of health and the Public Health Service could act whenever the health and safety of the local population was thought to be at risk. This support led to policies with significant ramifications for ethnic or socioeconomic minorities. Groups from outside the Anglo-Saxon, middle-class mainstream in America were aggressively scrutinized and quarantined throughout the late nineteenth and early twentieth centuries.[17] In similar fashion, early in the war public health officials targeted working-class single women and associated them with venereal disease.

Crumbine initially followed the lead of the federal Commission on Training Camp Activities (CTCA) and focused specifically on prostitutes. The CTCA had done this in areas where military camps were close to large urban centers. When the incarceration and treatment of prostitutes in Kansas failed to cut infection rates, Crumbine met with the Kansas City political boss Tom Pendergast in an attempt to shut down prostitution in Kansas City, Missouri, the closest city with significant entertainment and organized prostitution. In Crumbine's version of the story, a threat to keep all Kansas and Missouri soldiers out of Kansas City produced cooperation from Pendergast. The city's prostitutes were soon locked up and receiving venereal disease treatment, but this intervention also failed to reduce the disease to acceptable levels.[18]

Crumbine and others recognized a "girl problem" involving women who moved to the small towns adjacent to Fort Riley, the largest army camp in Kansas. Officials considered these women, though not yet prostitutes, to be at high risk for eventual prostitution. These "camp followers" became the eventual focus for social investigations by Crumbine and his staff. By 1919 Crumbine felt that an understanding of the life circumstances and social conditions of such women would be the best way to motivate behavior change and reduce reinfection. He believed this information could be used to provide jobs, education, and other supervision that would enable women to avoid vice and return to "straight living."[19]

Darlene Doubleday Newby recorded the history of a seventeen-year-old, "fairly characteristic of the young, wayward girl," and many similar reports in a description of the Kansas State Industrial Farm for Women. Crumbine had requested Newby's assistance after early control efforts were deemed inadequate and convinced her to go undercover as a "sexually delinquent girl" and spend two weeks interned with inmates. Newby's report gave case histories for four hundred women. The report categorized home conditions and prior living arrangements as well as employment and sexual histories. Newby and other social workers contacted women after release and obtained follow-up information to assess responses to treatment and farm rehabilitation. Officials paid special attention to environmental influence and individual predisposition in Kansas. The case histories recorded in Newby's report describe girls as young as thirteen and many women from small Kansas towns with fewer than five hundred inhabitants.[20] Newby and Crumbine considered small-town girls particularly vulnerable to corruption.

Crumbine and his associates believed many of the women quarantined at the state farm were simply "innocent young girls" swept up in wartime excitement and patriotism. They thought stress and upheaval caused "promiscuity" and "delinquency" because of their harmful effects on women. Crumbine saw Newby's undercover investigation as a partial solution to this "influx of seemingly normal girls into the ranks of the morally delinquent."[21]

Incarceration of women early in the war did not include case work. Crumbine saw social work as a novel and important weapon in the fight to control disease. With the adoption of this socially focused and contextual approach, Crumbine, county health officers, and military physicians in Kansas shifted the responsibility for venereal disease from "promiscuous" women to what they saw as the social and environmental root causes of sexual behavior. Officials continued to view women as passive victims of venereally diseased men and made few attempts to change or intervene in social environments, but social conditions and backgrounds were now viewed as crucial to shaping behavior.[22]

Julia Perry, the superintendent of the Kansas State Industrial Farm for Women, insisted that punishment not be the farm's focus. She believed quarantine and protection of the public health should take a backseat to training and preparation for the active duties of life. According to Perry, "the awakening of noble ambitions and forming of correct ideas" was the primary goal of farm internment. Crumbine and Perry considered farm work and activities therapeutic, and the superintendent set up courses in typewriting, shorthand, and domestic science for the women.[23]

These new approaches for venereal disease allowed Crumbine and other officials in Kansas to balance competing views. Physicians, military officials, and women's advocates could support a range of opinions with the data produced by caseworkers such as Newby. Social workers hoped to shift blame away from women and toward social circumstances as a way to encourage voluntary behavior change without the use of incarceration. Military officials saw social data as a helpful investigative tool and a justification for continued police repression under hopeless social conditions.[24] Moderate public health authorities, including Crumbine, continued to favor punitive repression of "sexual promiscuity" but shifted blame for venereal disease to social circumstance. Crumbine and even Newby were unable to consistently describe how social behavior, past experiences, upbringing, economic circumstance, and germ theory could be integrated. By the end of the war Crumbine was using a system of venereal disease control in which germ theory, a coded sexual morality, and social causation were all viewed as contributing to targeted actions. This sociobehavioral focus contradicted some of Crumbine's earlier public health work that utilized laboratory discoveries to justify the destruction and separation of germs or germ-carrying individuals from the "germ-free," but it was certainly consistent with the adapted approaches he had used going back to the Pratt smallpox epidemic of 1902.[25]

Prior to the outbreak of the world war, Crumbine had been remarkably successful at translating bacteriologic laboratory discoveries into statewide legislative action for control of infectious disease. Crumbine facilitated the passage of many laws over the decade preceding the war in an attempt to protect public health by implementing germ-theory doctrine and breaking the chain of transmission.[26] His background as a Dodge City physician prepared him for his work as a public health official because he understood rural communities and the influence of poverty and drought on such communities. He believed populist-style campaigning would help round up support for laboratory science and bacteriology, and he was quite interested in improving the way government handled health-related issues. The radical brand of Kansas politics created a foundation upon which Crumbine could eventually build a large, state-funded public health enterprise.

Eventually Crumbine became a nationally prominent public health figure. In 1923 he was pressured to vacate his position as secretary by state Democrats, in the person of newly elected governor Jonathan M. Davis, who felt his department had grown too large to be run by a nonappointed official. The national Republican administration asked Crumbine to take a position in New York with the American Child Health Association (ACHA). Crumbine accepted and was soon appointed secretary. Quickly he introduced his usual methods of popular education, focusing directly on the individual behavior of mothers and infants. He stayed with ACHA for over twenty years, gaining in the process a reputation as a New York novelty with his Dodge City stories of gunfights and gambling.

Samuel Crumbine played an integral role in changing the image of the housefly and in bringing a socially focused, contextual approach to venereal disease control during World War I. He used charismatic educational methods to attract interest and spread his message and to promote ideas that helped germ theories gain widespread acceptance. Crumbine adjusted policies to the reality of social circumstances and thus found ways to effect behavioral change among the infected. He was unique because he succeeded in influencing popular perceptions with slogans and campaigning.

The "new" public health that Crumbine and others created in the early twentieth century was possible because citizens were ready to be sold on sanitary and hygienic practice. Crumbine's public health emphasis on individual education and behavior change was well received in an era of progressive reform, government activism, and agitation for individual justice. In addition, changing social customs led to changes in personal behavior. Both social forces and synergistic discoveries by bacteriologists motivated these changes. The "new" public health of this era legitimated the links that were established between proper social behaviors and germ-caused diseases. Crumbine pushed this process of legitimization with the force of a Populist and the insights of a pharmaceutical marketing agency. He helped establish a Progressive Era style and educational methodology that remained the standard for philanthropic and governmental public health promotion throughout the twentieth century as the focus of public concern shifted from infectious to chronic diseases.

Kate Richards O'Hare: A Life of Dissent

Sally M. Miller

One of the best-known Kansans of a century ago was Kate Richards O'Hare. By the first decade of the twentieth century O'Hare, born and bred on the plains of central Kansas, was a well-known speaker, journalist, and agitator on behalf of a myriad of radical causes. A household name in the Great Plains and the Southwest, she built a national reputation as a leader of the Socialist Party of America, a minor party then demonstrating impressive growth in all regions of the country. As her fame spread, O'Hare came to epitomize Kansas' reputation as a haven for a series of reform-minded political movements, lively alternative newspapers, dozens of cooperatives, and individualists and radicals of various persuasions. Indeed, Kansas at the turn of the twentieth century could be described as an environment of movement cultures, with O'Hare as its poster child.

In the last quarter of the nineteenth century, Kansas was caught up in a boom-and-bust cycle in which thousands plunged from optimism to despair as they suffered through hard times and sometimes lost their land. Consequently,

Kate Richards O'Hare (March 26, 1876–January 10, 1948), born on an Ottawa County farm, was an advocate for labor and a Socialist Party organizer; in 1908 she named her twin sons Eugene and Victor after Eugene Victor Debs, her party's perennial presidential nominee. Courtesy of the William R. Perkins Library, Duke University.

the state offered fertile soil to a variety of reform movements. Greenback advocates, prohibitionists, Populists, woman's rights proponents, cooperatists, millenarians, and even "sex radicals" peopled the state, offering panaceas for social, political, and economic grievances. The *New York Times* in 1887 termed Kansas "the great experimental ground of the nation," and a more recent author likened it to "a laboratory for experiments."[1]

Proponents of these various causes began to flirt with socialism—more frequently in Kansas than in many other states—and indeed, threads of socialism wove through the culture of the state from an early date. New York socialists established the Thompson Colony of cooperative farming near Salina in the

1870s, and in 1887 two Danish social democrats organized a commune near Hays. Summer encampment meetings, originally a Populist institution but increasingly a socialist phenomenon, became annual events drawing thousands of rural families for days of revivalist-style political rallies. Among other socialist institutions to emerge at the end of the century was the *Appeal to Reason,* the weekly with the greatest circulation in the nation. It was located in Girard, Kansas, and became the center of a socialist media publishing empire. Finally, in the new century the People's College for workers was established at Fort Scott and included on its staff Eugene V. Debs, the most famous American socialist and the party's perennial candidate for the presidency of the United States.[2]

Such a menu of options taught Kansans that a multiplicity of choices existed and that they could shape their own futures. They could be free citizens choosing their own political and economic paths and could regain control over their lives in the face of any threats from economic downturns or monopolistic exploitation.

Born on March 26, 1876, Carrie Kathleen Richards grew up in Ottawa County, Kansas, during this volatile era. Branches of her extended family had settled in the area on the eve of the Civil War, and her father had fought in the Union army. Andrew and Lucy Richards and their five children grew wheat and corn and were enmeshed in a community network in which neighboring farmers helped each other with labor-intensive tasks. They traded and bartered among themselves, sharing the solidarity of what anthropologist Robert Redfield termed a "folk society," and maintained close ties even though scattered fairly far apart from one another. They joined together in barn- and roof-raisings, ice cream socials, dances, picnics, bazaars, parades, and other patriotic commemorations. It was a close-knit society of face-to-face contacts in which staunch individualists supported one another.[3]

The Richards family managed life on the land, not only through wheat and corn sales but also through vegetable gardening; egg and berry gathering; making breads, pies, jams, and butter; and hunting small game and fishing. It is clear from Kate Richards O'Hare's later writings that she and her siblings had a strong sense of security, however limited the diet and sparse their wardrobes and furnishings, and that the family must have felt that, through its own hard work, Kansas was a good place to build its life. However, 1887 introduced an era of severe drought and economic collapse, and many homesteaders were forced to abandon their land, while others participated in a wave of third-party activism through the Farmers' Alliance and then the Populist Party. Falling crop prices had led to a loss of independence in an increasingly impersonal society of corporate domination, with the marketplace replacing the personal ties of the past.[4]

Andrew Richards discussed with his neighbors various political tracts promoting solutions for the hard times faced by farmers and workers, such as the best seller *Progress and Poverty* by Henry George, with his daughter Kate sometimes taking notes. But at the end of 1887 Andrew Richards was among those who pulled up stakes, and the family relocated to Kansas City, Missouri. Kate, who managed to finish high school, was shocked by her family's setback and by the startling sights in Kansas City of unemployed workers and begging tramps. She later recalled, "The poverty, the misery, the want, the wan-faced women and . . . workless workers . . . will always stay with me as a picture of [an] inferno such as Dante never painted."[5]

She joined the ranks of many religious young women of the era and participated in voluntarist networks seeking to raise up slum-dwellers, alcoholics, abandoned women, and prostitutes. She worked for the Florence Crittenton Mission and Home in the red-light district but soon decided that she was doing little to address serious social ills.[6] Because of her Kansas background she was open to the possibility of more ambitious solutions to society's problems; like some of her peers, she began to seek a secular path to end the "proletarianization and a concomitant loss of political power" of those she saw around her.[7]

Richards felt intrigued by the socialist speakers and writings that she encountered, as were thousands of others at the beginning of the twentieth century, and she was particularly impressed by J. A. Wayland, the publisher of the *Appeal to Reason*. In 1901 she enrolled in a school in Girard for socialist organizers. The three-month course, administered by Kansan Walter Thomas Mills, a minister, author of socialist tracts, and veteran of many minor party movements, concluded for Kate with her marriage to one of her classmates, Francis Patrick O'Hare of St. Louis. Together they won instant fame through the socialist press when they combined their honeymoon with an organizing tour for the Socialist Party.[8] As Kate Richards O'Hare later described that aspect of their lives: "We have followed the stony, rough hewn path from that day to this. From the coal fields of Pennsylvania and West Virginia and Indian Territory, to the farms of Kansas and Iowa and Missouri, through the plains of Texas and into the cotton fields of Oklahoma and Arkansas and Tennessee, from the Ghetto of New York to the Rocky Mountains we have gone wherever and whenever the economic pressure has made men and women receptive to the philosophy of Socialism."[9]

Kate and Frank O'Hare had commenced a twenty-five-year odyssey of party organizing, writing, lecturing, and office holding in the Socialist Party of America. Within the party, also organized in 1901, Kate O'Hare quickly became a star attraction. She loved the hustings and spent months of every year on the road. The O'Hares lived in Oklahoma with their four children from 1904 to 1909, then established a new home base from 1909 to 1911 in Kansas City, Kansas, where in 1910 Kate ran on a Socialist ticket for the U.S. House of Representatives in the Second Congressional District. The O'Hares moved in 1911 to St. Louis, where in 1916 she became the first woman to run for the U.S. Senate. She toured constantly, spreading her socialist message of the collective ownership of the means of production within a democratic system in order to achieve equality for working people. She drew crowds of farmers, urban workers, and others. Those particularly receptive to her message were working farm families because she clearly knew their circumstances, unlike the majority of the party leaders who focused their attention on factory workers in Eastern and Midwestern cities. The highlight of every year was the summer season, which she spent addressing farmers at the great encampments across the West. There O'Hare, Eugene V. Debs, May Harris "Mother" Jones, and other crowd-pleasers among the party's agitators spoke before thousands of families who joined in a week of camping and listening to socialist lecturers and musicians. The participants also shared games and craft activities in settings suggesting both revivalist meetings and Chautauqua classes. They made new friends, found spouses, and educated their children. The encampments were part of a culture of shared experiences through which their emerging socialist allegiances and views were nurtured.

Kate O'Hare's views were shaped by her party's ideology. The dominant view upheld by American socialists was a revision of Marxist revolutionary teachings. While the party tried to minimize or even deny that it had diluted Marxism, as was also true of many overseas socialist parties, in fact only a hardcore minority of American socialists clung to the orthodox view that a violent revolution was necessary to transform American society from capitalism to socialism. Instead most socialists believed that competitive capitalism bore within it the seeds of its own destruction, and that therefore the party faithful needed only to encourage the breakdown of the system, pressing for a variety of reforms within it. They argued that the increasing concentration of industry was itself straining and modifying capitalism. Through propaganda and electoral campaigns, the party must educate the masses of workers to the extent of their own exploitation and to the possibility of an egalitarian and democratic future in which the people themselves owned the means of production. Thus, O'Hare and the majority of her comrades pursued a policy of reform whereby they promoted social and economic measures to ease the lives of workingpeople while expecting the eventual triumph of socialism, opposing those Marxists who believed that ameliorative reforms would only sustain capitalism. They favored shorter workdays, protective legislation such as public pensions, child labor laws, public ownership of utilities and transportation networks, cooperation with unionists, and the expansion of the electoral franchise.[10]

In her lectures on the stump and articles in the socialist press, O'Hare discussed these and other topics, in many instances reflecting the era's muckraking journalism in a socialist frame of reference. She detailed deplorable working conditions, political corruption, organized vice and its connections to "honest" businesses, the hypocrisy of religious institutions, and race relations, among many other issues. O'Hare often highlighted the plight of workingwomen, who "worked because they were compelled to work." She described such women as wage slaves who were breeding another generation of wage slaves, "feed[ing] their children until they were old enough to work." While women had always worked, O'Hare noted that "Priscilla of old owned her loom and spinning wheel, and though she wove but little, it was all hers. Priscilla's loom to-day is owned by a capitalist and though she weaves much it is not hers, but belongs to the man who owns her loom, who gives her only a very little in return and calls it wages."[11]

The lives of farmers were also a frequent O'Hare topic, including the role of farmers' wives, whose toil and exploitation seldom won attention. She tried to convince her urban comrades that farmers were mistakenly viewed as property owners and employers when instead they should be seen as laborers, even though they might own or lease their land. Her background in Kansas homesteading led her to become a key voice in Socialist Party debates over the formulation of an outreach program to farmers. She forcefully argued against a party policy recommending the collectivization of the land, a certain path to deter farmers from becoming socialists. After a few years of wrangling over the issue at various meetings, the party agreed on a policy aimed at rural Americans that mandated public ownership of the means of transportation, storage facilities, and other institutions upon which farmers depended. The party also recommended, like the reformer Henry George, the taxing of land held out of cultivation.[12]

Without a doubt Kate O'Hare was her party's leading woman agitator, or in the perhaps overly dramatized phrase of a contemporary author, she was "the first lady of American socialism." Her constant activism and her popularity with rank-and-file members resulted in O'Hare holding almost every party position. She was elected a delegate to virtually all party conventions and congresses, and as mentioned later, in April 1917 she chaired its most crucial committee. She served on the party's executive body, was appointed to ad hoc committees, was elected to its Women's National Committee, and was in the running twice for its vice-presidential nomination. Perhaps the position she most prized was her 1913 election as the party's representative to the international congress of socialist parties held in London.[13]

Attending the congress, and then visiting with trade unionists there and in Ireland, she clearly was thrilled to stand on stage beside such world-renowned figures as Karl Kautsky of the German Empire; Jean Jaures and Jean Longuet of France; and the British socialist leaders, including the Scotsman Keir Hardie. (She did not meet Vladimir Lenin, who did not attend this congress.) Her proudest moment came when the French leader Jaures invited her to come to France sometime in the future to help teach socialists there how to construct a successful policy of outreach to their farmers. Unfortunately, the outbreak of war the next year prevented her making any such visit.

Ironic in hindsight was a demonstration by those socialist leaders, about which O'Hare enthusiastically reported, with speakers from England, Belgium, Germany, and France—and herself representing American socialists—joining together to condemn war. She wrote, "One of the most impressive and interesting happenings . . . was the public demonstration against militarism. The British comrades took advantage of the presence of Socialists from abroad to hold a huge anti-militarist demonstration in . . . London." O'Hare described the event as "a wonderful plea for world peace."[14]

Her whirlwind activities must be seen against the backdrop of her monthly columns and her annual speaking tours. But her popularity was not universal among party members. Indeed, the dominant Eastern party leaders held her in contempt, characterizing her as a hayseed, an ignorant Westerner unlettered in party theory who only embarrassed the party before its overseas comrades. These leaders, especially Morris Hillquit of New York City and Congressmen Victor Berger of Milwaukee, both European immigrant intellectuals, had long loathed O'Hare, and even Gene Debs, whom they considered unlearned in Marxist ideology as well as too radical for the reformist message of

the party. They eventually labeled O'Hare "Red Kate," a name that caught on
with some of the American press. For many of the party's urban Eastern elite,
Westerners were by definition uneducated, unreliable, and erratic, and they
tarred O'Hare with that brush. That she was a woman made it easy for them
to dismiss her. At the same time, they had to acknowledge her popularity and
repeated election to positions they expected to monopolize. Hence, they
groused among themselves against "Red Kate" even though she was their
ideological soulmate.[15]

After fifteen years as a socialist agitator, O'Hare was well settled into her
life work. By 1915 she was a Socialist Party leader with a national following.
She continued to reflect her Kansas roots through her easy relationships with
American farmers and her deep commitment to helping them find a way to
ease their burdens. Her chosen political path also made her a representative
of the America of her times, the so-called Progressive Era, when hundreds of
thousands joined movements and organizations in the belief that they could
shape the nation's future toward greater democratization, social justice, and
economic independence.

But O'Hare's attention was increasingly drawn overseas. She was one of
the first American columnists to warn against the possibility of the United
States being drawn into the European war that erupted in the summer of
1914. She predicted that commercial ties with England and France could easily transform "their" war into "our" war and later commented bitterly that
American youth would soon be sent "to the trenches of France to fight the battles of the Bank of England."[16]

In her monthly column in the St. Louis–based *National Rip-Saw* she wrote
that every day brought war just a little closer to American shores and "nearer
our firesides, our sons, our daughters and our means of life. Already we can
see the lurid flames of War lighting our horizons." In fact, she added, "War is
striding in seven-league boots across the Atlantic." She explained to her readers, "War rages in Europe today because the bankers, armament makers and
powerful groups of capitalists know that when the world is glutted with unsold
goods and the highways are filled with unemployed men, war and destruction
becomes a far more profitable game than peace and production."[17]

Not limiting herself to her usual talks and newspaper columns, in a frantic
effort to prevent U.S. involvement, she and husband Frank drafted an antiwar
play, *World Peace*. It was performed in 1915 and 1916 on the Socialist lecture
circuit and also issued in booklet form.

O'Hare was aghast that the majority of European socialists, despite their long history of emphasizing international brotherhood, supported their governments at war. O'Hare also condemned those party comrades who endorsed President Woodrow Wilson's preparedness campaign. By spring 1917, with ever closer ties to the Allied economies as well as with the resumption of unlimited submarine warfare by the German government, U.S. readiness to enter the war was evident. O'Hare stood with her party's majority in opposition to that path. She chaired a Socialist Party committee at an emergency convention that passed an antiwar statement in April 1917, the same week that the United States declared war on Germany and Austria. O'Hare had no second thoughts. She boldly declared, "I am a Socialist, a labor unionist and a follower of the Prince of Peace, FIRST, and an American second. I will serve my class before I will serve the country that is owned by my industrial masters." She was not even fazed by the Espionage Act passed by the U.S. Congress in May, which mandated limitations on any speech that might invite military insubordination or obstruct conscription.[18]

She traveled across the country that spring and summer delivering essentially the same antiwar speech, often aware of government agents taking notes in the audience. After perhaps its seventy-fifth presentation, this time in the hamlet of Bowman, North Dakota, on July 17, 1917, Kate O'Hare was indicted under the Espionage Act. It now seems evident that the indictment was a by-product of local political rivalries involving the farmers of the populist-inspired Nonpartisan League. O'Hare was convicted following a short trial before a hostile judge and a jury of antagonistic businessmen, and featuring perjured testimony.

The prosecution had called her "a dangerous woman," and in her address to the court before her sentencing, O'Hare declared, "I am dangerous to the invisible government of the United States. I am dangerous to the white slaver and to the saloonkeeper, and I thank God that I am dangerous to the war profiteers of this country who rob the people . . . but no jury or no judge can convince the people that I am a dangerous woman to the best interests of the United States."[19]

This feisty challenge resulted in a longer sentence than the judge had originally intended, even with the Justice Department itself ambivalent about the value of a prison term for this famous woman with young children. She was sentenced to five years in the Missouri State Penitentiary (there not yet being a federal prison for women).

O'Hare entered prison in April 1919, a forty-three-year-old woman who had never led a sedentary life. She was confined to a small cell surrounded by other inmates with whom she was forbidden to speak under the silence system, by then abandoned by most American penitentiaries. The majority of her peers were illiterates, mentally ill, or "dopers," and many were African American. However, there were three other political prisoners, including Emma Goldman, the leading American anarchist. O'Hare, like the other inmates, worked five and a half days a week in the prison's industrial shop, under terrible conditions of excessive heat and lack of light and ventilation. Her robust health began to decline, and because of the harsh conditions as well as the uncooperative prison administration, she gave up her plans to conduct case studies of her fellow inmates.

While incarcerated O'Hare was able to use her celebrity to win a few positive changes in the prison conditions. She convinced the warden to order the meals delivered hot, to install showers, to segregate individuals with venereal diseases, and to allow women inmates access to the library books available to the male prisoners. She shared with her fellow prisoners the floral bouquets and the dozens of packages of food she received weekly from supporters across the country, read to and wrote letters for the illiterates, and offered to teach a few classes (permission was, however, refused). She wrote letters constantly to her husband and children—as often as the authorities would permit—and Frank issued them in booklet form as *Kate O'Hare's Prison Letters*. She also read voraciously, especially in the field of modern penology.[20]

During her enforced separation from her family and her life's work, the socialist movement itself underwent a cataclysmic collapse. Under pressure from the newly organized American communist movement, which emerged after the Bolshevik Revolution, the Socialist Party fragmented. It lost some of its leaders, many of whom had earlier broken with it to support the war effort; many others resigned at this time, and still others had to concentrate on defending themselves from federal prosecution. By 1920 the party had lost three-fourths of its membership. O'Hare began to hope that groups on the left would coalesce and form a new political party. She envisioned labor unionists, Nonpartisan Leaguers, socialists, and even communists joining together. In fact, splinters of groups were merging during her incarceration. Former Bull Moose Republicans, representatives of the railroad brotherhoods, socialists, farmers, and others formed a Farmer-Labor Party in the upper Midwest, and some of these same groups nominated Progressive Republican senator Robert

M. La Follette of Wisconsin for president in 1924. To O'Hare, clearly drawing on her nineteenth-century Kansas background, it seemed logical that a new party could offer Americans policies that could compete effectively with those of the Republicans and Democrats. As she wrote to Frank, she hoped that these groups would "work out some intelligent plan whereby ALL of the radical and progressive forces of the country can combine to sweep the forces of reaction from the places of political power all over the country. I don't think anyone can question my loyalty to the Socialist movement, yet I am ready to join hands with all forces that are willing to help remove the political barnacles from the ship of state."[21]

What O'Hare did not know was that American politics in the twentieth century was settling into a firmer two-party system in which third-party appeal was seldom effective. Some socialists tried to capture the party's 1920 vice-presidential nomination for Kate O'Hare, but the leadership's obviously luke-warm interest in O'Hare's plight deepened the sense of alienation that Kate and Frank had always felt toward many party leaders. Lacking official party co-ordination of their struggle for a commutation of her sentence, the O'Hares concentrated on orchestrating a campaign among a wide range of their political, civic, media, and other contacts, some of whom wrote letters and appeals to the president, formed committees, and held rallies on her behalf. On May 29, 1920, after having served fourteen months of her five-year sentence, O'Hare won a commutation of her sentence from President Wilson (and would later receive a full pardon and the restoration of her civil and political rights from President Calvin Coolidge). She was free to resume her life and was cheered by editorials that celebrated her release with comments that she had been an innocent victim of the Red Scare.[22]

O'Hare's incarceration marked more of a break in the pattern of her life than she might have anticipated. The collapse of the Socialist Party and the tensions within it meant that she could not return to the movement as she had known it. She resumed touring for a few years for the party and for the release of political prisoners until she and Frank were dropped from party membership, on a trumped-up charge of failure to pay party dues. But her priorities had changed, and her speeches and writings began to focus on prison reform and labor education. She was instrumental, with others, in winning congressional legislation to undermine the convict labor system in 1929. By then she and Frank had divorced, and Kate lived in California with a new husband, Charles C. Cunningham, a businessman. She remained engaged as a speaker on civic issues, with her last minor party activism on behalf of Upton Sinclair's Depression-era campaign to end poverty in California and her final public official role that of a gubernatorial appointee seeking to modernize the California prison system. As a postscript, in 1943 Governor Earl Warren invited her to sit in on sessions of the State Crime Commission.[23]

As should be clear, Kate Richards O'Hare may easily be seen as an agitator and reformer grounded in the Kansas of her youth, a state with a multitude of political parties and various reform movements. A pioneer in the image of her forebears, she was shaped by her time and place. She was also a product of the Progressive Era of her early adulthood, when Americans of virtually all classes embarked on an ambitious effort, not unlike the New Deal of the next generation, to make the country more equitable, more representative, and more just.

O'Hare's activities offered Americans a sense of possibilities and suggested a variety of paths and alternatives to enhance the promise of America. She pursued her work through a minor party, with little chance of winning elections. But the classic role of third parties in the United States has always been to offer new ideas that the Republicans or the Democrats might eventually adopt and fashion into law. Thus, to a public seeking solutions for some of the problems of twentieth-century life, the socialist O'Hare offered programs, among others, to help working farmers and factory workers and promote safe working conditions, public pensions, and other elements of a safety net. Some of these suggestions would later become the law of the land.

O'Hare's historical role was that of shaking up the status quo and planting seeds of change, especially in the American West. She encouraged a view that the government must assume new responsibilities in American life in order to soften some of the harsher elements of a modern industrial and technological society. While her socialist perspective did not prevail, the public eventually accepted many of her proposals for reform.

Finally, Kate O'Hare was also a pioneer as a woman in politics. She signaled to women that a life in the public sphere was possible and pointed the way for later generations in which women in politics and even in high office became a familiar sight. O'Hare, the first woman to run for the U.S. Senate, could be seen as a foremother to the many women now serving in the U.S. Congress. At least in part, as a result of Kate Richards O'Hare's pioneering activism and agitation, women in contemporary political life are able to find wider possibilities in their own time and place.

PART FOUR

REACTION, DEPRESSION, AND WAR, 1920–1945

Kansas, once referred to as "Bleeding Kansas," is all steamed up. Kansas once more is in a mood to go back to the advice given the people of that state by the late Mary Ellen Lease, one-time Populist leader, to "raise less corn and more hell."

Senator [Arthur] Capper rushes down to Washington to plead with the President to make the federal farm board announce a definite policy on wheat. Vice-President [Charles] Curtis deserts his place on the fence for a place in the antifarm board boat that he may lend an oar to Senator Capper.

"I will stand by the farmers to the end," announces Capper. That has an ominous sound for the administration. It begins to look like Mr. Curtis will desert Hoover and run for senator again. Yes, Kansas is getting steamed up.

The Baltimore Sun takes occasion to poke fun at Kansas, predicting that, come what will, Kansas will be back in the

Republican fold again next year. The Baltimore oracle shouldn't be too sure about that. Kansas has kicked over the traces in former elections and may do so again.

Kansas went Democratic in 1916. Kansas has a Democratic governor right now. Kansas has elected Populist governors and senators and Democratic governors and senators in the past. When Kansas starts to bleed, anything political can happen in the Sunflower state.

And Kansas is bleeding right now, don't think it isn't. With 30-cent wheat, 10-cent oil and other commodities in proportion, Kansas is doggone hard up. And when Kansas gets hard up the natives recall the advice of Mrs. Lease about corn and hell. Right now Kansas can't see any profit in raising corn.
—Kansas City Star, *July 25, 1931*

15

Emanuel and Marcet Haldeman-Julius:

An Innovative Partnership

in Publishing

M. H. Hoeflich

There can have been few more fascinating couples in the history of Kansas than Emanuel and Marcet Haldeman-Julius. Emanuel Julius was born on July 30, 1889, in Philadelphia, the son of emigrant parents. His father was a bookbinder and a nonobservant Jew; his mother was a housewife. The family was far from wealthy, but like many Jewish emigrant families it valued learning and reading. Emanuel attended school through the eleventh grade and then dropped out to find work. He was, in most respects, an autodidact. Throughout his life Emanuel was obsessed by words and ideas and was both a voracious reader and a prodigious writer.[1]

Anna Marcet Haldeman came from a very different family background. She was born in 1887 in Girard, Kansas. Her father was both a doctor and the

Emanuel (July 30, 1889–July 31, 1951) and Anna Marcet (June 19, 1887–February 13, 1941) Haldeman-Julius, ca. 1920, pursued careers in journalism, publishing, and social reform from their home in Girard, Kansas; among their best-selling book titles were *What Married Women Should Know, Modern Aspects of Birth Control,* and Marcet's *Why I Believe in Companionate Marriage.* Courtesy of Special Collections, Leonard H. Axe Library, Pittsburg State University.

president of the State Bank of Girard. Her mother was the president of the Board of Education of Girard and, after her husband's death in 1905, succeeded him as president of the bank. Her aunt was Jane Addams, the prominent Chicago feminist and advocate of the poor. Marcet was educated in Girard, then in Chicago and, between 1905 and 1908, at Bryn Mawr College. From 1908 until 1910 she was a student at the American Academy of Dramatic Arts in New York City and later worked as a professional actress around the United States. She returned to Girard in 1915 to work at the bank with her mother.[2]

Although Marcet Haldeman came from small-town Kansas, she did not suffer from a rural, conservative upbringing. Both her parents were well educated, and her aunt was a famous urban reformer. Girard itself was not a rural backwater. On the contrary, it was a center of progressive publishing and the home of the *Appeal to Reason,* a popular socialist periodical.[3] Thus, Emanuel, the urban son of Jewish immigrants, and Marcet, the daughter of middle-class Kansans, actually had much in common.

Emanuel Julius early chose a career as a working journalist within the confines of the then extensive socialist press. As a teenager he began freelancing in Philadelphia. He then moved to New York and worked as a general reporter for the socialist weekly the *Call,* whose most famous staff writer was John Reed. Next came the *Leader,* a Milwaukee socialist newspaper, where Julius came to know Carl Sandburg, then the paper's labor reporter. Later in life Haldeman-Julius recalled his relationship with Sandburg in *My First Twenty-five Years.* After a year in Milwaukee Julius moved to Chicago to write for the *World,* but it was not to his liking, and he soon left the Midwest for Los Angeles. In California he wrote for the *Citizen* and then edited a magazine, the *Western Comrade.* In Los Angeles Julius became acquainted with Jack London and Upton Sinclair, many of whose works he was later to print. Perhaps most important for his future publishing activities, during Julius's time in California he also became friendly with Clarence Darrow, whose politics and combativeness made him a hero to Julius. In 1914, when he was twenty-five, Julius returned to New York to continue his writing and editorial career, but his stay in New York was to be relatively short. In October 1915 Emanuel Julius left New York for Girard, Kansas, to assume an editorship at a socialist newspaper founded by J. A. Wayland in 1895.[4]

The *Appeal to Reason,* although located in a small southeastern Kansas town, was a major socialist weekly and a principal media outlet for Eugene V. Debs and his Social Democratic Party. In 1905 the *Appeal* commissioned

Upton Sinclair to write a serialized novel, which became his landmark muck-raking work, *The Jungle*. The newspaper had a circulation in excess of 500,000 and a printing plant capable of producing as many as 25,000 copies per hour.[5]

In 1912 Wayland committed suicide and was succeeded by his long-term deputy, Fred Warren. He stayed on until 1914, when W. H. Wayland, the son of the founder, took over as publisher and Louis Kopelin, a former New York colleague of Emanuel Julius, was named editor. Kopelin invited Julius to join the staff of the *Appeal* the following year. The paper went through a series of changes in editorship and position as a result of the split in the Socialist Party over the U.S. entry into World War I in 1917 and was never again quite as successful as it had been under J. A. Wayland's guidance.[6]

In the meantime Emanuel Julius met Marcet Haldeman. They were married in 1916, and Emanuel Julius became Emanuel Haldeman-Julius. His wife's wealth enabled him to take over the financially ailing *Appeal to Reason,* and soon he began what was to become his greatest publishing venture, the Little Blue Books.

Haldeman-Julius maintained throughout his life that the idea for the Little Blue Books came from an experience he had when he was about fifteen and still living in Philadelphia. He often recounted how he had frequented bookstores in the city; on one visit to a store owned by Nicholas Brown he had found a small booklet that contained a copy of Oscar Wilde's *Ballad of Reading Gaol*. Years later he remembered his reaction to reading this booklet: "I thought, at that moment, how wonderful it would be if thousands of such booklets could be made available."[7] If the story is true, or even if it is not, there can be little doubt that Haldeman-Julius's passion for reading, belief in the importance of education for the workers of the world, and innate business sense led him, from an early age, to his fate.

Soon after Haldeman-Julius took over the *Appeal* in 1919 he not only changed the name of the newspaper to the *Haldeman-Julius Weekly* but also began a separate publishing venture: the Appeal Pocket Series. His notion was to produce large quantities of small booklets, like the Wilde poem he had read as a boy, priced for mass consumption. Wilde's *Ballad* was number one in the series, and the second was Omar Khayyam's *The Rubaiyat*. These first two pocket books set the model for the later volumes. They were each 3.5 by 5 inches in size and contained a multiple of thirty-two pages. They were originally priced at twenty-five cents, but soon Haldeman-Julius hit on the idea of selling them in lots, fifty for $5. He advertised the new series in the newspaper and sent circulars to 175,000 names on his subscriber list. The series bailed out the troubled business. Haldeman-Julius sold five thousand subscriptions to the first series—even though he had yet to publish the fifty volumes (or even select them all)—and five thousand additional subscribers for a second series of fifty volumes soon followed. The income generated by these ten thousand subscriptions permitted Haldeman-Julius to pay off his debt for the purchase of the *Appeal* and develop further his fledgling publishing empire.[8]

The success of the Haldeman-Julius publishing ventures derived from the remarkable diversity of skills possessed by Emanuel and Marcet Haldeman-Julius. Over the course of several decades they produced a number of periodicals, including the *Haldeman-Julius Monthly* and the *Debunker.* But these were only an ancillary activity. Their main publishing project was the Little Blue Books and, later, the Big Blue Books. The success of these two ventures came from a combination of savvy marketing, brilliant selections and constant selection updating, the creation of a stable of writers not seen since eighteenth-century England's Grub Street, and an understanding of the American public's hunger for inexpensive reading material.[9]

Emanuel Haldeman-Julius was obsessive about success, and he closely managed every aspect of his publishing enterprise. Each Little Blue Book was either written or edited so that it would fit into the optimal length for his presses. There was nothing sacred about the pamphlets or anything that could not be changed in the name of marketing. The books were first called the Appeal to Reason Library. Then they became, among other titles, the Five Cent Pocket Books; then, as the price rose, the Ten Pocket Books. Finally Haldeman-Julius settled upon the title the Little Blue Books. Each book was numbered, but the numbers were often reassigned if a book's sales did not live up to expectations. Haldeman-Julius generally wanted his books to sell a minimum of ten thousand copies to remain in print, although he made exceptions. Sales of individual volumes were constantly monitored. Often, if a book were not selling well, he would first change the title; if a title change did not help, the book might well be dropped from the list.[10] By the time of Haldeman-Julius's death, more than two thousand titles had been published in the Little Blue Book series alone, and many of his titles had sold more than fifty thousand copies.

Both of the Haldeman-Juliuses were unconventional in their social, political, and religious views. They were freethinkers who often characterized religion as "bunk." Marcet was a champion of women's rights, companionate marriage, and comprehensive sex education.[11] Emanuel retained his socialist beliefs throughout his life and always championed the "little guy" against the wealthy, large business, and government. During the Depression and the years thereafter, their views on these matters found both passionate supporters and dedicated opponents. In their periodical publications and in their selection of works for their book series, they followed their beliefs.

The Little Blue Books represent the diversity of the Haldeman-Juliuses' interests and beliefs quite well. Many of the books were simply abridged versions of popular classics of both American and European literature.[12] But an extensive run of books on sex education and on the problems of organized religion, as well as a substantial number of works on science and natural history, rolled off the Girard press. They published abridged editions of Shakespeare, of poetry, of horror stories, even of collections of jokes. There was virtually no subject of human endeavor not represented by a title in the Little Blue Books. Among the authors whose books were abridged and included in the series were Oscar Wilde, H. G. Wells, Edgar Allen Poe, Henrik Ibsen, Henry David Thoreau, the great Russian anarchist Pyotr Alekseyevich Kropotkin, Anton Chekhov, Edward Bulwer-Lytton, Jack London, Leo Tolstoy, and, of course, Karl Marx and Friedrich Engels. The classics, though not his best sellers, did sell. By 1928 Ibsen's *The Doll House* had sold fifteen thousand copies. Euripides' *Bacchantes* had sold twelve thousand copies.[13]

Among Haldeman-Julius's best-selling books were, not surprisingly, those on sex. The basic manuals sold best. *What Married Women Should Know* sold 112,000 copies by 1928. *What Married Men Should Know* was not far behind, with 97,500 copies sold. *Modern Aspects of Birth Control* sold a remarkable 73,000 copies, and *The Art of Kissing* sold 60,500 copies. Havelock Ellis's books did exceptionally well. His *Plain Talks with the Married* and *The Love Rights of Women* sold 60,500 and 39,000 copies, respectively. Marcet Haldeman-Julius's volume *Why I Believe in Companionate Marriage* sold 64,000 copies. Even such obscure titles as *Phallic Elements of Religion* and *Sex Obsessions of Saints and Mystics* sold over 35,000 copies each.[14] Clearly these volumes helped to finance the literary works that sold in far smaller quantities.

One of Haldeman-Julius's greatest achievements was the creation of a stable of writers who wrote specifically for him. These ranged from writers who attained international prominence in literature, the arts, and other fields to others who were hacks, but hacks who could produce a substantial number of decent books that sold solidly. Haldeman-Julius had a genius for friendship and for spotting talent. His home at Girard became a stopping-off place for some of the greatest personalities of his era. Upton Sinclair, Clarence Darrow, and Abraham Walkowitz, one of the finest artists of his day, all spent time in Girard with the Haldeman-Julius family.

Among the more notable contemporary authors published by Haldeman-Julius, none was better known than Upton Sinclair. Ten of his books were published in abridged form as Little Blue Books, and an additional twenty-five appeared as Big Blue Books. Haldeman-Julius and Sinclair eventually found themselves at odds over the latter's interest in spiritualism, which Haldeman-Julius blamed on Sinclair's wife. Even more fruitful were Haldeman-Julius's relations with Frank Harris. Although Harris had spent time in Kansas, his relationship with Haldeman-Julius began after he left the state. Haldeman-Julius always remained a great admirer of Harris's literary talents, if somewhat skeptical about his personal habits. A number of Harris's works were published as Little Blue Books, and several did well. His essay *Has Life Any Meaning?* had sold over 133,000 copies by January 1949. His short story "A Daughter of Eve" sold 105,000 copies. His volumes on Shakespeare did not do so well, but Haldeman-Julius, against his usual practice, kept them in print anyway. All told, Haldeman-Julius estimated that he had sold a total of 587,000 copies of the eight Little Blue Books authored by Harris. He expressed regret in 1949 that he had not published Harris's autobiography, but he explained that he did not think he could have published the book without running afoul of the U.S. antiobscenity laws.[15]

Both Marcet and Emanuel Haldeman-Julius maintained a close friendship with Clarence Darrow. Emanuel had met Darrow during his time in Los Angeles, and the friendship remained strong throughout their lives. Haldeman-Julius published many of Darrow's writings, and Marcet published analyses of Darrow's greatest cases. Darrow was a welcome guest in Girard, where he could find peace and shelter from the turbulence of his life. Darrow's works never sold large numbers of copies, but that seems to have meant little to Haldeman-Julius, for they, like Harris's works, always remained in print. Although Haldeman-Julius was a hard-boiled businessman, he continued to print the works of friends and others whom he admired, regardless of how they sold.[16]

In addition to the famous authors whom he published, Haldeman-Julius had a number of "house authors" who provided substantial numbers of Little Blue Books. Of all of these, Joseph McCabe, a British scholar and writer, was perhaps the greatest contributor. He began his quarter-century collaboration with Haldeman-Julius by agreeing to produce no fewer than fifty volumes on religion. By 1949 McCabe had written 121 Little Blue Books, which had sold a total of 2,347,000 copies. Another writer who began to write for Haldeman-Julius while still obscure, but who eventually achieved prominence, was Will Durant. Durant, whose collaborative works with his wife became a mainstay of the Book of the Month Club, began writing for Haldeman-Julius in 1922. He produced a series of works on great philosophers, which foreshadowed his first national success, *The Story of Philosophy,* published by Simon and Schuster.[17]

Of course Haldeman-Julius was not only the editor of all of his publications, he was also a frequent contributor. As of 1949 he had authored 108 Little Blue Books. He had also published a novel with his wife titled *Dust.* His first Little Blue Book, Number 72, was a collection of his short stories, *The Color of Money.* His last, Number 1758, was titled *Was Adolph Hitler a Maniac?* In between he published volumes on Russia and Henry Ward Beecher; attacks on Herbert Hoover, Warren G. Harding, and Henry Ford; and a study of the mathematician Sir James Jeans.[18] No subject was taboo to Haldeman-Julius.

Marcet contributed far fewer volumes to the series, but her books were very popular. She published a one-act play, volumes on companionate marriage, and a fascinating volume called *What the Editor's Wife Is Thinking About.* She also was a frequent contributor to their magazines and wrote several volumes in the Big Blue Book series.[19]

Haldeman-Julius recognized from the start that no matter how good the content of his books and magazines, he needed more to be successful. He was a pioneer both in literary advertising and in mail-order sales. He combined the dedication to popular education of John Ruskin with the marketing savvy of Sears and Roebuck. Indeed, Haldeman-Julius considered advertising and marketing to be so important that he published a book on the subject in 1928, *The First Hundred Million.* Haldeman-Julius established a marketing formula that was later adapted throughout the book publishing industry; he combined intense media advertisements with easy mail-order availability and advance sales.

From the beginning of his publishing enterprise Haldeman-Julius devoted care and attention to building a large database of potential customers. He used newspaper and magazine advertisements extensively, running advertisements in the socialist press as well as in mainstream magazines such as *Colliers,* the *Nation,* and *Liberty.* Advertisements ran in large urban newspapers such as the *New York Times* and the *Detroit Free Press* and in smaller papers such as the Fort Wayne, Indiana, daily, even though Haldeman-Julius believed these were rarely profitable. Wherever advertisements appeared they had but one purpose: to get readers to send in an order and thereby get their names onto Haldeman-Julius's mailing lists. Once there, these buyers were never again left alone: "Once the name gets on my mailing list the customer is put through the wringer. He is hit often and hard, so that frequently where a new customer comes in with $1, he ends up by buying regularly."[20]

Haldeman-Julius, whose books were not available in stores, carefully developed the mail-order business and was a pioneer in market demographics. He knew the sales of each title on his list; that 75 percent of his customers were male; that the average sale was for $1.50. He referred to his advertising methods as "coupon advertising." In order to purchase his books, a buyer would mail a coupon with payment to Girard. Each coupon carried a specific "key" number, which permitted Haldeman-Julius to identify the magazine or newspaper from which it had been removed. In this way it was possible to adjust advertising to match titles to a particular newspaper or magazine. Haldeman-Julius kept detailed statistics on what the readers of each magazine and newspaper ordered. He was a pioneer in another aspect of this market research: not only did he use his mailing list and detailed market research to sell his own publications but he also rented out this information to others.[21]

Haldeman-Julius produced frequent catalogs, often arranged by author or subject. He was proud that many of his customers gave him names of friends to whom he might send a catalog. Catalogs were included in orders sent out from Girard and could be obtained free by sending in a magazine or newspaper inquiry form. The advertisements themselves were often specially tailored to a particular audience. For instance, Haldeman-Julius ran an advertisement for the complete works of Upton Sinclair in the October 10, 1934, issue of the *Nation,* then the country's leading politically liberal magazine. Its readers were the perfect market for Sinclair's muckraking works. In addition to these media advertisements, many of the Little Blue Books carried advertisements and partial catalogs printed on blank pages at the end.[22]

Haldeman-Julius encountered one major problem with his advertising. His politics were well known and often repugnant to the owners of newspapers and magazines. Furthermore, many of the Little Blue Books on sex or religion were controversial. As a result, many periodicals—the *Chicago Sun-Times,* for example—simply refused to carry Haldeman-Julius's advertisements if they mentioned his name.[23]

Haldeman-Julius was a marketing genius. He adopted tactics and methods that had been the province of hucksters and patent-medicine purveyors to the far more genteel world of book publishing. He developed mail-order marketing and demographic research to a point far more sophisticated than any publisher had before. By 1949, when he published the first installment of his autobiography, Haldeman-Julius had a mailing list containing 550,000 names. He employed a dozen workers to stuff envelopes with circulars and catalogs.[24] He developed printing plates that permitted him to print names directly onto envelopes for rapid and inexpensive mailings. No year passed when anyone on his list received fewer than four mailings from Girard. In many years they received six. Once an individual made himself known to Haldeman-Julius, he could count on a steady stream of mail and book offerings for the rest of his life.

At the height of its existence the Haldeman-Julius publishing empire achieved international fame. Customers literally came from all over the world and from all classes. He sold books to farmers in Canada and a maharajah in India. Haile Selassie, the emperor of Ethiopia, was a loyal customer. According to Haldeman-Julius, the emperor ordered a wide range of titles, including several on sex. Even Hollywood yielded to his marketing: Charlie Chaplin and Gloria Swanson were both customers.[25]

In spite of the success of Haldeman-Julius Publishing and close editorial and writing collaboration of Emanuel and Marcet, all did not go smoothly. They had three children (two biological and one adopted), but by 1933 tensions over finances had divided the couple, and Marcet sued Emanuel for separate maintenance. The courts granted her request, but, oddly, she did not leave the family home in Girard. Instead the couple lived together until her premature death in 1941; soon afterward Emanuel married his secretary.

Emanuel Haldeman-Julius made many enemies. He was opinionated and outspoken and never backed away from a fight; his publications attacked organized religion, Wall Street, capitalism, Republicans, and anyone he believed was a purveyor of "bunk." In a good cause he was not afraid to stretch the truth or go for the jugular. He also supported Marcet's progressive views on sex, birth control, and women's rights. Indeed, when their adopted daughter, Josephine, entered into a companionate marriage with her parents' blessing, a national scandal erupted, and Haldeman-Julius found himself opposed by such notables as William Allen White of the *Emporia Gazette*.

In the end his own success may have well been his downfall. In 1951 the federal government prosecuted Haldeman-Julius for tax fraud, and in April of that year he was found guilty and sentenced to pay a fine and serve six months in a federal prison. He never lived to serve his sentence, for on July 31 he drowned in his swimming pool. It was the end of an era in American publishing history and of one of the most colorful figures in Kansas history.[26]

Emanuel and Marcet Haldeman-Julius are all but forgotten now, even in their home state. The Little Blue Books are found only in used bookshops, at estate auctions, and in some library collections. There is a Haldeman-Julius Society, but it numbers fewer than fifty members. Neither Marcet nor Emanuel Haldeman-Julius has yet found a biographer. The closest they have come is a collection of writings edited by Albert Mordell, a Philadelphia lawyer who wrote a number of Little Blue Books. But their legacy nonetheless continues to gain strength. Although it is always difficult to estimate influence, there can be little doubt that through their publishing activities Emanuel and Marcet Haldeman-Julius played a large role in the intellectual history of the United States during the mid-twentieth century. They sold over 500 million Little Blue Books during their lives. They published numerous magazines championing progressive causes. They even spawned imitators. Can one simply ignore the fact that Clifton Fadiman, the founder of the Book of the Month Club, visited the Haldeman-Julius publishing offices years before he started his own publishing empire?[27] Their legacy to Kansas and to the world was great.

Alfred M. Landon: Budget Balancer

Peter Fearon

In early 1936 the general public knew little of the man who soon was to challenge Franklin D. Roosevelt for the presidency. Those who were politically literate could recall that he was the only Republican governor reelected in 1934. Indeed, this feat had propelled him to the fore amongst his party's prospective presidential candidates. The other element of electoral appeal was that he had managed to balance the Kansas budget at a time when the federal budget seemed mired in persistent deficit. The failure to achieve a budget balance deeply concerned the incumbent president. At heart he was a fiscal conservative who believed that deficits were fundamentally destabilizing to the economy. Moreover, during the election campaign of 1932 candidate Roosevelt had accused President Herbert Hoover of presiding over an administration that had failed to control government spending, with a resulting budget deficit that Roosevelt, when elected, would swiftly correct. Balance, however, proved elusive. As the 1936 election approached, the president and his advisers thought that he was extremely vulnerable to an attack in this re-

Alfred M. Landon (September 9, 1887–October 12, 1987), Kansas oil man and politico, was elected governor in 1932 and, in large part because of his successful reelection campaign (a rare thing among Republicans in 1934), received the GOP's 1936 presidential nomination. Courtesy of the Kansas State Historical Society.

spect, especially when his opponent could boast that what he had achieved in his own state could be replicated in Washington.

The man who in 1936 sought the opportunity to address the nation's fiscal problems was born in West Middlesex, Pennsylvania, on September 9, 1887, but raised in Marietta, Ohio. The development of Alfred Landon's political and moral philosophy owed much to the influence of his father, John Landon, a businessman who was heavily involved with the Ohio oil industry. The elder Landon introduced his son to Republican Party politics at a very early age. He was, however, a man of independent thought who was more likely to do what he thought was right than to instinctively grasp at what appeared politically expedient. Perhaps the family's commitment to Methodism can at least partly explain the refusal of John, and later Alf, Landon to be bound in strict ideological chains. In 1904 the family moved to Independence, Montgomery County, Kansas, where John Landon had secured employment with the Kansas Natural Gas Company. Almost immediately Alf Landon entered the University of Kansas to begin his undergraduate studies.[1]

During his school days in Marietta, Landon was a popular but not an academically gifted student. Nor did he demonstrate intellectual distinction while studying law on the Lawrence campus. He was, however, an assiduous scholar who was clearly influenced by some of his teachers. Indeed, historian and biographer Donald R. McCoy reported that during this formative period Landon became deeply committed to the view that power tends to corrupt. From this point on, he saw the accumulation of power as a threat to democracy as well as a danger to the competitive business environment he supported. As a result, Landon retained a suspicion of monopolists and an admiration for the operators of small businesses; he remained a champion of the independent proprietor throughout his long life. Although Landon had a deep-seated commitment to individual liberty, he saw many political issues in shades of gray rather than in stark black and white. He was a natural negotiator whose inclination was to seek compromise even if it meant that his own carefully argued position would require moderation. For example, although leaning toward the "dry" cause he was willing to risk antagonizing the powerful Kansas antiliquor forces by advocating a state referendum on prohibition in 1933.

Landon's character developed during his time at the University of Kansas. He was deeply involved in student affairs, displaying both the energy and the capacity to prosecute his views with vigor but to do so without antagonizing his peers. His bonhomie, his sense of humor, his sensitivity and gregariousness were all assets that later were to prove immensely valuable as he climbed up the greasy pole to high political office.

After graduating in 1908 Landon chose to work as a bookkeeper in several local banks rather than practice law. In spite of a modest salary of $75 to $90 per month, he was able to invest in several oil-drilling projects with such success that in 1911 he decided to join the oil industry as a full-time independent operator. Alfred Mossman Landon had entered a highly volatile industry that had always attracted many flamboyant speculators. However, he was a cautious operator who could not be seduced into excessive risk-taking by the lure of an instant fortune. To achieve even modest success in the oil business, Landon had to acquire a great deal of knowledge, possess sound judgment, quickly establish a network of trusted contacts, and have the confidence to make quick decisions.

In 1912 both John and Alf Landon defected to the Progressive Party and campaigned to secure the election of Theodore Roosevelt. After the failure of this campaign Alf Landon spent a few years in the political wilderness before gravitating back to the progressive wing of the Republican Party. Landon enlisted in the army after the United States entered World War I and received a commission in the chemical warfare corps; only the Armistice of November 1918 prevented his departure for the battlefields of Europe.

During the 1920s Landon consolidated his interests in the oil and gas industry and became one of the state's leading oilmen. The industry was enjoying a period of prosperity, and by the end of the decade Landon was comfortably affluent.

He also became increasingly active in Republican Party politics while retaining a pronounced independent streak. Landon endorsed Emporia editor William Allen White's Independent gubernatorial candidacy in 1924 rather than giving his support to the Republican standard-bearer, Ben Paulen, whom Landon considered weak in his opposition to the Ku Klux Klan. Although Paulen emerged a comfortable winner, Landon's credentials as an independent-minded progressive were firmly established before he played the lead role in Clyde M. Reed's successful 1928 campaign for governor.

Reed's victorious campaign owed much to the organizational skill and drive of Alf Landon, who chaired the election committee. Unfortunately for Landon, Reed became a one-term governor after his candidacy was rejected by Republican voters in the 1930 primary. Having supported a candidate who was ousted by his own party, it seemed that Landon's political rise had gone into reverse. It was, however, his and the state's good fortune that he distanced himself from politics at the very time when his skills and energy were needed by the oil industry.

In 1930 Kansas oil producers faced ruinously low prices caused by a Depression-induced decline in demand and the discovery of new fields. Landon was drawn into a battle between the big oil interests, organized into the American Petroleum Institute, and the smaller independent producers who formed the Independent Petroleum Producers of America. An active senior official in the latter group, Landon was instrumental in persuading Kansas to accept the regulation of oil production so that output could be kept more closely in balance with demand. Landon's role as an oil industry leader gave him valuable publicity, and his concern that small-scale operators should not fall victim to the might of corporate power struck a chord with the public. As a result, Landon became an attractive gubernatorial candidate in 1932.[2] His experience in successfully coping with excessive oil production showed Landon that regulation of output could also ensure a balance between supply and demand for farm products.

After 1929 the rapidly worsening Depression played havoc with the state's public finances, which were heavily dependent upon property taxes.[3] In 1930, even before the Depression began to bite, fifty-three counties recorded budget deficits caused primarily by declining property values. Tax delinquency on farm real estate more than doubled between 1928 and 1931, and there was no improvement during the following year. As early as 1931 over one-third of the total farm acreage of the state was tax delinquent. Democratic governor Harry H. Woodring implemented an economy drive that resulted in considerable savings, the result of which enabled him to substantially reduce the burden of the general property tax. In 1932 Woodring was proud to announce that in spite of worsening economic circumstances, he had achieved a small budget surplus and had become the only governor in Kansas history to spend less than the sum appropriated by the legislature.[4]

As a result of rising unemployment, short-time working, and low farm prices, an increasing number of Kansans were unable to care for themselves and their families. Though obliged to do so, counties could not meet the needs of all the distressed people who applied for assistance. Fortunately, private charities played a key role in helping the destitute, and these organizations began to raise additional funds for that purpose. Private welfare agencies increased their spending from $542,000 in 1929 to just over $1 million in 1932. During the same period county expenditure on relief rose from $1.8 to $2.9 million.[5] These figures give a clear indication of the mounting social costs of the Depression and must be viewed in the context of the effect of falling property values, which eroded the tax base of many counties. By late 1931 many counties and other taxing units were facing a desperate situation, having reached the limit of their bonded indebtedness while the demands of the needy were still rising.

Congress recognized the impossibility of the task facing many states and local governments. In July 1932 the Emergency Relief and Construction Act made available, via the Reconstruction Finance Corporation (RFC), $300 million as loans to the states for the purpose of direct relief. All governors had to make detailed applications for federal funding showing that all sources of revenue, including private charitable contributions, had been fully exploited and that these sources were now exhausted. It was made clear that federal funds were a supplement to local efforts, not a substitute for them, and that the money had to be repaid. For the last three months of 1932 Kansas received over $1.1 million in loans from the RFC, a sum so substantial that the state's politicians could not afford to antagonize the source of this flow.

In spite of Woodring's fiscal success, Alf Landon, the Republican Party's nominee, was victorious in November 1932 at a time when the nation as a whole moved solidly to embrace the Democratic Party. Landon stressed his commitment to further reductions in spending and also his desire to seek alternative sources of revenue that would lessen the property tax burden that he deemed unfair. However, it is important to stress that Landon frequently reassured the victims of the Depression that although he would significantly reduce the cost of government, all legitimate welfare claims would be honored.[6] His compassion for the victims of the Depression was articulated clearly.

Governor Landon's early state-house actions demonstrated his intention to keep those campaign promises. Wherever possible, public sector jobs were cut and salaries, including his own, reduced, but he was not in mindless pursuit of a lower spending target. Where people could no longer care for themselves and their families, the state and the federal government had a supporting role to play. Landon recognized the importance of the developing relationship between the state and federal governments and anticipated that this relationship would be an even more complex one once the New Deal was fully in place. The governor moved quickly to establish a good working relationship with the Democratic administration. One of Landon's first executive actions was to inform the RFC that he would urge his 1933 legislature to find the means of raising additional revenue for relief purposes. That January meeting of the legislature, and the special session that took place in October and November, laid the foundations for Landon's claim that he was the nation's foremost budget balancer and his successful 1934 reelection campaign.

In the November 1932 elections, voters had expressed a clear wish that the state adopt an income tax. The legislature obliged, and as a result the general property tax, which had contributed 72 percent to state revenue during the 1920s, made a contribution of only 54 percent between 1930 and 1937. The state's tax base became broader, and tax demands were more closely linked to the ability to pay. To cope with the current crisis Landon advocated that for a two-year period counties be allowed to levy an emergency relief tax if their commissioners could convince the State Tax Commission that a need existed. The new governor conceded that his recommendation was based on the fear that without additional revenue the state's entitlement to federal funds might be compromised.[7]

Landon was determined to limit the spending powers not only of the state but also of its subdivisions. The 1931 budget law required cities, boards of education, and a number of other taxing units to prepare their budgets in a way that showed the amount of money each anticipated raising from taxes and from other sources and the planned amount to be spent during the ensuing financial year. After publication of the budget, all taxing authorities were obliged to hold a public hearing so that the spending plans could be subject to local scrutiny. This was the sort of practical democracy that appealed to Landon, and the legislature agreed that this practice be strengthened, clarified, and adopted by all taxing units so officials would be forced to plan expenditure carefully and be prepared to defend their spending plans when confronted by their taxpayers.

Taxing units faced further pressure from Landon's request that the legal limitations designed to restrict tax levies should be examined to reflect the straitened times. The new governor believed that officials could rarely resist the temptation to always tax to the maximum and that if taxes were to be reduced, so must the ceiling on levies. The legislature put Landon's proposal into law with the passage of the Tax Limitation Act.

With missionary zeal Landon preached that all taxing units should live within their income. Cities of the first and second class had to observe that rule, and Landon was determined to see this restriction in place everywhere taxes could be raised. Excess spending would be illegal, and it would no longer be possible for officials to exceed their levies and create outstanding warrants and indebtedness. This restrictive fiscal initiative became known as the cash basis law. Once it was adopted by the legislature, school boards, county commissions, indeed all political units had to limit their spending to no more than the actual income on hand during the current financial year. Once a contract was executed or a purchasing order issued, the money in the fund to cover this expense was frozen, even if the payment was not due immediately. Some exceptions could be made, such as an emergency relating to relief expenditures, but only on a temporary basis and only after approaching the State Tax Commission. Or, of course, the electorate could authorize further indebtedness through the ballot box, provided the legal limit on bonded indebtedness was not exceeded.

When the legislature adjourned, Landon had every reason to feel a sense of triumph because his fiscal package was in place. The governor regarded the cash basis law as crucial in his fight to reduce expenditure, lower taxes, and achieve a balanced budget. Legislation that limited the amount of the tax levy and a budget law that forced transparency certainly contributed to his economy drive, but they were refinements of existing legislation. The cash basis law, on the other hand, imposed a straitjacket by making it very difficult for taxing units to spend more than their allotted budget. Furthermore, any public officer who violated the provisions of the law risked being automatically removed from office.[8]

When the Federal Emergency Relief Administration (FERA) replaced the RFC in May 1933, states could look forward to grants-in-aid rather than loans. However, the FERA, like the RFC, expected each state to make a full contribution toward aiding the needy, and it was again made clear that federal grants were a supplement to state and local efforts, not a substitute for them. Landon informed the special session of the legislature in advance of its October meeting that Kansas would need $7 million to fund its total relief obligations until June 30, 1934. The counties had the power to provide $2 million of this sum by tax levies, and Landon was confident that the FERA would contribute an additional $2.8 million. The shortfall could be made up, so the governor advised, by giving the counties additional bond-raising powers to the value of $2.2 million, which, together with federal funds, would be spent on jobs building and repairing roads and streets (a type of relief work). By this means the full quota of federal relief could be anticipated, without the creation of any new tax burden.[9]

Under the New Deal all states came to rely heavily on financial assistance from Washington. A total of $23 million was spent on relief in Kansas during 1934. Of this sum, the federal government contributed $15.4 million and the counties $5.6 million, with an additional $1.8 million worth of surplus commodities being distributed to those in need. The state's contribution was a mere $331,000. Looking at a different period, Washington was responsible for 72 percent of funding for emergency relief in Kansas between January 1933 and December 1935; the counties' proportion was 26 percent and the state's 2 percent.[10] Kansas counties were responsible for the distribution of allocated federal funds, but they also had to support the substantial numbers who, although eligible, could not secure a place in federally funded programs. In addition, local resources had to support unemployables, who were ineligible for work relief, and the heads of large families whose work relief wages were insufficient. Another task given to county officials was to generate work relief projects that would satisfy federal scrutiny and to raise the necessary sponsor's funds to support the projects. Those counties that possessed a strong tax base and had a team of highly competent and energetic officials could operate effectively under this system, but others with financial or staffing deficiencies could not. For example, Crawford and Cherokee Counties faced great difficulty because of heavy unemployment among coal and lead miners, extremely depressed property values, and a volatile population that made life difficult for relief officials. The concentration of acute social hardship created a series of problems that were beyond solution by local effort.

State tax receipts rose from $22.9 million to $28.1 million during Landon's tenure as governor. On the other hand, the local tax burden fell from $81.5 to $74.5 million, and as a result, the per capita cost of government declined marginally, from $56.84 to $55.74. The fact that under Landon's leadership Kansas had achieved a balanced budget attracted first local and then, when the feat was repeated, national attention. Editors were quick to point out that not only was the state budget in balance but the cash basis law had ensured that all taxing units operated in the black. Kansas presented a sharp contrast to the national government, where, argued critics, New Deal profligacy gave rise to persistent and deeply worrying deficits.[11]

During the summer of 1935 the *New York Times* was lavish in its praise for the cash basis law, which it described as a "pay as you go plan." Landon, the newspaper pointed out, had reduced the cost of government, cut property taxes, and shown that it was possible to have a balanced budget in spite of the formidable relief problems imposed by serious drought and a depressed economy. William Randolph Hearst, desperate to find a presidential candidate who could topple Roosevelt and impressed with Landon's apparent fiscal success, instructed his newspapers to promote the Kansas man.[12] Landon was beginning to emerge as a Republican hero at a time when there were few political figures whom the party could call on to fill that role.

The governor's increasing public exposure did not escape the attention of leading New Dealers. In November 1935 Harry Hopkins, the administrator for the Works Progress Administration (WPA), accused Kansas of having "never put up a thin dime for relief" and added that Landon had managed the state budget by "taking it out of the hides of the people."[13] This was the first time that Landon had the satisfaction of being singled out for attack by a senior administration Democrat. The governor remained aloof, but his state relief administrator, John G. Stutz, a man with a towering reputation in his field, mounted a robust defense. Stutz pointed out that if state and local government contributions were taken together they amounted to 26 percent of all federally funded work and work relief costs, which was about the national average. Furthermore, the state's local political subdivisions had always paid in full the relief costs for unemployables, and Kansas had used all RFC and FERA funds entirely for work relief rather than direct relief. Within a few days Hopkins had distanced himself from what had been an instant and thoughtless response to a journalist's question about Landon's skill as a budget balancer.[14] But Hopkins's quick abandonment of this line of attack was surprising; Congress had after all stipulated in the Federal Emergency Relief Act of 1933 that the ability of both states and localities to contribute to relief programs should have been exhausted before federal funds were made available.

Although Hopkins could have legitimately criticized the manner in which the burden of relief provision had been thrust on Kansas counties, he could not have faulted the quality of the state's relief administration. As early as February 1934 federal field agents reported that the relief administration created under Stutz's leadership was exemplary. Indeed, at the close of the Civil Works program, the organization of relief in Kansas was described as one of the best in the country, and Stutz was personally singled out for praise.[15] It was not possible for New Dealers to attack on these grounds when experienced agents had frequently identified the state as an example of best practice.

From late 1935 on it was increasingly common to find Landon's name linked with the words "budget balancer." In general the Kansas governor was praised for what he had accomplished, though a perceptive piece in the *New Republic* emphasized the costs of the austerity program he had implemented. The state's school system, for example, was unique in that it relied on local taxes for virtually all of its funding. Compliance with the cash basis law had imposed savage salary cuts on teachers and had led to the closure of many schools. Other public services, such as institutions that cared for the mentally handicapped, were unable to offer assistance to all who needed it.[16] These criticisms were not easily dismissed, especially in counties whose local economies had been hardest hit.

As Landon moved to the center of the political stage it was clear that he had a problem. The Kansan did not share the visceral hatred of Roosevelt that many of his more extreme fellow Republicans exhibited, and he found it impossible to inject into his speeches the notion that the president was the devil incarnate. Moreover, he supported some key elements of the New Deal. No son of a wheat state could fail to appreciate the assistance given to farmers from a variety of programs, such as the generous allotment payments that flowed from the Agricultural Adjustment Act or the rescheduling of farm debts and the many initiatives designed to lift drought-stricken operators out of their despair. Landon was also a fan of the Civilian Conservation Corps, and he had urged the president to continue that most expensive of work creation initiatives, the Civil Works Administration, when it was being run down in the spring of 1934. The governor viewed dole payments as a sure route to an un-American dependency culture, and he was a strong supporter of work relief for the able-bodied unemployed. He was an advocate of rigorous means testing to ensure that federal and state benefits were enjoyed only by the needy. None of these ideas, however, differed from the views of committed New Dealers such as Harry Hopkins. Indeed, as governor Landon had willingly cooperated with New Dealers and had striven to maximize federal funding for Kansas. It was, therefore, difficult for him to ideologically distance himself from his opponent on all occasions.

From a distance, the well-informed British journal the *Economist,* in a review of the White House contest, claimed, "The budget is the only issue on which the Republican and Democrat platforms differ by more than shades of emphasis."[17] It is not surprising that Landon's presidential campaign stressed economy and efficiency, since the highest federal deficit ever was recorded in June 1936. The federal budget could be balanced, Landon argued, with the elimination of wasteful spending and the discontinuance of political favoritism, which increasingly influenced New Deal resource allocations. He singled out the WPA as a clear example of undesirable political involvement in relief. However, he also pledged that any reordering of federal finances would not be at the expense of the provision of relief for the nation's needy unemployed or the nation's stricken farmers. The New Deal, he insisted, had retarded recovery by displaying hostility to business, appealing to class prejudice, and excessively taxing consumers and employers. Landon believed that his more cooperative approach to the nation's Chambers of Commerce would encourage business to create more jobs. However, he never displayed an unqualified admiration for big business. He also castigated the Democrats for presiding over a mounting public debt and advocated a return to the discipline of the gold standard at the earliest opportunity. In his intolerance of public debt one can see the mind-set of the small businessman. Although the candidate was clear in his promise that so long as the need for relief remained the necessary funds would be provided, he was vague about where the axe would fall to achieve the economies necessary for budget balance. Indeed, a *New York Times* headline, "Landon Pledges Strict Economy but Full Relief to Those in

Need," was, perhaps intentionally, an oxymoron. The Kansan's case was further weakened when he confessed that he did not know how many unemployed there were.[18]

The notion that Landon's tax policies as governor could form the core of a fiscal program to balance the federal budget was misguided. The governor demonstrated naïveté by drawing parallels between the federal budget and the household expenditure of a typical family.[19] Private and public expenditure are not the same. The federal budget should have been used as a force for economic recovery, but in Landon's defense, the economics profession had not yet provided a robust intellectual case to justify an expansive fiscal policy.

It would have been economically unwise and perhaps politically disastrous for a Landon administration to try to impose the equivalent of the cash basis law on Congress. Indeed, it is hard to envisage a Congress so compliant and so willing to surrender the opportunity to gain credit from the voters back home. Any critic could have pointed out that Alf Landon had been able to balance the Kansas budget without incurring unacceptable social costs because of the money that had flowed into the state from Washington in unprecedented amounts. Federal relief to Kansas came in the form of general and special emergency relief programs, substantial subsidies to farmers, and the Civil Works program. During the winter of 1933–1934, Washington's contribution to the latter program was $12.2 million; that of the state was $159,259 and the localities $2.4 million. In 1935 alone payments to young men in the Civilian Conservation Corps enabled 4,760 families to be removed from the relief rolls.[20] There were many other New Deal initiatives, a number of which did not call for local financial support, that pumped much-needed cash into the drought-stricken state or gave vital assistance to those perilously in debt. It is not possible to assess the way in which the Kansas budget was balanced without taking into account the substantial social safety net the New Deal provided. It was federal spending that enabled many Kansans to pay their taxes and made Governor Landon's balanced budgets possible. Furthermore, as Landon was a supporter of continuing federal assistance to farmers and also had promised to support relief for the needy unemployed, balancing the nation's budget would have been a much more complex task than managing the finances of a single state.

The cash basis law endured as a lasting legacy, but a commitment to balanced budgets could not save Landon from political annihilation at the polls in November 1936. It is a great irony that although his contemporaries worried greatly about the size of the federal deficit, modern economic analysis shows that their concern was misplaced. In fact a larger deficit would have helped to eradicate some of the cyclical unemployment plaguing the nation.[21] And had his contemporaries accepted aggregating federal, state, and local budget information, the deficit would have disappeared and with it much that made Landon's presidential candidacy attractive. It was not until the economy struggled in the aftermath of the disastrous depression of 1937–1938 that economists were able to convince President Roosevelt that the deficit he disliked and Landon criticized could be used as a positive tool to aid recovery.

In the 1936 presidential election Landon won only the states of Maine and Vermont, losing not only Kansas as a whole but also his home county of Montgomery. Landon remained phlegmatic about the scale of his defeat, however. He never again stood for public office and instead devoted his formidable energies to building up his oil and other business interests. Alf Landon also remained active in his political party and was always ready to give his opinion on important political matters. His stature was sufficient to guarantee press attention, and sometimes his views did not reflect those of the Republican leadership. His capacity for independent thinking was sometimes an embarrassment to members of the Republican Party, but he never flinched from providing an opinion. Thus, he was a critic of U.S. isolationism in the 1930s, an advocate of generous assistance to Britain in the fight against Nazi Germany, a firm supporter of the Marshall Plan in the late 1940s, and an advocate for Medicare and other Great Society programs in the 1960s. Alf Landon, who in later years was also known as the father of Kansas senator Nancy Landon Kassebaum, died on October 12, 1987, shortly after celebrating his one-hundredth birthday, with his reputation for straight talking and dedication to public service undiminished.

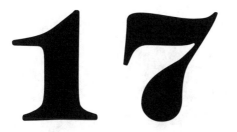

Walter A. Huxman: Leading by Example

Virgil W. Dean

"Our schools must be . . . open to all classes of citizens," wrote then governor Walter A. Huxman to Chancellor E. H. Lindley on July 11, 1938. Reacting to an allegation that "no colored student has ever been permitted to graduate from the Medical School," the governor asked that the matter be investigated and "corrected" if the charge were true. It was, and within a month, on the governor's direct instruction, the board of regents unanimously resolved "that colored students with the necessary scholastic standing should be admitted to the Medical School of Kansas University at Kansas City, Kansas."[1]

Thirteen years later Walter Huxman, then a judge on the U.S. Court of Appeals for the Tenth Circuit, had yet another opportunity to strike a blow against "Jim Crowism." This time, however, his action was more circumspect. As presiding judge on the three-judge federal district court panel that tried *Brown v. Board of Education of Topeka* in June 1951, Judge Huxman sided with the African American plaintiffs, but his decision for the unanimous court was for

Walter A. Huxman (February 16, 1887–June 25, 1972), a one-term Democratic governor of Kansas, attended the April 1937 Midwestern premiere of *The Good Earth,* a movie based on the novel by Pearl S. Buck, with the first lady, Mrs. Eula Biggs Huxman, at the Orpheum Theatre in Kansas City, Missouri. Courtesy of the Kansas State Historical Society.

the defendants. The Kansas jurist had long believed the U.S. Constitution was "pliable," but it was vitally important that it "be approached with a sense of responsibility." Judicial responsibility, to Judge Huxman, meant a commitment to the rules of stare decisis. Since *Plessy v. Ferguson* and *Gong Lum v. Rice* had "not been overruled," they remained the "authority for the maintenance of a segregated school system in the lower grades."[2]

Much has been written about the landmark Brown decision and many of the now famous individuals involved. Few writers, however, have really focused on the opinion rendered by the U.S. District Court at Topeka, and fewer still have examined the role or background of its presiding judge, whose attitudes and actions with respect to race, segregation, and other mid-twentieth-century issues tell us a great deal about Kansans and one man who sought to lead them in the right direction.[3]

Born on the family farm in Reno County, Kansas, on February 16, 1887, Walter August Huxman was the eldest son of Mary Graber and August H. Huxman. His mother was of Mennonite heritage, and his father was a part-time Swedenborgian preacher in Pretty Prairie; thus, the younger Huxman was raised in a relatively liberal, socially conscious household. He was educated in the rural public schools and then attended the county Teachers Institute. At age eighteen Huxman received a teaching certificate, and after four years teaching in his home county's elementary schools he attended the Kansas State Normal School at Emporia before moving to Lawrence and the University of Kansas Law School.[4]

After graduating in 1914 Huxman launched his legal and political careers almost simultaneously, while assuming some additional familial responsibilities. He campaigned for the Democratic candidate for Reno County attorney and subsequently received a position as assistant county attorney. Early in 1915 Huxman passed the bar exam, married Eula E. Biggs, and opened a law office in Hutchinson, where the couple lived and worked for the next twenty-two years.

Huxman remained active in party politics and served on the state tax commission during the administration of fellow Democrat Harry Woodring. Prior to his 1936 gubernatorial race, however, Huxman sought elective office for himself only once—an unsuccessful 1928 bid for a position on the Kansas Supreme Court.[5]

Eight years later, amid the Democratic tidal wave that engulfed even Alf Landon's Kansas, Huxman bested the Republican standard-bearer by some 22,000 votes, 433,000 to 411,000. During the primary and general election campaigns, Huxman proved a gifted speaker and enthusiastic champion of President Franklin D. Roosevelt. The press characterized Huxman as "a political progressive" and was favorably disposed toward this exceptionally popular Kansas Democrat.[6] "People in general have been impressed by his sincerity," reported the *Kansas City Times* soon after the general election. "In the campaign he indulged in few promises as a means of vote-getting. Repeatedly he pledged himself to give the state 'a sane, sensible and sound administration.' He spoke of the need of a wider distribution of taxes so that each citizen would bear his due share, but he promised no drastic reduction of taxes. He spoke of farm and school problems and expressed his support of fair and workable old-age pensions in the state."

The *Times* found Huxman, "by virtue of training and experience, as well as personal qualities, . . . one of the best equipped men ever chosen for the office of governor of Kansas." The governor elect's simple honesty and integrity also impressed the *Kansas City Star,* which described Huxman as "quite Kansan and quite American . . . a consistent liberal Democrat. The new deal to him is neither Utopia nor bedlam, but a progressive attempt to bring political service up to the level of today's changed social structure."[7]

The twenty-seventh governor of the state of Kansas was a man devoted to the legal profession who came of age during the dynamic period of Progressive Era politics and thus developed a deep interest in government. In his inaugural address Governor Huxman acknowledged the importance and difficulty of the job upon which he embarked and asked all Kansans to help him rise to the challenge. He called for "an unselfish, patriotic devotion to the best interest of the state" and a realization "that our own individual prosperity depends upon the general prosperity of all." Boldly Governor Huxman announced, "In the solution of the problems that confront us it will be necessary to raise new and additional revenue, additional tax burdens will be laid upon the people. It cannot be otherwise. Let me say to you that it should be the earnest endeavor of us all to see that these additional tax burdens are equitable and fair, and lie less heavily on those least able to pay."[8]

Two days later Governor Huxman called the legislature's "attention to the major problems which lie before us." He called for full state participation in the "social security" program (old age assistance and unemployment), ratification of the child labor amendment to the U.S. Constitution, and the passage of legislation to equalize funding of schools, to force necessary consolidations, and to provide free schoolbooks for all children, not just the poor. Huxman called for the repeal of the state law under which citizens had to "take an oath" that they were "unable to provide their children with school books" before they could qualify for such assistance. "It is rather degrading to ask any person to take what amounts to a pauper's oath, to provide his children with what every child is entitled to as a right."9 Overall the governor experienced significant, if limited, success with his moderate, progressive agenda during his single two-year term of office.

For purposes of this essay, one entirely unrelated but notable incident, occurring during the summer of 1938, deserves mention. Historian Nancy J. Hulston skillfully uncovered and told this story in a 1996 article for *Kansas History,* so the details can be omitted. Suffice it to say, when confronted with a blatantly discriminatory state practice, the governor acted decisively. In the face of stiff opposition from University of Kansas administrators, the governor effected change. He insisted, reported Kansas City's *Plaindealer,* an African American newspaper, that since the university and the medical school were state-supported public institutions, "'the Negroes are entitled to admittance the same as any other person, and that no public institution has the right to set any bars against them.'" According to the *Plaindealer,* Huxman continued, "'I hate intolerance. We are all of one blood and neither democracy nor the true American spirit is in the heart of any man who seeks to array class against class, race against race, or the people of one religious belief against the people of another.'"10 The African American student in question, Edward Vernon Williams, was immediately admitted to the junior class of the University of Kansas School of Medicine with little or no fanfare and completed his clinical training at the school's Kansas City facility.

Meanwhile, the governor was in the midst of a reelection campaign that seems to have been unaffected by the medical school affair. Huxman had "made a fine record in the statehouse" and was universally praised for his conduct in office. But like his four Democratic predecessors in the state's executive office, Governor Huxman was denied a second term. The governor experienced some success with his legislative program, but, opined Emporia editor William Allen White, Huxman simply "could not overcome the [Kansas] jinx" against Democratic reelection. He "has been a wise, brave, honest man, personally and politically. . . . He goes out of office as he came in—a clean-handed, high-visioned Kansan—a gentleman and a scholar. . . . Governor Huxman's name will remain in Kansas a symbol of all that is decent and fair and fine in Kansas history." Zula Bennington Greene, alias "Peggy of the Flint

Hills," agreed: "I doubt that a more sincerely friendly, a more warmly gracious man than Walter Huxman has ever occupied the Governor's chair, nor one more liked and respected."[11]

Immediately after his defeat, observers began to speculate about Huxman's future. Longtime political columnist for the *Topeka State Journal* A. L. Shultz wrote on November 10 that all signs indicated Huxman was "pretty certain to find himself attached to a federal lifetime judgeship before the next election." As it turned out, in less than six months a position on the U.S. Circuit Court of Appeals opened, and Huxman was everyone's first choice. The *Kansas City Times* thought Huxman, whose private and public record was "notable for two things—intelligence and integrity," was a sure thing for Court of Appeals appointment. "Personally unassuming, thoroughly honest, possessor of a fine legal mind and an abiding sense of justice, he will make, if he is appointed, an ornament to the circuit bench of the United States."[12]

Later the same day, April 24, 1939, the "calm, deliberative, mild-mannered" Walter A. Huxman was indeed nominated to the Tenth Circuit, which encompassed Colorado, Wyoming, Utah, Kansas, Oklahoma, and New Mexico. And within a month Kansas Republican senator Arthur Capper had led the way for a speedy, unanimous Senate confirmation.

Thus, former governor Walter A. Huxman became U.S. Circuit Court Judge Walter A. Huxman, launching a new career that would span a quarter century. The new judge, reported the *Star*, was "a student of corporation law as well as other forms of civil law, and his approach to the statutes has always been from the standpoint of the people. The famous Katy [Missouri, Kansas & Texas Railroad] case which he won for Kansas [while a member of the state tax commission] is an example of his brilliance in one of the most complicated branches of jurisprudence." Huxman described his own judicial philosophy as follows: "I hope to be sound, just, progressive with the times and adapt myself to changing conditions. The Constitution is pliable, but it must be approached with a sense of responsibility."[13] It seems that Judge Huxman diligently sought to apply this moderately progressive approach to the law throughout his judicial career.

Nowhere, perhaps, was this more evident than in the Kansas jurist's 1951 opinion for the court in *Oliver Brown, et al., v. Board of Education, Topeka, Kansas*. A dozen years after accepting his lifetime appointment to the federal bench, Judge Huxman came face to face with the "American dilemma," which might also be called the Kansas dichotomy—the existence of an openly Jim

Crow practice and law in "free" Kansas.[14] It surely must have put his sense of fairness and justice to the test. The result was an eminently defensible, if not boldly egalitarian, decision that both condemned discrimination and upheld legal precedent.

In *Brown v. Board* the plaintiffs asked that the Kansas state statute allowing separate schools be declared unconstitutional, "contend[ing] that apart from all other factors segregation in itself constitutes an inferiority in educational opportunities offered to negroes." The two-day trial, which was held in Topeka on June 25 and 26, 1951, focused on the equality or inequality of the educational opportunities available to the black plaintiffs and the expert educational and psychological testimony presented to challenge the practice of segregation in the elementary grades. Since it was reasonably clear to all concerned that the facilities, instruction, and educational materials provided for the education of black and white children were essentially equal, plaintiffs clearly "relied primarily upon the contention that segregation in and of itself without more violates their rights guaranteed by the Fourteenth Amendment."[15]

During the month of July, while the court worked on its ruling and opinion, Topeka and much of the nation focused on the great flood of 1951, which hit the Kansas River valley with devastating effect during the second week of July. Of course the nation's attention also focused on events thousands of miles from home on the Korean peninsula. Perhaps as a result, surprisingly little media attention was given the five civil rights cases—called collectively, in retrospect, "the case of the century"—as they worked their way through the District of Kansas and four other jurisdictions.[16]

An exception was the *Plaindealer,* which followed developments throughout the nation. On July 6, 1951, in a page 1 item titled "Dixie Papers Approve S.C. Jim Crow School Decision," the newspaper reported that by a two-to-one vote, the federal court at Charleston had upheld the state's right to maintain segregated schools. The paper assured its readers that the U.S. Supreme Court would be reviewing this decision, but in the meantime, and on the positive side, the South had "no alternative"; if it expected to maintain separate schools, it would have to invest millions of dollars "to bring Negro schools to the same level or nearer to the level of white schools." Nevertheless, segregation per se was "wrong," insisted editor James A. Hamlett Jr. "It is sinful and will only lead to damnation of our government. . . . The whole pattern is wrong and arguments, words, court decisions based on points of law, editorials from prejudice newspapers and its general promotion can't change segregation to right."[17]

For the Huxman court, however, the legal issue was not "black and white." The judges had to address a difficult question, and they did so in a unanimous decision issued on August 3, 1951. At the heart of Huxman's dilemma was one stark reality: the U.S. Supreme Court had clearly spoken to this issue, and his tribunal, reasoned the Kansas judge, was clearly "a subordinate court in the federal judicial system." The Supreme Court had consistently refused to overturn *Plessy,* which was the ruling precedent here, and in *Gong Lum v. Rice* (1927), a Mississippi case involving a Chinese child, "the court held that the question of segregation was within the discretion of the state in regulating its public schools," but it also had ruled that separating black students in a graduate school setting was unconstitutional. "If the denial of the right to commingle with the majority group in higher institutions of learning as in the Sweatt case and gain the educational advantages resulting therefrom, is lack of due-process, it is difficult to see why such denial would not result in the same lack of due process if practiced in the lower grades." This point was made even more explicit in the accompanying "Finding of Fact No. VIII," where the court stipulated:

> Segregation of white and colored children in public schools has a detrimental effect upon the colored children. The impact is greater when it has the sanc- tion of the law; for the policy of separating the races is usually interpreted as denoting the inferiority of the negro group. A sense of inferiority affects the mo- tivation of a child to learn. Segregation with the sanction of law, therefore, has a tendency to retard the educational and mental development of negro chil- dren and to deprive them of some of the benefits they would receive in a racial integrated school system.

Nevertheless, reasoned Judge Huxman, since the U.S. Supreme Court specif- ically chose to narrowly focus its decisions in past cases, *Plessy* and *Lum* had not been overturned, and they applied in *Brown.*[18] Basically, in his own subtle (or perhaps *not* so subtle) way, Huxman told the Supreme Court it was time to overrule *Plessy* and declare school segregation unconstitutional, but the high court, not a lower one, had to do so.

Curiously, in dissenting from *Briggs v. Elliott* just weeks before, South Carolina District Court Judge J. Waties Waring, confronting the same dilemma that caused the Kansas court to decide for the defendants, had ruled for the plaintiffs. He boldly, if somewhat creatively, declared that the

Supreme Court already had "definitely and conclusively established the doctrine that separation and segregation according to race is a violation of the Fourteenth Amendment." Judge Waring simply ignored *Lum* and asserted that *Plessy,* which concerned railroad accommodation only, was irrelevant; the ruling precedent in *Briggs,* he insisted, was *Sweatt v. Painter* (1950) and *McLaurin v. Oklahoma State Regents* (1950). Especially in light of the expert testimony showing "beyond a doubt that the evils of segregation and color prejudice come from early training," Waring insisted "the place to stop it is in the first grade and not in graduate school." This same testimony made it perfectly clear "that segregation in education can never produce equality and that it is an evil that must be eradicated. This case presents the matter clearly for adjudication and I am of the opinion that all of the legal guideposts, expert testimony, common sense and reason point unerringly to the conclusion that the system of segregation in education adopted and practiced in the State of South Carolina must go and must go now." In the judge's view, segregation was *"per se inequality."*[19]

Judge Waring was correct. By 1951 "any thoughtful person" should have concluded that it was time "to strike at the cause of the infection [i.e., segregation] and not merely at the symptoms of disease," and the "place" to strike was "in the elementary schools where our future citizens learn their first lesson to respect the dignity of the individual in a democracy." But his legal reasoning was, to say the very least, imaginative. In contrast, Huxman, the temperamentally moderate Kansas jurist, condemned the practice of segregation but wrote the only opinion he could have written. Walter A. Huxman was not J. Waties Waring. Although Huxman had a copy of the South Carolinian's uncompromising dissent in his possession during deliberations, he counseled patience.[20] It was, in Huxman's opinion, important to follow the proper legal procedures. Both men were correct—the time for change was *now,* but real, pervasive change had to be effected by the nation's highest tribunal.

Perhaps Judge Huxman knew, or believed, in 1951 what Judge Jean S. Breitenstein, U.S. Circuit Court of Appeals, Denver, observed some two decades later: "Judge Huxman wrote good opinions which clearly defined the facts, the issues, and the controlling law. They were understandable." Huxman, according to Breitenstein, was recognized on several occasions by the justices of the U.S. Supreme Court as "a distinguished member of the Kansas bar" whose opinions/decisions carried considerable weight. Reportedly, the judge himself simply "felt" he "had no choice, in the light of past decisions, but to uphold the Kansas law. If I were on the Supreme court," said Huxman some years later, "I would vote to overrule the decision I had made. I do not believe in segregation."[21]

In the final analysis, it is difficult, perhaps, to improve on the January 1973 observations of Kansas Supreme Court Justice Richard H. Kaul. According to Kaul, Huxman's application of his long-held judicial philosophy that "the Constitution is pliable, but it must be approached with a sense of responsibility" was clearly

> illustrated in his opinion for the Tenth Circuit in the landmark case of *Brown v. Topeka Board of Education.* Judge Huxman was torn between his own philosophical beliefs and judicial responsibility dictated by the rules of *stare decisis.* A long line of United States Supreme Court decisions, commencing with *Plessy v. Ferguson,* without deviation compelled adherence to the then prevailing separate, but equal doctrine. Judge Huxman, however, so constructed the opinion that it served, at least in part, as a vehicle for later reversal by the Supreme Court when it overthrew the long-standing doctrine in its momentous decision.

Certainly there is no reason to doubt that the Kansas jurist was just as convinced as was his South Carolina colleague that the time had come for "separate but equal" to go. And so it did, on May 17, 1954.[22]

As "the case of the century" made its way through a first and second hearing in the U.S. Supreme Court to that final landmark decision written by Chief Justice Earl Warren, Judge Waring became progressively more outspoken in his antisegregationism, and in 1952, "in the face of local hostility," Waring and his wife left Charleston for New York City.[23] Huxman's post-*Brown* life and career were far less tumultuous. The Kansan remained on the federal court until 1957, when he assumed senior status, retiring completely from the bench and closing his Topeka office in May 1964. In retirement and at the time of his death, which came on June 25, 1972, Huxman was "esteemed as a great judge" by his associates, and, said Judge Breitenstein, "had a keen sense of justice and worked indefatigably to attain what he deemed to be the correct result in every case." [24]

Walter A. Huxman was not free of prejudice any more than Kansas was free of prejudice, but as governor and as a federal judge he was out front, motivating others to make the *right* decisions. It is perhaps telling that his closest friends and colleagues were unaware of his decisive role in the desegregation of the medical school, prior to reading about it in the 1990s. Huxman seldom spoke of his pivotal role in *Brown*.[25] The judge was not a self-promoter but a modest, mild-mannered man—some might say a quintessential Kansan, who led by example and thus moved Kansas and the nation slowly forward, leaving it a little better and fairer place for all.

Gerald B. Winrod: From Fundamentalist

Preacher to "Jayhawk Hitler"

Leo P. Ribuffo

During the 1920s Gerald Burton Winrod enjoyed regional prominence as a Protestant fundamentalist preacher and publisher based in Wichita, Kansas. By the late 1930s he was nationally notorious as the "Jayhawk Hitler," a proponent of an extraordinary anti-Semitic conspiracy theory, an admirer of Nazi Germany, and a target of Federal Bureau of Investigation (FBI) surveillance. Although Winrod's transition from fundamentalism to the political far right was not inevitable, his religious beliefs predisposed him to accept sweeping conspiracy theories and influenced his brand of anti-Semitism.[1]

Winrod grew up in the fundamentalist movement. He was born on March 7, 1900, the first child of John Wesley and Mabel Craig Winrod. According to family folklore, the Winrods' faith had been molded by two events. First, John had been moved to give up his job as a bartender when Carry Nation smashed his saloon. Second, in 1910 Mabel had been healed of breast cancer through

Gerald B. Winrod (March 7, 1900–November 11, 1957), a Wichita fundamentalist, evangelist, and anti-Semitic publisher, known to many as the "Jayhawk Hitler," was the center of much unwanted attention in 1942 when a District of Columbia grand jury indicted him for conspiring to cause insubordination in the armed forces. Courtesy of the Kansas State Historical Society.

divine intervention. The family became increasingly devout. Around 1918 John felt called to preach, and by 1925 he and Mabel had established the Healing Temple in Wichita.

Also according to family lore, Gerald was even more devout than his parents. He passed through a conversion experience at age eleven (at roughly the same time that the family thought Mabel had been miraculously healed) and preached his first sermon a year later. His formal schooling apparently ended after the fifth grade, but the noted revivalist Newton N. Riddell subsequently tutored him in theology. After combining preaching with a job as a bookkeeper, Winrod became a full-time evangelist in his early twenties. In November 1925 he convened a meeting in Salina, Kansas, where thirty theologically conservative clergymen and laymen voted to create the Defenders of the Christian Faith with Winrod as executive director. He began to publish the *Defender* magazine in April 1926.

Winrod soon established a routine that lasted until his death in 1957. His chief goal was to build up the Defenders as an interdenominational parachurch organization. With the exception of 1930–1931, when he led an Oklahoma City tabernacle and contemplated settling into that pastorate, he used Wichita as his home base. In addition to editing the *Defender*, he began preaching over the radio and supervised Defender missionary activities abroad. Typically Winrod left home for weeks or months at a time, delivering hundreds of sermons in pulpits elsewhere. Even critics conceded that the six-foot-two–inch evangelist exuded an impressive platform presence. Unlike the stereotypical flamboyant fundamentalist, personified for the news media of the era by Billy Sunday, Winrod preferred a calm presentation and a dignified demeanor.

By the mid-1920s the conflict between Protestant theological liberals and theological conservatives—the most prominent of whom had begun to call themselves fundamentalists—had attracted national attention. Individuals often struggled with the intellectual issues, and the spectrum of Protestant opinion was less clear than rival polemicists charged. Broadly speaking, however, theological conservatives affirmed the "inerrancy" of the Bible, the divinity of Jesus Christ, and the validity of biblical miracles while theological liberals expressed varying degrees of doubt. In addition, a small minority of theological liberals invoked Jesus' name on behalf of a politically liberal regulatory or welfare state. Usually eschewing this social gospel, theological conservatives stressed the necessity of personal conversion; when commenting on public affairs they focused on personal rather than social sins, notably prostitution, divorce, and the consumption of alcohol. In 1919 Rev. William Bell Riley, a Minneapolis Baptist, took the lead in creating the World's Christian Fundamentals Association (WCFA) in order to more effectively combat Protestant "modernists," as opponents usually characterized theological liberals. Equally important was the group's campaign to bar the theory of evolution from being taught in public schools. In 1926 Winrod assisted Riley's unsuccessful effort against Darwinism in Minnesota and became the WCFA extension secretary. In addition to Riley, many other prominent fundamentalists worked alongside Winrod at religious conferences or joined the *Defender* editorial board. Although scorning fellowship with Roman Catholics and Protestant "modernists," Winrod was more willing than many other strict fundamentalists to cooperate with Pentecostals, whose belief in faith healing seemed to him to be a virtue rather than a heresy. He also cultivated good relations with the large Mennonite community in Kansas. Even after he became an outspoken anti-Semite, he remained sufficiently respectable among theological conservatives to receive an honorary doctorate from the Bible Institute of Los Angeles in 1935.[2]

Until Winrod made his transition to conspiratorial anti-Semitism during 1932–1934, the chief arguments presented in his magazine and books were commonplace among theologically conservative Protestants. For instance, he attacked evolution for two familiar reasons. First, evolution was a false materialist philosophy rather than verifiable science. Second, this philosophy fostered brutality and immorality ranging from German atrocities during World War I to the pervasive "moral sag" of the postwar Jazz Age. For Winrod, as for most theological conservatives, immorality meant personal vices rather than greed, graft, or economic exploitation. He especially condemned Hollywood movies, loosening sexual mores, and violations of prohibition.[3]

The current moral decline was only the latest manifestation of human sinfulness that had persisted since Adam and Eve. The only antidote was what Winrod called "old-fashioned holy ghost religion." Salvation required the acceptance of Jesus Christ as one's personal savior. Even the embrace of Jesus did not obliterate the human propensity to sin. But God's agents in this world—angels—helped true Christians to reject the temptations offered by the demons who served as Satan's earthly agents.

By the 1920s many fundamentalists, including Winrod, employed a complicated method of biblical interpretation known as premillennial dispensationalism. Properly construed, the Bible explained all human history—past, present, and future. During five previous epochs—dispensations—God had offered prosperity and salvation, but each time, starting with Adam and Eve, sinful humanity had reneged on the covenant. The sixth dispensation had begun with Jesus' crucifixion and was still in progress. Once again humanity would fall short, and this time the dispensation would end with God's final judgment. Satan would temporarily rule through his human agent, the Antichrist (or Beast), whose crimes would include creation of a dictatorial world government and a false international religion, which, Winrod joined other fundamentalists in inferring, would combine Roman Catholicism and Protestant modernism. True Christians would suffer persecution during this period of "tribulation." Then Jesus would return, defeat the Antichrist in battle at Armageddon, and rescue the true church of believers. After a thousand years—the millennium— Satan would again rally the forces of evil but suffer inevitable defeat. The final judgment of all souls and inauguration of God's kingdom would follow.[4]

The biblical citations used to support this interpretation of human history might have seemed strained, occasionally even to Winrod, but premillennial dispensationalism was immediately consequential. Along with many other fundamentalists, Winrod believed that the temporary triumph of the Antichrist and Jesus' second coming would occur in his lifetime. Accordingly, he searched scripture and the news media for signs that prophecy was being fulfilled. The Antichrist was probably alive already, and Winrod joined many other fundamentalists during the 1920s in believing that his name was Benito Mussolini.[5]

Dispensationalism prepared the way for Winrod's transition to the far right in two important ways. First, it disposed him to believe that there were no accidents in history. Rather, history in the broadest sense could be explained as the conflict between God's children and a satanic conspiracy. Second, Jews played a crucial role in these events, especially in the last days. Shortly before Jesus' return, some of them would reestablish their ancient kingdom in Palestine—a prophecy confirmed by the British capture of Jerusalem in 1917, the Balfour Declaration, and the Zionist movement. At the same time, a minority of Jews would convert to Christianity. To help along this prophecy, so to speak, Winrod pursued missionary work among Jews and welcomed "Hebrew Christians" into fundamentalist ranks.

Although Winrod examined world events for signs of prophecies fulfilled, during the 1920s he only occasionally paid attention to politics in the conventional sense. In 1928 he joined fundamentalists and many theological liberals in opposing the presidential candidacy of Democrat Alfred E. Smith, a Catholic and "wet" foe of prohibition. Until late 1930 the *Defender* paid scant attention to the Great Depression, which Winrod viewed primarily as a divine judgment on an immoral nation and yet another sign that the last days were at hand. Instead of economic tinkering, the United States needed a religious revival. In 1932 Winrod endorsed the Prohibition Party's presidential candidate.

There was never any possibility that Winrod would approve of President Franklin D. Roosevelt and the New Deal. As Winrod made clear in 1933, he was appalled by the administration's repeal of prohibition and recognition of the atheistic Soviet Union. Moreover, as a small businessman—a religious publisher—he belonged to a class generally opposed to federal regulation and the welfare state. By early 1933, however, Winrod combined standard conservative complaints about FDR with an argument that the New Deal represented the latest phase in a conspiracy at least as old as human history. These charges increasingly appeared in the *Defender*, in pamphlets and radio addresses, and between May 1934 and January 1937 in a second, more conventionally political magazine called the *Revealer*.

Borrowing themes from conservative publicists and members of Congress, Winrod accused the Roosevelt administration of using federal relief jobs to buy votes, denounced excessive bureaucracy, perceived parallels between the New Deal and Soviet communism, and speculated that the United States teetered on the verge of tyranny. Yet such complaints supplemented an updated version of Winrod's denunciation of the country's moral decline. Simply put, the New Deal institutionalized the moral sag. As Winrod lamented, Roosevelt's cosmopolitan advisers drank alcohol, used foul language, and allowed themselves to be photographed surrounded by worshipful young women. When a drunk driver ran into Winrod's car in 1936, he telegraphed the White House and, holding Roosevelt "PERSONALLY RESPONSIBLE" for the return of the saloon, demanded $100 for the repairs.[6]

Winrod placed his political analysis within the prophetic context of premillennial dispensationalism. For instance, the blue eagle, the symbol of the New Deal National Recovery Administration, resembled the Beast described in the Book of Revelation. As proliferating signs signaled the approaching tribulation, Winrod contemplated how much Americans would suffer during the inevitable conflict between Christ and the Antichrist. Reading scripture through the lenses of patriotism, Winrod inferred that God blessed the United States more than other nations. Perhaps if a revival began at last, the country might be spared from the worst suffering.[7]

The role of Jews in the prophetic scenario looked more important than ever. In 1932 Winrod announced that he had recently "learned of a HIDDEN HAND consciously preparing the way" for the rise of the Antichrist.[8] The phrase "hidden hand," as well as the framework for Winrod's subsequent elaboration, came from *The Protocols of the Learned Elders of Zion. The Protocols,* a vicious anti-Semitic tract written by Russian royalists in the early twentieth century, ostensibly recorded the deliberations of an international Jewish conspiracy dedicated to the destruction of Christian civilization. The elders not only spread liberal ideas to undermine morality but also secretly controlled both communism and international capitalism. When this iniquitous fiction reached the United States shortly after World War I, no one embraced it with greater credulity than Henry Ford. Ford's newspaper, the *Dearborn Independent,* ran a long series, *The International Jew,* in which the anti-Semitic central theme of *The Protocols* was adapted to "explain" American developments ranging from the Federal Reserve Act to the popularity of jazz.

Winrod hedged on the question of the authenticity of *The Protocols,* but his writings after 1935 reveal a belief in their accuracy. Dispensationalism had disposed him to view events in orderly terms without contingency. Here was an even simpler scheme to explain everything, a scheme, moreover, that also highlighted Jewish actions. Winrod used *The Protocols* as if they were a newly discovered biblical text. He combined *The Protocols;* dispensationalist prophecy; and venerable anti-Semitic stereotypes, lore, and language to tell a story of alleged Jewish perfidy that stretched across millennia.

According to Winrod, both the Old Testament and the New Testament showed Jews disobeying God's will. Forebears of the contemporary elders of Zion manipulated a Roman "gentile front" to crucify Jesus Christ. The Talmud was a precursor of *The Protocols.* Disguised Jewish ideas corrupted Christianity during the Middle Ages and Reformation. Adding an anti-Semitic twist to a classic Protestant countersubversive myth, Winrod claimed that a Judaized Society of Bavarian Illuminati had fomented the French Revolution. Using *The International Jew* as his authority, Winrod charged Jacob Schiff, a Jewish capitalist, with financing the Communist revolution in Russia. Joseph Stalin was merely a "gentile front" that obscured control of the Soviet Union by a Jewish cabal. Moreover, despite Soviet rhetoric promoting world revolution, this cabal lived like exploitative capitalists. Similarly, Jews were the chief force behind the New Deal. In the mid-1930s Winrod joined many other far-right activists in claiming that FDR was descended from Jews. At roughly the same time he broke with prevailing dispensationalist opinion to predict that the Antichrist himself would be Jewish. The Jewish conspirators who operated over the millennia served Satan's evil ends—often unknowingly. Yet that foreordained role did not absolve them of responsibility for their actions.

Winrod's attitude toward Jews as flesh-and-blood human beings during the 1930s is hard to pin down. In a letter to the FBI Mrs. Jim Craig, a cousin by marriage, reported hearing Winrod say, "If he had his way every Jew would be annihilated!" Such an outburst was certainly possible, though the FBI seems to have been unimpressed by Mrs. Craig as an informant. Certainly Winrod accepted anti-Semitic stereotypes that had circulated for centuries in Christian culture: Jews were unusually tricky, greedy, and immoral. Yet Winrod's public statements contain little of the joyous invective against Jews that characterized such of his far-right contemporaries as Silver Shirt leader William Dudley Pelley; "radio priest" Charles Coughlin; or Coughlin's Protestant counterpart, Gerald L. K. Smith.[9]

Dispensationalism not only disposed Smith toward anti-Semitism but also shaped the kind of anti-Semitism he preached. Without any sense of inconsistency, Winrod denounced an alleged international Zionist conspiracy and continued trying to bring Jews to Jesus. In a strict sense, there was no inconsistency, since unconverted Jews were less than fully virtuous and destined to face God's punishment. Yet Winrod was genuinely puzzled that converted Jews viewed him as an anti-Semite rather than an unbiased interpreter of Bible prophecy.

Between the mid-1930s and U.S. entry into World War II, Winrod repeated his favorite themes over and over, often reprinting whole paragraphs from earlier issues of the *Defender.* His views underwent two significant changes. First, he muted his criticism of those Catholics, including Father Coughlin, whom he regarded as de facto allies in his battle against Roosevelt, communism, and/or the Jewish conspiracy. Much more important, he grew increasingly sympathetic to Adolf Hitler and Nazi Germany. In a 1933 pamphlet called *Hitler in Prophecy,* Winrod had speculated that Hitler's brutality and infatuation with Teutonic mysticism offered a taste of what life would be like during the Antichrist's reign. But the next year he began to look favorably on Nazi Germany as a bulwark against the Jews who controlled international communism and international capitalism. Moreover, Germans were defending their culture against lustful Jews even worse than their counterparts in Hollywood. While excessive sympathy was lavished on German Jews, the suffering of Christians persecuted in the Soviet Union was barely noticed. Finally, Winrod decided that Hitler was a good Catholic rather than a Teutonic mystic. The FBI reported that Winrod destroyed all remaining copies of the hostile *Hitler in Prophecy.*[10]

Rumors have circulated for seven decades that Winrod changed his mind about Nazism because Nazi officials courted him during a 1935 trip to Germany. An informant, apparently for the B'nai B'rith Anti-Defamation League, quoted Winrod as saying not only that he had met Hitler and propaganda chief Joseph Goebbels but also that he planned to do their work in the United States. Given Winrod's relative obscurity at that point, meetings with Hitler and Goebbels seem highly unlikely. The FBI was able to ascertain "very little detail" about his visit to Germany and nothing about alleged meetings with Nazi officials. When Winrod visited several European countries in 1934–1935, anti-Semitism was already very much on his mind. For example, while in France he discussed the authenticity of *The Protocols* with the son of one of the Russian royalists who had introduced them into the United States. Winrod publicly insisted that his four days in Germany were spent primarily in religious studies at Wittenberg. Somewhere along the line he befriended Otto Melle, a German Methodist bishop who showed more enthusiasm for Nazism than was typical among German clergy. Winrod entertained Bishop Melle in Wichita in 1939.[11]

In 1938 Winrod ran for the Republican nomination for U.S. senator from Kansas against three other candidates: former Governor Clyde Reed, former state senator Dallas Knapp, and Methodist minister Jesse Fisher. His decision to seek public office followed several years of increasing attention to state politics. In 1932 Winrod endorsed the independent gubernatorial candidacy of Dr. John R. Brinkley. Subsequently he chided Governor Alfred M. Landon and Senator Arthur Capper for insufficient zeal in criticizing the New Deal. Brinkley's strong showing in the gubernatorial races of 1930 and 1932 suggests an additional motivation that could not have been lost on Winrod: even a candidate as unconventional as he might actually win the nomination in a four-person race. Anti-Semitism would not necessarily disqualify him among the many Kansans who had belonged to the Ku Klux Klan during the 1920s. He was a skilled speaker both on the platform and over the radio, and he had many loyal supporters in and out of state, though the strength of this network remains uncertain. In 1937 Winrod claimed to have secured one million signatures on petitions opposing FDR's plan to expand the U.S. Supreme Court.

Winrod toured Kansas and spoke often on radio stations WIBW and KCKN. Although he continued to assert that a national moral sag was the ultimate source of Depression-era problems, Winrod sounded for the most part like an ordinarily conservative Kansas Republican. He assailed New Deal bureaucracy, promised a better program for farmers than the Agricultural Adjustment Administration, and appealed to state pride. He presented himself as a small businessman. He contrasted Kansas' relatively strong Christian morality with the decadent ethos of New York and San Francisco. He said nothing specifically about an international Jewish conspiracy stretching back to the biblical patriarchs, about FDR's putative Jewish ancestors, or about Hitler's virtues as a bulwark against communist Jews.

Because many recalled that these issues had recently ranked among Winrod's favorite themes, his promising candidacy attracted national attention. President Roosevelt asked *Emporia Gazette* editor William Allen White how an "openly" fascist agitator could stand a good chance of winning the Republican Senate nomination.[12] FDR need not have worried. Those who recalled a less cautious Winrod mobilized to publicize his devotion to a bigoted conspiracy theory. Former Governor Landon and John D. Hamilton, the Republican national chairman, nudged their party behind Clyde Reed. No critic was more zealous, or ultimately more damaging to Winrod's reputation, than Leon M. Birkhead, a former Unitarian minister from nearby Kansas City, Missouri, with whom Winrod had feuded since the early 1920s. In 1937 Birkhead had founded Friends to Democracy to combat an expanding far right, and now he singled out his old adversary Winrod as a leader of a formidable party "friendly to Hitler."[13] Despite this array of opposition Winrod attracted 53,149 votes in the Republican primary (21.4 percent), finishing third behind Clyde Reed and Dallas Knapp. He received strong support from Mennonites and also from districts where the Ku Klux Klan had been popular during the 1920s.

After attributing his defeat to Jewish influence, Winrod returned to watching the deteriorating world situation through a dispensationalist lens. Even as he had grown to admire aspects of the Nazi regime, Winrod had had trouble placing Germany into a prophetic scheme that, according to his reading of scripture, required an alliance with Russia that seemed implausible for most of the 1930s. The Nazi-Soviet Pact of 1939 resolved this problem, as he proudly announced in a special prophetic edition of the *Defender*.

During the next two years Winrod worked against U.S. entry into World War II. Perhaps due to the influence of Kansas Mennonites, he showed more respect for pacifism than did other far-right activists. Yet most of his arguments were borrowed from secular noninterventionists rather than from religious pacifists: war profiteers favored intervention, war to save democracy abroad would destroy democracy at home, and FDR could not be trusted. But this standard fare was adapted to fit Winrod's conspiratorial anti-Semitism. According to Winrod, the Jewish conspiracy that had lured the United States into World War I was promoting intervention again, but Americans must not shed their blood just because these conspirators wanted to save German Jews.

Energetic as ever in his writing and speaking, Winrod nonetheless faced mounting difficulties during 1939–1941. With increasing frequency the news media portrayed him as a key figure in the international fascist movement. Subscriptions to the *Defender* declined. Responding to citizen inquiries about

Winrod, the FBI began regular surveillance in 1939. With the exception of William Bell Riley, who shared Winrod's belief in *The Protocols,* prominent fundamentalists distanced themselves from him. Although Northern fundamentalists typically looked askance at the New Deal, most spent the 1930s building a religious infrastructure of radio stations and Bible colleges instead of engaging in far-right politics.

Winrod's family life deteriorated too. On May 27, 1940, his wife, Frances, went to the Wichita police for protection. Not only did she consider her husband's political views unchristian, but she also thought him dangerously unstable. She said that Winrod expected to be "nominal head of the country" after a revolution and had acquired a pistol to fight his enemies. Frances was granted an emergency divorce, with Winrod agreeing to pay a $5,000 lump sum and monthly support for their three children. In March 1941 FBI director J. Edgar Hoover placed Winrod on a list of persons "to be considered for custodial detention in the event of a national emergency."[14]

After U.S. entry into World War II in December 1941, Winrod muted both his criticism of the Roosevelt administration and his anti-Semitism. Although subscribers to the *Defender* would have had no trouble reading between the lines to find old themes, patriotism affected his actions and his interpretation of scripture. He organized a national network of followers who pledged to pray at least fifteen minutes each day for the United States; he also inferred from the Bible that the country would not be invaded. Winrod's wartime restraint did not mollify his opponents. FDR repeatedly prodded his attorney general to prosecute the "seditionists." In July 1942 a grand jury impaneled in the District of Columbia indicted Winrod along with more than two dozen other men and women under the Smith Act for conspiring to cause insubordination in the armed forces.

After much legal maneuvering, the trial of Winrod and twenty-nine other far-right activists, German American Bundists, and publicists for Nazi Germany began in Washington in April 1944. As defense counsel stressed, the government case was weak even by the loose standards of conspiracy cases. The defendants had almost never disseminated their writings among the armed forces, and few knew each other. They sometimes bonded during the trial, however, with Winrod trying to convince his fellow defendants that the Antichrist stalked the earth. Cooperating with the prosecution, the FBI checked Winrod's mail for secret codes and messages in invisible ink but found nothing. The trial ended in November 1944 when the presiding judge died suddenly of a heart attack.[15]

By the time a federal court of appeals ruled out a retrial in 1947, Winrod had begun to feel a sense of vindication. As the Cold War escalated, he presented himself as a pioneer anticommunist. He fitted new national concerns into familiar frameworks. Violent television programs offered the latest evidence of an American moral decline. The Korean War, flying saucers, and nuclear weapons—the "stone of fire" prophesied in the Book of Ezekiel—signaled the Antichrist's imminent but temporary triumph. Although less vehement than before World War II, Winrod still discerned a satanic Jewish conspiracy that in the 1950s destroyed Senator Joseph R. McCarthy, prevented President Harry S. Truman from effectively fighting communism, and threatened President Dwight D. Eisenhower when he sided against Israel during the Suez crisis.

Winrod and Frances had reconciled before the sedition trial, and apparently their home life remained stable. Although Winrod remained a fixture on the residual anti-Semitic far right, Defender enterprises thrived during the post–World War II religious revival. *Defender* subscriptions climbed to 100,000, almost reaching the peak of 110,000 claimed before the 1938 Senate campaign. Defender missionary activities grew in the Caribbean, Mexico, and the Middle East. As always, Winrod spent much time on the road.

According to the recollections of his associates, Winrod's health visibly declined during the 1950s. Perhaps worries about his own health contributed to his last crusade—on behalf of dissident physicians and full-fledged quacks who promoted spurious cures for cancer. The memory of his mother's cancer had never left Winrod. He believed that he had developed tumors decades earlier and had been saved by one of the quacks he subsequently championed. But this last crusade was energized by more than memories of Mabel Winrod's suffering and concern about his own health. At least as important was the fact that the quacks were scorned by federal regulators and remained open to the possibility of supernatural healing.

Not cancer but influenza and his own rejection of orthodox medicine cost Winrod his life at a relatively early age. He came down with the flu during the 1957 epidemic but refused to consult a doctor. Finally, too late, he agreed to see an osteopath, a personal friend. He died on November 11, 1957.

Winrod was a Kansan who made a difference, but not in the way he hoped. He wanted to bring Kansas, the Midwest, and ultimately the United States "back" to conservative Protestant morality in general and fundamentalist doctrine in particular. In the end, ironically, his career reinforced two stereotypes from the 1920s and 1930s. The first posits that all theological conservatives are "paranoid" bigots, and the second presumes that provincial Kansans are particularly susceptible to such forms of bigotry. Both stereotypes survive among ostensibly cosmopolitan intellectuals who continue to wonder, on the basis of superficial investigation, what's the matter with Kansas.

19

John Steuart Curry: A Portrait of the Artist as a Kansan

Marjorie Swann and William M. Tsutsui

During his lifetime John Steuart Curry was no hometown hero—at least not to the folks who actually lived "back home" in Kansas. For the artistic opinion-makers of the Northeast, Curry's value as a painter was inextricable from his identity as a Kansan: he was "Curry of Kansas," the "greatest painter Kansas has produced." Kansans, however, dared to think otherwise. They found Curry's depictions of tornadoes and fanatics thematically offensive and technically flawed: his subjects ranged from "gloomy to morbid," his cows looked like "they were painted with lipstick," and his pigs were anatomically incorrect. Kansans' attitude toward their would-be artistic "messiah" was summed up trenchantly by one visitor to Curry's 1931 exhibition at the Kansas City Art Institute: "I wouldn't want any of these pictures on my walls."[1]

Since the 1990s, however, Kansans seem to have reconsidered their relationship to John Steuart Curry. A resolution passed by the Kansas Senate in

[handwritten margin note: cite for Kansas dislike b Curry]

John Steuart Curry (November 14, 1897–August 29, 1946), an estranged native son of Kansas, seen here at his University of Wisconsin studio easel in May 1941, achieved fame and success as a member of the great triumvirate of Midwest Regionalist painters. Courtesy of the Kansas State Historical Society.

1992, for example, declares the state's "homage" to the artist, and the Native Sons and Daughters of Kansas have given Curry a posthumous Kansan of the Year award.[2] The hype Curry generated outside the state during his career has been recast as a kind of legitimate "fame" that Kansans should respect, and Curry's once ridiculed images have become cherished symbols of the state's identity. Indeed, Curry's reputation has been so dramatically rehabilitated that the artist is now as much a Kansas icon as the wild-eyed John Brown he painted on the walls of the capitol in Topeka.

Yet it is questionable whether John Steuart Curry deserves such esteem. Other Kansas artists have achieved fame; have better claims to be considered primarily as "Kansans"; and, because their artistic visions have resonated more strongly with the residents of Kansas, have been more beloved in the state. Thus, our current tendency to celebrate "Curry of Kansas" should be understood as the revival and belated home-state embrace of a mystique that was first created on the East Coast more than seventy years ago. This essay will explore the origins of the Curry myth, analyzing how John Steuart Curry came to be promoted as a native Kansan whose "authentic" vision of life in the state propelled him into a leading role in the American Regionalist movement. Stripped of this protective swaddling of mythology, Curry's status as the definitive "Kansas artist" becomes all the more dubious.

The basic outline of Curry's life and career is well known. John Steuart Curry was born on November 14, 1897, near Dunavant in northeast Kansas, the eldest child of Margaret and Thomas Smith Curry. Curry attended local public schools until he dropped out at the end of his junior year of high school. Having spent one month at the Kansas City Art Institute, Curry left Kansas for good in the fall of 1916, moving to Chicago to study at the School of the Art Institute. After briefly majoring in football at Geneva College in Pennsylvania, Curry next headed to New Jersey to study with the acclaimed illustrator Harvey Dunn. Under Dunn's tutelage Curry became especially skilled at producing "lusty blood-and-thunder scenes," and he was able to support himself during the first half of the 1920s by illustrating stories in magazines such as *Boy's Life*.[3] During this period Curry also married his first wife, Clara Derrick, and took up residence in the chic artists' colony of Westport, Connecticut. When his career as an illustrator flagged, Curry left for Paris to study drawing, his remedial training in draftsmanship bankrolled by a wealthy New York patron.

Ironically, it was only after he had returned from Europe that John Steuart Curry became inspired by Kansas. In financial straits, Curry retreated to his

Westport studio and in August 1928 painted *Baptism in Kansas,* a depiction of a young woman about to be ritually immersed in a farmyard water tank. This painting became a milestone in Curry's career. Regarding *Baptism in Kansas* as "a gorgeous piece of satire," the East Coast art cognoscenti savored the exotic primitivism of Curry's subject matter. *Baptism in Kansas* quickly garnered critical accolades, and Curry soon found himself patronized by the influential New York art maven Gertrude Vanderbilt Whitney, who also purchased the painting for the permanent collection of her new Whitney Museum of American Art. Curry had discovered his sales hook, and to reacquaint himself with the hinterland he had not visited for years, he spent six weeks in Kansas in the summer of 1929. More paintings of Kansas promptly appeared, including the now famous *Tornado,* which portrays a farm family scurrying into a storm cellar as a funnel cloud whirls toward them. After viewing Curry's 1930 solo exhibition at New York's Ferargil Galleries, the art critic for the *New York Times* proclaimed, "Kansas has found her Homer."[4]

Embarrassingly, however, Kansas seemed uninterested in acquiring any of the paintings produced by "her Homer." To enhance the artist's down-home image, Ferargil Galleries launched a campaign to persuade Kansans to open their hearts—and their pocketbooks—to John Steuart Curry. In 1931–1932 Ferargil arranged for exhibitions of Curry's paintings to be staged in Topeka, Kansas City, Lawrence, Manhattan, Emporia, and Wichita. Having seen two of these displays, Mrs. Henry J. Allen, the wife of a former governor, objected to Curry's obsession with "freakish" subjects and surmised that only New Yorkers' ignorance of the Midwest allowed them to believe that Curry's images were "peculiarly typical of Kansas soil."[5] It seems that Mrs. Allen's lack of enthusiasm typified most Kansans' response to Curry's work, for no individual or institution in the state would buy one of Curry's paintings until the Kansas State Agricultural College purchased the landscape *Sun Dogs* in 1935—although Curry did manage to persuade a garage owner in Kiowa, Kansas, to accept a watercolor as payment for some car repairs.

John Steuart Curry briefly abandoned Kansas subject matter—and his wife—in 1932, when he ran away from home to join the circus. In financial difficulties yet again and afflicted by a drinking problem, Curry found the ailing Clara "unreasonable" and was "desperate to free [his] mind." So Curry became an embedded artist with the Ringling Brothers–Barnum and Bailey Circus for several months, sketching the animals, freaks, and acrobats; he returned to Westport shortly after his wife died. Curry quickly got the circus out of his system, however, and was once again promoted by Ferargil Galleries [*rise to fame* — handwritten annotation] as a Kansas painter. By exhibiting his work alongside the canvases of Grant Wood of Iowa and the Missouri native Thomas Hart Benton, Curry emerged as a leading "Regionalist" artist. Ostensibly unsullied by European experiments in abstraction and inspired by their firsthand knowledge of the agrarian Midwest, Benton, Curry, and Wood became poster boys for American Regionalism, a kind of artistic nationalism that flourished during the mid-1930s. As Benton memorably observed, "We came in the popular mind to represent a home-grown, grass-roots artistry which damned 'furrin' influence and which knew nothing about and cared nothing for the traditions of art as cultivated city snobs, dudes, and *ass*thetes knew them." When Curry briefly visited Grant Wood at his Stone City Colony and Art School in the summer of 1933, he and Wood donned overalls for a publicity photo; this image of the artist as a corn-fed rustic reached a national audience in the December 1934 issue of *Time,* illustrating the magazine's cover story on the rise of Regionalism and cementing Curry's status as the painter laureate of Kansas.[6] [*earlier form Regionalism* — handwritten annotation]

Personally and professionally, Curry was on the upswing. In June 1934 he married Kathleen Gould Shepherd, the British ex-wife of one of Curry's Westport friends. A solo exhibition of recent work opened at the Ferargil Galleries in 1935, and critics enthusiastically hailed Curry's return to his Midwestern roots. M. Sue Kendall noted that Curry then began to cultivate his identity as a Kansan "by deliberately affecting the persona of a down-home Kansas farmer, and by stressing his associations with the heartland whenever he was interviewed"—by wearing overalls for the camera, as it were. Yet this program of image management could not be entirely successful as long as Curry lived in Connecticut, so his supporters launched a campaign to repatriate Curry to the land of his birth. Although Curry seems to have taken no active part in this effort, his boosters energetically twisted Midwestern arms on Curry's behalf. No universities in Kansas could be persuaded to create a faculty position for him, but the College of Agriculture at the University of Wisconsin was willing to designate Curry "artist-in-residence." Thus, in 1936, two decades after he had left Dunavant, John Steuart Curry returned to the Midwest. A poem from his new friends in Wisconsin assured the refugee from Westport that he would still be able to keep abreast of the latest trends by reading the *New Yorker* every week.[7]

But Wisconsin was not Kansas, as Curry and the proponents of Regionalism were all too aware. An article about Curry in the first issue of *Life* magazine pointedly observed, "Wisconsin's apparent object is to steal Curry from

[*1936* — handwritten annotation]

his native Kansas, which has notably failed to buy his pictures."[8] Just how "authentic" was John Steuart Curry's vision of Kansas if the state remained stubbornly aloof? So a new scheme was hatched to bring Curry home—this time to paint murals in the Kansas State Capitol in Topeka. Although Kansas schoolchildren would be encouraged to donate their pennies to help pay for the paintings, the murals were never a grassroots initiative. William Allen White of Emporia had been enlisted in previous attempts to reconcile Curry with Kansas, and White now became a driving force behind the murals project. With the blessing of the governor, the Kansas Editorial Association agreed to raise $20,000 for the state-house murals, and a Murals Commission, made up largely of influential newspapermen, was quickly created to oversee the endeavor—and to ensure that John Steuart Curry was chosen to be the artist.

Curry conceived his Kansas murals as three related units. Each section would depict one aspect of the state's history: European colonization, culminating in the territorial period (*Tragic Prelude,* located in the east corridor); the experience of homesteaders (not executed, to have adorned the rotunda); and the contemporary farm family (*Kansas Pastoral,* displayed on the walls of the west corridor). Curry's preliminary sketches were released in November 1937, giving rise to a chorus of complaints that would accompany all of the artist's work on the murals. Members of the public ridiculed Curry's images in *Kansas Pastoral:* the stance of the bull was wrong, the pigs' tails were not properly curled, and the farm wife's skirt was too short. *Tragic Prelude* elicited disapproval on a more broadly thematic level. Predictably, Curry's towering figure of an apocalyptic John Brown, brandishing a rifle in one bloody, outstretched hand and a Bible in the other, occasioned the strongest protests. One state senator called *Tragic Prelude* a "wall of horror" and fumed that John Brown "was an erratic, crazy old coot and a murderer. I don't see any reason to perpetuate his memory."[9]

In the spring of 1941 Curry's plans for his state-house murals hit a wall of marble. During his time in Wisconsin Curry had become an advocate of soil conservation, and as the literal centerpiece of his Kansas murals Curry intended to paint in the rotunda images of drought, a dust storm, and soil erosion—damning emblems of irresponsible farming practices. When an opportunity arose to prevent Curry from thus painting yet another "wall of horror" in the capitol, some powerful politicians seized it. To create sufficient space for his murals in the rotunda, Curry needed to remove the panels of Italian marble above the wainscoting. The State Executive Council refused to take down the marble, de facto killing the rest of Curry's project; in response, Curry petulantly refused to sign the completed panels. One keen observer noted several years later that the artist would have better understood Kansans' reactions to his murals "had Curry spent more time in the state."[10]

By 1941 Curry's career was already in decline. He had returned to doing illustrations, and he made no sales from his last solo exhibition of new work held in 1938. After struggling for years with high blood pressure, John Steuart Curry died of a heart attack in Madison, Wisconsin, on August 29, 1946. Decades later his widow insisted that Curry's experience working on his murals in Topeka was, in part, responsible for killing him; however, it seems likely that Curry's habitual smoking, drinking, and "chunky" physique contributed more significantly to his chronic health problems.[11] Curry now lies buried in Winchester, Kansas; only with the paintbrush removed from his hand could John Steuart Curry finally come home again.

The image of Curry as the iconic Kansas artist—the image that warrants his inclusion in this book—was, as we have seen, scornfully rejected by Kansans during Curry's lifetime. Yet for the art establishment of the Northeast, "Curry of Kansas" was a dyed-in-the-wool Midwesterner whose paintings had value precisely because they depicted the artist's intimate knowledge of life in the atavistic heartland. Throughout his career the rhetoric used to lionize Curry reiterated two themes: Curry's status as a "native" Kansan and the resultant "authenticity" of the exotic events and landscape he documented. New York reviewers, praising the artist's "accurate, convincing portrayal of locality," asserted that "Kansas is Mr. Curry's state, and the pictures could only have been painted by a native son."[12]

However, Curry's identity was more complex and ambiguous than his East Coast audience cared to acknowledge. For starters, Curry's family did not live solely in Kansas. Curry's parents owned land in Arizona as well as their property near Dunavant, and as a youngster Curry spent one winter and "several summers" on his family's farm in Arizona. By the late 1930s Margaret and Thomas Curry were spending all their winters in the Salt River valley to avoid cold weather, and writing from Arizona in February 1938, Margaret Curry seemed unperturbed by the prospect of losing their farm in Kansas to foreclosure: "We are getting on comfortably here. . . . So we hate to throw good money into the gap." His family's physical and emotional detachment from Kansas was paralleled by Curry's own long-term residency in the Northeast. Although his loyal hagiographer, Laurence Schmeckebier, insisted that Curry's work was infused by a "homesick yearning" for the Midwest, Kathleen Curry would later admit that "John left the farm [in Kansas] as quickly as he could." Many of the artists active in Kansas during Curry's lifetime—such as William Dickerson, Herschel Logan, and Lloyd Foltz—had, like Curry, left the state to pursue training in Chicago but then returned home to forge their careers. Curry, by contrast, voluntarily lived far from the heartland until he had no choice but to accept the position offered to him in Wisconsin, and after his arrival in Madison, Curry confessed that he was suffering from "a state of worry over our removal from the East." Curry may have been "farm-reared"—in Arizona as well as Kansas—but he enjoyed the sophisticated social life of Westport, and he exhibited no burning desire to exchange this urbane existence for what New Yorkers regarded as "the aching monotony of life" in Kansas.[13]

Curry's depiction of Kansas was likewise more complicated than his supporters could appreciate. In East Coast art circles, Curry's status as a Regionalist painter rested on the assumption that he realistically documented his lived experience of the Midwest. However, rather than providing "a vigorous registration of observed fact," it seems that Curry created images of Kansas that fulfilled the expectations of his Eastern audience. Curry maintained, for example, that *Baptism in Kansas* accurately depicted a real event that occurred on a neighbor's farm, down to the credulity-stretching "doves descending in the ray of light from heaven." Although no eyewitness accounts disproved such an unlikely, symbol-ridden conjunction of avian behavior and atmospheric conditions, the very topography of Curry's painting calls its veracity into question. In a laudatory *New York Times* review, Edward Alden Jewell noted how Curry's landscape enhanced his depiction of the "religious fanaticism of the hinterland": "On all sides spread the flat Kansas prairies, stretching to a horizon that fences from the outer world this shut-in frenzy of the human soul." Although Northeasterners may well believe that Kansas is flatter than a pancake, the countryside around Dunavant does not, in fact, resemble a billiard table but, rather is marked by rolling hills. As Jewell's analysis suggests, in *Baptism in Kansas* Curry strove for psychological effect—designed to satisfy East Coast stereotypes—at the expense of realism and accuracy.[14]

The "authenticity" of Curry's depiction of Kansas is even more problematic in his celebrated 1929 painting, *Tornado*. Many commentators over the years have blithely assumed that *Tornado* originated from Curry's childhood memories. Yet as Kathleen Curry acknowledged, her husband "never really encountered a tornado." Not until May 1930—the year after Curry created *Tornado ridiculous are there tornados in KS*

in his Westport studio—did a funnel cloud touch down near his family's farm in Kansas. Curry's own mother had so little experience of tornadoes that she regarded the storms as fictions: "I had come to believe that tornadoes and caves [storm shelters] in Kansas were myths and believed by Easterners who don't know better." Given his complete lack of any personal observations of twisters, it seems likely that Curry modeled his painting on some of the first photographs of a tornado ever published: art historian Henry Adams argued persuasively that both the shape of the funnel cloud and the overall composition of Curry's *Tornado* replicated photographs of a Kansas storm taken in 1929. Thus, we find displayed in *Tornado* not the "authenticity" of personal memory but rather the love of melodrama that Curry had developed as an illustrator specializing in "blood-and-thunder scenes."[15]

So how did an artist with such a tenuous relationship to the Midwest become "Curry of Kansas"? With his typically acerbic insight, Thomas Hart Benton acknowledged that Curry, along with Wood and Benton himself, was just following a Regionalist script: "A play was written and a stage erected for us. Grant Wood became the typical Iowa small towner, John Curry the typical Kansas farmer, and I just an Ozark hillbilly. We accepted our roles."[16] Two Svengalis—both of them, ironically, Kansans—were central to creating the down-home image of Curry that the Northeastern media avidly promoted. To understand "Curry of Kansas," then, we must analyze the men most responsible for fashioning this mythologized figure: the writer Thomas Craven and the art dealer Maynard Walker.

merit in this argument

Thomas Craven was born in Salina, Kansas, in 1889. After graduating from Kansas Wesleyan University in 1908, Craven headed to Paris to study art; upon his return from Europe, he traveled extensively and worked as a reporter, teacher, railroad clerk, and sailor. Craven arrived in New York in 1912 and spent eight years trying, unsuccessfully, to become a poet. In 1920 Craven finally discovered his vocation when he published his first essay in art criticism; never one to be constrained by either diffidence or tact, the novice critic gleefully gave the British artist Frank Brangwyn "the drubbing of his life." Over the next two decades Craven would become a highly popular and influential critic, "a sort of H. L. Mencken of art" whose fierce yet caustically funny diatribes made him a best-selling author.[17]

It was Thomas Craven who most forcefully articulated the intellectual framework of the Regionalist movement. Simultaneously attacking European influences and championing the rise of an indigenous American art, Craven lambasted Americans' tendency to worship "the annual crop of chlorotic plants nurtured in the Bohemian slums of Europe." For Craven, great art was not "a universal practice" but instead responded to "a specific environment, the impression of a special civilization." Thus, rather than the ability to ape the latest European fads, the American artist "must have firsthand knowledge . . . sustained by observation and habitual intimacy with American life." Great art must also be representational rather than abstract; abstraction, according to Craven, was "the last resort of failure, a compensation for mental impotence and social maladjustment."[18]

Through his writings Craven created the image of the Midwestern Regionalist triumvirate that persists to this day. A reviewer judiciously observed in 1939, "If not the discoverer of Benton, Curry and Wood, [Craven] certainly has been their most persistent and effective advocate." In Craven's opinion, Midwesterners, naturally infused with a "melancholy, sharp-seeing interest in hard facts" and suspicious of foreign influences, were most likely to produce a truly "American" art; in the Regionalists, Craven insisted, he had found artists who lived as "an organic part" of their society, thus allowing their work to reflect "the color and character" of a uniquely American experience. To support his nativist ideology, Craven proclaimed Curry the embodiment of Kansas. Craven argued that Curry's childhood in the state had permanently imprinted him, "entered his blood and determined the direction of his art"; with Kansas thus hardwired into Curry's DNA, his paintings were necessarily rooted in "things directly observed and experienced." Brandishing his own childhood in Salina as the source of his intellectual authority, Craven brushed aside suggestions that Curry's paintings were not realistic but "theatrical": "I know better—I grew up in Kansas."[19]

Despite his paeans for the heartland, Craven spent his entire writing career in the Northeast. However, his own preference for life in New York did not prevent Craven from pushing John Steuart Curry to return to Kansas—and pushing Kansans to welcome their prodigal son home with a suitable sinecure. Craven, who was a friend as well as an ally of Curry, personally campaigned on the artist's behalf, although his letters suggest that Craven was unlikely to win any battle for Midwestern hearts and minds: "Don't let the impotent bastards bother you," he commanded Curry in 1935, "I shall be in Wichita late next month and will tell them a few things." Characteristically, Craven sat down at his desk on Long Island, wrapped himself in the Kansas flag, and howled with outrage when the "impotent bastards" frustrated his plans to repatriate Curry:

"As one Kansan to another, I cannot remain silent in the face of my state's refusal to seize upon . . . the talents of so sterling a character and so eminent an artist!"[20]

Using his own essentialism against him, one contemporary described Thomas Craven as "a red-haired Kansan capable of tornadoes of indignation." Unlike the arbitrary behavior of a tornado, however, the formidable storms of propaganda that Craven unleashed on behalf of John Steuart Curry were calculatedly self-serving. Craven needed an indigenous artistic hero, and so he created one using the materials at hand, transforming Curry into a Moses of the Great Plains, "destined to lead our art out of the wilderness of French imitation into the promised land of American independence." "Curry of Kansas," oozing Midwestern authenticity from every pore, was an essential prop in Craven's attempt to stage the triumph of Regionalism and thus establish his own position as the intellectual arbiter of American art.[21]

Maynard Walker likewise needed "Curry of Kansas," but to market paintings rather than fulfill an ideology. A New York art dealer originally from Garnett, Kansas, Walker regarded John Steuart Curry as an important member of his stable of artists, and he needed the imprimatur of Curry's "nativeness" and "authenticity" to sell Curry's canvases. A founding member of the Topeka Art Guild, Walker worked as art editor for the *Kansas City Journal-Post* in the late 1920s before moving to New York to become director of paintings at Ferargil Galleries. In this position Walker strove tirelessly to market Curry's work, enlisting his contacts among Kansas journalists, politicians, and art organizations to try to exhibit and sell Curry's paintings in the state.

When Walker left Ferargil in 1935 to strike out on his own, Curry, along with Benton and Wood, went with him, the trio of Regionalist artists becoming the "three-sided cornerstone" of the new Walker Galleries. Like Craven, Walker believed that Curry should not linger in the "too effete East," so he joined in the effort to relocate Curry to the heartland. (In the 1970s Walker briefly considered moving—with his cat, Figaro—back to Garnett but quickly abandoned the scheme and remained in the Northeast for the rest of his life.) Despite Walker's decade-long campaign on Curry's behalf, the artist decided to switch to another gallery early in 1941; as Benton and Wood had previously decamped, Curry's departure was a great blow to Walker, and Walker Galleries was never again a leader in the New York art scene. After Curry died Walker's published tributes stressed Walker's own role in promoting the artist, and he was hailed as "one of the first to appreciate the genius of John Steuart Curry."[22]

Walker gave many p[?]ys to library n Garnet, Very nice collection— I've been here

During the years that he represented Curry, his correspondence with the artist revealed Maynard Walker's unwavering focus on the bottom line. Although Walker enthusiastically supported Curry's decision to paint murals in the capitol in Topeka, he was also concerned that Kansas would exploit Curry financially and offered to help Curry negotiate a reasonable salary. With similar pragmatism, Walker repeatedly advised Curry that he would be able to sell more if he would price his work realistically and produce paintings that were not consistently "as big as a barn." Such hard-nosed practicality vanished, however, in Walker's public remarks about Curry. As James Dennis observed, Walker promoted Curry with "Cravenesque fervor and form," jumping aboard the Regionalist bandwagon to make his sales pitch. The leitmotifs of Craven's rhetoric—nativism and authenticity—recurred throughout Walker's puff-pieces on Curry. "Curry's art has its roots in the American soil" and springs directly from "his own native existence," Walker wrote in 1937. In his paintings of Kansas, Walker asserted, Curry "has created immortal epics from homely scenes hitherto wholly neglected" and "has been an ambassador at large, bringing honor to his native state." When dealing with skeptical Kansans, Walker was quick to cite his own Midwestern origins as the source of his "deep personal interest" in Curry and his belief that "as an interpreter of the Kansas life he knows, [Curry's] paintings are unique and are the work of a true and sincere artist." Underpinning these high-blown sentiments was, of course, the same concern with money that led Walker to urge Curry to paint smaller canvases. Maynard Walker's professional and financial success rested, in large part, on his ability to market Curry effectively, and thus for ten years he allied himself with Thomas Craven in creating and promoting "Curry of Kansas."[23]

In the end John Steuart Curry appears less like a "Homer," a "messiah," or a "painter laureate" than a cipher. As a persona manufactured in the Northeast, "Curry of Kansas" served a variety of agendas: to affirm stereotypes of the agrarian heartland, to legitimize a particular brand of art criticism, and to make money. In a self-congratulatory eulogy, Maynard Walker declared that without Curry, "Kansas would have no lasting artistic identity."[24] Yet this figure of a heroic John Steuart Curry rescuing Kansas from cultural oblivion obscures a more complex vision of both the state's artistic heritage and the conflicted, uncertain artist from Dunavant. By paying knee-jerk homage to "Curry of Kansas," we do justice neither to the history of Kansas nor to the life and work of John Steuart Curry.

why is this so damned evil - artists + dealer must make a living.

I totally disagree - so now we are but the propagandists on harassing

R. H. Garvey: "Operations Are Interesting"

Craig Miner

The word "operator" can have a conniving connotation. To Ray Hugh Garvey, however, it implied only the highest type of realistic responsibility. "Operations are interesting," he would say.

Sprung from a farm background in Phillips County, Kansas, where he was born in 1893, Garvey had early success as an attorney and owner of and dealer in wheat land. He later operated a group of filling stations; an investment company; a home construction, sales, and rental company; a petroleum exploration company; and numerous terminal grain elevators. He became controversial, but Garvey seemed to fear nothing except boredom. An outgoing, hard-driving man, visionary and practical, he impressed his associates as a force of nature. When he died in an automobile accident near Salina in 1959, there were many in Kansas who could not imagine the state without him.[1]

Garvey was temperamentally unsuited to bureaucracy. He ran many of his businesses as individual proprietorships or partnerships in which his personal responsibility, liability, and control were nearly unlimited. He was a person of

Ray Hugh Garvey (January 2, 1893–June 30, 1959), an attorney from western Kansas who turned his attention to real estate and large-scale wheat farming, became an entrepreneur extraordinaire with major interests in the petroleum, construction, and grain storage industries. Courtesy of the Kansas State Historical Society.

action, delighting in shaping the materials of his businesses to make a permanent contribution. "Here Today, Here Tomorrow," he would quip. To understand the entrepreneur and manager thus involves studying the man—his personality, philosophy, and experience—and what he made of the varying circumstances in which he found himself.

Several characteristics stand out: energy, intellectual curiosity, optimism, enthusiasm, common sense, family loyalty, emotional toughness, confidence, sense of humor, unassuming lifestyle, and interest in people.

Lest this seem a wholly positive list, it might be noted that he drove many of his managers to distraction. In their view he talked as a proponent of decentralized authority but acted as a micromanager, even an autocrat. A combination of preparation, instinct, and optimism led to a preternatural calm in facing risk, which could be disturbing to associates. Garvey's early farming partner John Kriss remembered that on a 1945 auto trip to eastern Colorado, where the two proposed to break tens of thousands of acres of grassland in the center of the Dust Bowl, R. H. went to sleep immediately at night while Kriss was wakeful and worried. The Garvey confidence could utterly convince. His wife, Olive, said, "My husband was a genius, and I never worried about a thing." But some saw his confidence as monomania, which resulted in unrealistic expectations and a tendency to oversimplify. R. H. could be blunt, even harsh. Garvey was dogmatic in his vilification of the New Deal and Franklin Roosevelt's internationalist foreign policy. William Allen White stopped corresponding with him the day after the Pearl Harbor attack. He sent Garvey an editorial titled "Don't Simplify Too Much." It said, "If you want to be happy in these days of turmoil when America is going through the valley of a dark shadow, don't be too cocky. Don't be too dead sure you are right." It was, White wrote, "the best way to end our discussion. You won't convince me and I wouldn't try to convince you."[2]

On the whole, however, people liked Garvey. In later years he was balding; his muscular frame, damaged by diabetes and heart trouble, tended to avoirdupois; and his face had a soft, good-humored look, which masked his intensity. His 1916 wedding picture, however, showed a slim Washburn College track athlete. By the Depression enough heft had been added to create a bull of a man. Garvey was always in motion—talking and gesturing, pounding a typewriter, calling on the telephone. Innocent of the snobbery of taste and class, he drove Ford cars and dressed casually. His multitrack mind was able to wrestle issues to a conclusion without fretting in a self-conscious way. He was sensitive to people's breaking points even when driving them to the brink. All the while he was engaging, disarming, friendly. He wrote his own ad copy and was a natural salesman. "If you take a negative attitude when you go out to sell an insurance policy," he wrote once, "thinking of the many reasons why you should not sell it or the many reasons why the customer should not buy it, you will not sell the policy." When he "put the pump handle" on people, as he phrased it, Garvey was capable of obtaining information without creating the feeling that the conversation had more than a social purpose. People loved to talk about themselves, and Garvey was a good listener with a retentive memory and a penchant to "copy the best." His speed in everything, along with his "human Univac" calculating intelligence, was beyond the capacity of most to fathom, though all could appreciate something special there. A *Kansas City Star* reporter who interviewed Ray and his son Willard in 1959 commented, "After a day with Ray Hugh Garvey, Kansas entrepreneur extraordinary, and one of his dynamic sons, a visitor feels like a ping-pong ball buffeted in a gale between two electric fans."[3]

It has been said that the entrepreneurial personality is one that thrives on change, enjoys feedback, is motivated by personal challenge more than money, and can abide loss and mistakes. These were all Garvey traits. He often used an educational image, noting that one must "pay tuition" to learn. R. H. emphasized that business was a full-time occupation for a person who wanted to devote to it every resource and skill available. "The making of money in itself was never a major concern," his wife recalled. "It was the game, the tantalizing magnetism of achievement."[4]

Garvey's career was shaped by a series of decisions made under conditions of uncertainty. His earliest moves showed typical independence. He went to college and law school, the first in his immediate family to have a higher education. He married Olive White, an extraordinary helpmate and later head of the Garvey enterprises. He moved to Colby in 1915. On his first day there he befriended a banker, W. D. Ferguson, who was to be a trusted confidant and investor for the life of both men. Garvey associated with a land dealer named A. A. Kendall. He studied the history of the weather and crops and learned dryland-farming methods, which were then far from universally employed. He talked to Asa Payne, the best practitioner of dryland techniques, and convinced himself that wheat farming in northwest Kansas could pay. Garvey formed the Garvey Land Company and moved into buying and selling land, retaining and farming it with tenants when land prices fell. He wrote ads for the *Colby Free Press* that contained lessons in farming, pieces of local history, and bits of philosophy and economics linking everything he had read to his current challenges, wondering out loud, for example, what Dante or Virgil would think of Thomas County's possibilities.

In 1924 Garvey purchased Service Oil Company and its regional gas stations. He understood that farming was a cyclic business and that gasoline sales might provide the income required to hold on to farm property. "It is a very smart thing to have a business diversified both as to locality and as to character," wrote Garvey in 1930.[5]

Garvey survived the Great Depression, even thrived in it in a sense, seeing opportunity in adversity. "This is an interesting period to live through," he wrote during those dark years, "if one lives through it."[6]

At the beginning of the Depression decade, however, it seemed he had made a series of mistakes. He moved to Wichita in 1929, seeking improved education for his children. Thus, he became an absentee landlord. The company he formed at Wichita, Amortibanc, provided retirement packages based on investment in farm and home mortgages. That model was legislated against, and both the value of the underlying investments and the interest of customers in retirement saving diminished. In 1930 he, Ferguson, and Dr. Jacob Geiger formed the Mutual Farming Company, but Kansas in 1931 outlawed farm corporations. This legislation was a blow to Garvey. "Large unit farming," he wrote in 1930, "is in the experimental stage, but it looks like a feasible method of raising grain."[7]

The situation seemed grim. Garvey reported to Ferguson in 1930 that men were working in Wichita for twenty-two cents an hour. Land he had bought for $90 an acre in 1920 was worth $27 in 1930. The wheat price, which had hovered between seventy-five cents and a dollar a bushel through the 1920s, dropped in 1932 to twenty-five cents. The Mutual Farming Company in 1931 abandoned 2,000 of its 9,000 acres of wheat. Garvey had, he wrote in 1931, "been preaching worse conditions for the past year than I really thought they were but they are turning out far worse than I was preaching."[8]

There was no question of walking away. Garvey had studied the history of economic cycles. The businesses that survived the periods of deflation and prospered in the upturn following, he observed, were run by people who "tightened up their belts, faced facts, and plugged away." The same had been true of the pioneers of western Kansas, where the "stickers" survived to prosper at the expense of the "kickers." Profit was the difference between income and costs. In a depression one cut operating costs and bought assets cheaply. The trick was adjusting quickly. Garvey quoted a sign he saw on the wall at a Wichita business, which read, "Nine-tenths of wisdom consists of being wise in time."[9]

Garvey believed people were spoiled. To the agents at Service Oil in 1933, he wrote, "If we can live as economically as our parents lived in 1890 or 1910, we probably will be as prosperous in 1933. . . . If you make $1,000 a year and spend $900 you are prosperous. . . . If you make $5,000 a year and spend $5,500, you are . . . going broke." He thought every business would be on an "intensely competitive basis" with a "margin of profit so small that each grocer will be wrapping his own groceries. . . . I would prefer trying to make the farming company pay than to make the Empire State Building pay."[10]

It is not true that Garvey bought up his land empire in the Dust Bowl days from starving farmers at giveaway prices. He said in 1931 that he had confidence that farmland in his region would be worth far more in fifteen to twenty years. But he was an operator, not a speculator, and he already had ten thousand acres, "quite a portion of which I have not been able to get good returns on."[11] His great expansion in landownership came in the 1940s. It is true, however, that he cut costs in a draconian way in the 1930s and changed his operating style. It was then that he developed his reputation as a low-cost producer.

A telling example of his discipline was his dismissal in 1933 of his farm manager from the corporate days, Claude Schnellbacher, and the formation of a partnership (G-K Farms) with John Kriss. Schnellbacher liked to keep machinery in perfect condition, farmsteads and fences painted and neat, and his cultivation attractive. Kriss was accustomed to poverty and making do. One was appropriate for expansive times, the other best for a crisis. Garvey wrote, "I think Claude is looking at gross profits rather than net profits and likes to visualize himself as a liberal fellow who passes a lot of business around to a lot of different people and they make a profit on it. If everyone would do this, it would be a very fine world to live in, but they don't all do it so a person must cut down costs as well as increase acreage and volume."[12]

Kriss and Garvey studied every possibility with reference to cost and return, from the use of rubber-tired versus steel-wheeled tractors to the desirability of irrigation and insecticide. They decided yes on the first and no on the latter two. They raised sheep as a way of gaining some income on growing wheat in the fall. They learned that business from the ground up, and it made a difference when Kriss's sheep became known by Chicago buyers as worthy of a premium price.

Garvey could adapt as well as innovate. After a year of negotiation about the terms, he and Kriss signed up for the Agricultural Adjustment Administration (AAA) farm subsidy program. The resultant large government payments to a wealthy absentee landlord with a strongly expressed antigovernment outlook were controversial enough in Colby that Kriss reported they were hanging Garvey in effigy there. However, to Garvey it was simple realism, necessary to compete on the same terms as others. One of his patented one-liners was, "We just operate under the program, we don't set it." He asked if the purpose of the federal AAA program was welfare or production. To him, the question was rhetorical. He asked in a letter to a newspaper editor in 1957 how the editor would like it if government aid for newspapers went only to "the family-operated paper, where the publisher lives over the shop, sets the type, runs the press, and he and his family mail out the editions?"[13]

Playing by government rules, however, was the source of much criticism of Garvey over the course of his career. The lead lines in national media coverage generally were about his being the largest recipient in the nation of government largesse from the farm program. "Big Kansas wheat growers had a front seat on the gravy train," wrote the *Chicago Daily News* in 1954 when Garvey Farms received a $700,000 federal subsidy check. *Time* magazine editorialized in June 1959, "Of all the harvesters of the U.S.'s scandalous farm subsidy program, none have harvested more profitably than a bulky . . . hearty Kansan named Ray Hugh Garvey." Garvey, the *Time* reporter wrote, annually got enough government subsidy money "to stagger the imagination—and he does it without bending either the letter or the spirit of the nation's farm support laws."[14] That pattern began in 1933.

At Service Oil, collections went on a cash basis. Garvey advised to delay expenses "until we see where we are riding." The same went for tax payments: "I would never send anything to the revenuers until they ask for it." He cut salaries, changed oil brands, found new wholesalers, and modified freight routes. There was no sentimentality in his approach. The next time a man came into the Colby bank "with a frog in his throat and tears in his eyes," Garvey wrote Ferguson, "I think you should take a walk around the block, else you are liable to be converting the lobby of the bank into a soup kitchen." When Ferguson as a Service Oil investor wrote that he did not think it was possible to build a filling station "we could be proud of" in two weeks, as Garvey demanded, Garvey shot back, "We are not building a service station at Colby to be proud of. We are building a service station at Colby to try to get a little gallonage." Garvey recommended also delivering quality and service. A better grease-job and a friendly attitude was the small-town company's advantage over its more distant and larger competitors with their larger advertising budgets.[15]

There were opportunities to expand for someone with cash operating in the low-cost environment. Garvey was interested in tourist camps and hamburger diners run by couples hired cheaply. Trucks were inexpensive, but people were afraid of investing in them, so there might be profit in trucking. Modest expansion of service stations was possible: "$25,000 Super-service Station layouts in towns of 2,300 people," Garvey wrote Kenneth Crumly, "is 1929 talk instead of 1931. . . . A $2,500 layout could be added to, but I think of nothing other than a well insured and well managed fire that would subtract any return from a $25,000 investment." Service Oil was profitable through the 1930s, adding the operation of regional Firestone stores in 1937.[16]

Garvey was restless and he was an entrepreneur, not a stand-pat defender of assets, so he did some low-cost plunging. He bought securities in troubled or bankrupt companies through Amortibanc, hoping that reorganization or government loans would make these worth more than the pittance he paid. He bought heavily in bonds of the St. Louis and the Phoenix land banks and the Bankers Mortgage Company of Topeka. These were investment firms with an underlying asset of real estate mortgages. He gained on the first two and lost heavily on the third. Garvey admitted, "Our planning on Bankers Mortgage was about as far off as the planning of the National planners on the Atlantic seaboard." He had fun learning, however, and said it was a "very interesting circus." And it was not all dross. By summer 1937 he had made $50,000 in bond speculation but was frustrated not to have made more. "Our chance of a big profit failed," he wrote Ferguson, "when our big shot on the Bankers Mortgage Company collapsed."[17]

Garvey also bought the assets of failed banks, driving over the United States in his Ford V-8 to attend small-town auctions. He would make an "if come" deal with a local attorney to try to sell buildings and furniture and collect on notes at some reduced figure. He seldom paid more than $700 for a bank and hoped to make a few hundred dollars on each deal. These investments broke even at best, not counting Garvey's time and effort. He wrote in 1937 that he doubted the banks would be profitable "unless a person gets a pretty good-sized bank at the right kind of price. Most of the banks do not have much left in them and it costs quite a bit of money to run back and forth."[18]

Still, it was an idea and an adventure. Garvey expressed interest in opening a Penney's store, in becoming a Fordson tractor dealer, in buying and selling truck beds, in opening an auto parts company. "The Amortibanc makes a little money in spots and then takes some severe losses in other spots," he wrote. "I believe the best business to get into right now is to become a labor organizer."[19]

During World War II Garvey proved that he could innovate and adapt in boom times. He opposed New Deal spending and programs and was an active isolationist at the approach of war. He called FDR a "grinning gargoyle." But when the war came, he changed his focus to how inefficient the war effort was. The emphasis must be on "factories turning out planes and tanks in mass production," not "a bunch of damn promoters and communists around Washington." He wrote Charles Lindbergh, "The needlecraft workers should go back to their needlecraft and the social workers back to their YMCAs. . . . Hard tough executives with imagination will be needed to win this war." His farming became profitable, the 1941 harvest of 91,000 bushels selling for $150,000. "This is probably the big year we have been hoping for for ten years," Garvey wrote Kriss. "Ain't it hell that it is necessary in order to make a profit to have a war."[20]

Garvey bought farms and ranches again, both in Kansas and in eastern Colorado, eventually accumulating about 100,000 acres. He had toyed with Colorado land as early as 1935, when the "beautiful level land" there that had been successfully farmed for wheat in the 1918–1920 era was grown up in Russian thistles and selling for as little as fifty cents an acre. Garvey thought it was a big opportunity and moved as soon as he could and before others got the idea. Working with Kriss, he began breaking land in Colorado in 1945, when land, labor, and equipment were scarce. He bought the land for between $1.00 and $2.50 an acre, negotiated and lobbied away the Soil Conservation Service restrictions on plowing, and in 1947 sold over a million bushels of wheat at $2 a bushel.[21]

When he had broken land in Sherman County twenty-five years earlier, Garvey remembered, he had been told that was not cropland either. He had bought that for $10 an acre, and in 1945 it was worth $40 an acre and raised good wheat. Garvey loved the feedback on his instinct and planned to test it again. He quoted Robert Louis Stevenson: "The world is so full of a number of things/I'm sure we should all be as happy as kings."[22]

Although such accomplishments in farming might seem a full-time job, it was not for R. H. Garvey. His hometown of Wichita doubled its population in the war years on the strength of major federal investment in aircraft production. Garvey saw the chance early. "I am speculating some on land around Wichita," he wrote Ferguson in the spring of 1941, "and I may need to borrow a hell of a lot of money. . . . I am beginning to believe our population is growing. Rents are going up and there is lots of building and this defense work is going on even though the British Empire falls as long as our Treasury holds out." Ferguson couldn't follow. "Your ideas have grown away from me since you moved into the city," he wrote.[23]

Garvey formed Builders, Inc., and built duplex houses, apartments, and shopping centers. He argued with the city about its rent and assessment rules and quarreled with the federal government about competing with private industry with its government housing projects, but he had fun. "How long a person will enjoy any suspected profits," he commented, "is problematical, but it is nice to keep busy and active." Once Garvey asked a Builders employee why the concrete pouring was going so slowly. His foreman said, "Can't control the weather, Mr. Garvey." To which R. H. replied, "Have you ever tried?"[24]

It is difficult to summarize in brief compass any of Garvey's projects, but perhaps the one for which brevity is most unfair was his last and possibly most innovative—the building of eleven concrete terminal grain elevators between 1950 and 1959 with a combined capacity of nearly 200 million bushels. There were several individual terminals of 30- to 40-million-bushel capacity, including the mile-long, twenty-seven-tank behemoth at Wichita, once considered the largest grain elevator in the world. For comparison, Cargill, Inc., which had been in the business since the nineteenth century and was an emerging leader in the global oligopoly in grain storage, had a terminal storage capacity in 1959 of 151 million bushels. Cargill built or acquired about 75 million bushels of storage in the decade of the 1950s, while Garvey expanded at over twice that rate. He constructed 60 million bushels of new storage in 1958 alone and by the end of that year owned tanks holding 162.4 million bushels. In 1959 he received $20 million from the federal government for grain storage. R. H. sent out postcards with a picture of an elevator and the message, "Aren't Elevators Beautiful?" He thought they were more beautiful than the Parthenon because that had been a monument to winsome gods, whereas his temples were useful devices to help feed the world.[25]

Garvey was in poor health by the time he started the elevator project and had more money than he could use, much of his income falling in the above-90-percent tax bracket. The tax situation forced him to form Petroleum, Inc., in 1948, only to have it become a successful oil company, creating more tax liability. He wanted his family to inherit not just money but the fun of operating businesses, and he still enjoyed operations. In 1947 Garvey began corresponding with Richard Cochener, husband of his daughter Ruth, about building elevators.[26]

The two started a partnership, C-G Grain Company, in 1949 with the construction of elevators at Brandon and Haswell, Colorado, mostly to store grain from Garvey farms. But Garvey had a broader vision based on the "rules" that had created a wheat surplus out of the government farm program, a severe shortage in cities of large terminal elevators of the type that collected grain, a near monopoly on such facilities in the region in and around Kansas City, and the unwillingness or inability of entrepreneurs to undertake the construction of new ones. There were also federal incentives. Congress in 1948 and 1949 passed laws providing that the Commodity Credit Corporation could give a partial guaranty of government grain storage and authorized the IRS to allow faster depreciation. A million-bushel section of the C-G elevator at Topeka began taking grain in July 1950. Garvey thereafter built terminal storage facilities at many "inland" locations (Topeka, Salina, Wichita, and Atchison, Kansas; Lincoln, Nebraska; Fort Worth, Texas; Fargo, North Dakota), in smaller towns than was customary, off the rivers but near the farmers—fundamentally modifying the way the harvest was handled.

His innovations in this area were many. Garvey's son Willard, who made the initial loan contact with Teacher's Insurance & Annuity Association, remembered that financiers thought elevators went up and down in tall buildings. Eventually some of the largest banks in the country (Harris Trust of Chicago and Chase Manhattan of New York, for example) would compete to loan to Garvey. R. H. and Willard personally guaranteed $50 million in notes for elevators. Always there was that confidence. "He moved fast," Willard recalled. "He didn't screw around. We got our elevators built and filled before most others got started. He hit when it was hot. The people who started after us got burned."[27]

It was important to do the construction well, cheaply, and in a timely way. Garvey built concrete storage for sixty cents a bushel capacity, compared to ninety cents at Kansas City. He worked with Chalmers and Borton Company in Hutchinson, a firm that was itself innovating in slip-form concrete construction. Expiration of the government's accelerated depreciation program in 1956 did not slow him. Half his capacity was constructed after that date. Before Garvey's death the Topeka elevator expanded to 7, 18, and then 30 million bushels. Salina started with 7 million in 1953 and reached 30 million by 1958. Wichita, using its flat-shed storage, could accommodate 40 million bushels.[28]

Garvey wrote in 1954 that the 7 billion bushels of wheat the United States grew then would expand to 10–12 billion bushels fifty years in the future, when the country would need to feed 300 million citizens. He told the Commodity Credit Corporation administrator in Washington, "We are probably a bit silly to extend ourselves. . . . We are in a position, however, to build these, we believe, as few others are, and feel that those who can should. We have an interest in this entirely separate from the financial incentive. While not easy, it is a lot of fun to build elevators." The *Southwestern Miller* in a 1959 article called the sixty-five-year-old R. H. Garvey "a dominant factor in the grain business in the Southwest and of the entire United States."[29]

Early in 1959, shortly before that fatal car trip, Ray Garvey was reading a book titled *Shaka, Chief of the Zulus*. He was impressed with that chief's leadership and perseverance against odds. He commented that he felt "somewhat like a Zulu myself."[30]

In 1953 the family dog Muggs died. R. H. wrote a tribute to him, which, maybe not accidentally, said much about Garvey himself. R. H. often wrote letters to the family signed by the dog, as "Pop confuses you with all the letters he writes." Garvey wrote that the dog's sight and hearing were gone at fourteen, "but his spirit was youthful as ever." Certainly Muggs was intent on the immediate. "People on the Eastern Seaboard would probably call Muggsy an isolationist, as he was not interested in international affairs or national affairs, or even in municipal affairs, but only in his own yard, his own home, and his own folks." He had a keen appreciation of the differences among those folks: "He would knock the paper out of my hands, but he didn't knock the paper out of Olive's because he knew who thought that was funny and who didn't." There was half a case of Pard in the garage and a red rubber bone in the utility room, but the great soul was gone.[31]

Garvey's friend Judge J. E. Alexander said of him, "R.H. has had the good judgment to recognize a favorable situation, and the courage to follow it up." It was a thing rarely done so well, and so singly. Garvey observed, "In every new business it is necessary to 'breathe the breath of life' into it, and to keep the breath in by somebody." He thought that was a privilege. "He doesn't have to now," son James commented the year R. H. died, "but Dad still likes to drive his own tractor."[32]

PART FIVE

KANSANS AND KANSAS SINCE WORLD WAR II, 1945–2004

Back in those days [at the turn of the twentieth century], Kansans were proud of their eccentricities. . . . But today, Kansas is busily engaged in trying to live down that reputation. It wants to conform. It is proud of its wheat (the automobile tags bear the words, "The Wheat State"), its oil and gas, its growing manufactures, and, to a more limited extent, its culture. . . .

The current tendency of Kansas legislation is to avoid "rocking the boat." A constitutional amendment provides for the initiative and referendum, but the legislature has never implemented it—and nobody seems to care. The state has a weak civil rights law, which there has been no effort to strengthen, perhaps on the ground that even the present law isn't enforced. Negroes and Mexicans are excluded from many theatres and most restaurants and hotels, and a good many towns operate segregated elementary schools. . . .

On the other hand, the legislature is on its toes when it comes to improving Kansas institutions. The 1948 session made unprecedented appropriations for education. Also, largely at the instance of the Menningers, native Kansas psychiatrists, it adopted plans for eventually bringing the state hospitals up to the standards of the American Psychiatric Association. . . .

In spite of the recent eclipse of the old crusading spirit, no one can predict when the people of the state will suddenly decide to follow the eloquent Mary Lease's advice and raise hell.

—*Nelson Antrim Crawford,* The American Mercury, *1950*

Esther Brown: In Pursuit of Human Rights

and Social Justice

Milton S. Katz

On May 18, 1954—the day after the U.S. Supreme Court announced its decision in the landmark school desegregation case *Oliver Brown, et al., v. Board of Education, Topeka, Kansas*—150 African American citizens of Topeka celebrated their victory. They applauded a white Jewish Kansas City housewife named Esther Brown when she reminded them that it had been "little people like us" who had brought about the most far-reaching achievement in the cause of civil rights since Abraham Lincoln's Emancipation Proclamation. When Hugh W. Speer presented a copy of his book *The Case of the Century* to Esther Brown, he wrote on the flyleaf, "With my compliments to the white Mrs. Brown of the Topeka case. If Abe Lincoln were around to shake your hand, he no doubt would say something like he did to Harriet Beecher Stowe, 'Is this the little woman who started it all?'"[1]

Esther Brown (September 19, 1917–May 24, 1970), ca. 1948, was a Jewish housewife and passionate social activist and agitator from Merriam, Kansas, who challenged segregation in the public schools of Kansas while raising her own family and contributed to the establishment of what became the Kansas Commission on Civil Rights. Courtesy of Susan Tucker, daughter of Esther Brown.

Although volumes have been written on "the case of the century," little has been written about the contributions of Esther Brown, who in 1947–1949 spearheaded the Kansas desegregation case *Webb v. School District No. 90.* Her determination to desegregate schools throughout the state took her to Topeka, where she became involved in the National Association for the Advancement of Colored People's (NAACP's) constitutional attack on segregation. For the next twenty years Brown organized and agitated full-time at the grassroots level for racial equality, human dignity, and social justice.[2]

Brown's involvement in the school integration struggle dated from the fall of 1947, but her social activism had deep roots. The daughter of Russian-Jewish immigrants, Esther Swirk was born on September 19, 1917, and grew up in a working-class neighborhood in Kansas City, Missouri. Esther was only ten when her mother died of cancer. Her father, Ben Swirk, a watchmaker, was not religious, but he was socially conscious and a member of several left-wing labor organizations. Brown identified with her father's radical politics and causes and with the ethical values of Judaism. During the turbulent Depression decade, while a high school student in Kansas City and later as a salesgirl at Marshall Fields in Chicago, Brown joined in a garment workers' picket, spent two summers at the leftist Commonwealth College in Mena, Arkansas, and supported the Spanish Loyalists and other progressive causes.[3]

Back in Kansas City, after losing a job with the Works Progress Administration (she believed for political reasons), she married a childhood friend, Lt. Paul Brown, who was home on leave from the Army Air Corps. After the war the Browns moved their two young daughters into a modest home in Merriam, Johnson County, Kansas, on the edge of suburban Kansas City. The family had lived there almost a year when Brown learned from her maid, Helen Swan, about the deplorable state of a black school housed in a sixty-year-old building in the adjoining largely rural township of South Park.[4]

Contrary to state law, South Park had established segregated schools in 1912, when a new school was built for white children; the black children remained behind in the original one-room building, soon called Walker School. In the fall of 1947 the school board built a modern $90,000 elementary school for the 222 white students but excluded the 44 black students, even though the parents of all the children had been taxed for construction of the new school. The African American community was incensed.

Brown visited Walker School, by then a dilapidated two-room structure with an outhouse, poor heating, and a flooded basement. As journalist Richard Kluger later wrote, Brown subsequently "went on a one woman crusade" to right this injustice. Through Helen Swan, Brown joined with the black residents of South Park, who were already demanding improvements.[5]

On October 8, 1947, Helen Swan and Alfonso Webb, a concrete contractor, father of nine, and a respected community leader, met with school authorities. They did not ask for integration, only for improvements to the Walker School and equal educational facilities for their children. The board advised them to ask their churches for donations to improve their school. Several months later the school board offered a new stop sign and a mailbox at Walker School.

Brown suggested that if South Park formed a local chapter of the NAACP, the chapter's demands would have national backing and carry more weight with the local board. In January 1948 Brown and Webb met with Rev. E. A. Freeman, president of the Kansas City, Kansas, branch, who helped them organize a local chapter. Dr. A. Porter Davis, president of the state NAACP, attended their first meeting and promised to take action. But the school board remained intransigent.

At one meeting in the South Park School gymnasium, the board chairman incited an angry reaction in the large crowd with his opening remark: "All of a sudden we seem to have a racial problem in South Park. Well, let me tell you that no nigger will get into South Park as long as I live." People shouted obscenities and racial slurs. The room grew quiet. It was clear that Brown was supposed to speak. Terrified, she pulled herself together, stood up, and said, "Look, I'm just a Kansas housewife. I don't represent these people. One of them works for me and I've seen the conditions at their school. I know none of you would want your children educated under such circumstances. They're not asking for integration—just a fair shake."[6]

But Brown's efforts to explain the facts and bring some sanity to the meeting were greeted with hostility. When she protested that she had been invited to the meeting, the chairman denied it and walked off the platform. Although the meeting had apparently been called to intimidate her, Brown later recalled that she came out of it "a changed woman." She was outraged at the injustice and vowed to fight it.

After the public meeting Brown was subjected to a twenty-four-hour barrage of threatening telephone calls. Additional threats and harassment followed. One neighbor pointed to a distant hill and warned Brown that the Ku Klux Klan had once burned crosses there. A few days later a cross was burned on the Browns' front lawn.

Brown refused to be intimidated, and the black parents of South Park organized their community for action. On April 9, 1948, Esther Brown, Alfonso Webb, and Helen Swan attended the annual meeting of the school board and made a formal demand that the black children be admitted to the new South Park Common Grade School. Faced with vicious opposition from the white community, the South Park NAACP decided to take legal action. With the financial and moral support of Kansas City, Kansas, NAACP leaders, they instructed their attorney to sue the school board. On May 25, 1948, William Towers filed a mandamus action before the Kansas Supreme Court to require the school district to admit black students to the new school.[7]

Although the South Park black community had started out merely asking for improved conditions at Walker School, it now demanded full integration in compliance with Kansas law. In May Towers filed the lawsuit that became *Webb v. School District No. 90,* but Brown believed he was pursuing the case with indifference. Impatient for action, she persuaded the local NAACP to fire

Towers, and on August 11 the chapter hired Elisha Scott, a noted civil rights lawyer from Topeka, who litigated the case more vigorously.[8]

Due largely to Brown's relentless organizing and public relations efforts, the local black press gave extensive coverage to the South Park case, which began to attract attention throughout the state. Brown addressed the assembled delegates at the September 1948 Kansas NAACP Convention in Osawatomie. She stressed the importance of making school desegregation the "top priority on the agenda for national defense. . . . Until Jim-Crow is abolished, the words 'democracy,' 'freedom' and 'justice' used so freely to support our foreign policy will ring hollow throughout the world." Following her speech, the state delegates voted full support for the lawsuit.[9]

When school opened on September 3, African American parents attempted to enroll their children in the new South Park School. The principal turned them away, saying he had no authority to admit them while the case was pending. Subsequently Brown helped persuade all but two black parents to boycott the segregated Walker School and to set up temporary schoolrooms in their homes. Money soon became an immediate and persistent problem. To finance the lawsuit and pay the salaries of two qualified teachers, Brown traveled throughout the state collecting donations. "If someone will put me up for the night," she wrote the NAACP branches across Kansas, "I have a story to tell."[10]

Brown also made personal appeals to friends, businessmen, and various organizations in the Kansas City area. Her letter-writing campaign was as determined as it was voluminous. Before the case was settled she had raised more than $3,000 and had contributed over $1,000 of her own money. A relentless activist, Brown also sent passionate and well-articulated appeals to Thurgood Marshall's NAACP Legal Defense and Educational Fund, and civil rights attorney Franklin Williams was dispatched to work with Scott on the case.[11]

As the case dragged on for a long and difficult year, Brown, with Alfonso Webb and other black leaders, worked to keep the people together and the boycott school in session. This became especially difficult when the school board tried to bribe parents with free school lunches and threatened not to graduate their children.

By the spring of 1949 Brown was receiving letters from around the country that nourished her spirit and reaffirmed her commitment. A letter addressed to "Dear Crusading Sister" from a sixty-year-old widow in Milwaukee, Wisconsin, assured her that she did not "stand alone" in her efforts "to civilize her community." A black minister from Oakland, California, wrote to congratulate her for the part she played "in making democracy work in Kansas." An editorial in the *Call* applauded her as a "Twentieth Century Joan of Arc, [for] 'spearheading the attack against segregated schools' [and for struggling] almost single-handedly against white obstructionists and economic hardship." Although her father-in-law called her a communist and fired Paul Brown from his job, and the Federal Bureau of Investigation tried to discredit her, Brown continued to travel, speak, and plead for money, declaring wherever she went, "We have to correct these conditions all over the state."[12]

Meanwhile, the state Supreme Court heard the case in April, and on June 11, 1949, the justices ruled in favor of the plaintiffs. The court held that the school board's policy "was arbitrary" and "unreasonable" and an attempt by "subterfuge" to bring about segregation, which the statutes of Kansas did not permit. It ordered the board to rebuild or make comparable Walker School and to develop a reasonable and logical zoning plan so black children and white children could attend both schools. In the interim, the South Park School was ordered to admit black pupils in September.[13]

The *Call* hailed the "victory won by children who went on strike" and called the court's decision "a victory in the fight against educational inequalities." A spokesman for the national NAACP predicted that *Webb v. School District No. 90,* the eleventh school segregation case to reach the Kansas Supreme Court, would set a precedent for eliminating segregation in public schools throughout the country. The *Plaindealer* and the *Call* gave generous credit to Esther Brown as the white woman who "was the guiding spirit behind the fight of South Park parents for admittance of their children to the new South Park School [and] who launched the fight and pushed it through to its final victory."[14]

On September 9, 1949, the black children presented themselves at South Park Common Grade School. The school's new principal, Charles H. Rutherford, greeted them warmly. He was called a "nigger lover" and a communist, but he insisted on completely integrating the children into all activities at the school. On the first day of classes, September 12, all the children in the district—black and white—attended the South Park School without incident, and another long and difficult step toward integration was accomplished.

Alfonso Webb, a lifelong resident and activist in South Park whose son was the lead plaintiff, later recalled that "if it had not been for Mrs. Brown, we would have not have gotten as far as we did as quick as we did. It took a white woman who had determination and contacts to spearhead the movement that would desegregate a school, which by law was illegally barring blacks from attending. Black people were just too scared, at least some of them were. Scared from history, scared from experience, scared from not enough experience."15

Bolstered by the victory in the *Webb* case, Esther Brown was determined to desegregate schools throughout Kansas. Wanting to challenge the legality of segregation in larger "first class" cities, she urged the NAACP in Wichita to launch a similar suit against segregation, but the black teachers who realistically feared for their jobs defeated her. Next she went to Topeka, where the local NAACP was aggressively fighting against "the inconvenience, injustice, and humiliation" imposed upon black children and their parents by segregation. The result of the Topeka struggle was the U.S. Supreme Court's historic *Brown v. Board of Education of Topeka* outlawing segregation in all American public schools. In 1990 eighty-year-old Lucinda Todd, who had been the secretary of the Topeka NAACP and worked closely with Brown during this period, said, "I don't know if we could have done it without Esther Brown."

Brown raised funds for the case, helped persuade Oliver Brown to be the lead plaintiff, and provided moral support. Extensive unpublished correspondence between her and the national NAACP's Roy Wilkins, Walter White, and Thurgood Marshall also shows that she helped influence the NAACP to shift its strategy from challenging segregated graduate schools to demanding universal desegregation of America's public schools. She also advocated for behavioral-science testimony to demonstrate the inequality of segregation, and she helped locate expert witnesses.16

Brown's heroic struggle for democracy embodied tremendous courage, deep conviction, and a stubborn persistence in the belief that, if pushed to do so, America could reform itself systemically to achieve justice and equality. Her politics were neither ideological nor academic; they came from the heart. Brown later explained that she became involved because it was "simply the right thing to do."17

Brown's involvement with the struggle for social justice did not begin in South Park, nor did it end with the Supreme Court's landmark 1954 decision. Over the next two decades she became a grassroots organizer and full-time agitator for racial equality and social justice. In early 1949 Brown worked with other civil rights activists in organizing the Kansas Clearing House on Civil Rights, whose primary focus was the problem of segregation in schools, discrimination in employment, bad housing conditions for minority groups, and civil rights in public accommodations. Brown was chosen to head the organization's activities against school segregation.

Due largely to the clearing house's efforts, the issue was brought to the Kansas legislature in the spring of 1949. Because legislators disagreed on the nature and extent of employment discrimination in the state, they passed a joint resolution establishing a temporary commission to study the problem, hold hearings, and submit a report to the governor and the legislature within two years. The Kansas Commission Against Employment Discrimination, as it was now called, reported its findings to the legislature on March 1, 1951. Not surprisingly, the commission concluded, "Employment discrimination exists in the state of Kansas . . . on the basis of race, religion, and national origin."[18]

As a result of these findings, Representative Myles Stevens introduced an antidiscrimination bill during the 1951 session of the legislature. Due to the persistent efforts of Esther Brown; the Kansas City, Kansas, branch of the NAACP; and other civil rights activists, the bill passed the House, but it died in committee in the Senate. Brown appealed to Walter White of the NAACP in New York for support in the campaign, and their combined efforts eventually achieved a positive result. During the 1953 session Representative Stevens finally got a diluted bill through both houses, and Kansas became the twelfth state in the nation to have a law against employment discrimination. The act, however, was limited to employment practices and contained no enforcement provisions. It was not until 1961 that it became an enforceable law prohibiting discriminatory practices because of race, religion, color, national origin, or ancestry.[19]

Although Brown realized great satisfaction from these civil rights campaigns, she passionately searched for an activity and organization that would represent many of the human rights concerns she cared about. Brown found what she was looking for in 1957 when she helped to develop the Panel of American Women through the Sisterhood of Temple B'nai Jehudah in Kansas City, Missouri. Here Brown found the cloak of respectability and acceptance that had eluded her in past campaigns. The panel was well suited to her style of operating through communication and understanding and gave her the independence, control, and platform to persuade people to bring about significant values changes in themselves, their communities, and the world.[20]

The panel was a unique and well-respected human relations program that created dialogue and an understanding among women of diverse ethnic, religious, and racial backgrounds. Its purpose was to appeal to the emotions of the audience in the belief that the establishment of a community of feeling could be the basis for a change in attitudes from prejudice to understanding. The initial format consisted of five middle-class women—a Jew, a Catholic, an African American, a white Anglo-Saxon Protestant, and a member from another minority group—who simply and candidly stated how they felt about prejudice and what they were doing about it. Brown, as moderator, would field probing questions from the audience and conclude the program with a plea for tolerance and understanding.[21]

What started as a one-time presentation gave rise to a national volunteer movement. Brown became the national panel coordinator and traveled throughout the United States and Canada setting up panels and often moderating their programs. Money was always tight, as panelists largely funded the panel out of their own household budgets. To preserve their independence, Brown and her colleagues refused to accept financial backing from any racial or religious organizations. The panel was incorporated and chartered in 1964 as a not-for-profit educational organization. During the 1960s interest in and publicity about the panel continued to spread. By 1970 Brown had managed to help women organize seventy-five panels involving 1,500 women in all parts of the United States and Canada, and there were requests from hundreds of other communities to set up panels.[22]

A direct result of these programs was a deepening commitment on the part of panelists to other efforts in the field of human rights work. Through their increasing contact and developing friendship with people outside their usual social groups, panelists often became involved in other activist programs. In their attempt to provide insightful answers to the questions of their audiences, they broadened their knowledge and became more sensitive to problems within their own communities. Many panelists became members of school boards, active in community projects, and looked to as leaders in their cities.

As race relations became more volatile and polarized in the late 1960s and some panel members pushed for greater militancy, Brown constantly reminded them that they must build bridges to those people whom some civil rights activists regarded as the "enemy." "Not by further alienating people," she declared, "but by drawing them into your warmth and concern, by making them aware that the human rights issue is respectable and important to women just like themselves." She deeply believed that in this way "you can get further than all the preachers of morality and angry militants put together."[23]

Asked what made the Panel of American Women successful when so many organizations working to eliminate prejudice failed, Brown identified several reasons. "People identify easily with us when they hear mothers speak to them as parents; we reach who are in the best position to reduce prejudice by the examples they set for their children; and we're not experts who talk down to them. We make controversial matters seem uncontroversial by discussing the problems in simple, neighborly terms." She derived strength from her conviction that women as a group were the world's most powerful force for change.[24]

Brown was intensely committed to social change and would not allow any barriers to get in her way. Impatient for progress, she firmly believed that the best way to get things done was "to starve the problem and feed the opportunity." According to a close colleague, her skill was bringing the future closer to the present—of making real a vision where persons of differing history and culture could support one another in a coalition based upon their common humanity. She knew that if people were to survive in this imperfect society, vested interests in conflict must reach reasonable compromises and progress toward new levels of shared human dignity. The foundation for all her human rights activism was a basic and pure assumption—that human potential can be fulfilled where there is love and justice.[25]

Esther Brown was fifty-two years old when she died of cancer in May 1970. An editorial by Thorpe Menn, book editor of the *Kansas City Times,* recalled the beauty of her unique spirit and suggested that her death "was a loss to all mankind, for she spoke for, and to, the best of humanity." The *Call,* which, along with the *Plaindealer,* had been reporting Brown's efforts and achievements for equal rights from the time of the South Park case, paid this final tribute to her: "Never did a human light shine so brightly as did the life of this young woman who devoted her time and talents in a never-ceasing struggle to make the world a better place for all of God's children. . . . If there were more like her in the world, the struggle for justice and equality would have been over long ago."[26]

In 1975, despite her unpopularity among the white residents where the school desegregation case was first played out, a new public park in South Park was named in her honor. Among members of the Urban Renewal Board who joined in the unanimous vote for the park's dedication was the former president of the school board who had refused to listen to Esther Brown. Julius Mc-Farlin, president of the local NAACP, installed a simple plaque to serve "as an everlasting memorial to her unselfish contribution to humankind." After visiting the park in 1976 while covering the Republican National Convention, Richard Cohen, a reporter for the *Washington Post,* wrote, "Around the corner from the park was the old black school and nearby was the former all-white school and in between was the park named after Esther Brown because she managed to make the two schools one."[27]

Movements for social change are driven by countless ordinary individuals whose struggle for equality and justice alter the course of human history. We often forget that history is actually made by people much like ourselves who commit their lives and their energies to obtaining freedom and equality for all. Esther Brown was one of these individuals whose remarkable courage, unswerving determination, and moral strength in the pursuit of human rights and social justice brought democracy in America a step closer to reality.

Dwight D. Eisenhower: His Legacy in

World Affairs

William B. Pickett

The most important event in the last half of the twentieth century was the peaceful end of the Soviet Union in 1991. The difficulties inherent in the Soviet system were the main cause, but the strategy of the United States and its allies was a contributing factor. This strategy, called containment, initiated by President Harry S. Truman, was also a legacy of his successor, the Republican president Dwight David Eisenhower, who during his two terms shaped and institutionalized it.

When Eisenhower entered the White House in January 1953, American foreign policy was in turmoil. The Truman administration had responded to communist aggression in Korea by mobilizing the armed forces and enlisting the support of allies and the United Nations. Eisenhower, however, devised a comprehensive approach to global affairs that, as carried out by him and his successors in the White House, brought about the above-mentioned result

Dwight D. Eisenhower (October 14, 1890–March 28, 1969), who led the Allies to victory in Europe in 1944–1945, is depicted here in 1946 on the porch of his boyhood home with his beloved mother, Ida Stover Eisenhower. Ike essentially remained, according to his personal White House secretary, "the boy from Kansas, and the values that his family taught him sixty years ago are as present today as then." Courtesy of the Eisenhower Library, Abilene, Kansas.

favorable to the spread of democracy. The relevance of this accomplishment in the year 2006 appears in the fact that the *Final Report of the National Commission on Terrorist Attacks upon the United States* concluded that the United States once again needs a global strategy.[1] It is thus worth asking what can be learned from the Eisenhower legacy.

Eisenhower's approach to the Cold War had its shortcomings. Indeed, some critics charged, in retrospect with considerable force, that it was needlessly militant and provocative. The strategy, after all, by the end of the Soviet era included alliances with oppressive military dictatorships; tolerated communist (though nationalist) regimes in North Vietnam and Cuba; involved an incredibly dangerous and expensive nuclear arms race; and, notably for present concerns, included support for anticommunist but also anti-Western Muslim extremist fighters. Other critics, including Senator John F. Kennedy and his supporters in 1960, countered, in retrospect probably correctly, that the strategy was insufficiently bold, allowing the Soviet Union to expand its missile program and geographical influence in Southeast Asia, the Middle East, and Latin America.[2]

The critics notwithstanding, the Cold War strategy institutionalized by Eisenhower during the 1950s, although not without missteps, was successful. An approach to life that harkened back to the president's Kansas childhood, it balanced strength and conciliation. Always seeking the best response to a given situation through diligent staff work and intelligence gathering, it remained focused on its objective: preserving a way of life. This focus involved developing military strength while avoiding both a garrison state and general war; attempting to understand the enemy's purposes while working closely with allies to bolster the forces of democracy; and, confident in the future, allowing time for the adversary to weaken.

It is difficult to imagine a beginning less auspicious than that of this son of the American prairie. A baby named David Dwight Eisenhower (later changed to Dwight David) was born on October 14, 1890, in Denison, Texas. His father, David Eisenhower, had moved his family there from Kansas two years earlier so he could take a job as a railroad laborer. In 1889 he had a streak of bad luck, including the failure of a general store that he owned and operated with a partner. The family returned to Kansas in 1892 when David Eisenhower found better employment maintaining the refrigeration unit at the Belle Springs Creamery in Abilene, a job he would hold for the rest of his life. It was the family's return to the place of its origin that made Dwight, or "Ike," a Kansan.[3]

The east-central Kansas of over one hundred years ago was a place where the flat, gently rolling land; hot, dry summer winds; and economic circumstances conspired to make much possible, but only for those who owned property and were willing to work. It was young Dwight's good fortune to have parents, David and Ida Stover Eisenhower, who had inherited little but nevertheless believed in hard work, Bible study, and a rigorous classical education, all within the framework of friendly neighbors and family ties. Dwight's grandfather had moved to Kansas from Elizabethville, Pennsylvania, in the 1870s as part of a community of the German Brethren in Christ, a sect of the Mennonite Church. They hoped to own land where they could raise wheat and improve their life.

Eisenhower recalled that his father was "a strong, active man, an avid reader," but also that he "always had the shadow of early failure [of the store] on him." David and Ida had little money when they returned from Texas, but with the help of a relative they were able to move into a modest house that had three acres of land on South East Fourth Street. To make ends meet, Ida and her children (who would number six boys in all—Ike was the third) milked cows and raised vegetables, which they sold at a stand in front of their small, square, two-story, three-bedroom, wood-frame home. Years later, when asked his definition of "capitalism," Eisenhower recalled growing these vegetables and a way of life that was, he believed, universally applicable. "I was a capitalist," he said, "and probably the poorest boy in America. . . . I [nevertheless] bought football equipment with the profits." Eisenhower, who never forgot the spirit of the Abilene community, would call himself a "Jeffersonian Republican . . . because once you take away from [a small town] its feeling of primary responsibility for its disabled and its hurt and its injured, then I believe the whole citizenry has lost something."[4]

Young Eisenhower loved wrestling and foot racing with his brothers and friends, but before long it had become clear that he had other advantages. He learned to fish in the nearby Smoky Hill River and to hunt, trap, and go camping. But perhaps more importantly for his later accomplishments, he loved team sports. A natural athlete, he played football and baseball with great intensity, becoming a high school sports hero. His parents, who had shifted their membership from the Brethren in Christ to the Jehovah's Witnesses—an affiliation that his mother continued to the end of her life—saw to it that their boys said morning prayers and memorized passages from the Bible. Eisenhower recalled that his mother "was absolutely certain that those who were honest and faithful Christians would have a perpetual life of happiness." The American form of government, he later would say, was a "deliberate attempt—so stated by our founding fathers—to translate into the political field something of our religious faith . . . that each individual created in the image of his God has rights and privileges that no government, no machinery, can take away from him."5

Another influence was history. From the time he was old enough to read, young Eisenhower devoured books about the wars of the Greek and Roman empires and the American Civil War; he especially admired the Carthaginian general Hannibal. He received good grades in high school—a rigorous curriculum that included three years of Latin, two of German, three of mathematics (both algebra and plane geometry), civics, economics, physics, English composition and literature, and history. He was a solid B-plus student. He excelled in mathematics and performed so well in history that the editor of the school yearbook predicted that he would become a professor of history at Yale.

In the years that followed, his friends and family often would note that for many practical purposes Eisenhower had never left Abilene. Ann Whitman, his White House personal secretary, knew him better than almost anyone. Near the end of Eisenhower's second term, one of his good friends asked Whitman to name a few of her boss's characteristics for a memoir he was writing. It was "his consideration for others," she replied, that caused people to trust him and was his most important quality. "Essentially," she said, "he is still the boy from Kansas, and the values that his family taught him sixty years ago are as present today as then: the honesty, the modesty, the independence, the integrity . . . the spiritual values."6

Such was the outlook that Eisenhower took with him in the summer of 1911 from the banks of the Smoky Hill to the gray granite fortress on the east bank of the Hudson River, the U.S. Military Academy. His four years at West Point imbued him, perhaps indelibly, with notions of "duty, honor, country." But it is probable that his later success stemmed more directly from his experiences as a junior officer. What was most striking about him in those years were his curiosity, openness to ideas, and quickness to take the initiative. In the years between his graduation from West Point in 1915 and—as he progressed through the ranks—the U.S. entry into World War II in 1941, in all the officers with whom he came in contact he constantly noted the traits that brought success. If possible, he maintained contact with those whom he considered the best. He thus learned the principles of leadership and the importance of planning, to consider what was in the mind of his enemy and the in-

terest not just of his unit or even the army but the nation. He mastered what
the foremost Western philosopher of war, Karl von Clausewitz, had taught
about war ("the use of force to cause the enemy to carry out one's will") and
its relationship to diplomacy ("nothing other than politics by other means").
He became aware of how military demobilization after the Spanish-American
War had hindered the ability of the United States to do anything about the
events that brought on World War I and how demobilization after that war
similarly precluded any ability to stem the international breakdown that led to
World War II.

During these years he gained the respect of many of the army's most capable officers, who later influenced his promotion to greater rank and responsibility. During these years he served as commanding officer of the army's tank
corps training center at Camp Colt near Gettysburg, Pennsylvania, and then
collaborated in the study of armor in warfare with Colonel George S. Patton, recently returned from command of U.S. tank forces on the battlefields of northern France. Eisenhower served as chief of staff to Brig. Gen. Fox Conner, who
became his mentor. The officer from Abilene graduated first in his class from
the army's Command and General Staff College, then traveled to France to
write the official army guidebook to the battlefields of World War I. He served as
War Department liaison and secretary of a congressional study of economic
mobilization for World War I and later was personal aide and report writer for
army chief of staff General Douglas A. MacArthur. Eisenhower accompanied
MacArthur to the Philippines as executive officer when MacArthur, at the end
of his tour as chief of staff, became military adviser to that country's president.
Finally, after returning to the United States, Eisenhower was chief of staff of
the victorious forces in the largest training exercise ever carried out, the
Louisiana maneuvers of 1939.[7] It was, accordingly, not surprising that after the
Japanese attack on Pearl Harbor on December 7, 1941, General George C.
Marshall, army chief of staff, appointed Eisenhower director of the War Plans
Division in the Pentagon and then, in consecutive order, European theater
commander; supreme commander of the Allied invasions of North Africa,
Sicily, and Italy; and finally supreme commander of the D-day invasion at Nor-
mandy and the Western Allied assault on the German homeland.

Eisenhower's wartime successes and the resulting adulation, it is important to note (as he was among the first to admit), obscured certain mistakes.
The North African campaign of 1942–1943 went badly at first because of ill-
trained and poorly led troops, and his "broad-front" strategy after the invasion

of Normandy in June 1944 was probably unnecessarily cautious. Eisenhower's skills, said his critics, were suited for holding together an allied coalition and for retaining the support of the civilian leaders but not for the operational control of troops in battle.[8]

Still, his victories revealed that he had mastered the military art—the importance of unity of command, deception, joint combined operations in an offensive, force protection, and the gathering and dissemination of intelligence (including that derived from code-breaking). He understood the necessity of controlling the air and the sea, the centrality of supply, and elements of speed and maneuverability in response to enemy movements. The amphibious operations and campaigns of 1942 and 1943—in addition to bringing about the fall of Mussolini's fascist government in Italy—would secure supply routes, the oil resources of the Middle East, and the North African littoral as a base of air operations. His successful strategy after D-day and the battle of Normandy, which the critics called "broad-front," reflected the principles of von Clausewitz and was in fact a two-pronged offensive, designed to move in pace with its logistical tail and to prevent the enemy from massing troops. Mistakes were made and setbacks occurred, but victory nevertheless came in early May 1945. It stemmed from Eisenhower's approach—a well-prepared, patient, responsive, yet bold and multipronged advance to unbalance, surround, and defeat the enemy.[9]

On D-day, June 6, 1944, however, that victory was by no means certain. The complexity of the task and the difficulty of the key decisions Eisenhower had to make are impossible for most of us to comprehend. He accepted the challenge and the responsibility. Before giving the order that only he could issue, in the privacy of his quarters he offered a prayer and then jotted down a message to his commanders for release to the press in the event of failure. "My decision to attack at this time and place was based upon the best information available. The troops, the air and the Navy did all that bravery and devotion to duty could do. If any blame or fault attaches to the attempt, it is mine alone."[10]

These words point to what in retrospect was perhaps the crucial reason for Eisenhower's success—a willingness to accept responsibility and an instinctive ability to select, delegate, work with, and get the very best from others. At the end of his presidency, in response to a query from a West Point cadet about the source of his accomplishments, Eisenhower without hesitation remarked that it was the system of decision-making and management. "An outfit like that can't make a decision for you—they can't do a thing for you except give you a greater comprehension . . . based on fact and on studied examinations and analyses. . . . You have to hear it debated." It was this understanding—the need for a constant flow of good information resulting from the initiative and independent advice of staff as a basis for making decisions—along with his professional competence and confidence that brought victory.[11]

Eisenhower might have defeated Germany more quickly. His failure to close the gap at Normandy between Falaise and Argentan in August allowed the escape of some forty thousand German troops. And failure to attack the base of the salient created by the Germans when they moved westward during their surprise offensive through the Ardennes (the Battle of the Bulge) in December prevented early encirclement and destruction of the German army west of the Rhine. Still, by the time German leaders surrendered, unlike their predecessors in 1918, they knew they were defeated. Their factories and cities were in ruins; their army and navy were nonexistent; and their leader, *der führer,* the practitioner of genocide, was reportedly dead by suicide. Eisenhower's strategy had liberated Western Europe and brought an end to fascist tyranny—an accomplishment of epochal proportions.[12]

The crisis facing the nation when Eisenhower became president in 1953, as mentioned, was located in Northeast Asia. Communist aggression in Korea—and preceding events such as Soviet intransigence regarding a postwar settlement in Germany, the USSR's acquisition of the atomic bomb, and Mao Zedong's victory on the Chinese mainland—had persuaded Eisenhower along with many of his countrymen that the American way of life was in jeopardy. President Truman's failure to develop strength sufficient to implement his policy of containing communist expansion, a project he had announced in March 1947, had resulted in public statements in early 1950 by the secretary of state that excluded South Korea from the U.S. defense perimeter. These statements, Eisenhower speculated, had caused the North Koreans and their communist allies, the Soviet Union and People's Republic of China, to miscalculate.[13]

Having lived through three American military demobilization-remobilization cycles, Eisenhower by 1951 had concluded that Truman, who had presided over the third—during 1946 and 1950—lacked the qualities the nation needed. The most likely Republican candidate for the presidency in 1952, however, was Senator Robert A. Taft. This ambitious Senate minority leader from Ohio believed the time had come for his neoisolationist brand of Republicanism. Eisenhower was dismayed at the prospect. Before leaving for his new assignment as supreme commander of the North Atlantic Treaty Organization

(NATO) in late 1950, Eisenhower had met secretly with Taft in a Pentagon office and conducted a test. He had sought the senator's support for congressional appropriations to assure European collective security, but the senator would not commit himself. A Taft candidacy, Eisenhower then determined, would bring either another four years of Truman or a truly ruinous approach to world affairs.

The general from Abilene felt he had no choice and in January 1952 announced publicly that he would allow his name to be entered as a Republican candidate in the New Hampshire primary. Astute maneuvering by his supporters at the convention in Chicago wrested the nomination away from Taft, and in November Eisenhower defeated his Democratic opponent, Adlai E. Stevenson, in a landslide.[14]

Summarizing his purposes and approach as president in a conversation with newsman and author Merriman Smith, Eisenhower said the problem with "politicians" (something he insisted he was not) was their outlook. He, Eisenhower, would make "smarter political decisions" than "a lot of the guys who are pros" because "they have gotten too used to the narrow quick advantage." "The great problem of the day," he said, "is foreign. . . . Everything you do at home is colored by the foreign picture. The success of the measures you take to nullify the Russian threat and eventually to bring about some way of increasing the strains within the iron curtain and so reaching a place where you [can have] a peace where you can have some confidence, even if it is not the perfect peace we would hope for. . . . All that, of course, is very difficult. . . . At home, your great object is to be stronger in every way in order to carry out that work abroad in confidence."[15]

Eisenhower's strategy emanated from a comprehensive staff study, code-named Solarium, that he initiated in the late spring of 1953. The objective was not to defeat or destroy but rather to change the behavior of the Soviet Union. The United States, the study determined, needed to restore political unity (including civil liberties and capitalistic prosperity) at home; retain a respectable level of conventional military power after the war; remain ahead of the Soviet Union in nuclear technology; establish treaties with other nations that opposed the spread of communism; and negotiate with the Soviets to bring arms control and reduction of tensions; and, as necessary, conduct covert and propaganda activities to weaken its empire.[16]

To this day it is uncertain exactly what brought about the Korean armistice restoring the *status quo ante bellum*, signed in July 1953. The death of Stalin in

March was an opportunity to probe Soviet intentions. Eisenhower responded in April at a meeting of the Society of American Newspaper Editors with his "Chance for Peace"—also known as the "Cross of Iron"—speech. It was, it turned out, the best of his presidency and reflected the values of his Kansas upbringing. He called upon Stalin's successors in the Kremlin to work with him to reduce hostility and the inordinate costs of the arms race. "The world in arms is not spending money alone. It is spending the sweat of its laborers, the genius of its scientists, the hopes of its children. The cost of one modern bomber is this: a modern brick school in more than 30 cities . . . two electric power plants, each serving a town of 60,000. . . . This is not a way of life at all. . . . It is humanity hanging from a cross of iron." The Central Intelligence Agency (CIA) distributed three million copies of the speech in Western Europe, Latin America, and India and sent them to 921 West German newspapers.[17]

Soviet leaders failed to respond to the president's overture. Stalin's death and the new Soviet leadership, Eisenhower's insistence that South Korea allow repatriation of communist prisoners of war, U.S. bombing of river dams in North Korea causing devastating floods, and Eisenhower's transmittal to China of a plan by the U.S. National Security Council for using nuclear weapons if no armistice was forthcoming all had occurred by the time an armistice was signed at Panmunjom in July 1953. By then the fighting in Korea had brought death to 36,500 Americans, three million Koreans, and one million Chinese.[18]

The armistice, of course, did not end hostile relations between North and South. Still, by the summer of 1955 Eisenhower had accomplished the mission he had begun five years earlier as the first NATO supreme commander. In the months leading to the president's July 1955 meeting at Geneva with the Soviet leaders Nikolai Bulganin and Nikita Khrushchev, Eisenhower expressed his belief that the "Soviets seem prepared to accept businesslike procedures." It was at this meeting that they agreed formally to a mutual withdrawal from occupation zones in Austria (and therefore to a neutral nation in the heart of Europe) and to "discuss a mutual verification of nuclear testing." Soon thereafter a united and rearmed West Germany joined NATO.[19]

The Geneva summit was nevertheless a disappointment. The most pressing issue in the new era of transcontinental bombers and missiles, the threat of surprise attack (a so-called nuclear Pearl Harbor), remained unresolved. Aware since his childhood study of the Battle of Cannae of the importance of superior technology, and having reflected upon the threat posed to his D-day strategy if the German V-2 rockets had been deployed, President Eisenhower initiated new American programs of scientific research and covert intelligence. In an effort at reducing tensions and, hopefully, averting the necessity on both sides of developing and deploying new systems, Eisenhower told the Soviet leaders that the United States was not going to attack them with nuclear weapons. "The world's winds go east and west, not north and south," he said. "If there is war, both of us will be destroyed. Only the southern hemisphere will be left." The president proposed that the United States and the Soviet Union exchange blueprints of their respective military installations and allow flyovers of each other's territory to assure themselves that their rival was not preparing an attack.

Eisenhower's efforts to bring reason to the table and to reassure his Soviet counterparts, we now know, backfired. They removed from the mind of Khrushchev any fear that the United States would attack the Soviet Union. Intending to continue his efforts to catch up to the United States in weapons technology, the general secretary's response was curt. Eisenhower's "open skies" proposal was, he said, "an attempt at espionage."[20]

As he had explained in his "Chance for Peace" speech, Eisenhower's Cold War objective was to guarantee the survival of a way of life. This meant, on the one hand, keeping defense spending from becoming so large that it both undermined the civilian sector and provoked the opponent and, on the other, preventing the Soviets from believing nuclear blackmail was a rational option. Without an agreement to reduce tensions, he needed a way to detect any Soviet preparations for a nuclear first strike and to monitor the USSR's aircraft and missile development. Eisenhower therefore ordered the air force and CIA to develop and deploy a high-altitude aircraft photo-reconnaissance capability, the U-2 program, and authorized the air force and navy to continue reconnaissance flights around the periphery of the communist land mass. These programs provided information on Soviet air defense vulnerabilities and mapped targets for the U.S. Strategic Air Command's contingency plans. They also monitored Soviet nuclear testing and bomber development as well as the Soviet economy. The effect was to help Eisenhower keep defense spending within realistic limits and provide a factual basis for negotiations.[21]

Eisenhower's strategy of balance guided his handling of foreign policy crises. He decided in 1954, for example, not to rescue France's colonial position in Indochina after French troops were surrounded at Dien Bien Phu but rather to sponsor a Southeast Asian mutual defense pact, the Southeast Asia

Treaty Organization. He used a congressional resolution, fleet movements in the Pacific, and a threat to respond with nuclear force in combination with certain concessions to end the Formosa Straits crises of 1955 and 1958. He insisted during the Suez crisis in 1956 on the rollback of a British, French, and Israeli invasion of Egypt but warned the Soviets after Khrushchev's threatened missile attack on London. That same month he refused to send U.S. aid to the Hungarians rebelling against communist rule in Budapest. He refused to be stampeded in 1957 into a crash program of military spending after the Soviet Union launched Sputnik, the first earth-orbiting space satellite, and Khrushchev bragged that the Soviet Union was ahead in missiles. In 1958, at the invitation of the prime minister of Lebanon, he landed U.S. marines on a temporary basis to restore order in Beirut. In the same year he decided not to respond to an ultimatum by Khrushchev to turn over West Berlin to East Germany, instead inviting the Soviet leader to the United States for a tour, state visit, and summit meeting.

By April 1960 Eisenhower's approach had brought a reduction of tensions and, no doubt, a safer world. The Khrushchev visit the previous year had gone relatively well. The two leaders had set aside the Berlin issue and had moved toward a treaty to ban nuclear tests in the atmosphere. They planned to meet again in Paris in June, after which, assuming nothing untoward happened, Eisenhower would visit the Soviet Union.[22]

Unfortunately, something did happen. On May 1, 1960—just a month before the planned summit—a Red Army surface-to-air missile detonated close enough to the U-2 spy plane of CIA pilot Francis Gary Powers some sixty thousand feet above Sverdlovsk, Soviet Union, to cause a horrific spiral. Bailing out with some difficulty, Powers floated to earth in his parachute and was almost immediately captured. Eisenhower, having been assured by the CIA that the pilot (and hopefully the plane) would not have survived the crash, authorized the release of a prepared cover story claiming that a weather flight had strayed off course. Khrushchev, whose motives had much to do with Kremlin politics—an effort to improve his stature as a hard-liner—then sprang his trap, producing the pilot, the plane's wreckage, and the camera and film containing photographs of Soviet weapons sites. Khrushchev—desiring not to appear weak and already sensing that he likely would not gain substantive concessions at Paris—launched a propaganda blitz, condemning Eisenhower as a hypocrite and the United States as a warmonger. Eisenhower's only regret, he later admitted, was that "we gave them a bad cover story." Khrushchev allowed the plans for the summit to go forward, but after the conference convened in early June, he said he would negotiate no further until Eisenhower both accepted responsibility for the flights, which he did—he was in fact dismayed and saddened by the turn of events—but also apologized. The latter Eisenhower refused to do, believing his actions, though admittedly provocative, had had peaceful intent and were, after all, nothing new. "Khrushchev," he recalled, "looked at me once as he was making the statement. He saw I was grinning so he put his face down behind his papers. He knew I knew he had his orders."[23] The summit, along with Khrushchev's invitation for a visit to the Soviet Union, came to an abrupt end.

Relations between the Soviet Union and the Western world, much to the satisfaction of the military-industrial complex of both sides, entered an era of renewed tension. Khrushchev, after the election of John F. Kennedy in 1960, again began his pressure on Berlin, increased his support to Fidel Castro's nationalist/communist government in Cuba, and lashed out at the United States after the aborted Bay of Pigs invasion of Cuba in April 1961. It was a new period of tension that brought an escalation of efforts by both sides to outdo the other in numbers of nuclear-warhead-tipped missiles (and also, of course, led to the Cuban missile crisis of October 1962).

The irony, for those critics who later believed that Eisenhower should have taken a softer, less risky line with the Soviets, was that Kennedy, in his campaign for election against the Republican nominee, Eisenhower's vice president, Richard M. Nixon, had accused Nixon (and Eisenhower's policies) of being insufficiently militant and bold. The senator from Massachusetts criticized the general-president not for being overly aggressive or provocative but rather for allowing the Soviets too many advantages—in Vietnam, Suez, the Formosa Straits, and Cuba as well as in numbers of nuclear-warhead-tipped missiles.

In hindsight after the opening of the Soviet archives, it is possible to conclude that Kennedy, while wrong in his accusation that the Republican president had allowed the Soviet Union to get ahead in missiles, was correct in his assertions that Eisenhower was, if anything, too conciliatory. Eisenhower, unfortunately, was never able to dissuade Khrushchev from bluffing and bullying. Looking always for signs of American weakness that he could exploit, Khrushchev, according to his biographer, William Taubman, suffered from an inferiority complex and believed that his rattling of rockets at London during the Suez crisis had brought about an outcome favorable to the Soviets (a naval base at Alexandria on the Mediterranean and influence in the Arab world).

This mentality also told him that Eisenhower's invitation to visit the United States in the face of the Berlin ultimatum in 1958 was a sign that the American president might give in, "a concrete result of the Berlin pressure [Khrushchev] had been exerting on the Western powers." Khrushchev respected Eisenhower's historic stature as a victorious general who had helped the Soviet Union defeat a common foe, but he misjudged Eisenhower the president—possibly because of Ike's personal warmth, self-confidence, desire to avert armed crises, and willingness to reassure him. Soviet ambassador Anatoly Dobrynin later wrote that Khrushchev's perception that Eisenhower would not allow war between the two countries "made it safer for [him] to threaten war in a crisis."

Eisenhower, for his part, knew from his mastery of warfare in the twentieth century that once both sides had a certain number of nuclear weapons and an ability to deliver them, neither could win a general war. Although he also engaged, one can say, in a kind of "nuclear diplomacy" in certain circumstances, as in Korea and the Formosa Straits, Eisenhower rejected a policy of resorting to force for fear that it would escalate to nuclear exchange. The situation, he believed, as the arms race continued, was becoming ever more costly and subject to a disastrous miscalculation. Khrushchev, for his part, believed that "if he had or seemed to have a minimum number of missiles and sounded prepared to use them, the Americans would be intimidated."[24] In Eisenhower's prudent approach Khrushchev saw an opportunity for intimidation. This outlook, of course, got him nowhere but prevented much progress toward arms control or détente.

According to one estimate, defense spending to implement Eisenhower's strategy, even with cuts in Pentagon budgets, cost the United States roughly $2 trillion in today's dollars. By 1960 Eisenhower had given U.S. commanders in Europe, in the event that they could not reach the president for a decision, permission to use nuclear weapons against attacking Soviet forces. On the other hand, despite his creation of the U.S. nuclear arsenal, Eisenhower initiated a test moratorium in 1958, reduced the number of spy flights over the Soviet Union in 1959 to two, placed limits on defense spending, and warned in his farewell address of the unwarranted influence of the military-industrial complex. Finally, by his willingness to pursue a verifiable arms control treaty, the first Republican president of the Cold War established a precedent that culminated in 1972 in the signing of the first Strategic Arms Limitation Treaty (SALT I).[25] In the years that followed, both sides negotiated treaties (START) to reduce the numbers of nuclear weapons.

Thus, Eisenhower's chief strategic failure was not the pursuit of provocative policies—he based his response on an accurate understanding of the foreign, domestic, and technological threats. Rather, it was his inability, during this time of transition from conventional to nuclear warfare, to persuade both his domestic adversaries and his Soviet antagonists that the new technological realities had rendered any decision to use force unacceptable. This lack of success, it seems clear in retrospect, may have stemmed from his Kansas upbringing, his belief in the essential rationality and goodwill of his fellow humans. But it also probably stemmed from the times as well as the mind-sets and ambitions of his opponents—the lag between technological innovation and the development of societal institutions within which they could be harnessed for the benefit of humankind.26 This humble yet confident, cautious yet farsighted and resolute son of the Kansas prairie used a strategy that took the correct lessons from the past and was appropriate to the task. It both drew upon and preserved a way of life—human dignity and independence within a caring community—instilled by his small-town Kansas upbringing. His was a remarkable feat that embodied numerous lessons for twenty-first-century leaders facing a new era of global conflict.

Gordon Parks and the Unending Quest

for Self-fulfillment

John Edgar Tidwell

This above all: to thine own self be true,
And it must follow, as the night the day
Thou canst not then be false to any man.
—*Hamlet*

That [Parks] is a poet with his camera as well as with his pen, shows, I
think, in his concentration on the image.
—*Stephen Spender,* Preface, *Gordon Parks: A Poet and His Camera*

Historians and biographers are generally mystified and con-
fused by the life and work of Gordon Parks, which accounts for the relative
paucity of critical commentary on him. Since he does not fit comfortably in a
literary or cultural movement like the New Negro Renaissance or the Black
Arts Movement, they simply do not know what to do with him. It is a problem

Gordon Parks (November 30, 1912–), whose life epitomizes the thoughtful dignity conveyed by this October 2004 photograph, has both "good and bad" memories of the Kansas town of his birth, Fort Scott, where he returned in the mid-1960s to film the movie version of his well-known autobiographical novel *The Learning Tree*. Courtesy of Bill Snead/*Lawrence Journal-World*.

that emanates from their disciplinary preoccupation with locating a subject within a single category, or "pigeonholing." Parks defies easy categorization by living out the spirit and meaning of "renaissance man." He immerses himself in different art forms and has achieved acclaim in photography, autobiography, poetry, cinema, classical music, fiction writing, painting, and essay writing.

Parks's achievement transcends disciplinary boundaries; blurs distinctions; and emerges with an innovative, malleable definition of art. The controlling theme animating most of his work is an effort to understand himself, his personal development, his driving force or motivation, and the demons that propel him on the road to his many successes. At times this means that his fear of failure has banished him to the isolation or loneliness frequently experienced by the creative artist. In those moments, he has confessed, success came with a terrible price. At other times Parks returns to Fort Scott, Kansas, where he was born on November 30, 1912, to unravel his layered, textured experiences in an effort to make sense of his life. He not only identifies Fort Scott as a land of uncertainty and contradiction, he also foregrounds it as his source of family values and his drive to succeed in a world made complicated by the peculiar social winds shifting the ever-changing dynamics of interracial relations. In striving to come to terms with his personal and racial identities and to understand the forces that motivated him to succeed, Parks inevitably turns intellectually and imaginatively to Kansas.

The youngest of Sarah and Andrew Jackson Parks's fifteen children, Gordon was the last to benefit from the uncanny wisdom of his mother. Although she was never the traditional matriarch or authority figure for the family, she clearly was its guiding force, instilling a sense of morality and family values. So important was her shaping influence in developing family unity that only later did Gordon come to know that Andrew Parks had brought five children with him to the marriage. Sarah Parks refused to allow distinctions created by labels such as "stepchildren" and "half-brothers and -sisters" to be used. She stressed the cohesiveness of the family because only through unity could the Parkses successfully counter the abject poverty that dogged them. Despite economic poverty, their home was filled with so much love that even hard times seemed tolerable.

A lack of money was not the only problem facing the Parks family. Fort Scott, like most Kansas towns, embodied the contradictory, confusing racial setting that belied the familiar historical idea of "free" Kansas. A peculiar combination of racial integration and segregation characterized the state, as in the example of its public schools. The common assumption was that black children did not need to progress beyond the eighth grade; as a result, few of them attended the almost exclusively white high schools. Guidance counselors discouraged even those few from seeking a college education. The reason, simply, was that a degree was unnecessary to be a Pullman porter, a redcap, a day laborer, a truck farmer, or a domestic servant. Against the potential bitterness that might have consumed Parks, Sarah reinforced one idea: if a white student could be successful, Gordon could be successful too. This encouragement was a powerful motivating force in Parks's determined drive for success. Even though his formal education was cut short, his self-education via voracious reading and tenacious practice more than compensated for the lack of a high school diploma or college degree. It eventually resulted in his being awarded over fifty-two honorary degrees. The foundational statement of these lessons that propelled him to a phenomenal record of success is clearly articulated in his first novel, *The Learning Tree*.[1]

Parks describes *The Learning Tree* as his first autobiography *and* as "a novel from life." In effect, what rescues the curiously blended narrative from an aesthetic tug-of-war is the form of novel that literary critics commonly identify as bildungsroman, a German term designating a coming-of-age novel or a tale of development. By definition, a "novel of becoming" traces the growth of a character from an earlier to a later point in his life, often the adolescent years. It sets up the expectation that the narrative traces the protagonist's emergence from a state of innocence into one of experience. Since the emphasis is on what and how the character learns, this kind of novel often has a didactic quality. *The Learning Tree* sacrificed historical and biographical accuracy for the thematic expression of lessons Parks learned from his life in Fort Scott.

For this autobiographical novel Parks created protagonist Newt Winger, a fictionalized version of himself, and traced Newt's development from about his twelfth to his sixteenth birthdays. In effect, the reader follows Newt as he develops an awareness of sex, love, death, religion, and racism. With the assistance of his various "teachers," Newt grows and matures through these experiences. Among many excellent sources of instruction, his mother, Sarah, and his Uncle Rob are especially crucial to his learning process. In one of her many pieces of advice, Sarah articulates the title's significance: "You can learn just as much here about people and things as you can learn any place else. Cherokee Flats is sorta like a fruit tree. Some of the people are good and some of them are bad—just like the fruit on a tree. . . . No matter if you go or stay, think of Cherokee Flats like that till the day you die—let it be your learnin' tree." Cherokee Flats, thinly disguised as the Fort Scott of Parks's youth, provides the site of Newt's coming-of-age. His father, Jack, has already described the town, and actually the whole state, as "a plateau of uncertainty." That is to say, Cherokee Flats embodies the contradiction between the American creed and America's practice of that creed. The laws that promise freedom to all its citizens are, for black people, restrained by the social custom of Jim Crow. In response, Newt's Uncle Rob, blinded years ago by an explosion, expresses arguably the most important piece of advice Newt hears in the novel: "Take the rest of your anger out on the piano."[2]

The philosophical vision engendered by Rob's blindness makes his advice especially poignant: "You've got to believe in yourself," he tells Newt. "Don't let the teachers or anyone else hold you back. Learn all you can, so when bigger things come you'll be ready for them." When Newt gets into a racially motivated fight with a white boy and his mother, Rob responds by imparting a foundational concept to which Parks would continually return: the value of developing and choosing weapons. With characteristic avuncular wisdom, Rob teaches Newt the most effective way to eliminate racism. The solution, simply stated, is through art, a concept Parks developed further in his second autobiography, *A Choice of Weapons*.[3]

The second installment of Parks's life story recorded the historical events and probed the meaning of his life in the years roughly from 1928 to 1943. In it he proclaims his life was nearly consumed by anger and bitterness, even though these qualities are not developed in the text with the emotional intensity they deserve. At the same time, a will to love, forgive, and understand asserts itself against the potential for bitterness to become all-consuming, for hatred to have a crippling effect on the shape and direction of his life. The reader is effectively guided in a more positive direction. In the prologue Parks recounts how he was invited to witness the execution of a convicted murderer. As if in a double-exposed photographic moment, Parks looks through the glass that separates the execution's observers from the prisoner and perceives his own image emerging from within the prisoner's image. Later, as he leaves after the execution, he reflects upon his own past. It is a past filled with discrimination, violence, and hatred—all of which beckoned him down the same road that the convict traveled. His saving grace, he says, was the several weapons he cultivated for protection: "I chose them slowly, with pain and infinite caution. Here now, in the chill of this frightful morning, their presence comforts me: how fortunate I was to have the privilege of choosing them."[4]

There is little doubt that Parks could have gone the way of this murderer. Following his mother's death when he was sixteen years old, he went to live with a sister in St. Paul, Minnesota. Arriving in the middle of Minnesota's fabled harsh winter, Parks found himself homeless and adrift when his brother-in-law kicked him out. Riding the trolley car back and forth from St. Paul to Minneapolis, he pondered his future, which looked as bleak as the raging snowstorm from which he sought refuge. In a climactic moment he took out his knife with the intention of killing and robbing the conductor. Something pulled his hand back, and the unsuspecting white conductor generously gave him a few dollars to get a meal and some clothes.

Parks continually found himself being rescued in a series of similar life-changing events, and he slowly built a refuge against a life of crime. He developed his earlier experiments on the piano, constructed his own notation system (he did not read music), and wrote "No Love," a song that was played on the radio by a nationally known band. While working as a busboy at the exclusive Minnesota Club in 1929, he began reading voraciously from its library as a way of augmenting his education. It was not until he discovered photography while working as a porter on a train that he cultivated one of his most important weapons.

For Parks photography proved to be salvation *and* creative expression. It was a weapon against discrimination *and* an instrument enabling personal growth and interracial healing. Of all his weapons, fashion and documentary photography were most responsible for saving Parks's life and for making the acquisition of his other weapons financially possible.

In a period of "apprenticeship," Parks studied copies of *Vogue* for their luxurious fashions. Without a portfolio or experience, he took one of his boldest chances. He convinced the owners of Frank Murphy's, the most impressive fashion store in St. Paul, to let him take pictures of their models. When he developed the photographs, Parks discovered that he had double-exposed all of the film except one image. With few options left, he enlarged and displayed the one picture. So impressed were the Murphys that another photo shoot was arranged. Marva Louis, an aficionado of fashion and the wife of heavyweight champion Joe Louis, thought Parks's display demonstrated an exceptional talent. She encouraged him to move to Chicago in the late 1930s and, with her assistance, engage in fashion photography in a more lucrative, appreciative place. Parks achieved a prominent place in the world of fashion photography, as attested by the freelance work he would later obtain for *Vogue* and *Glamour* magazine.

In between his fashion sessions and his runs on the railroad between St. Paul and Chicago, Parks took time to explore and document the "bums warming at bonfires, [and] beggars wandering the windswept streets." His many photos led him to probe the different ways in which meaning could be conveyed through pictures. For an answer he turned to the painters who spent a great deal of time at the Chicago Southside Community Center. They had asked the same questions and responded by representing their subjects in a number of ways: graphic protest, grim realism, and merciless satire. "In purpose, and execution," he wrote, "the two kinds of expression [realism and satire] tended to oppose each other." Mike Bannarn, a friend who was both a painter and a sculptor, helped Parks resolve the contraries. "I get just as riled up over preserving the beauty of things as I do about destroying the ugliness of them," he said to Parks.[5] The same aesthetic impulse or emotional engagement that motivates destruction also inspires preservation. Although at this point in his apprenticeship Parks understood how the same principle could work in photography, his most protracted education in the subject would come a bit later.

Without question, the two most important events in Parks's growth and development as a photographer were his apprenticeship under Roy Emerson Stryker at the Farm Security Administration (FSA) and his employment at *Life* magazine. The former was made possible in 1941 when he received the first Julius Rosenwald Fellowship for Photography, which carried a monthly stipend of $200. In January 1942 Parks began training under Stryker. What made this period arguably the most significant one for Parks was his discovery of the "camera as a documentary weapon."

The FSA was a program implemented by the Roosevelt administration to assist farmers who had been adversely affected by the Depression and the severe drought that created the "dust bowl." As a way of documenting the devastation wreaked upon the lives of these farmers, the FSA created a photography section, of which Roy Stryker became head. Stryker, Parks recounted, was "a remarkable man with sparse technical knowledge of cameras but an acute awareness of their power to communicate."[6] Parks drew this conclusion from the first assignment Stryker gave him.

Parks found Washington, D.C., to be a decidedly Southern town with a form of racism more virulent than he had experienced in Kansas and Minnesota. In the nation's capital, the site and symbol of American democratic principles, Parks was shocked into realizing the depth of discriminatory practices when he was denied service at a restaurant, a department store, and a movie theater. These insults so angered him that his first impulse was to expose bigotry through photographs. With Uncle Rob's avuncular wisdom, Stryker first counseled Parks to prove himself a good craftsman with a camera so that he would become "accepted as another photographer—not just as a Negro photographer." Then, in an especially important directive, he advised Parks to go home and "to put it on paper." What he meant was: "You can't take a picture of a white salesman, waiter, or ticket seller and just say they are prejudiced. . . . You've got to verbalize the experience first, then find logical ways to express it in pictures. The right words too are important; they should underscore your photographs. Think in terms of images and words. They can be mighty powerful when they are fitted together properly."

The next day, when Parks returned with a narrative of nearly every racial injustice he had undergone, Stryker acknowledged the horrible experiences and then advised Parks "to simplify all this material."[7] He assigned Parks to go through hundreds of photographs to see how Dorothea Lange, Carl Mydans, Walker Evans, and other FSA photographers had fought the evils of poverty and racism with a camera. Their pictures were "full of the intolerance [for] the poor, indicted America." Then Parks began to understand: "There were some [victims of disaster] no doubt who laid these tragedies to God. But research accompanying these stark photographs accused man himself—especially the lords of the land. . . . I began to get the point."[8]

However, the point proved difficult to implement. Stryker assigned Parks the task of talking with Ella Watson, an African American woman who cleaned offices and mopped floors at the FSA. The result was *American Gothic,* arguably Parks's best-known photograph. The Grant Wood–style picture of Watson with a broom in one hand and a mop in the other as she stood before the American flag, looking directly into the camera, was, by Parks's own admission, "unsubtle." Still, it represented a major shift in his aesthetic. He began to understand what the other FSA photographers had learned: how to make photos reveal the depth of their subjects' humanity and dignity, which, in turn, severely indicted the sources of the subjects' oppression. Parks saw how to make his camera a means of protest.

The Southern faction of Congress and some Republicans were offended by such displays and increasingly attacked the heart of the FSA budget. They exerted so much pressure that by the fall of 1942 the photographic section was absorbed into the Office of War Information (OWI). Parks remained long enough with the OWI to have his efforts to document the valor of the 332nd Squadron of all-black pilots frustrated. Ending *A Choice of Weapons* at this point, Parks reminded the reader that the sacrifices made by these pilots were quite high, even for "the price [of] a questionable equality."[9] But Parks did not succumb to defeatism or disillusionment. From Roy Stryker he had gained discipline and a sense of direction. He remembered that his mother had freed him from believing in a curse of inferiority simply because he had been born black; he knew that the ambition and purpose she had taught him would enable him to stay the course. Even though he did not know what the future might bring, he confidently faced the unknown with a choice of weapons to fight what might come.

After working with Stryker for three years at Standard Oil, Parks, beginning in 1948, achieved a long-held dream of working at *Life* magazine as a documentary and fashion photographer. *To Smile in Autumn,* his autobiography covering the years 1944–1978, recounted many of his experiences. *To Smile in Autumn* is the most experimental of Parks's autobiographies. It combines poetry, journal entries, letters, and narrative into a text with a modernist feel. Parts of it recast material dealing with the 1960s earlier presented in his book *Born Black.* In organizing his life story this way, Parks revealed some of the maturity of thought and surety of vision that characterized the diversity of assignments he undertook at *Life.* En route to achieving the height of aesthetic prowess, Parks wrestled with a number of personal and professional issues. Among many other issues, he had to confront the question of whether he was *Life*'s photographer and reporter or whether he was *Life*'s black photographer and reporter. On a much deeper level, he had to come to terms with the meaning of his own blackness. Following a nearly two-year stint in Paris, Parks returned in 1952 to a United States on the brink of interracial turmoil. But a personal turmoil bothered him as well: "I had returned an unlikely loner still driving failure from my dreams, still being pulled by something up ahead— something that hinted there was more luck in store, but that first I would have to pay for it. I recall hours in shadowy bars, drinking, searching the years for some connection to whatever it was that was moving me. It wasn't enough simply to be moving; I wanted to know what was making it happen."

In escaping the confining or limiting existence that had trapped so many other African Americans, Parks felt he had lost many black friends along the way. Blackness, though, could not dictate his work or his aspirations. Despite all the trappings of financial success, he wrote, a "hunger still gnawed at me." He concluded that there was no future in the past and resolved to look only at what lay ahead. In truth, he had little choice because something still deeply troubled him: "I couldn't understand why I felt so troubled, *and so alone.*"[10]

As a photographer, Parks was assigned every conceivable topic. Race was not a consideration unless the editors felt he could bring a special significance to the story. Even then, he wrote, "I went in as a *Life* reporter—not as *Life*'s 'black' reporter."[11] In the midst of these considerations Parks found himself suddenly liberated to gather his own research and photograph his subjects when a white reporter assigned to work with him committed a major faux pas at a black church in 1953. By not removing his hat when he entered the church, the young reporter unwittingly insulted the church and the congregation. His heartfelt apologies were insufficient to mollify those who considered his error just another indication of white disrespect for black people. Parks took advantage of the opportunity given him by the reporter's withdrawal from the assignment. He added doing his own research to his arsenal of weapons and over the next fifteen years shot and wrote his own stories.

In those years Parks's stories covered a broad range, from the heiress Gloria Vanderbilt to Malcolm X and the Nation of Islam, Muhammad Ali, the Fontenelle family in Harlem, the Causey family in Alabama, and Flavio de Silva in Brazil. In assigning racial topics to Parks, *Life,* to its credit, was admitting its ignorance about such matters and expressing a sense that the magazine needed to learn more about the one-tenth of the nation that was effectively disenfranchised. When the embers of the civil rights movement in the 1950s erupted into the flames of Black Power in the 1960s, the staff at *Life* asked the question "Why?" Why did young African Americans feel the need to reject racial integration as a social goal in favor of establishing a separate nation within a nation? Why were these young insurgents so angry? By looking to Parks for answers, the magazine was unknowingly looking to a man who felt he was on a tightrope. "Where the 'tightrope' came was knowing that the militancy that was out there somehow was seeping into my bones," Parks told an interviewer. "I, as a reporter, had to be careful if I wanted to hold an honorable position with the editors of *Life* and an honorable position with the militants I was covering. . . . The 'tightrope' was not falling for everything the militants wanted me to believe and not letting *Life* push me in the direction they wanted me to go while I was writing a story."[12] At times the tightrope seemed less precarious because Parks constantly reminded himself that he "had chosen [his] camera as a tool of social consciousness." He had to remember that he was a journalist first. After a while this mantra proved to be difficult to sustain. The problem was that he also had to remain true to his own convictions. As a consequence, he would "have to bear the anguish of objectivity, and try to avoid those intellectual biases that subjectivity [could] impose upon a reporter."[13] Despite the personal anxiety, Parks walked the line with true professionalism and created a reportorial style that was not biased and that also enabled him to be true to himself.

In 1968 Parks received another opportunity to add to his arsenal of weapons when Hollywood finally decided to make *The Learning Tree* into a film. After a series of disappointments, Parks was given virtual control over the movie by being selected to be its director, screenwriter, producer, and composer of the musical score—an assignment only Charlie Chaplin and Orson Welles had previously received.[14] In accepting these roles, Parks became the first African American to be given a directorship of a major Hollywood motion picture. The success of the movie made it possible for Parks to be selected to direct *Shaft* (1971) and its sequel, *Shaft's Big Score* (1972). *The Super Cops* (1974) and *Leadbelly* (1976) followed. In retrospect, his directing of the Shaft movies was an especially big challenge because they departed so dramatically from *The Learning Tree* and its autobiographical themes. The ethos engendered by the Kansas prairies seemed incapable of mirroring the urban geography of Harlem. However, the part of Parks that continually stretched and strove to conquer new horizons no doubt led to his success with these two films.

Parks's life and career are littered with "firsts." He was the first recipient of the Rosenwald Fellowship for Photography; the first black photographer hired at *Life, Glamour,* and *Vogue;* the first black man to direct a major Hollywood motion picture; and more. But listing or cataloguing his "firsts" is a poor substitute for defining the shifting focus of his art. After his tenure with *Life* ended in 1972, a combination of art photography, musical composition, and poetry resulted in the expansion of weapons that enabled Parks to choose how to confront the world and represent his emotional responses to it. Through his intermittently appearing autobiographies, Parks invited readers into his inner sanctum, into the interrogation of self that revealed itself in poetry, painting, classical music, and more. This aesthetic shift from overtly social concerns did not signal abrogation or surrender; instead his art became more intensely personal. This revised, almost confessional, voice probed the autobiographical impulse that compelled him to strive, to seek, to discover what lay over the next horizon. In so doing, he conducted experiments that resulted in an inescapably distinctive aesthetic vision. This vision is expressed in such books as *Whispers of Intimate Things* (1971), *Moments Without Proper Names* (1975), *Arias in Silence* (1994), *Glimpses Toward Infinity* (1996), and the remarkable retrospective *Half-Past Autumn* (1997).

The highly respected poet Stephen Spender once observed that Parks "is a poet with his camera as well as with his pen." In making this claim, Spender introduced what he perceived as one of the most important features of Parks's books combining poetry and artwork: a concentration on the image. There is little question that Spender's analysis represented a culmination of sorts. Prior to winning his Rosenwald fellowship, Parks spent time talking aesthetics with the famous painter Charles White and other artists who worked out of the Southside Community Center in Chicago. Through these interactions he came to understand the importance of image in art. Roy Stryker had wisely counseled Parks to focus on making the image communicate the idea. Thus, when Spender continued his preface by saying that Parks's "photographs nearly always leave a single, strong, clear image in the mind or else contrasted images," he called attention to Parks's years of practice and experimentation.[15]

Parks himself has much to say about his own aesthetic practice. In one of his most compelling statements, written as a foreword to *Arias in Silence,* he wrote:

> The pictures that have most persistently confronted my camera have been those of crime, racism and poverty. I was cut through by the jagged edges of all three. Yet I remain aware of imagery that lends itself to serenity and beauty, and here my camera has searched for nature's evanescent splendors. Recording them was a matter of devout observance, a sort of metamorphosis through which I called upon things dear to me—poetry, music and the magic of watercolor. . . . Paint, music and camera came together like souls touching—lifting me from earth to the sky.[16]

This self-description was what friend and fellow *Life* photographer Philip B. Kunhardt meant when he talked about Park's "poet's sense—his eye, his ear, his soul."[17] For some, such as the art historian Philip Brookman, this shift makes his formal expression more abstract. For Parks, though, his newest mode of expression represents a deepened, more intense exploration of an interior landscape. It allows him new choices in trying to reach that something that continuously pulls him toward the future. Having sacrificed himself to the loneliness of the artist, his latest work enables him to find new ways of interrogating who he is and where he is going. The aesthetic spirit still calls him at age ninety-two years, and he feels he must continue to answer.

The Gordon Parks of the twenty-first century is obviously quite different from the Parks of the Depression years and World War II, when he was trying to find his voice. At the same time, he remains rooted in the values he learned growing up in Fort Scott, Kansas. Kansas, as he said in the Prologue to *Half-Past Autumn,* has always been his touchstone.[18] He fully accepted his mother's teaching that race could never be an excuse for failing; if a white person could be successful, so could he. She taught him strength of character, thus encouraging him to strive to reach the limits of his potential. In so doing, he would not follow blindly or uncritically; instead, he would always be true to himself. In a magnificently poignant poem titled "Parting," he used his father's voice to express this same idea. A portion of it reads:

> And you will learn
> that
> All the same things
> Are really not the same,
> that
> You must select your friends
> With the same care I gave
> to choosing your mother
>
> . . .
>
> Avoid things that die too easily
> And get your own soul ready
> to die well.
>
> . . .
>
> Remember most that everything
> I have told you might very well
> amount to everything
> Or
> Perhaps nothing. But be most thankful, son
> If in autumn you can still manage a smile.[19]

In giving consideration to Parks as an innovator, one must be prepared to shadow a life that even in "half-past autumn" continues to strive, to seek, to do, and above all to be true to itself.

Vern Miller: Kansas' Supercop

Brian Moline

In the early 1950s a restless Wichita college student began a youthful flirtation with law enforcement that would quickly evolve into a lifelong passion. Vern Miller's vague ambition to become a lawyer would be postponed for over a decade while he pursued a career that would ultimately border on legendary. Known by friend and foe alike as "Supercop" and "Supersheriff," Miller would arguably become the best-known Kansas lawman since Wyatt Earp and "Bat" Masterson. His hands-on style and feats of derring-do were avidly chronicled in the local and even national media. Miller parlayed his enormous popularity into a statewide political career that would, for a time, redefine the politics of the state. He was the first Democrat elected attorney general in eighty years and, when he sought reelection, carried all 105 counties in the state. In 1974 he came within four thousand votes of being elected governor of Kansas. Miller's credo that all the laws, no matter how symbolic or inconvenient, should be vigorously and equally enforced won him a loyal bipartisan following but also a fierce and vocal opposition.

Vern Miller (August 28, 1928–), the unlikely victor in the 1970 campaign for state attorney general, who became a symbol for those who favored aggressive and visible enforcement of the state's drug and liquor laws during a turbulent era, was first attracted to law enforcement by his love of motorcycles. This 1969 photograph was taken while the Democratic sheriff of Sedgwick County worked a Haysville parade. Courtesy of Vern Miller.

It is no accident that Miller's meteoric political career coincided with the 1960s. The politics of this turbulent era were defined by an escalating fear of crime, racial tension, antiestablishment turmoil on college campuses, and a revolution in sexual mores and moral values. Fear and uncertainty divided the electorate along racial, gender, and generational lines and created a climate made to order for candidates such as Miller.

LaVerne Adilmon Miller was born August 28, 1928, in Wichita, Kansas.[1] He was raised in a rough-and-tumble neighborhood known as Hoover's Orchard, attended a rural elementary school, and entered Wichita High School North in 1943. An indifferent student, Miller was a stellar athlete despite his average height and weight. He loved sports and physical activity and participated in football, basketball, and track. In his junior year in high school he acquired a secondhand motorcycle, which would trigger another lifelong passion. The motorcycle became an integral part of his law enforcement career as well as his private persona. At every opportunity he would take to a motorcycle to hunt down an escaped prisoner, search for a lost child, or patrol a picket line to head off violence.[2]

Shortly after his high school graduation in 1946, Miller enlisted in the U.S. Army and was shipped to Korea prior to the breakout of hostilities. While in Korea he contracted rheumatic fever, which left him with a persistent heart murmur.

Miller returned to Wichita after military service and enrolled at Friends University. His plans to study law were temporarily sidetracked by his love of motorcycles and a newspaper advertisement seeking candidates for the Sedgwick County sheriff's newly created motorcycle unit. Miller applied, was hired by Sheriff Bob Gray, and for the next few years combined motorcycle traffic duties with his college studies. During Tyler C. Lockett Sr.'s four-year tenure as sheriff, Miller worked his way up to captain of the road patrol, the youngest ever at the time. But when Floyd Shroeder was elected sheriff in 1954, Miller was not retained.[3]

For the next four years Miller continued his college studies and operated a service station. He would later observe that the service station was more lucrative than any of the public offices he held. During this period he graduated from Friends and enrolled at the University of Oklahoma City Law School, one of the very few accredited programs offering a law degree that could be completed with night courses.

By law Shroeder could not succeed himself in 1958, and Denver Bland, a captain of the road patrol, was the Democrat candidate for sheriff. Anxious to return to law enforcement, Miller decided to make his first political effort as candidate for marshal of the Court of Common Pleas. A controversial "right to work" constitutional amendment incited organized labor to get out the vote, and both Miller and Bland were elected in a virtual Democrat sweep of the Sedgwick County courthouse. Miller's two terms (four years) as marshal would prove tumultuous and put him at odds with his fellow Democrat Sheriff Bland.

The office of marshal had traditionally been little more than a minor political sinecure. The Court of Common Pleas, since abolished, had jurisdiction in civil disputes under $2,500 and criminal misdemeanors. It also handled the first stages of criminal felony matters. Miller lost no time in pushing the envelope of his authority. He quickly recognized the statutory powers granted to the marshal but never fully exercised before and transformed the office from a sleepy backwater to an aggressive force for law enforcement. Twelve years later he would duplicate that performance by making the attorney general's office the top law enforcement office in the state—something it had always been in theory but never in practice.

Miller was sworn in for a second term on January 9, 1961. Within days he and his deputies began a campaign to arrest scofflaws who had failed to pay fines and costs. The newspapers were soon filled with stories of Marshal Miller's exploits, from foiling a jailbreak to acting as an undercover operative to purchase drugs. During this period Miller developed a technique he was to use often in drug investigations and surveillances and that would become his trademark. He would hide in the trunk of an operative's car, and when his agent appeared to be in danger with no way to get help—at the right moment, when the buy was made or the suspect had made contact—Miller would leap out of the trunk and personally make the arrest.[4]

Tension developed early between Miller and Sheriff Bland. Kansas had strict liquor laws that several sheriffs had been notoriously lax in enforcing. And it had not escaped Miller's notice that certain private clubs seemed to operate slot machines and other gambling devices with impunity. Miller complained to Bland on several occasions about lax and selective law enforcement, with no success. On January 12, 1962, volunteers from the attorney general's and county attorney's offices joined the marshal in raiding several Wichita nightclubs. The sheriff, whose department was conspicuously absent from the raid, was furious.[5]

Bland was unable to succeed himself in 1962, and Miller announced his candidacy for sheriff; soon Bland announced that he would be a candidate for marshal. The open and public antagonism between Miller and Bland left damaging political scars, and both men were defeated in the general election. For the next two years Miller worked in a plastics factory and continued to commute to night law school. The 1964 election for sheriff was a rematch between Miller and the incumbent, Tommy Tomlinson, and Miller won handily; subsequently, the two-term limitation was abolished, and Miller served three two-year terms.

During the late 1960s the Miller legend began to evolve in earnest. From almost his first day in office, the new sheriff made it clear that he intended to be much more than a desk-bound administrator. His aggressive hands-on style of law enforcement, frenetic energy, and friendly, engaging manner combined to make him one of the most admired and certainly most recognizable figures in Wichita.[6]

Miller usually led the motorcycle patrol on occasions demanding crowd control or conducting manhunts. Often in the midafternoon he would exchange his white shirt and tie for a uniform and ride a motorcycle to one of Wichita's four aircraft-manufacturing plants. There he would be observed by thousands of potential voters personally directing traffic during the shift changes. And many a bereaved family suddenly noticed that the motorcycle escort for the funeral cortege was none other than the sheriff himself.[7]

Miller's willingness, even eagerness, to put himself in harm's way inspired a loyalty among his deputies that was legendary. He refused to sit behind a desk and order others to take risks he would not take himself. Time and again Miller faced the same dangers as the street cops. The examples are legion.

One hot August night in 1967 Miller was wounded in a shotgun attack, narrowly missed crashing into a freight train during a high-speed pursuit, and single-handedly faced the threat of an angry mob. This harrowing series of events occurred when the summer heat and escalating racial tensions combined to create a dangerous situation in the predominantly black area of northeast Wichita. Miller was conversing with a group of young black men when a carload of white youths fired a shotgun into the group. Despite wounds to his neck and hand, Miller pursued but lost the suspects after a high-speed chase. Still bleeding from his wounds, Miller spent several hours defusing an angry and volatile crowd that had gathered at the scene of the crime. He later apprehended the perpetrators.

On another occasion Miller received a tip that the home of a wealthy Wichita jeweler was going to be robbed. He arranged with the jeweler to vacate the premises for the night and for several hours lay quietly on a narrow beam in the living room. Long after midnight two men broke in the house through a sliding glass door. As the loot-laden duo was about to leave, Miller swung down from his perch and arrested the flabbergasted thieves.[8]

Another well-publicized arrest occurred in May 1965 when Richard Lee McCarther, a prisoner awaiting transfer to the state penitentiary, managed to escape from the Sedgwick County jail. It was the second escape for McCarther from the same jail in less than a year. McCarther was facing a sentence of 119 years plus life when he escaped the second time. McCarther's wife told Miller, "You won't take him alive this time. He'll kill you first."[9]

For two months Miller personally pursued the fugitive, usually on all-night surveillance and sometimes hiding in the trunk of McCarther's wife's car while she toured the escapee's late-night haunts. After many false leads, suddenly, by sheer coincidence, Miller spotted McCarther casually strolling down the street. A foot chase, fistfight, and gun battle ensued, but Miller finally captured McCarther and delivered him to the Kansas penitentiary.[10]

Miller faced his closest brush with death in a long series of such encounters on a June evening in 1968. Two men and two women, suspects in the brutal murder and robbery of an elderly Missouri farmer, were thought to be aboard a Transcontinental bus due to pass through Wichita. Miller and two deputies flagged down the bus. Miller explained the situation to the bus driver and started down the aisle looking for a face that matched the descriptions. The narrowness of the aisle forced the party to proceed single file, with Miller in the lead. Near the back of the bus, convicted killer and fugitive Marvin Fisher slumped in his seat next to his girlfriend. Across the aisle were their two companions. Miller first spotted Fisher, whose right hand was concealed in his shirt. When Miller asked for identification, Fisher suddenly produced a loaded and cocked .45-caliber pistol. As the pistol swung upward toward Miller's head, he grabbed Fisher's arm. The bus driver, directly behind Miller, clutched at Fisher's head, pulling him forward. For several seconds the three struggled for possession of the gun. "He almost had it between my eyes," Miller recalled, "when a shot rang out and almost deafened me. For a moment I thought I had been shot." But Deputy Art Stone, third in line, had fired one shot just inches under Miller's armpit, which killed Fisher instantly. The other three suspects were captured without incident and returned to Missouri to face homicide charges.[11]

In 1966 Miller received his law degree and was admitted to the Kansas bar. As the end of his third term approached in 1970, he quietly made plans to retire from public life, to give up politics and law enforcement, and to enter private law practice. It would turn out, however, that his political career had just begun.

That same year Governor Robert Docking sought an unprecedented third term. The Democratic governor faced stiff opposition from Attorney General Kent Frizzell, who had been a popular state senator from Wichita. Anxious to shore up his Wichita base, Docking approached Miller to join him on the state ticket as candidate for attorney general. The approach caught Miller by surprise. Although technically a lawyer, he had never practiced a single day. Party loyalty and personal affection for Docking, however, ultimately caused him to agree.[12]

Richard Seaton of Manhattan won the Republican primary, and the outcome of the general election seemed a foregone conclusion. Kansas, after all, had not elected a non-Republican attorney general for over eighty years. Seaton was a Harvard Law graduate who had risen to chief of the attorney general's criminal division, whereas Miller, by his own admission, was "just a cop with a law degree." Miller's self-definition was highlighted just weeks before the election during a racial conflict at a Wichita high school. In newspaper accounts Miller was featured prominently wading into a group of rioting youths and fighting hand to hand with them for over an hour. A front-page photograph of the disheveled and bleeding sheriff was a timely and graphic reminder of Miller's campaign slogan—"Vern Miller—He'll Be There."[13]

With just weeks left in the campaign, 50 percent of likely voters listed themselves as undecided. But Miller's promise to emphasize the law enforcement role of the attorney general's office proved to be a persuasive message, and he won the election by over seventy-five thousand votes. Miller ran well not only in Sedgwick and the surrounding counties but also in the traditionally Republican western counties that were part of the Wichita media market.

Miller wasted no time in demonstrating that his promise to bring the full power of the attorney general to street-level law enforcement was no idle boast. Throughout his campaign he had consistently spoken of his alarm at the escalating drug culture, particularly on college campuses. His campaign against drugs produced his most memorable quotation: "If elected, one of my first moves will be to land in the middle of the drug-ridden, hippie culture of Lawrence with both feet."[14]

And that was exactly what he did less than two months after taking office. On February 26, 1971, thirty-three residents of the Lawrence area were arrested and charged with drug violations. In July raiding parties personally led by the attorney general struck simultaneously in fifteen Kansas cities at 4:00 A.M. and arrested fifty people on various narcotics charges. The nineteen-year-old son of the Council Grove mayor was arrested when a search of the mayor's basement yielded a freshly cut batch of marijuana.

Miller had made another campaign promise that did not seem particularly significant at the time. "If a law is on the books," he remarked, "it's my job to enforce it. A law officer does not have the right to pick and choose what laws to enforce and what laws not to; and the private citizen does not have the right to choose which laws to obey and which to ignore. The law is for everyone and I intend to enforce it fairly and impartially."[15]

The first hint that Miller was serious occurred when he suggested that "tailgate" parties and office World Series pools were illegal. The law in Kansas at the time said lotteries were illegal. Since bingo was a lottery and lotteries were against the law, the attorney general shut down all the civic club and church-sponsored bingo games. Predictably there was a howl of outrage from all over the state. "If you don't like the law, change it," Miller replied.[16]

The law said gambling was illegal, but some social and country clubs had slot machines and dice tables. Many of the same businessmen who had applauded the attorney general's crackdown on the youth-dominated drug trade were indignant when Miller moved against their private clubs, seizing gambling equipment, making arrests, and challenging local law enforcement to stop looking the other way while the law was being broken. Miller's concern about local law enforcement was legitimate. The gamblers surprised in a raid on a Great Bend social club included an assistant chief of police. The chief of police was summoned and attempted to arrest the attorney general for trespass.[17]

This commitment to enforcing the letter of *all* laws led Miller to the logical but controversial conclusion that even out-of-state entities should follow Kansas law while in Kansas. Consequently, Miller asked the Amtrak Corporation to stop serving mixed drinks on its trains while traveling through Kansas since the practice violated a state law prohibiting the open saloon. Amtrak, a federally funded corporation, simply ignored the request.

On a July evening in 1972 Miller personally boarded a train temporarily stopped in Newton, Kansas. In an unprecedented move, the Kansas attorney general raided a common carrier, arrested three Amtrak employees, and put the federal government on notice that it too must answer to the laws of a sovereign state.

The next question, of course, was what to do about the airlines that had traditionally offered wine and spirits along with coffee and tea. When Miller suggested that the airlines cease and desist from serving alcohol while flying over Kansas, much of the nation scoffed. But for Vern Miller the answer was as clear-cut and enforceable as the ban on narcotics and gambling—cease and desist or pay the penalty. Perhaps cognizant of the Amtrak affair, the airlines for the most part complied with the request. For a time coast-to-coast airline passengers were startled to learn that no alcohol was available as the aircraft passed through the skies over Kansas. Miller's simple but effective credo was attractive to many Kansans but also earned him the scorn of some editorial

writers and occasionally made the state the butt of late-night television come-
dians. However, his relentless enforcement of increasingly unpopular laws
forced the legislature to confront changing public attitudes and modernize an-
tiquated laws on alcohol consumption and even gambling.[18]

Miller sought reelection in 1972. His opponent was Robert Hoffman, a former assistant attorney general and longtime Republican activist. The race set
several political records. It was the first time in Kansas history that a candidate
for attorney general carried all 105 counties in the state. Miller received 67
percent of the vote and three out of four votes in Sedgwick County. He was the
first candidate to receive over 600,000 votes, and his majority was the largest
of any candidate for any office in the history of the state.[19]

Miller's second term as attorney general was pretty much a replay of his
first. The most controversial event in his second term was an investigation into
an alleged 1972 political bribery case that embarrassed his old friend and ally
Robert Docking. The complicated case revolved around six trials involving
eighteen individuals and five corporate defendants accused of diverting
$30,000 to Robert Docking's campaign fund in return for a $500,000 contract
for architectural design work at the University of Kansas Medical Center.
Miller's office conducted an inquisition that ultimately uncovered links to the
Docking administration. Robert Brandt, former secretary of administration
under Docking, implicated former Docking aide Richard Malloy and the governor's brother, George R. (Dick) Docking, in the scandal. Although Governor
Docking was never personally tarnished, the incident soured the relationship
between Docking and Miller.[20]

In 1974 Robert Docking decided to retire to private life at the end of his unprecedented fourth term. Miller's immense popularity and lopsided reelection
win inevitably created the belief that he would be the next governor. However,
the attorney general routinely denied gubernatorial ambitions. He had observed the governor's job at close hand, and the administrative detail and political intrigue did not attract him. In the end he felt he owed it to his supporters to run, and he reluctantly committed to the race.

Robert Bennett, a state senator from Johnson County, won the Republican
primary for governor that year and prepared to face the popular attorney general in the fall. The contrast between the two men was stark. Bennett was a
bearded, erudite corporation lawyer and president of the state senate. He had
an encyclopedic knowledge of the budget and operations of state government.
Miller cheerfully admitted to knowing very little about the details of state gov-

ernment beyond his law enforcement sphere. Bennett was a poised and force-ful public speaker who spoke in paragraphs and radiated gravitas. Miller was an energetic and ebullient campaigner but had never been comfortable as a public speaker. In fact, Miller was never a natural politician and tended to be impa-tient with what he saw as the often evasive and devious nature of politics.[21]

Early polls indicated that Miller enjoyed a comfortable lead, but the num-bers turned out to be shallow. As the campaign evolved Miller's lead slowly but steadily eroded. The attorney general continued the relentless style of per-sonal law enforcement for which he was renowned, but polls continued to show increasing public skepticism that Miller could make the transition from supercop to governor. On election day Bennett narrowly defeated Miller by a little under four thousand votes.[22]

After the election Miller claimed that he had had a "gut" feeling he would lose the contest. He believed his aggressive investigation into the architect scandal had split the Democratic Party and fatally damaged his chances. He also believed negative press, particularly the *Hutchinson News,* and the hostile climate on college campuses had contributed to his defeat. He observed that his strict enforcement of the drug laws had produced fifteen-to-one vote mar-gins against him in some university precincts. And indeed, it seemed that many college students, faculty, and recent graduates had not forgotten or forgiven Miller personally ordering the arrests of dozens of antiwar demonstrators when they refused to clear the streets after several warnings.[23] In January 1975 Vern Miller retired from public life and returned to Wichita to practice law.

His retirement was short-lived. Soon Miller was once again in the thick of Sedgwick County politics, challenging the incumbent district attorney, Keith Sanborn, in the 1976 Democratic primary. Miller's promise to reduce crime and establish closer working relationships with law enforcement agencies seemed to connect with the electorate, and he easily won the primary and general elections.

After the election and shortly before he assumed office, Miller revealed plans to involve the district attorney's office in the strict enforcement of ob-scenity and drug laws. He promised a vigorous effort to close nude dancing es-tablishments and so-called adult movie theaters, and within weeks of taking office he made clear his belief that state obscenity statutes covered books as well as pictures and performances. Miller's office had already removed certain offending magazines from commercial establishments, and Miller warned that enforcement could extend into private homes.[24]

Unlike his detached, almost clinical enforcement of alcohol, gambling, and even drug laws, Miller made no effort to conceal his intense personal beliefs regarding moral issues and their links to criminal activity. "I feel strongly that if we are a good moral community, we're going to see less crime," he said. In an appearance before the Glenville Bible Baptist Church, Miller promised "a war against obscenity" and told the congregation "it was an honor and privilege" to enforce a law he personally considered right. Miller also spoke out openly on two other "moral" issues—a proposed city ordinance banning discrimination against homosexuals and a county ordinance banning nude dancing in taverns.[25]

There were those, of course, who were critical of Miller's moral crusade and claimed that he was inappropriately injecting his personal moral values into his official conduct. Miller replied that while it was not against the law to be a homosexual, it was against the law to commit homosexual acts, and he intended to strictly enforce that law, as he had always done. Moreover, he firmly believed that nude dancing invited prostitution, which in turn led to narcotics abuse, theft, and violence. Some members of the American Civil Liberties Union called Miller "a dictator with little respect for civil liberties." Students protesting seizure of an alleged obscene film at a Wichita State film festival displayed a sign stating, "Miller is an obscenity to educational freedom." On the other hand, over two thousand people cheered and applauded the district attorney at a public rally against obscenity.[26] At the end of his four-year term Miller again returned to private life.

The contrasting reaction to Miller's obscenity crusade neatly illustrates the duality of the man and his career. He seemed to embody the unambiguous frontier values embedded deep in the Kansas culture and collective psyche—honesty, courage, morality, integrity, and determination. But in an increasingly diverse and pluralistic society, many of his critics saw the reverse image of those same values—intolerance, impatience with subtleties and shades of gray, rigidity, and even recklessness. Typically, Miller never doubted or wavered and continued to do what he had always done—thrill his supporters and infuriate his opponents. At age seventy-six Vern Miller still practices law and rides his motorcycle—a genuine Kansas character.

Wes Jackson: Kansas Ecostar

James E. Sherow

Ad astra per aspera—to the stars through difficulties—now, that's the Kansas way of doing things. Wes Jackson has proven himself a fit exemplar of this motto. He has encountered more than his share of travails and hardship, and even though his story is still unfolding, he has reached at least one star among many as he has become a, if not the, Kansas "ecostar." *Life* magazine included Jackson's name among eighteen other illuminati who would in all likelihood number among the one hundred most influential people of the twenty-first century.[1] In any case, as Jackson himself will quickly tell anyone, he has not yet reached his yearned-for stars.

What is an "ecostar"? Jackson coined this term as he reflected on one particular event that caused him great anguish. The board of directors of the Friends of Earth found itself in a quandary in 1984. The directors felt that David Brower, as executive director, routinely followed his own path rather than adhering to the board's directions. Worse for the financial viability of Friends, Brower ignored fiscal realities in favor of protecting the earth. "What

Wes Jackson (June 15, 1936–), whose Kansas roots go back to territorial days and a great-grandfather who fought alongside John Brown at the battle of Black Jack, June 2, 1856, is at home among the perennials that thrive at his Land Institute, where this photograph was taken in 2005 and where he has become a pioneer in the sustainable agriculture movement. Courtesy of the Land Institute, Salina, Kansas.

good was a financially stable organization," Brower often asked, "if the planet's ecosystems lie in ruin?" The board, Jackson included, decided it had little recourse but to call for a membership vote on whether to dismiss Brower.

Style, not content, had gotten Brower into trouble. Jackson saw a public infatuated with Hollywood-type stardom, a trend plaguing universities, government, and the environmental movement itself. In Brower's case, Jackson saw a man whose "eyes were not on [the board], or for that matter on the environment. His eyes were on the camera." To listen to Brower was to listen to a revivalist calling his flock "to love mother earth and go solar." Although tent preachers such as Brower were necessary to win converts to the cause, the word needed a solid base upon which to rest. Jackson reluctantly came to the conclusion that Brower, the ecostar, had to go if the Friends of Earth were to survive, and a majority of the membership reached the same conclusion.[2]

Now, twenty years later, has Jackson reached a pinnacle in his career where the ecostar has consumed the ordinary mortal? A quick glance at his laurels and public activities may incline one to think so. Heady stuff, receiving a MacArthur Genius Fellowship, a Pew Conservation Scholar Award, or a Right Livelihood Award (the "alternative Nobel Peace Prize"). Hard to remain fixed on the problem at hand when so many universities want him to speak; nationally syndicated television news programs seek to feature him; and national, state, and local magazines and newspapers constantly write lead stories about his endeavors.[3]

Although it is probably correct to label Jackson an ecostar, one qualifying modifier is critically important: *Kansas* ecostar. The Kansas ecostar is a different breed of environmentalist than Brower was. Perhaps Jackson best summed up the qualities of the Kansas type when he said: "I don't like priesthoods. I like *mortals* who develop their skills, learn their craft, *humbly* set out to understand the world and how it works, and are satisfied to go to bed tired."[4] In many respects this is an accurate picture of Jackson himself.

What is this astral plane Jackson seeks? What has propelled him on his journey? Where has he met his successes, obstacles and failures? William Clugston once wrote an insightful critique of typical Kansans, who, he believed, were so firmly fastened on achieving the practical and economical that they forewent the artistic or philosophical.[5] In short, Kansans were fixated upon the art of making a living to the exclusion of practicing the art of living. Yet somehow Jackson has blended the arts with the pursuit of the practical to become the type of Kansan Clugston yearned to see.

Jackson's heritage, grounded in the practical guided by a deep and abiding religious faith, shaped his early childhood. His great-grandfather Robert Hall Pearson farmed a quarter section near present-day Baldwin, Kansas, and there, on the same land alongside John Brown, fired what many consider to be the opening shots of the Civil War at the battle of Black Jack on June 2, 1856. Other ancestors came from a variety of places and backgrounds—some on his mother's side had ties to the Eisenhowers of Abilene. His mother's father had a sister named Ida Stover who married David Eisenhower, and out of this union was born Ike. Others hailed from Pennsylvania Dutch country. These immigrants into Kansas uniformly pursued farming.

Most of Jackson's ancestors fared decently, neither becoming wealthy nor sinking into abject poverty. The Taylor-Hummer family on his father's side made an adequate living tending a tree nursery. Grandfather Albert Jackson, who married one of the Taylor girls, had a more difficult time of it. Frightfully commonplace, he developed a severe drinking problem that eventually led to a divorce. His life of dissipation convinced Jackson's mother and father to lead the life of strict teetotalers. A sober hard-work ethic characterized their style of living, and this ethic rubbed off on their son.[6]

Jackson's parents, Nettie Stover and Howard Taylor Jackson, farmed a quarter section of land just west of Topeka. In the rich second bottomlands of the Kansas River valley, the Jacksons developed a small yet highly diverse farm. This sixty-two-acre farm had thirty-seven acres in an experimental irrigation project under the auspices of the Topeka Chamber of Commerce and Kansas State Agricultural College (see Table 1). Such a farm required the hard work of all the family members, and the five Jackson children labored picking strawberries and tending flowers and vegetable crops for local markets.[7]

The farm was a place where one did not waste steps, parents seldom if ever praised children, and everyone conserved his or her energy in order to achieve the daily tasks at hand. Wes's parents, true Kansas Republicans and regular churchgoing Methodists, despised unions. They feared that worker collectives might lead to a life of dissipation—"eating out, taking breaks, and drinking pop." Work was a purifying endeavor, and temptations of the flesh were actively discouraged. Like many Kansans who believed it reasonable to regulate or prohibit immoral behavior such as smoking, drinking, or lewd movies, the Jacksons forbade their son to see more than two movies a year, and of course these had to be preapproved.

Even Jackson's public schooling mirrored his family's and neighbors' preoccupation with the practical. Through the eighth grade Jackson attended a two-room schoolhouse in Indianola District 93. As he remembers it, first through fourth grades were combined, followed by fifth through eighth. His teachers placed little emphasis on grades, and he scarcely acquired the rudiments of math, reading, and writing. Seamen Rural High School offered little more academic grounding than his elementary schooling. Rural folks regarded farming as the highest calling. Following in this tradition, Jackson joined the

Table 1. A Census of Howard T. Jackson's Experimental Irrigated Farm Acreage, 1936

Acreage	Crop	Yield
4.75	Strawberries	65 crates
6.60	New strawberries	good stand
1.72	Asparagus	too young to cut
0.70	Rhubarb	poor stand
0.26	Blackberries	red spiders destroyed the crop
5.30	Bluegrass pasture	10 head of livestock all summer
3.00	Potatoes	554 bushels
2.59	Tomatoes	7700 lbs.
1.72	Radishes .1 acre	40 doz.
	Table beets .5 acre	130 bushels
	Peas .5 acre	50 bushels
	Onions .16 acre	insects destroyed the crop
	Parsnips .1 acre	45 bushels
	Sugar beets .16 acre	1900 lbs.
	Carrots .2 acre	grasshoppers—no yield
5.00	Sweet clover and Oats	good hay crop
5.00	Alfalfa	28 tons
2.00	Field corn	65 bushels
0.60	Cucumbers	245 bushels
0.70	Popcorn	none

Source: "Topeka Chamber of Commerce Irrigation Project: Report on Costs and Results for 1936," provided by Wes Jackson.

Future Farmers of America (FFA), became its president, and excelled in judging livestock competitions. During his junior year he became discontented with the new vocational agriculture teacher, and he quit his FFA endeavors in his senior year. After that he spent more time honing his football skills, and when he graduated he showed little promise of future achievement.[8] Jackson entered Kansas Wesleyan with one attitude and emerged with another. At first academics seldom engaged his full attention; playing football and simply enjoying college life occupied most of his time. For some reason unknown even to himself, he declared biology his major during his sophomore year. Yet he rarely studied, and as a result he earned a D in his general botany class—hardly an auspicious beginning for a stellar career in genetics. Something clicked in Jackson's mind, and he petitioned his professor, Al Robinson, for a chance to retake the examination. Jackson made an A on his retake, and Robinson changed his grade to a C for the course.

From his junior year until graduation he took his course work more seriously. By the time of Jackson's graduation in 1958, a budding academic biologist had burst into bloom. Professor Robinson, impressed by Jackson's onset of dedicated study, wrote a glowing letter of recommendation to accompany his student's request for admission into the botany department at the University of Kansas. Also contributing to a more serious attitude toward academics might have been meeting and dating Dana Percival, whom he married in December 1957. She followed Wes to Lawrence, where Wes pursued his master's degree and Dana completed her B.S. degree, with honors, in language arts education.

Teaching seemed the path for Jackson, but work in the public schools proved a difficult profession. "The hardest work I've ever done" is the way Jackson remembers his high school teaching days in Olathe. Preparing for five classes a day was hard enough without the additional responsibility of coaching football and track. Jackson enjoyed coaching because he relished the physical. Teaching, however, and especially creating good teacher-pupil relationships, was difficult. This problem became apparent when the school superintendent, whose daughter had received an F in Jackson's class, rebuked the young biology instructor. Jackson recalls the gist of the letter this way: "When a student fails, you have failed!" Although filled with "self-righteousness" at the time, forty years later Jackson readily admitted that the superintendent had a valid point. Yet he quickly added that public education too often weakens the "near holy" relationship of master and student by eroding the authority of teachers and contributing to the loss of standards.[9]

His dislike of public school work convinced Jackson to pursue other educational avenues. Jackson received an offer to return to his alma mater, and he spent two years teaching biology, first as an instructor and then, a year later, as an assistant professor. Then an aspiring professor, Jackson applied for graduate school and was accepted into the Department of Genetics in the College of Agriculture at North Carolina State University. During his time there, Professor Ben W. Smith may have planted an idea when he casually mentioned the value of maintaining wild ecosystems as a gauge against which agricultural practices can be judged. Smith's idea would later play a central role in shaping Jackson's most notable undertaking, the Land Institute.[10]

In 1967 Jackson received his Ph.D. in genetics and returned to Kansas Wesleyan, this time as an associate professor in biology. By 1970 he had enjoyed three years not only as a professor but also as the cross-country and track coach. The small liberal arts college environment nurtured close ties among professors in varied disciplines.

The college atmosphere of the late 1960s, shaped by concerns with civil rights, the Vietnam War, and mounting environmental problems, gave rise to student demands for "relevance" in course work. Jackson provided such connections in his biology classes as he "clipped, tore, Xeroxed and filed" information for his students. From this exercise, Jackson identified three linked problems: population/food, resource depletion, and environmental pollution.[11]

These insights and "relevant" material became the core of his first book, *Man and the Environment,* published in 1971. In the foreword Paul R. Ehrlich sounded an environmental alarm: "Attitude change is the key," he asserted, and Jackson's collection of readings provided paths for a more simple and joyous life. Jackson had become a nationally recognized environmentalist.[12]

Jackson's growing reputation as an accomplished academic and writer caught the attention of several universities that offered him attractive positions. One by one Jackson refused them until one notable offer ignited his imagination. California State University (CSU) at Sacramento had just received authorization from the regents to create a Center for Environmental Studies, and Jackson was offered the opportunity to organize it. This was an offer too good to refuse, so Wes and Dana put aside their plan of building a country house on twenty-eight acres of prairie and packed the family for the move to California in 1971.

Jackson quickly climbed the academic ladder at CSU, and he seemed destined for a respectable career as a dean, provost, or even higher-ranking administrator. In directing the center, he hired his own faculty and collaborated with professors in creating an interdisciplinary curriculum. Out of this approach grew Jackson's contribution to television programming on environmental impact statements and the creation of the Lake Tahoe Environmental Consortium. The latter endeavor, of which Jackson became the first director, bound seven colleges and universities to undertake three goals centered on the Lake Tahoe environment: ecosystem analysis, community development, and continuing ecological education.[13]

Jackson, however, found himself the proverbial fish out of water. The deeply rooted Kansan kept hearing a clarion call to return to the land that had nurtured him. Wendell Berry explained the Jacksons' return this way: California proved to the Jacksons that Kansas was their home, "where they know the talk 'in sale barn or capitol.'" To remain in California, Berry opined, would have created too many "unanswered questions about [the Jacksons'] place and their work." So in 1974 Jackson turned his back on a most promising academic career, returned to his prairie house near Salina, Kansas, and began building the Land Institute.[14]

Berry's insights fail to describe fully why Jackson left California. What calls a person to set aside what, by most people's judgment, is an eminently successful profession in order to take up what appears to be at best a difficult burden and at worst a quixotic quest? Jackson can only say, "It's a mystery," which is what always lies at the heart of a calling. When a two-year leave of absence from CSU was exhausted, Jackson wavered about whether to return to California. His daughter Laura decided the issue when she recited her father's own words back to him: "We're not called to success, but obedience to vision." Jackson knew tremendous difficulties lay in his path and that he might never reach his goals, but his life journey lay before him. Moreover, Jackson had sensed something out of place in the abiding purpose of academics. He made his critique clear twenty years later in his *Becoming Native to This Place*. Jackson dedicated this work to his longtime friend, Wendell Berry, whose work, both in prose and in the soil itself, speaks to learning from the land how to live with it. Jackson too had become concerned with creating coherent and sustainable human communities "embedded in the ecological realities of [the community's] surrounding landscape." Universities simply did not train students for this type of life. Too often the sole focus of higher education was upward mobility. In striking, nearly biblical prose, Jackson called for ending the "binge the developed world has enjoyed" in order "to find our way home and use what little time is left for partial redemption of this prodigal generation." Jackson had found his purpose: the development of perennial polyculture agriculture.[15]

Jackson first became intrigued with this idea while pursuing his Ph.D. Now, as Professor Ben Smith's peer, he engaged his former professor in the problems of creating perennial crops. As a young man Smith had been intrigued by the work of the Soviet geneticist N. I. Vavilov, who reportedly had developed a perennial wheat in the 1920s. The results were never duplicated in the United States, but many researchers were fascinated by the possibilities. American farmers specialized in raising and harvesting annual monocultures such as wheat, oats, rye, corn, sorghum, and soybeans. For centuries these crops were grown in separate fields and harvested separately; because these plants could not reseed themselves, farmers replanted them the following season. Prairie grasses and forbs, in contrast, reseed themselves year after year in close proximity. In fact, these plants have evolved symbiotic relationships. Some, such as eastern grama grass *(Tripsacum dactyloides),* show yet unrealized harvest potential. The promise lies in the better nutritional value of its seeds over that of traditional cereal crops; the liability rests in the fact that it produces far fewer pounds per acre than either corn or wheat.[16]

Nonetheless, if hybrids of prairie plants could be propagated, Jackson believed, then a variety of mutually beneficial species could be sown together in one field, harvested, and left to proliferate for the following season. In the wake of such practices would come a substantial reduction of machinery, petrochemicals, soil erosion and depletion, water pollution, and crop-destroying insects. Farms would tend toward smaller sizes, which would mean a repopulation of the American farmscape and a revitalization of small, rural community life.[17]

By mimicking prairie ecosystems, these farms would mirror the nature of wild grasslands. Such a method contradicted the established practice of eliminating and replacing prairie ecosystems with monocrops. This practice, Jackson maintains, has led to severe ecological problems such as nonpoint stream pollution, soil nutritional depletion, evolution of pesticide-resistant insects, and groundwater depletion as well as economic dislocations associated with the ever-rising capital costs of industrial, mechanized agriculture. These problems have resulted in increasingly large operations in a depopulated farmscape dotted by abandoned houses and withering communities in an ecologically debased environment. Jackson embraced perennial polyculture agriculture as his passionate goal in life, and with modest means he and Dana launched the Land Institute against the prevailing winds of industrial agriculture. With some friendly financial backing, the Jacksons took up residence in their prairie home and began working earnestly to research the problem of perennial polycultures, both through Wes's own work and that of promising graduate students who came to labor literally in the field. Jackson hoped that within twenty-five to fifty years viable perennial polycultures would be found. To date, tantalizing results have pointed the way, yet without reaching the stars. Consequently, to many Jackson appears a prophet rather than a reliable researcher. Still, the Land Institute has not been bereft of tangible results as a steady stream of published scientific research has flowed from its confines.[18]

Like the Land Institute itself, as well as the more recent endeavor of revitalizing the nearly defunct Flint Hills town of Matfield Green, Jackson's literary work expresses the need to blend the art of living with the art of making a living. Among his many articles and public presentations, Jackson has authored or coauthored six books, all hammering home the same themes. Especially in *Altars of Unhewn Stone* (1987), the thinking of Francis Bacon and René Descartes is taken to task for the "de-sacralization of nature" and for seeking "power over nature." This ideology has resulted in a cadre of researchers and economists who explore narrowly defined subjects conforming to modern scientific analysis rather than taking on broader problems resistant to this methodology.[19] Moreover, capitalism works as the economic engine of this system and produces incredibly efficient means for consuming fossil carbon stores of energy. This approach, Jackson maintains, undercuts itself. In counterdistinction, the course of the Land Institute "challenges the fundamental philosophical cornerstone of modern science as advanced by Francis Bacon around 1610, that to achieve the benefits of science we must 'bend nature' to our will. Our work, therefore, is not just the restructuring of agriculture, but a restructuring of the scientific paradigm itself." As far as Jackson is concerned, to continue industrial capitalistic agriculture, an outgrowth of the modern philosophical tradition, results in calamity for both land and the human community.[20]

This proposition has created some problems for Jackson and the Land Institute. One notable instance was the divorce of Wes and Dana in March 1993. Dana went on to pursue her own advocacy career in sustainable agriculture, and in 1994 she became the associate director of the Land Stewardship Project based in White Bear Lake, Minnesota. Her thinking was most clearly reflected in *The Farm as Natural Habitat: Reconnecting Food Systems with Ecosystems,* a collection of writing coedited by her and Wes's daughter, Laura. Her and Laura's views of sustainable agriculture are far more comfortable with various forms of diversified monocropping than are Wes Jackson's.[21]

Jackson's views have also often put him in conflict with the direction taken by agricultural education at land grant universities such as Kansas State University. Bluntly, Jackson has seen the simplification of agricultural ecosystems leading to the simplification and weakening of agricultural education. An acquaintance of Jackson, Professor Don Wise at the University of Minnesota, once had over 150 students in his weed management classes. By 2004 he had an enrollment of less than ten. Petrochemical herbicides have nearly killed the need for students to learn weed management practices that go beyond chemical applications, which recently have been taught by the chemical companies themselves. Corporate agribusiness's reach into colleges has become so acute that the dean of agriculture at Iowa State University once quipped to Jackson that he worked for Pioneer, a seed company owned by Dupont Chemical.

Still, from time to time Jackson and land grant institutions have attempted cooperation. These endeavors have shown few tangible results. From Jackson's perspective, the schools, often under the increasing burden of cuts in their appropriations by state legislatures, have sought cooperative arrangements with the Land Institute primarily to augment their own budgets. This downward-spiraling public support has made Jackson realize that schools of agriculture need allies, much as they may have deserved the criticisms leveled at them by such writers as Jim Hightower. Industrialized agriculture, Jackson fears, simplifies and destroys not only the land, small farmers, and communities but also the public outreach and service commitments that have long been a part of the land grant school heritage. By 2004 Jackson wished he had been more sympathetic to the plight faced by these venerable institutions.[22]

Sustaining Jackson through these travails has been an enduring friendship with Wendell Berry. The two are kindred spirits who seek a simpler, more fulfilling life based upon a mutually beneficial relationship with the land. As Jackson once wrote to Berry, "You and I have an important mission before us, I think, and that is to contribute to the discussion and practice of agriculture which is about the only potentially non-exhaustible exercise underway." They also share a pessimism regarding the condition of American society. "I was a long time coming to the conclusion," Jackson mused, "that our culture is probably too manic to experience the quiet drama of a falling leaf. The likes of you and [Gary] Snyder do your best to help but most of us aren't even calm enough to read." Hope for change still heartens Jackson: "Though I am an intellectual pessimist, I am also a glandular optimist." Their relationship continues to affirm and sustain their drive to improve human life.[23]

Wes Jackson, the Kansas ecostar, continues his labors on the land. "The agriculture I promote depends on the information of a community which has evolved an information system that allows the possessors of the information to occupy a middle place between, for all practical purposes, two infinite resources—the sun and the rocks."[24] Jackson reaches for his own stars, a self-renewing agriculture engendering and nurturing human communities. In this effort Clugston's incomplete Kansan is made whole in Jackson, who has pursued the art of making a living while practicing the art of living. To the stars through difficulties—that is the Kansas way of life, and few people know it better than Wes Jackson.

Robert J. Dole: Driven to Perform,

Destined to Motivate

Burdett Loomis

I think I've been tested. I have a vision. *It's trying to keep things together,* trying to make the government more responsive, more sensitive to the needs of a lot of people who haven't had the opportunity. It's strong sensible leadership, prudent . . . and what you see is what you get.
—*Bob Dole, 1986*

For almost his entire life Robert J. (Bob) Dole has motivated those around him, to say nothing of legions of individuals who do not know him personally. At the same time, he appears an unlikely motivator. He is a witty but scarcely inspirational speaker, and his lacerating sense of humor often undercuts any full-blown attempt to motivate others. His legions of former staff members remain loyal supporters, but many find him a too-tough taskmaster. He remains a fierce, and sometimes careless, partisan, yet he

Robert J. Dole (July 22, 1923–), seen here with some Kansas farmers in 1974, the year of his most bitterly contested reelection campaign, was born and raised in Russell; although he spent most of his adult life in the cosmopolitan environs of Washington, D.C., his down-home style and wit served him well with his rural Kansas constituents. Courtesy of the Robert J. Dole Institute of Politics, University of Kansas.

stumps for civility. Though a driven worker, eager for results, many of his hard-won accomplishments have come behind closed doors in highly complex negotiations. Bob Dole has won some, lost some. He can see the pitfalls ahead, can understand the difficulty of achieving one's goals, and can often imagine himself in the other fellow's shoes. These are not hallmarks of a conventional political motivator.

Yet Bob Dole does motivate, does inspire others to do good works, and does offer an example, albeit imperfect, of a public man, all in a time when such a figure seems to have gone out of fashion. In the end Bob Dole's life serves as a *model* for others—not to emulate but to respect his continuing struggles against adversity, whether physical, ideological, or political. Ironically, Americans may have come to admire Dole most in the years since he has left elected office and lost his bid for the presidency. In his eighties, when he could ease up, he has embraced public life all the more enthusiastically. Indeed, a lingering doubt remains that there is any truly private side to Bob Dole, so thoroughly has he led his life within the public sphere. As he said in announcing his 1988 presidential candidacy, "What you see is what you get."[1]

Bob Dole is a Kansas icon, and certainly his home-state roots have remained visible throughout his life, with special emphasis on the four occasions when he ran for national office. In the main, however, Dole's legacy as a motivating figure has largely played out in Washington and in national and international politics. The traditional Kansas Republican Party that rewarded Bob Dole with eight years in the House of Representatives and almost twenty-eight in the Senate has ceased to exist, replaced by a thoroughly divided party that social conservatives have increasingly come to dominate. Dole's interests, his wide connections, and his style of partisanship make him more welcome in Washington than in many parts of his native state. Over the years Dole has motivated Republican allies and adversaries in Kansas to become active in party politics, and the latter may well outnumber the former. Such are the ironies ingrained in his lengthy public life.

But such observations move the Dole story ahead too far, too fast. This essay will track Bob Dole as a model and motivator from his early days through his war days (and the long rehabilitation), his political career and its various stages, and his evolution into the unique combination of pitchman-statesman that frames his post-1996 career.

The Bob Dole story has been told and retold for more than fifty years. Dole was born in Russell, Kansas, on July 22, 1923; his first political manifestation was as a local officeholder (one term as state legislator, eight years as district attorney, from 1951 to 1961). The compelling narrative of local golden boy turned wounded war hero and gritty veteran was part and parcel of his existence. Russell's 5,500 citizens bore witness to Dole's promise as an athlete and his almost miraculous recovery from severe World War II wounds.

Although Dole would influence countless others, the first person he had to motivate was himself. His ambition would soon propel his rise in politics, but his initial fuel was even more powerful—a fear that drove him toward physical health and only then toward public office. Biographer Richard Ben Cramer wrote, "Sometimes [Dole] could actually *see* himself on Main Street, Russell, in a wheelchair, with a cup. That was his private vision of hell, the spur to get him up again, trying again."[2] In his postwar undergraduate and law school studies, Dole discovered an immense capacity for work, both to compensate and to overcome. This style—developed and honed as prosecutor, representative, senator, presidential candidate, and lawyer/public figure—has served as a hallmark of the Dole persona. His personal motivations made him a model; others knew they would not outwork him, but at least they might emulate him.

Most directly affected over time were the hundreds, even thousands, of members of his various staffs, who became Dole loyalists not because of his praise for them, which was rare to nonexistent, but because of his willingness to work longer hours, at a higher pace, than anyone else. In constant motion, Dole kept driving, kept working, always "trying to keep things together."[3] He became an almost entirely public man; there was no time to lose, and such a responsibility would overwhelm an ordinary mortal. No wonder his staff often could not keep up.

If it hadn't been for his war wounds Bob Dole might well have channeled his immense energy and capacity for work into the role of rural physician–cum–local mover and shaker. Eighteen-hour days would have filled such a life with tangible results, social stature, and reasonable wealth. Perhaps ambition, and a sense of limitation in western Kansas, would have moved Dole into politics, but a full-blown political career seemed unlikely.

However, once he started his legal career, even before he graduated from law school in 1952, Dole's capacity for work, his driven nature, and his ambition dictated a life in the public sphere. As county attorney he could work limitless hours on behalf of Russell's citizens, demonstrating by his dedication, skills, and results how one could make the most of such a modest position. Biographer Jake Thompson noted, "Dole . . . was the hardest working county attorney Russell County had ever seen" as he "handled county business all day and turned to his private cases only at night."[4] The political payoff for Dole's long hours came in the oft-told story of the legendary Republican Party leader Huck Boyd, the publisher of the Phillipsburg newspaper, who saw the courthouse lights on at midnight and found the county attorney hard at work. He told the story around the state, and Bob Dole had found a political sponsor to move his career toward the U.S. House of Representatives.[5]

In Dole's initial forays into Kansas politics his focus had to remain on his own career, his own advancement, as he sought, again and again, to prove himself. As Dole put it, "I guess I was very competitive anyway and even after the disability I was more competitive."[6] The Congress stood as the logical next step for an ambitious Kansas politician, and the 1960 election offered him the chance as the incumbent (conservative Republican Wint Smith) stepped down after having won the GOP primary in 1958 by a mere fifty-one votes over state senator Keith Sebelius.

With backing from Boyd and wealthy GOP kingmaker Dane Hansen, Dole campaigned with imagination (the singing Bob-o-Links), energy, and a relatively hard conservative edge. Although his 1960 campaign cost less than $20,000, the prospective congressman did find it necessary to mortgage the family home.[7] Dole won the primary by about one thousand votes and followed up with a convincing general election victory. Given the Republican nature of the district and Dole's willingness to work tirelessly, one might assume that the new House member would find reelection a simple task. Although Dole did win three more House races, the first two were anything but easy. First, in 1962 the Kansas congressional delegation shrank from six to five seats in response to the state's slow rate of population growth. The Kansas legislature paired first-termer Dole with Democratic representative Floyd Breeding in a district that covered 58 of 105 counties. Typically, Dole campaigned hard and won handily. But the district was still not secure because in 1964 GOP presidential candidate Barry Goldwater, backed by Dole, ran very poorly in Kansas, with the normally Republican state delivering its seven electoral votes to Lyndon Johnson as part of a Democratic landslide. In his most difficult general election campaign, Dole won by just 5,126 votes of a total of more than 221,000 and probably benefited from a visit by Richard Nixon, who was in the process of rebuilding his own political career. Only in 1966 did Dole score the kind of huge victory that has become the hallmark of Republicans in the "Big First" district over the past forty years. He had made his seat safe, but his ambitions pushed him forward once again.

Under different circumstances Bob Dole might well have remained in the House of Representatives for a long and successful career. Given his legislative skills, he would have become a first-rate congressman, but this kind of service would eventually have proved frustrating. Indeed, Dole would have found some outlet for his ambitions, perhaps a shot at the governorship, rather than continuing to serve as a House member who was part of a seemingly permanent Republican minority. Luckily for the congressman, his opportunity came relatively quickly when Republican senator Frank Carlson retired in 1968 and encouraged Dole to seek the seat. He won an overwhelming primary victory over former governor William H. Avery, and the general election was little more than a formality. At age forty-five Bob Dole entered the U.S. Senate—a body that rewarded individual political skills far more than the House, with its reliance on seniority. Though it would take Dole a decade to hit his stride as a senator, he was entering a body that could use all the talent and ambition he could muster.[8]

In many ways Dole's steady climb from the Kansas state house in 1951 to eight years as county attorney to eight more as a U.S. representative, while impressive, was relatively ordinary for a talented politician. He had developed a style that relied on partisanship, personal contacts, and hard work, and he had prospered. But the Senate would be different; to succeed there one had to do more than survive and rise through the ranks. One had to accumulate power and use it, and there were no manuals on how to build majorities and motivate your fellow senators to come together in productive ways. Dole's learning process in developing into a major national politician was about to begin.

Twelve years later Ronald Reagan became president, the Republicans captured the U.S. Senate, and Dole rose to chair the powerful Finance Committee. But in 1969, as a first-term senator from a rural section of a small state, Robert Dole, as he called himself in those days, was just one more politician who had taken a major step up the electoral ladder. Moreover, as biographer Thompson would write, the 1970s proved a "stomach-churning decade" for the new senator, whose previous political career had reflected steady advancement: "In the 1970s Bob Dole championed President Nixon; divorced his first wife Phyllis; vigorously headed the Republican National Committee [1971–1972]; was, in effect, kicked off the RNC; watched his president be driven from office; battled himself against Watergate; barely won re-election to the Senate in 1974; re-married, to Elizabeth Hanford in 1975; lost his father; ran as a hell-for-leather vice-presidential nominee; and lost [badly] a presidential contest of his own."[9]

Such a summary, while accurate, is incomplete in that Dole used the 1970s to hone a legislative style that would serve him well when he was given the opportunity to lead in the wake of the 1980 election. During the 1970s the senator worked with a number of Democrats, most notably George McGovern

(D–S.D.), to expand and streamline food stamps policy, a project that culmi-
nated in the Food Stamp Act of 1977. Even as Dole was becoming a partisan
icon as party chair and vice-presidential candidate, he was finding ways to pass
well-considered, hardheaded legislation, such as food stamps, that could win
support across the political spectrum.

While Dole polished his motivational skills inside the Senate as a member
of the Agriculture and Finance Committees, he simultaneously demonstrated
his willingness to take on "agitator" and "innovator" roles. Indeed, in the
1970s Dole's ambition moved him more toward "agitation" and away from
"motivation" as a dominant style. Between 1971 and 1976 Dole did become a
national figure, but at a price. The American public saw a Dole who, as national party chair, energetically defended a president who would resign in
shame within two years; ironically, Nixon treated Dole badly despite the fact
that the senator soldiered on in support of the president. Even more telling
was Dole's highly visible run as vice-presidential candidate in 1976, in which
he helped create his own long-lasting "hatchetman" image by, among other
things, blurting out an ill-considered statement about "Democrat wars" in the
vice-presidential debate. Twenty years later, during the 1996 presidential campaign, Dole's favorability ratings stood at just 45 percent, or ten points less
than Bill Clinton's.[10] Only in the wake of the 1996 campaign and his retirement from electoral politics did Dole's public reputation truly overcome the
image that emerged from that period, and especially from the 1976 campaign.

One other event helped define Dole during the 1970s, at least in Kansas.
His 1974 challenge from Representative Bill Roy, a two-term Topeka Democrat, stands as the most difficult legislative race of his career. Down in the
polls with six weeks to go, the Republican candidate and his campaign made
abortion an issue because Roy, a physician, had performed the procedure a
handful of times. In many ways the 1974 race became a prototype for the social issue–based campaigns that have become standard Republican fare over
the past thirty years. Still, Bill Roy may have gotten it right with his final assessment: "Bob Dole wanted it more than I did."[11] With his defeat of Roy in
the year of Watergate, Dole demonstrated the depth of his resolve, his willingness to engage in harsh campaign tactics, and his overall strength as a senatorial candidate; he would never receive more than a perfunctory reelection
challenge in subsequent campaigns. At the same time, with the election of
Nancy Landon Kassebaum to the Senate in 1978, Dole would remain the sec-
ond-most-popular Kansas senator for the rest of his time on Capitol Hill.

The Dole experience during the 1970s offers some clues as to the two most prominent driving forces behind his actions in politics. First is his ambition, which has continually led him to seek and take on a series of prominent positions, whether running for the Senate, accepting the chairmanship of the Republican National Committee, or engaging in a poorly executed race for president in 1980. By the late 1970s, however, he had begun to demonstrate a profound understanding of how the U.S. Senate operated. Whether through food stamps legislation or in extended Finance Committee negotiations, under the tutelage of Senator Russell Long (D–La.), Bob Dole used his traditional Kansas Republicanism to good advantage. Though a conservative, he understood that the national government—through farm subsidies, veterans' hospitals, and the interstate highway system (which ran right past Russell), among other programs—was often indispensable in serving both specific constituencies, such as farmers, and the broad public interest.

Dole's emergence as a patient legislator may well have been assisted by his marriage in 1975 to Elizabeth Hanford, then serving on the Federal Trade Commission. In her Dole found a highly compatible soul who had come to know him as a powerful national politician. Moreover, she had her own career, which she pursued vigorously. Again, for Dole, the public and the personal had become intertwined, which was, in the end, inevitable.

With Ronald Reagan in the White House and the Senate in Republican hands, Dole could bank his presidential ambitions for a time and allow his legislative strengths to grow. Although the next fifteen years would bring many ups and downs for the senator, this period would demonstrate how an individual legislator could motivate his colleagues through his own behavior; Dole would not always win, but he would always be in a position to legislate, to defend his institution, and to work with (or not) both Republican and Democratic presidents.

Although Dole mounted a halfhearted, ineffective campaign for president in 1980, his destiny for the next fifteen years was to lead the Senate, which Republicans had come to control for the first time in twenty-five years. Dole was ready for the challenge. A student of the Senate from early in his career, Dole learned much from its older, Democratic leaders. "Watching [Russell] Long operate was an education in itself," wrote Dole a few years later. "Some chairmen call meetings; others orchestrate them. Russell was of the latter school. The ability to conciliate different viewpoints is at least as important for success on Finance as knowledge of the federal tax code. For all the power granted him by formal rules, a chairman leads by consensus, not command. Those were lessons I intended to put to use in the chairman's seat."[12]

When the Congress convened in January 1981, Dole's immediate role as the new Finance Committee chair was to help move Ronald Reagan's historic tax cuts through the Congress. Although Dole voiced both public and private doubts as to the size of these proposals, especially the 30 percent reduction in income taxes, he proved a highly competent field commander for the administration as he negotiated effectively with the Democratic House and its Ways and Means Committee chair, Dan Rostenkowski (D–Ill.). In the end, much to the surprise of most observers, Dole helped forge a 25 percent income tax reduction as part of a large package that grew to irresponsible levels after House partisans from both sides of the aisle increased the numbers of tax-avoiding provisions.[13] The ultimate result scarcely reflected old-fashioned Kansas fiscal prudence, yet Dole had served his president both skillfully and faithfully.

Unsurprisingly, Dole found himself immediately addressing the revenue losses caused by the 1981 legislation. Faced with historically high—and growing—deficits, he saw a need for additional tax revenues, but such a conclusion ran against the Republican tide that had carried Reagan into office in 1980. Dole's old-fashioned fiscal conservatism did not mesh with the ideological approaches to taxing and spending put forward by such representatives as Jack Kemp (R–N.Y.) and Phil Gramm (R–Tex.).[14] Remarkably, in 1982 he put together a Republican-only majority that generated $100 billion over several years. Because the 1982 election was fast approaching, no Democrats agreed to help Republicans reduce the deficit that they had helped to create. Dole demonstrated his ability to motivate his fellow GOP senators to demonstrate serious fiscal restraint, even if it meant raising some taxes before an off-year election.

Dole's other two major accomplishments of the 1981–1986 GOP majority period involved fostering bipartisan coalitions that addressed two seemingly intractable policy issues: Social Security reform in 1983 and major income tax reformulation in 1986. No matter how difficult, these represented ideal issues for Dole's pragmatic, tough-minded approach to policy-making and obtaining results.

As a member of both formal and informal groups dedicated to reforming Social Security and as Finance Committee chair in the early 1980s, Dole recognized his responsibility for the health of Social Security and the political obstacles that faced any major overhaul. Still, Dole could look coldly at facts, which led to an inescapable conclusion: after June 1983 the Social Security trust fund would be broke. Dole worked effectively to develop a proposed fix within a small group of congressional and White House leaders—the so-called Gang of Nine—who privately put together a package that served as the ultimate basis for the legislation that passed. Although Dole did not begin the informal negotiations, his presence was essential to their success. But having a workable proposal was just a first step; he then needed to ensure Senate passage of the reform measure. Dole's ability to hold his committee together, with an eighteen-to-one vote to move the bill, contributed mightily to Senate passage.[15]

If placing Social Security on sound financial footing was a difficult chore, restructuring the income tax system seemed an impossible task. After all, by the mid-1980s, the federal tax code was a highly complex body of law that effectively benefited hundreds upon hundreds of organized interests. Although Dole was originally unenthusiastic about comprehensive tax reform, he understood that good timing could produce legislative breakthroughs. As the proposal to reduce tax rates and eliminate a host of specific tax breaks took shape, Dole did what a good leader often does: he maneuvered himself to the head of the pack to guide the intricate package to final passage. As the definitive study of the 1986 tax bill concluded: "Dole began to change his mind. He was intrigued and impressed. During a private briefing on the intricacies of the proposals, he repeatedly brushed aside reservations expressed by his aide. 'This thing,' he said, 'is going to pass.' . . . Dole's opinion carried a lot of weight. His support for the tax-reform effort would be crucial not only for its success in the Finance Committee, but also for its reception on the Senate floor."[16]

Even as a latecomer to the tax reform bill, Dole knew that his backing could make the difference between passage and defeat. And making laws was central to the Dole style, especially when there were dozens of opportunities to tweak the legislation in ways that would benefit his state, his constituents, and his increasing number of friends, who might well be valuable in the 1988 presidential campaign.

As he reflected on his Senate leadership period in a 2000 speech, the former majority leader assessed not only his victories but also his losses. "Looking back on my career," Dole said, "it is clear that defeat is as much a part of my life as victory." He then recounted a story in which his long-term nemesis and friend, Senator Robert Byrd (D–W.Va.), reversed his position to vote against sustaining a 1987 highway bill veto by President Reagan. "In the end, our one-vote majority turned into a one-vote loss. *Yet while we may have lost on the highway bill, the bigger loss would have been to do nothing.*"[17] For Dole, leadership meant staying in the game, pressing the issues, and trying to do what he thought was both right and possible. The active leader modeled behavior as his means of motivating his colleagues.

As majority leader in 1985–1986 Bob Dole could combine his aggressive, partisan side with a pragmatic approach to building majorities. As a legislator, Dole again proved an apt model for an era of profound change in the Senate, which moved from a "good ol' boy" chamber of the late 1960s to its more partisan, more polarized manifestation of the 1990s.[18] As GOP floor leader between 1985 and 1996, Dole ushered in a new era while maintaining the Senate as a distinctive, individual-oriented body. In contrast to the House, where speakers Jim Wright (D–Tex.) and Newt Gingrich (R–Ga.) ratcheted up partisanship in both style and substance, Dole played a different game, mixing his natural partisanship with his equally natural Kansas-born pragmatism. His relationships with Senate Democratic leaders Byrd, George Mitchell (D–Maine), and Tom Daschle (D–S.Dak.) were cooler than those between majority leader Mike Mansfield (D–Mont.) and minority leader Everett Dirksen (R–Ill.) in the 1960s, but their ties were positively cordial compared to his successors' links to Daschle in an increasingly hostile legislative environment.

In the end Bob Dole found that his Senate responsibilities conflicted with his duties as a presidential candidate; resigning from the Senate in June 1996 ended his twenty-eight-year tenure. But the body he left was far different from the one he had entered, and even though Dole adapted well to the growing polarization and decline in civility, he seemed to depart from the Senate with relative ease, perhaps almost happy to have an excuse to move on. In fact, Dole was merely the first of fourteen U.S. senators—many of them moderates in both style and substance—who would retire in 1996, leaving the chamber to even more partisan debate and even less civil discourse.

F. Scott Fitzgerald famously said, "There are no second acts in American lives." Of course he was wrong, at least about politicians. As Abraham Lincoln, Richard Nixon, Jimmy Carter, and scores of others have demonstrated, Americans are suckers for second and even third acts from their political leaders. Carter reinvented the job of an ex-president, Nixon spent almost twenty years seeking political rehabilitation and redemption, and Bob Dole has created a new role for defeated presidential candidates.

In his eighties, almost a decade removed from leading the Senate and running for president, Bob Dole has a website: http://www.bobdole.org, with a biography page labeled "The Bob Dole Story." At the end of his career Dole has grown wealthy, has continued to participate actively in political life, and has religiously tended his personal narrative. He may not refer to himself in the third person, as he did in the 1996 campaign, but he continues to work on the public image that he has constructed over the past fifty years. Although millions of words have been written about Bob Dole, in the end he has managed to tell his own story, create his own persona, and relentlessly use that persona in the same driven style that defined his almost fifty years of public service. At the same time, his distinctive combination of drive, emotion, and wit combine to limit his ability to control his own story. After all, he remains the partisan Republican who fought for Nixon, defeated Roy, campaigned for Ford, and ran—in a generally civil race—against Clinton.

On the website Dole divides his life into the categories of politics, charity, international, business, radio/television, and books. All senators develop "enterprises" that act on their behalf, and Dole has continued to build his enterprise, partly in concert with his law firm work but more generally on his own. As in his legislative days, Dole mixes his public life with his private affairs to the point that almost nothing remains private. The result is an often disconcerting mix of the serious, the partisan, the uplifting, and the crass.

Take, for example, Dole's highly public involvement in erectile dysfunction treatment, which has combined a desire to address an important problem, commercial opportunities, and his willingness to be part of a widely disseminated, self-deprecating joke. Thus, he followed up his involvement in a clinical trial study of Viagra with a series of ads that addressed the serious issue of impotence; subsequently, he made a famous Pepsi ad, aired during the Super Bowl, in which he played off his Viagra role in a commercial that featured the gyrations of nineteen-year-old Britney Spears. One conservative critic observed, "It's hard to imagine, say, Michael Dukakis pulling it off. Dole can, simply because he's universally known not just as a former politician, but as a septuagenarian pitchman for an erection drug."[19]

Dole's pop culture persona, buttressed by a couple of best-selling books of collected political humor and fed by frequent appearances on television, has meshed thoroughly with his other roles, largely because he brings humor to almost all his undertakings. Having left the Senate behind, he found himself at loose ends after the failed and generally uninspired 1996 presidential campaign, but he landed on his feet, both financially and emotionally, as he threw himself into a host of private, partisan, and public activities.[20] Dole had been on the public payroll for almost fifty years and had accumulated a substantial pension through his congressional service, but his most important initial move was to reach for a whole new financial stratum as he became "of counsel" at the Washington law firm of Verner Lipfert Bernhard McPherson and Hand, which paid him an annual salary of $600,000 and provided space and positions for several staffers. Dole did not lobby, as the practice is conventionally (or legally) defined. Rather, like other big names at Verner Lipfert, such as former Senate majority leader George Mitchell and former Texas governor Ann Richards, he operated as both client-producing "rainmaker" and high-level influence. He might not hang around the Senate hearing rooms, but a timely phone call to a key player was certainly within his repertoire. And Verner Lipfert's clients used Dole's visibility to place op-ed pieces that were written for him. Thus, he addressed such issues as local phone competition and Microsoft's policies at the request of GTE and Oracle, respectively.[21]

At the same time, Dole has given voice to various causes that he has long championed; his public backing and private fund-raising support for the World War II memorial could scarcely have been more appropriate or heartfelt. Likewise, his frequent calls for civility in politics, made concrete in his truly cordial relationship with Bill Clinton, have found receptive audiences, as at the dedication of the Clinton Presidential Library in 2004 and in the Dole Institute of Politics, established at the University of Kansas in the wake of the 1996 election. Further cementing Dole's relationship with his former rival was their joint effort to raise $100 million for the Families of Freedom Scholarship fund, which benefited surviving family members of those who died in the September 11, 2001, terrorist attacks. And he has continued to work as chair of the International Commission on Missing Persons, speaking out on the need for united Western action in Kosovo in order to stop the mass killing of innocent civilians.

In short, Dole has evolved from local politician to national figure to Senate leader to presidential candidate to highly visible statesman-pitchman, always leading by example, winning some and losing some. His creation of an octogenarian public persona fits both his own driven personality and the celebrity-obsessed nature of the times. At the same time, Dole's burgeoning career as an author led him, in 2005, to publish the detailed story of his war wounds and recovery and allowed him to come to terms with his most personal of experiences in the most public of ways.

In the end Bob Dole remains the partisan Republican, yet he strives for broad acceptance. He remains the public figure but has incorporated himself as Bob Dole Enterprises. He urges civility, yet his tongue remains as sharp as ever. With a senator for a wife, and television hosts clamoring for his services, Bob Dole soldiers on, motivating others through the sheer strength of his example.

Notes

Kansas State Historical Society, Topeka, is abbreviated as KSHS throughout the notes.

Introduction: Kansas History, Kansas Biography

1. Edwin C. Manning, "Kansas in History," *Kansas Historical Collections, 1911–1912* 12 (1912): 10.
2. William E. Connelley, *James Henry Lane: "The Grim Chieftain" of Kansas* (Topeka, Kans., 1899), 7; Julie Courtwright, "'A Goblin That Drives Her Insane': Sara Robinson and the History Wars of Kansas, 1894–1911," *Kansas History* 25 (Summer 2002): 102.
3. Elliott West, "A Story of Three Families," *Kansas History* 19 (Summer 1996): 112–123; William E. Unrau, *Indians of Kansas* (Topeka, Kans.,1990).
4. Unrau, *Indians of Kansas,* 51–74; see especially the maps on pages 66 and 67; Nicole Etcheson, "The Great Principle of Self-Government: Popular Sovereignty and Bleeding Kansas," *Kansas History* 27 (Spring–Summer 2004): 14–29.
5. Bill Cecil-Fronsman, "'Advocate the Freedom of White Men, as Well as That of the Negroes': The *Kansas Free State* and Antislavery Westerns in Territorial Kansas," *Kansas History* 20 (Summer 1997): 102–115; Bill Cecil-Fronsman, "'Death to All Yankees and Traitors in Kansas': The *Squatter Sovereign* and the Defense of Slavery in Kansas," *Kansas History* 16 (Spring 1993): 22–33; Kevin Abing, "Before Bleeding Kansas: Christian Missionaries, Slavery, and the Shawnee Indians in Pre-Territorial Kansas, 1844–1854," *Kansas History* 24 (Spring 2001): 69.
6. *Fountain City Herald,* June 10, 1856; see also James R. Shortridge, "People of the New Frontier: Kansas Population Origins, 1865," *Kansas History* 14 (Autumn 1991): 162–185.
7. Nicole Etcheson, *Bleeding Kansas: Contested Liberty in the Civil War Era* (Lawrence, Kans., 2004).
8. *Kansas Farmer,* May 1, 1863; Governor Thomas Carney's Messages to the State Legislature, January 1864, Public Documents of Kansas, Library and Archives Division, KSHS; Albert Castel, *Frontier State at War: Kansas, 1861–1865* (Ithaca, N.Y., 1958).
9. Charles L. Wood, *The Kansas Beef Industry* (Lawrence, Kans., 1980); Richard L. Douglas, "A History of Manufacturing in the Kansas District," *Kansas Historical Collections, 1909–1910* 11 (1910): 125.
10. Norman Saul, "Mill Town Kansas in the Age of Turkey Red," *Kansas History* 23 (Spring–Summer 2000): 26–41.

11. See, among others, Robert Smith Bader, *Prohibition in Kansas* (Lawrence, Kans., 1986); Wilda M. Smith, "A Half Century of Struggle: Gaining Woman Suffrage in Kansas," *Kansas History* 4 (Summer 1981): 74–95.

12. Peter H. Argersinger, *Populism and Politics: William Alfred Peffer and the People's Party* (Lexington, Ky., 1974), 6; O. Gene Clanton, *Kansas Populism: Ideas and Men* (Lawrence, Kans., 1969).

13. William Allen White, *The Autobiography of William Allen White* (New York, 1946), 215.

14. James A. Henretta, W. Elliot Brownlee, David Brody, and Susan Ware, *America's History* (Chicago, 1987), 646; Robert S. LaForte, *Leaders of Reform: Progressive Republicans in Kansas, 1900–1916* (Lawrence, Kans., 1974).

15. Paul S. Sutter, "Paved with Good Intentions: Good Roads, the Automobile, and the Rhetoric of Rural Improvement in the *Kansas Farmer,* 1890–1914," *Kansas History* 18 (Winter 1995–1996): 284; R. Alton Lee, "The Little White Slaver: A Century-Long Struggle against Cigarettes in Kansas," *Kansas History* 22 (Winter 1999–2000): 258–267; Gerald R. Butters Jr., "The Birth of a Nation and the Kansas Board of Motion Pictures: A Censorship Struggle," *Kansas History* 14 (Spring 1991): 2–14; Sally M. Miller, "Kate Richards O'Hare: Progression toward Feminism," *Kansas History* 7 (Winter 1984–1985): 263–279; Gene Clanton, "Populism, Progressivism, and Equality: The Kansas Paradigm," *Agricultural History* 51 (July 1977): 565.

16. "Wall Street and the Devil," *Topeka Daily Capital,* May 17, 1914; "The Future of American Individualism," *Topeka Daily Capital,* August 3, 1925.

17. "'Bleeding Kansas' Again," *Kansas City Star,* July 25, 1931; Richard Lowitt, *The New Deal and the West* (Bloomington, Ind., 1984); Broadus Mitchell, *Depression Decade: From New Era through New Deal, 1929–1941* (New York, 1947).

18. Virgil W. Dean, "Another Wichita Seditionist? Elmer J. Garner and the Radical Right's Opposition to World War II," *Kansas History* 17 (Spring 1994): 50–64.

19. Craig Miner, "The War Years in Wichita," in *Kansas Revisited: Historical Images and Perspectives,* ed. Paul K. Stuewe (Lawrence, Kans., 1990), 271. See also Patrick G. O'Brien, "Kansas at War: The Home Front, 1941–1945," *Kansas History* 17 (Spring 1994): 6–25; Peter Fearon, "Ploughshares into Airplanes: Manufacturing Industry and Workers in Kansas during World War II," *Kansas History* 22 (Winter 1999–2000): 298–314.

20. Craig Miner, *Kansas: The History of the Sunflower State, 1854–2000* (Lawrence, Kans., 2002), 320–326, 353–399.

21. "The Strength of Kansas," an address by Milton S. Eisenhower, president, Kansas State College, January 28, 1949; Kenneth S. Davis, "That Strange State of Mind Called Kansas," *New York Times Magazine* (June 26, 1949): 52; Kenneth S. Davis, "What's the Matter with Kansas?" *New York Times Magazine* (June 27, 1954): 12.

22. Thomas Frank, *What's the Matter with Kansas? How Conservatives Won the Heart of America* (New York, 2004), 8–9.

23. Richard Kluger, *Simple Justice: The History of* Brown v. Board of Education *and Black America's Struggle for Equality* (New York, 1976); Nelson Antrim Crawford, "The State of Kansas," *American Mercury* 70 (April 1950): 465–472; *Plaindealer,* October 15, 1948.

24. Arthur Capper, "The 'Family Size Farm,'" *Thirty-second Biennial Report, State Board of Agriculture, 1939–1940* (Topeka, Kans.,1940), 56–60; Kansas Department of Agriculture, *1999 Farm Facts for Kansas* (Topeka, Kans.,1999).

Chapter 1. John Brown of Osawatomie

1. Lawrence *Weekly Journal,* May 12, 1900; *Topeka Daily Capital,* September 25 and October 10, 1897.

2. *Topeka Journal,* January 28, 1941.

3. John Brown to Henry L. Stearns, July 15, 1857, reprinted in Franklin B. Sanborn, ed., *Life and Letters of Captain John Brown* (Concord, Mass., 1885), 12–17.

4. John Jr.'s remembrance in ibid., 91–93. See also Stephen B. Oates, *To Purge This Land with Blood: A Biography of John Brown* (Amherst, Mass., 1970), 23–24.

5. *Liberator,* January 1, 1831.

6. Brown to Frederick Brown, November 21, 1834, in Sanborn, *Life and Letters of John Brown,* 40–41.

7. Louis Ruchames, ed., *A John Brown Reader* (London, 1959), 179–181. See also Oates, *To Purge This Land with Blood,* 41–42.

8. Philip S. Foner, *Life and Writings of Frederick Douglass,* 4 vols. (New York, 1955), vol. 2, 49–50; see also Oates, *To Purge This Land with Blood,* 62–63.

9. See Michael Morrison, *Slavery and the American West: The Eclipse of Manifest Destiny and the Coming of the Civil War* (Chapel Hill, N.C., 1997).

10. *New York Times,* May 27, 1854.

11. John Brown to John Brown Jr., August 21, 1854, in Zoe Trodd and John Stauffer, eds., *Meteor of War: The John Brown Story* (Maplecrest, N.Y., 2004), 80–81.

12. John Brown Jr. to John Brown, May 20 and 24, 1855, in ibid., 82–83.

13. John Brown to Mary Brown, October 13, 1855, in Sanborn, *Life and Letters of John Brown,* 200–201.

14. On the complex chronology of events in May 1856, see Salmon Brown, "John Brown and Sons in Kansas Territory," *Indiana Magazine of History* 31 (June 1935): 142–150. See also Oswald Garrison Villard's masterful *John Brown: A Biography Fifty Years After* (Boston, 1910), 151–152; Oates, *To Purge This Land with Blood,* 128–130.

15. Testimony from both sides leaves little doubt that John Brown was involved, even if he did not himself participate in the slaying. See Villard, *John Brown,* 148–151; Oates, *To Purge This Land with Blood,* 133–137.

16. Manuscript, James Hanway Collection, Collection 372, KSHS (1856), 6–7.

17. James Redpath, *Public Life of Capt. John Brown* (Boston, 1860), 112–114.

18. Villard, *John Brown,* 248.

19. Dale E. Watts, "How Bloody Was Bleeding Kansas? Political Killings in Kansas Territory, 1854–1861," *Kansas History* 18 (Summer 1995): 116–139.

20. Nicole Etcheson's *Bleeding Kansas: Contested Liberty in the Civil War Era* (Lawrence, Kans., 2004) is an excellent overview of Kansas' territorial history.

Chapter 2. James H. Lane: Radical Conservative, Conservative Radical

1. William Elsey Connelley, *James Henry Lane: The "Grim Chieftain" of Kansas* (Topeka, Kans., 1899), 46; see also John Speer, *Life of Gen. James H. Lane, "The Liberator of Kansas" with Corroborative Incidents of Pioneer History* (Garden City, Kans., 1897). For an overview, see Nicole Etcheson, *Bleeding Kansas: Contested Liberty in the*

Civil War Era (Lawrence, Kans., 2004). Rollin M. Richmond to Judge E. D. Briggs, March 31, 1858, Rollin M. Richmond Collection, KSHS.

2. Wendell Holmes Stephenson, *The Political Career of General James H. Lane* (Topeka, Kans., 1930), 6–7.

3. Ibid., 15, 16.

4. Ibid., 19–27, 61–67; *New York Times,* April 16, 28, 1856; *Herald of Freedom,* Lawrence, Kans., May 10, 1856.

5. *New York Times,* June 14, 19, 24, 25, July 2, 9, 1858; J. H. Lane to the People of Kansas, March 17, 1859, James Henry Lane Papers, University of Kansas Library, Lawrence, Kans.; *Herald of Freedom,* July 3, 1858.

6. *New York Times,* December 20, 1855, June 26, 1856; Stephenson, *Political Career of General James H. Lane,* 71–76; Alice Nichols, *Bleeding Kansas* (New York, 1954), 135–137, 142–143; George A. Root, ed., "The First Day's Battle at Hickory Point," *Kansas Historical Quarterly* 1 (November 1931): 24–49, esp. 38–49; J. H. Lane to Charles Robinson, September 13, 1856, box 1, Richard Hinton Papers, KSHS.

7. *Congressional Globe,* 35 Cong., 1 sess. (Washington, D.C., 1858), 541; Albert Castel, *A Frontier State at War: Kansas, 1861–1865* (Ithaca, N.Y., 1958), 46–56; *The War of the Rebellion: Official Records of the Union and Confederate Armies* (Washington, D.C., 1880–1901) (hereafter *War of the Rebellion*), ser. 1, vol. 3, 163–164; J. H. Lane to Capt. W. E. Prince, Sept. 17, 1861, *War of the Rebellion,* ser. 1, vol. 3, 196; J. H. Lane to Major-General Frémont, September 24, 1861, *War of the Rebellion,* ser. 1, vol. 3, 196, 506.

8. H. W. Halleck to Maj. Gen. George B. McClellan, December 19, 1861, *War of the Rebellion,* ser. 1, vol. 8, 449; A. L. Gilstrap to Maj. Gen. W. S. Rosecrans, February 27, 1864, *War of the Rebellion,* ser. 1, vol. 34, pt. 2, 440; L. Thomas to Major-General Hunter, January 24, 1862, *War of the Rebellion,* ser. 1, vol. 8, 525–526; D. Hunter to Maj. Gen. W. H. Halleck, February 8, 1862, *War of the Rebellion,* ser. 1, vol. 8, 829–831; J. H. Lane to Montgomery Blair, October 9, 1861, reel 21, Blair Family Papers, Library of Congress, Washington, D.C.

9. Report of Brig. Gen. Thomas Ewing Jr., Kansas City, Mo., August 31, 1863, *War of the Rebellion,* ser. 1, vol. 22, pt. 1, 580; Report of Maj. Gen. J. M. Schofield, September 14, 1863, *War of the Rebellion,* ser. 1, vol. 22, 573–574; "Events in the Dept. of the Missouri," John McAllister Schofield Papers, Library of Congress, Washington, D.C., 71–78; J. M. Schofield to Maj. Gen. H. W. Halleck, September 3, 1863, *War of the Rebellion,* ser. 1, vol. 22, pt. 2, 508; H. W. Halleck to Major-General Schofield, September 10, 1863, *War of the Rebellion,* ser. 1, vol. 22, pt. 2, 521; C.M.C. to ___, August 29, 1863, Lela Barnes, "An Editor Looks at Early-Day Kansas: The Letters of Charles Monroe Chase," *Kansas Historical Quarterly* 26 (Summer 1960): 113–151, esp. 148–149.

10. Report of Maj. Gen. Samuel R. Curtis, January 1865, *War of the Rebellion,* ser. 1, vol. 41, pt. 1, 473–478; Report of James H. Lane, *War of the Rebellion,* ser. 1, vol. 41, pt. 1, 567–570.

11. Ben to Father, November 14, 1861, box 1, folder 8, Benjamin and Harriett Carr Papers, Colorado Historical Society, Denver; F. B. Sanborn, *The Life and Letters of John Brown, Liberator of Kansas, and Martyr of Virginia* (1885; reprint, New York, 1969), 338.

12. Lecompton Union, August 30, 1856; G. W. Brown to William E. Connelley, January 4, 1911, George W. Brown Papers, Illinois State Historical Library, Springfield, Ill.; *New York Times,* February 27, 1856.

13. Albert D. Richardson, *Beyond the Mississippi: From the Great River to the Great Ocean . . . 1857–1867* (Hartford, Conn., 1867), 44–47; *New York Times,* March 20, 1856; *Herald of Freedom,* March 26, 1859.

14. Speer, *Life of Gen. James H. Lane,* 84; J. L. Lovejoy to Editor, March 4, 1859, "Letters of Julia Louisa Lovejoy, 1856–1864: Part Four, 1859," *Kansas Historical Quarterly* 16 (February 1948): 40–75, esp. 54–55; S. C. Smith to Dr. [Robinson], January 6, 1859, Robinson Papers, KSHS; S. Medary to J. W. Denver, January 13, 1859, James William Denver Collection, KSHS.

15. Connelley, *James Henry Lane,* 75; *Congressional Globe,* 33 Cong., 1 sess. (Washington, D.C., 1854), 923.

16. Speer, *Life of Gen. James H. Lane,* 143.

17. John W. Geary to Wm. L. Marcy, September 9, 1856, John W. Geary Letters and Executive Minutes, KSHS; Sam. F. Tappan to Charles Sumner, March 9, 1856, Edward Lillis Pierce Collection, KSHS; *New York Times,* July 17, 1857; *Congressional Globe,* 39 Cong., 1 sess. (Washington, D.C., 1866), 3903–3904.

18. Benjamin to Father, July 1, 1858, folder 4, box 1, Carr Papers.

19. Box 65 of the Ewing Family Papers, Library of Congress, Washington, D.C., contains the complex maneuvering of the senatorial balloting. Speer, *Life of Gen. James H. Lane,* 223; *Congressional Globe,* 37 Cong., 2 sess. (Washington, D.C., 1862), 263, 341, 360–361; Castel, *Frontier State at War: Kansas,* 46–56, 65–77, 86–89; Thos. Ewing Jr. to Brig. Gen. Schofield, June 23, 1863, box 68, Ewing Family Papers.

20. Craig Miner, "Lane and Lincoln: A Mysterious Connection," *Kansas History* 24 (Autumn 2001): 186–199.

21. *New York Times,* October 22, 1855; House of Representatives, Report No. 200, 34 Cong., 1 sess., serial 869, vol. 2 (Washington, D.C., 1856), 612–616.

22. September 4, 1856, entry, Henry Miles Moore Journals, Yale University Library, New Haven, Conn.; *New York Times,* June 6, 1862, June 4, 1857; *Congressional Globe,* 33 Cong., 1 sess. (Washington, D.C., 1854), 610–611; *Daily Times,* Leavenworth, Kans., October 2, 1864.

23. Connelley, *James Henry Lane,* 76; Journal, Topeka Constitutional Convention, October 31, 1855, History, Constitutions, KSHS.

24. *Congressional Globe,* 38 Cong., 1 sess. (Washington, D.C., 1864), 672–675; 37 Cong., 1 sess. (1861), 187.

25. Lane to General S. D. Sturgis, October 3, 1861, *War of the Rebellion,* ser. 1, vol. 3, 516; *Congressional Globe,* 37 Cong., 3 sess. (Washington, D.C., 1863), 215–219; Michael P. Johnson, "Out of Egypt: The Migration of Former Slaves to the Midwest during the 1860s in Comparative Perspective," in *Crossing Boundaries: Comparative History of Black People in Diaspora,* ed. Darlene Clark Hine and Jacqueline McLeod (Bloomington, Ind., 1999), 223–245, esp. 232.

26. Dudley Cornish Taylor, *The Sable Arm: Negro Troops in the Union Army, 1861–1865* (New York, 1966), 69–75, 77–78; Ira Berlin, Joseph P. Reidy, and Leslie S. Rowland, eds., *Freedom: A Documentary History of Emancipation, 1861–1867,* series II: *The Black Military Experience* (Cambridge, 1982), 19; Dudley Cornish Taylor, "Kansas Negro Regiments in the Civil War," *Kansas Historical Quarterly* 20 (May 1953): 417–429; Joseph T. Glatthaar, *Forged in Battle: The Civil War Alliance of Black Soldiers and White Officers* (New York, 1990), 176, 122; Benjamin Quarles, *The Negro in the Civil War* (Boston, 1953), 113–115, 120.

27. *New York Times,* June 6, 1862; Stephenson, *Political Career of General James H. Lane,* 132; *Daily Times,* August 6, 1862.

28. *Congressional Globe,* 37 Cong., 2 sess. (Washington, D.C., 1862), 334; Stephenson, *Political Career of General James H. Lane,* 132–133; Senate, *Bills and Resolutions,* 38 Cong., 1 sess. (Washington, D.C., 1864), Bill 45; *Congressional Globe,* 37 Cong., 1 sess. (1861), 190; 38 Cong., 1 sess. (1864), 672–675.

29. *Congressional Globe,* 37 Cong., 2 sess. (Washington, D.C., 1862), 852; 38 Cong., 1 sess. (1864), 90–91, 606; 38 Cong., 2 sess. (1865), 300–301; 38 Cong., 1 sess. (1864), 449, 320; 38 Cong., 2 sess. (1865), 141; 38 Cong., 1 sess., 841.

30. *Congressional Globe,* 39 Cong., 1 sess. (Washington, D.C., 1866), 1026, 1257, 1799, 1803, 1804, 2865; 38 Cong., 1 sess. (1864), 2458–2459, 2866, 2904–2906; Connelley, *James Henry Lane,* 124.

31. Connelley, *James Henry Lane,* 38; "Journals of Abelard Guthrie," April 9, 1862, in William E. Connelley, ed., *The Provisional Government of Nebraska Territory and the Journals of William Walker* (Lincoln, Nebr., 1899), 145. For a description of the bipolar personality, see Kay Redfield Jamison, *Touched with Fire: Manic-Depressive Illness and the Artistic Temperament* (New York, 1993), 12–17. For the psychopathic personality, see Hervey Cleckley, *The Mask of Sanity* (Saint Louis, Mo., 1976), 337–364.

Chapter 3. William H. Russell: Proslavery Partisan and Western Entrepreneur

1. Raymond W. Settle and Mary Lund Settle, *Empire on Wheels* (Stanford, Calif., 1949), 6–8, 10, 11, 132; Raymond W. Settle and Mary Lund Settle, *War Drums and Wagon Wheels: The Story of Russell, Majors, and Waddell* (Lincoln, Nebr., 1966); Walker Wyman, "Freighting: A Big Business on the Santa Fe Trail," *Kansas Historical Quarterly* 1 (November 1931–1932): 17–27.

2. Settle and Settle, *War Drums and Wagon Wheels,* vii; Robert Richmond, *Kansas: A Land of Contrasts,* 3d ed. (Arlington Heights, Ill., 1988); Kenneth S. Davis, *Kansas: A History* (1976; reprint, New York, 1984); Craig Miner, *Kansas: The History of the Sunflower State, 1854–2000* (Lawrence, Kans., 2002); Nicole Etcheson, *Bleeding Kansas: Contested Liberty in the Civil War Era* (Lawrence, Kans., 2004).

3. Settle and Settle, *Empire on Wheels,* 5; Settle and Settle, *War Drums and Wagon Wheels,* 33.

4. Ray Allen Billington and Martin Ridge, *Westward Expansion: A History of the American Frontier,* 5th ed. (New York, 1982), 379–380, 405–408, 474–475, 574–576; Leroy R. Hafen and Carl Coke Rister, *Western America: The Exploration, Settlement, and Development of the Region beyond the Mississippi* (New York, 1941), 255–258, 260, 494–495; Arrell M. Gibson, *The West in the Life of the Nation* (Lexington, Mass., 1976), 237, 278–280, 298, 375; Robert M. Utley, *Frontiersmen in Blue* (Lincoln, Nebr., 1967), 64–68, 72; Elliott West, *The Contested Plains: Indians, Goldseekers, and the Rush to Colorado* (Lawrence, Kans., 1998), 230–234.

5. Settle and Settle, *War Drums and Wagon Wheels,* 32, 36, 38, 39.

6. Ibid., 41, 44; Settle and Settle, *Empire on Wheels,* 16; Russell, Majors & Waddell, Co-partnership Agreement, December 28, 1854, William B. Waddell Collection, Huntington Library, San Marino, Calif.

7. Settle and Settle, *War Drums and Wagon Wheels,* 42, 44, 45–46, 47, 48; *Kansas Weekly Herald,* May 1, 1855.

8. Paul Wallace Gates, *Fifty Million Acres: Conflicts over Kansas Land Policy* (New York, 1966), 114; Rita G. Napier, "Squatter City: The Construction of a New Community in the American West, 1854–1861" (Ph.D. diss., American University, 1976), 63, 66, 69–70.

9. Settle and Settle, *War Drums and Wagon Wheels,* 45.

10. Napier, "Squatter City," 34–37; Gates, *Fifty Million Acres,* 49, 54, 56, 62–63.

11. Settle and Settle, *War Drums and Wagon Wheels,* 46–47; Gates, *Fifty Million Acres,* 50, 67, 114.

12. Settle and Settle, *War Drums and Wagon Wheels,* 48; Elmer L. Craik, "Southern Interest in Territorial Kansas, 1854–1858," *Kansas Historical Collections, 1919–1922* 15 (1923): 360, 378.

13. U.S. Congress, *House Report 104,* 36 Cong., 2 sess. (1860), "The Testimony of Benjamin Luce," 232, "Testimony of John J. Luce," 510, "Testimony of William Haller," 234–235; Napier, "Squatter City," 89–118.

14. Napier, "Squatter City," 60, 62, 58, 66–67, 69, 71–72; "Executive Minutes of Governor John W. Geary," *Kansas Historical Collections, 1886–1888* 4 (1888): 657–658.

15. Settle and Settle, *War Drums and Wagon Wheels,* 49–72, 50, 222–239.

16. Ibid., 53–54.

17. Ibid., 66–67, 77; "Statement of the Claims of Majors and Russell, for Transportation, 1857," December 7, 1859, William B. Waddell Collection.

18. Settle and Settle, *War Drums and Wagon Wheels,* 80, 82–85, 92.

19. Ibid., 108; see, among others, Fred Reinfeld, *Pony Express* (New York, 1966).

20. Settle and Settle, *War Drums and Wagon Wheels,* 127, 133, 135, 137.

21. Ibid., 30, 143–145, 151–156, 169.

Chapter 4. Clarina Irene Howard Nichols: "A Large-Hearted, Brave, Faithful Woman"

1. Elizabeth Cady Stanton, Susan B. Anthony, and Matilda Joslyn Gage, eds., *History of Woman Suffrage* (Rochester, N.Y., 1881), vol. 2, 229, 232, and vol. 1, 171.

2. Karlyn Kohrs Campbell, *Man Cannot Speak for Her: A Critical Study of Early Feminist Rhetoric* (New York, 1989), vol. 1, 92. See Joseph G. Gambone, ed., "The Forgotten Feminist of Kansas: The Papers of Clarina I. H. Nichols, 1854–1885," *Kansas Historical Quarterly* 39 (Spring 1973): 12; Diane (Eickhoff) Barnhart, "The Forgotten Feminist: Clarina Irene Howard Nichols Carried the Cause of Women's Rights in Kansas," *Kansas City Star,* November 5, 1999. See also Marilyn Schultz Blackwell, "Meddling in Politics: Clarina Howard Nichols and Antebellum Political Culture," *Journal of the Early Republic* 24 (Spring 2004): 27–63. See *Reprint of the Proceedings and Debates of the Convention Which Framed the Constitution of Kansas at Wyandotte in July, 1859* (Topeka, Kans., 1920), 169, 580, 588, cited in Gambone, "Forgotten Feminist of Kansas," 24. The constitution guaranteed the right for women to vote in school board elections, the right for married women to own property, and equal guardianship of children in cases of divorce

3. Nichols to Anthony, March 24, 1852, quoted in Gambone, "Forgotten Feminist of Kansas," 14, n.8.

4. Stanton et al., *History of Woman Suffrage,* vol. 1, 66, 172; Gambone, "Forgotten Feminist of Kansas," 15, 18; see *New York Daily Tribune,* October 17, 1851, cited in Campbell, *Man Cannot Speak for Her,* 90. For women's property rights, see Blackwell, "Meddling in Politics," 39.

5. Nichols to editor, Springfield (Mass.) *Daily Republican,* November 2, 1854, cited in Gambone, "Forgotten Feminist of Kansas," 34, 33.

6. *Herald of Freedom,* March 8, 1856, cited in ibid., 238, 241–242.

7. *Herald of Freedom,* April 26, 1856, cited in ibid., 243, 244.

8. Nichols to Emma ——, May 24, 1856, cited in ibid., 253.

9. Nichols to Thaddeus Hyatt, October 15 and October 4, 1856, Thaddeus Hyatt Papers, 1843–1898, KSHS; Gambone, "Forgotten Feminist of Kansas," 21. See also Blackwell, "Meddling in Politics," 52–53.

10. Nichols to "The Women of the State of New York," *New York Daily Tribune,* November 8, 1856, cited in Gambone, "Forgotten Feminist of Kansas," 259.

11. Receipt and "schedule of goods," George L. and Mary E. Stearns Correspondence, 1860, KSHS.

12. *Chindowan,* May 30, 1857, cited in Gambone, "Forgotten Feminist of Kansas," 394.

13. Stanton et al., *History of Woman Suffrage,* vol. 1, 191.

14. Nichols to Susan Wattles, July 14 and July 25, 1859, Augustus Wattles Collection, KSHS; Mills S. Reeves and John B. Bunch[?] to Nichols, July 14, 1859, Clarina I. H. Nichols Papers, 1843–1946, KSHS.

15. Charles Robinson to Nichols, August 5, 1876, cited in Gambone, "Forgotten Feminist of Kansas," 28, n.70.

16. Nichols to the editor, *Vermont Phoenix,* cited in Gambone, "Forgotten Feminist of Kansas," 519; Susan Wattles to Nichols, April 1, 1859, in Nichols Papers, KSHS; see also Ellen Carol DuBois, *Feminism and Suffrage: The Emergence of an Independent Women's Movement in America, 1848–1869* (Ithaca, N.Y., 1978), 79–104.

17. Nichols to Susan Wattles, May 2, 1859, Wattles Collection.

18. Nichols to Susan and Esther Wattles, November 6, 1859, Wattles Collection.

19. Nichols to *Kansas Daily Commonwealth,* September 1, 1869, cited in Gambone, "Forgotten Feminist of Kansas," 124.

20. Nichols to Susan B. Anthony, February 15, 1870, cited in Gambone, "Forgotten Feminist of Kansas," 250.

21. Nichols to *Woman's Journal,* July 1877, cited in ibid., 425.

22. Nichols, "Early Reminiscences of My Life, Written in Her Invalid Hours," 1880; Nichols to Worcester Woman's Suffrage Convention, October 9, 1880, cited in ibid., 455–456, 446.

Chapter 5: Joseph G. McCoy and the Creation of the Mythic American West

1. Ralph P. Bieber, ed., "Introduction" to Joseph G. McCoy, *Historic Sketches of the Cattle Trade of the West and the Southwest* (Glendale, Calif., 1940), 17–19, 68.

2. Ibid., 17–19, 65–67.

3. Ibid., 19; Joseph G. McCoy, *Historic Sketches of the Cattle Trade of the West and the Southwest* (Kansas City, Mo., 1874; reprint, Columbus, Ohio, 1951), 20.

4. McCoy, *Historic Sketches,* 74–75.

5. Ibid., 50; Bieber, "Introduction," 52; Robert R. Dykstra, *Cattle Towns* (New York, 1968), 21; David Galenson, "Cattle Trailing in the Nineteenth Century: A Reply," *Journal of Economic History* 35 (June 1975): 461.

6. McCoy, *Historic Sketches,* 65.

7. Ibid., 121; Bieber, "Introduction," 53; Dykstra, *Cattle Towns,* 18–19, 98–99.

8. Dykstra, *Cattle Towns,* 20, 154; McCoy, *Historic Sketches,* 184–185, 206–214.

9. Dykstra, *Cattle Towns,* 80; McCoy, *Historic Sketches,* 42, 52, 108, 150, 190–191, 249.

10. McCoy, *Historic Sketches,* 55, 138.

11. Ibid., 137; Joseph G. Rosa, *They Called Him Wild Bill: The Life and Adventures of James Butler Hickok* (Norman, Okla., 1964), 123; Bieber, "Introduction," 61–62.

12. Bieber, "Introduction," 62; Dykstra, *Cattle Towns,* 27, 294–297, 306.

Chapter 6. Theodore C. Henry: Frontier Booster and Nostalgic Old Settler

1. Stuart Henry, *Conquering Our Great American Plains: A Historical Development* (New York, 1930).

2. T. C. Henry, "The Story of a Fenceless Winter-Wheat Field" and "Thomas James Smith, of Abilene," *Kansas Historical Collections, 1905–1906* 9 (1906): 502–506, 526–532.

3. Emerson Hough, *North of 36* (New York, 1923); Henry, *Conquering Our Great American Plains,* 353–381, 4, 61, 193, 341.

4. James C. Malin, *Winter Wheat in the Golden Belt of Kansas: A Study in Adaptation to Subhumid Geographical Environment* (1944; reprint, New York, 1973), 35–36; see Henry, *Conquering Our Great American Plains,* 197–198. See also Stuart Henry, *Winter Wheat in the Golden Belt of Kansas: A Reply and Critique by an Eyewitness* (ca. 1946), and *Kansas State Historical Society: A Moral Lapse in Bureaucracy* (ca. 1951).

5. Robert R. Dykstra, *The Cattle Towns* (reprint, Lincoln, Nebr., 1983), especially, 26–28, 117, 294–297, 300–306.

6. David M. Wrobel, *Promised Lands: Promotion, Memory, and the Creation of the American West* (Lawrence, Kans., 2002), 2–3, 6–7, 121.

7. Henry, "Story of a Fenceless Winter-Wheat Field," 502–503: Dykstra, *Cattle Towns,* 294–295; U.S. Census, 1870, Dickinson County, Grant Township, 1870; obituary, T. C. Henry, *St. Louis Daily Globe-Democrat,* February 4, 1914, clipping in Vertical File, KSHS; Frank Hall, "Henry, Theodore C.," *History of the State of Colorado,* 4 vols. (Chicago, 1895), vol. 4, 464–465; Henry, *Conquering Our Great American Plains,* 47.

8. Dykstra, *Cattle Towns,* 294–295; Henry, *Conquering Our Great American Plains,* 47.

9. Henry, "Story of a Fenceless Winter-Wheat Field," 503; U.S. Census, 1870, Dickinson County, Grant Township; Dykstra, *Cattle Towns,* 294–295.

10. See Dykstra, *Cattle Towns,* 26–27; *Junction City Herald,* April 11, 1868.

11. Henry, "Thomas James Smith," 528; Henry, *Conquering Our Great American Plains,* 61–62; Joseph G. McCoy, *Historic Sketches of the Cattle Trade of the West and Southwest* (reprint, Washington, D.C., 1932), 203, 206, 229.

12. Henry, "Thomas James Smith," 527–532; Henry, *Conquering Our Great American Plains,* 87–89, 123–161; Dykstra, *Cattle Towns,* 117, 297–303; Malin, *Winter*

Wheat in the Golden Belt of Kansas, 32–34; *Abilene Chronicle,* November 10, 1870, September 15, 1870, and January 19, 1871; U.S. Census, 1870, Dickinson County, Grant Township; *Abilene Reflector,* January 26, 1871, and May 25, 1871.

13. Narrative sources, even obituaries, are strangely silent about details of Henry's family life. See Kansas State Census, 1875, Dickinson County, Grant Township; U.S. Census, 1880, Dickinson County, Grant Township; "Birds Eye View of the City of Abilene," *The Official State Atlas of Kansas* (Philadelphia, Pa., 1887); *History of the State of Kansas* (Chicago, 1883), 689; *A Gem: "The City of the Plains": Abilene: The Centre of the "Golden Belt"* (Burlington, Iowa, 1887), 18, Dickinson County Pamphlets, vol. 1, no. 1, KSHS.

14. Kansas State Board of Agriculture, *First Biennial Report, 1877–78,* 176–180.

15. Malin, *Winter Wheat in the Golden Belt of Kansas,* 66–70; Henry, "Story of a Fenceless Winter-Wheat Field," 502–506, quotations, 505.

16. *Kansas-Colorado Suit: Supreme Court of the United States: Direct Testimony of T. C. Henry before Supreme Court Commissioner Granville A. Richardson, October 20–21, 1904* (Denver, Colo., 1904), 3–21.

17. T. C. Henry, *Addresses by Hon. T. C. Henry of Abilene, Kansas, on "Kansas Stock Interests" and "Kansas Forestry"* (Abilene, Kans., 1882), 1–2.

18. *Dickinson County, Kansas: Henry's Advertiser,* vol. 1 (Spring Edition 1875), Dickinson County Pamphlets, vol. 1, no. 6; vol. 2 (Spring Edition 1878), Dickinson County Pamphlets, vol. 1, no. 7, KSHS; "Historical Address Delivered by Hon. T. C. Henry, at the Fourth of July Celebration in Abilene, 1876," *Abilene Chronicle,* July 14, 1876, Kansas Scrap-Book: Biography, H, vol. 3, 182–189, KSHS.

19. Theodore C. Henry, *An Address to the Old Settlers Re-union at Enterprise, Kansas, October, 1902,* Dickinson County Pamphlets, vol. 1, no. 9, KSHS; "Historical Address Delivered by Hon. T. C. Henry, at the Fourth of July Celebration in Abilene, 1876," *Abilene Chronicle,* July 14, 1876, Kansas Scrap-Book: Biography, H, vol. 3, 182–189, KSHS. For Henry's activities in Colorado, see James E. Sherow, "Agricultural Marketplace Reform: T. C. Henry and the Irrigation Crusade in Colorado, 1870–1914," *Journal of the West* 31 (October 1992): 51–58.

20. C. M. Harger, "A Wheatfield His Throne: Theodore C. Henry, Kansas's First 'Wheat King,' Is Dead," reprinted from *Abilene Daily Reflector* in *Kansas City Star,* February 17, 1914, Kansas Scrap-Book: Biography, H, vol. 15, 147–148, KSHS; *St. Louis Daily Globe-Democrat,* February 4, 1914, clipping in Vertical File, KSHS. Thanks to the Dickinson County Historical Society, Abilene, for confirming Henry's date of death and his burial in Abilene.

21. John Lewis Gaddis, *The Landscape of History: How Historians Map the Past* (New York, 2002).

Chapter 7. Frederick H. Harvey and the Revolution in Nineteenth-Century Food Service

1. Harold L. Henderson, "Frederick Henry Harvey" (master's thesis, University of Kansas City, 1942); James David Henderson, *"Meals by Fred Harvey": A Phenomenon of the American West* (Fort Worth, Tex., 1969).

2. Henderson, "Frederick Henry Harvey," 6, 7.

3. Henderson, *"Meals by Fred Harvey,"* 2.

4. James Neal Primm, *Lion of the Valley: St. Louis, Missouri, 1764–1980,* 3rd ed. rev. (St. Louis, Mo., 1998), 159.

5. Henderson, "Frederick Henry Harvey," 10, 12; Henderson, *"Meals by Fred Harvey,"* 3.

6. Henderson, "Frederick Henry Harvey," 11; *Leavenworth Times,* February 10, 1901.

7. Henderson, *"Meals by Fred Harvey,"* 3–4; Henderson, "Frederick Henry Harvey," 13; H. Roger Grant, *"Follow the Flag": A History of the Wabash Railroad Company* (DeKalb, Ill., 2004), 28–37; Richard C. Overton, *Burlington Route: A History of the Burlington Lines* (New York, 1965), 55–56, 75.

8. Henderson, *"Meals by Fred Harvey,"* 4; *Topeka Daily Capital,* February 10, 1901.

9. *Topeka Daily Capital,* February 10, 1901.

10. James Redpath and Richard J. Hinton, *Hand-Book to Kansas Territory and the Rocky Mountain's Gold Region . . .* (New York, 1859), 29. See John H. White Jr., *The American Railroad Passenger Car* (Baltimore, Md., 1978), 311–322.

11. Henderson, *"Meals by Fred Harvey,"* 10.

12. Ibid.; Keith L. Bryant Jr., *History of the Atchison, Topeka & Santa Fe Railway* (New York, 1974), 109.

13. *Fred Harvey Meal Service* (Chicago, Ill., 1926), 5–6.

14. Henderson, "Frederick Henry Harvey," 27; Bryant, *History of the Atchison, Topeka & Santa Fe,* 109.

15. *Florence Herald* (Kansas), February 23, 1878; Henderson, *"Meals by Fred Harvey,"* 11–12.

16. Bryant, *History of the Atchison, Topeka & Santa Fe Railway,* 109–152, quotation on 111.

17. Henderson, "Frederick Henry Harvey," 36.

18. George H. Foster and Peter C. Weiglin, *The Harvey House Cookbook: Memories of Dining along the Santa Fe Railroad* (Atlanta, Ga., 1992), 182–190. The Santa Fe lost control of the Frisco later in the 1890s, after the Santa Fe entered a short receivership following the panic of 1893.

19. Henderson, "Frederick Henry Harvey," 35–36; Lesley Poling-Kemples, *The Harvey Girls: Women Who Opened the West* (New York, 1989), 38; Whitefield Avery, "The Dining Room That Is Two Thousand Miles Long," *Capper's Magazine* (September 1930): 23.

20. Henderson, "Frederick Henry Harvey," 34–35.

21. Ibid., 46–48; Clifford Funkhouser and Lyman Anson, "Cupid Rides the Rails," *American Mercury* (September 1940): 42–46; James Marshall, *Santa Fe: The Railroad That Built an Empire* (New York, 1945), 100–101; Bryant, *Atchison, Topeka & Santa Fe Railway,* 114, 116; Poling-Kemples, *The Harvey Girls,* 42–44.

22. *Fred Harvey Meal Service,* 29–30.

23. Henderson, "Frederick Henry Harvey," 56, 57–58; *Topeka Daily Capital,* February 10, 1901.

24. Henderson, *"Meals by Fred Harvey,"* 35–37; "Ford Ferguson Harvey," *The National Cyclopedia of American Biography* (New York, 1953), vol. 38, 455, 457; Marta Weigle and Barbara A. Babcock, eds., *The Great Southwest of the Fred Harvey Company and the Santa Fe Railway* (Phoenix, Ariz., n.d.); William Patrick Armstrong, *Fred Harvey: Creator of Western Hospitality* (Bellemont, Ariz., 2000), 24–26.

Chapter 8. Bernhard Warkentin and the Making of the Wheat State

1. A useful work on the Mennonite migration and Warkentin is David A. Haury, "Bernhard Warkentin: A Mennonite Benefactor," *Mennonite Quarterly Review* 49 (July 1975): 179–202. See also Martin H. Schrag, *The European History of the Swiss Mennonites from Volhynia,* 2d ed., ed. Harley J. Stucky (Newton, Kans., 1999).

2. For an excellent historical geography of Mennonite movements and settlements, see William Schroeder and Helmut T. Huebert, *Mennonite Historical Atlas* (Winnipeg, Ontario, Canada, 1980).

A groundbreaking history is C. Henry Smith, *The Coming of the Russian Mennonites: An Episode in the Settling of the Last Frontier, 1874–1884* (Berne, Ind., 1927). For more recent updates, see Cornelius Krahn, *From the Steppes to the Prairies* (Newton, Kans., 1949); and Norman Saul, "The Migration of the Russian-Germans to Kansas," *Kansas Historical Quarterly* 40 (Spring 1974): 38–63.

3. Johann Cornies was the most respected and best-known leader of the Russian Mennonites during the first half of the nineteenth century. A progressive scholar, he contributed numerous articles—in excellent Russian—to the *Journal of the Ministry of State Domains* (the ministry that administered agricultural affairs) and was respected by Russian officials as a leading expert on the subject. Not surprisingly, prominent Russian Mennonite families were interconnected. Bernhard's sister married Johann Wiebe, a grandson of Cornies. David Goerz, two years younger than Warkentin, tutored the children of Johann Cornies Jr. Smith, *The Coming of the Russian Mennonites,* 37–40; Cornelius Krahn, ed., "Some Letters of Bernhard Warkentin Pertaining to the Migration of 1873–1875," *Mennonite Quarterly Review* 24 (July 1950): 249–250.

4. Smith, *The Coming of the Russian Mennonites,* 44–50. For the Jansen role, see Gustav E. Reimer and G. R. Gaeddert, *Exiled by the Czar: Cornelius Jansen and the Great Mennonite Migration, 1874* (Newton, Kans., 1956), 61–72.

5. Warkentin letters to Goerz during 1868 to 1871 and April to June, 1872, f. 7, box 1, Warkentin Papers, Mennonite Library and Archive, Bethel College; Krahn, "Some Letters," 250. The Warkentin-Goerz correspondence is a valuable record of immigration history, which, unfortunately, ends in 1874 with Goerz's own emigration to America.

6. Warkentin to Goerz, July 29/August 10 and August 6/18, 1872 (using Russian dating), Warkentin Papers. One of his first 1872 summer impressions in Illinois and Kansas was that of "lightning bugs."

7. Warkentin (Summerfield) to Goerz, January 8, 1873, March 3 and 28, 1873, in Krahn, "Some Letters," 251, 253–254; Smith, *The Coming of the Russian Mennonites,* 60–66.

8. Warkentin (Topeka) to Goerz, January 6, and Warkentin (Halstead) to Goerz, January 21, 1874, f. 9, box 1, Warkentin Papers. He added that the mill was to be built in March after a trip through Pennsylvania to New York; see also Board of Guardians Correspondence, f. 3, box 1, Warkentin Papers; Warkentin (Lancaster, Pa.) to Goerz, February 20, 1874, f. 9, box 1, Warkentin Papers; engagement announcement, f. 8, box 4, Warkentin Papers.; U.S. Census, 1880, Kansas.

9. Obituary, Bernhard Warkentin, *Yearbook and Almanac, 1909* (Philadelphia, 1909). Sources also vaguely mention a return to Russia in 1885, which may have been with his father.

10. "Bernhard Warkentin: Entrepreneur and Benefactor," *Bethel College Bulletin,* June 1987.

11. Sanborn maps of 1884, 1891, 1896, 1901, and 1908 for Halstead, and 1884, 1886, 1891, 1896, and 1901 for Newton. The Sanborn insurance maps are an excellent source for documenting mill expansion. The Spencer Research Library at the University of Kansas has a nearly complete set for the state. For an inventory, see *Fire Insurance Maps in the Library of Congress: A Checklist Compiled by the Reference and Bibliographic Service of the Geography and Map Division* (Washington, D.C., 1981). The Blackwell Milling and Elevator Company was registered in 1901 with Warkentin as president and David Goerz as vice president. Folder 6, box 4, Warkentin Papers.

12. "Warkentin House Museum," Newton Visitor Information, http://www.info newtonks.org/tourism/history.php.

13. The arrival of Turkey Red in Kansas has long been cited in Mennonite folklore, such as the Anna Barkman story, with little factual evidence. See Norman Saul, "Myth and History: Turkey Red Wheat and the 'Kansas Miracle,'" in *Kansas Revisited: Historical Images and Perspectives,* 2d ed., ed. Paul K. Stuewe (Lawrence, Kans., 1998), 161–175. Though Warkentin obviously had little to do with this "importation" and was actually surprised to learn about it, he emphasized the importation of 1873 in a 1900 letter to Mark Carleton. Warkentin to Carleton, November 9, 1900, f. 20, B/box 2, Warkentin Papers.

14. Unfortunately, the Center for Historical Research, KSHS, has only partial holdings of the Kansas Millers' Association's monthly publication, *Kansas Miller and Manufacture,* which began in 1888 and was headquartered in Enterprise. Warkentin was apparently the first president, served subsequently as treasurer, and served again as president in 1891. *Kansas Miller and Manufacture* 4 (January 1891).

15. Paul Lawrence, "Newton Mills and the Santa Fe: Early Mennonite Immigrants from Russia Brought the Seeds that Have Made Kansas Wheat Famous throughout the World," *Santa Fe Magazine* 26 (June 1932): 23.

16. Carleton to Warkentin, August 14, 1899, and *Newton Weekly Kansan,* August 25, 1899, f. 21, box 2; Warkentin to Carleton, November 9, 1900, f. 20, box 2, Warkentin Papers. Carleton was immortalized in the opening chapter, "The Wheat Dreamer," of Paul de Kruif, *Hunger Fighters* (New York, 1928), 3–30; see also Thomas D. Isern, "Wheat Explorer the World Over: Mark Carleton of Kansas," *Kansas History* 23 (Spring/Summer 2000): 12–25.

17. "Bernhard Warkentin," http://skyways.lib.ks.us/genweb/archives. Carl Warkentin also died tragically at his Overland Park home—by self-inflicted gunshot—in 1942. "Milling His Heritage," *Kansas City Times,* May 1, 1942; see also Norman Saul, "Mill Town Kansas in the Age of Turkey Red," *Kansas History* 23 (Spring/Summer 2000): 26–41.

Chapter 9. Mary Ann "Mother" Bickerdyke: A Gilded Age Icon

1. *Dodge City Times,* October 8, 1885.

2. Charles M. Correll, "Some Aspects of the History of the GAR in Kansas," *Kansas Historical Quarterly* 19 (February 1951): 63–74; Kyle S. Sinisi, "Veterans as Political Activists: The Kansas Grand Army of the Republic, 1880–1893," *Kansas History* 14 (Summer 1991): 89–99; Patrick J. Kelly, *Creating a National Home: Building the Veterans' Welfare State, 1860–1900* (Cambridge, Mass., 1997), 181–183; Randall M. Thies,

"Civil War Valor in Concrete: David A. Lester and the Kinsley Civil War Monument," *Kansas History* 22 (Autumn 1999): 164–181.

3. Dixon Wecter, *When Johnny Comes Marching Home* (Cambridge, 1944), 127.

4. Fred R. Berger, "Gratitude," *Ethics* 85 (1974–1975): 298–309; Andre Comte-Sponville, *A Small Treatise on the Great Virtues: The Uses of Philosophy in Everyday Life,* trans. Catherine Temerson (New York, 2001), 132–139. The liberal mood is discussed by Craig Miner, *Kansas: The History of the Sunflower State, 1854–2000* (Lawrence, Kans., 2002), 143–189. For women's political activism, see June O. Underwood, "Civilizing Kansas: Women's Organizations, 1880–1920," *Kansas History* 7 (Winter 1984–1985): 291–306; Michael Lewis Goldberg, *An Army of Women: Gender and Politics in Gilded Age Kansas* (Baltimore, Md., 1997).

5. Margaret B. Davis, *Mother Bickerdyke: The Woman Who Battled for the Boys in Blue* (San Francisco, 1886); Nina Brown Baker, *Cyclone in Calico: The Story of Mary Ann Bickerdyke* (Boston, 1952).

6. *Bunker Hill News,* February 28, April 8, November 25, December 16 and 23, 1887. Davis, *Mother Bickerdyke;* Baker, *Cyclone in Calico.* On Bickerdyke's early Kansas years, see Craig Miner, *West of Wichita: Settling the High Plains of Kansas, 1865–1890* (Lawrence, Kans., 1986), 20, 60.

7. *Russell Record,* May 21 and June 25, 1891; Bickerdyke to Chas. H. Blinn, April 27 and May 18, 1891; Bickerdyke to Hon. P. B. Plumb, April 4 and 24, 1891; Chas. H. Blinn to Bickerdyke, May 4 and 12, 1891; Anna Young to Bickerdyke, May 17, 18, 22, 27, and June 23, 1891; Bickerdyke to W. W. Broughton, June 2, 1891; Mary A. Perry to Bickerdyke, June 20, 1891, Personal Correspondence, Papers of Mary Ann Bickerdyke, Library of Congress, Washington, D.C.

8. *Bunker Hill Gazette,* June 7, 1888; *Russell Journal,* October 15, 1890.

9. *Western Veteran,* August 6, 1890; *Russell Record,* March 7, 1895; *General Order No. 4 Mother Bickerdyke Day,* Bickerdyke Papers.

10. Mary A. Livermore, *My Story of the War* (1887; reprint, New York, 1995), 544–546.

11. Baker, *Cyclone in Calico,* 243; Florence Shaw Kellogg, *Mother Bickerdyke As I Knew Her* (Chicago, 1907), 96.

12. Baker, *Cyclone in Calico,* 243; Julia A. Chase, *Mary A. Bickerdyke, "Mother"* (Lawrence, Kans., 1896), 103–107; Livermore, *My Story,* 542; Margaret Burton Davis, "A New Book of Thrilling Interest. Mother Bickerdyke . . ." (San Francisco, 1886), promotional pamphlet, Bickerdyke Papers.

13. *Kansas Knight and Soldier,* September 1884; *Topeka Daily Capital,* November 21, 1885, January 28, 1886.

14. *Russell Record,* November 16, 1901, October 3 and September 12, 1895.

15. Copied in *Russell Journal,* July 25, 1895; *Russell Record,* August 29, 1895.

16. Chase, *Mary A. Bickerdyke,* 101–107; Julia A. Chase, "Mother Bickerdyke," *Kansas Historical Collections, 1901–1902* 7 (1902): 197.

17. Chase, "Mother Bickerdyke," 197–198.

18. *Ellsworth Messenger,* December 24, 1896; *Western Veteran,* June 10, 1891.

19. *Ellsworth Republican,* May 6, 1897; Chase, "Mother Bickerdyke," 198; *Ellsworth Messenger,* May 13, 1897; *Constitution and Rules of the Mother Bickerdyke Home and Hospital at Ellsworth, Kansas,* Bickerdyke Papers, 5–6; Kellogg, *Mother Bickerdyke As I Knew Her,* 113–114; Baker, *Cyclone in Calico,* 244.

20. *Ellsworth Reporter,* October 7, 1897; *Russell Record,* February 23, 1901; Chase, "Mother Bickerdyke," 198.

21. *Russell Reformer,* July 23, 1897; *General Order No. 4.*

22. *General Order No. 4; Western Veteran,* July 1897.

23. *Western Veteran,* July 1897; *Russell Journal,* July 23, 1897.

24. *Russell Record,* July 17, 1897; Chase, "Mother Bickerdyke," 197; *Russell Journal,* July 23, 1897, quoted in Baker, *Cyclone in Calico,* 248.

25. Kellogg, *Mother Bickerdyke As I Knew Her,* 111; Baker, *Cyclone in Calico,* 250–251.

26. *Russell Record,* November 16, 1901.

27. Ibid.

28. Julia A. Chase to Mr. A. H. Thomas, January 9, 1905, Bickerdyke Papers.

29. Kellogg, *Mother Bickerdyke As I Knew Her,* 124.

Chapter 10. Mary Elizabeth Lease: Advocate for Political Reform

1. The best short account is Dorothy Rose Blumberg, "Mary Elizabeth Lease, Populist Orator: A Profile," *Kansas History* 1 (Spring 1978): 3–15. See also Michael L. Goldberg, *An Army of Women: Gender and Politics in Gilded Age Kansas* (Baltimore, Md., 1997).

2. Mary Clyens's pension file, No. 107,643, and records of Patrick H. Clyens, Private Co. I, 42d Penn. Infantry, and Joseph P. Clyens, Private Co. B, 147th New York Infantry, National Archives, Washington, D.C.; reminiscences in *Wichita Beacon,* July 21, 1892; clippings, n.d., *Kansas City Star,* Mary Lease entries, Biographical Scrapbooks, KSHS. A typewritten memoir by Lease's niece Josephine Clyens Ross, in author's possession, is immensely helpful in corroborating accounts, and I am grateful to Ellen Roth Pensinger and James Wray for sharing it.

3. Reminiscence in *Wichita Independent,* January 26, 1889; the Leases appear in many issues of *Neosho County Journal, Osage Mission Journal,* and *Osage Mission Transcript,* 1871–1874. On Lease's background, see entry for his brother J. T. Lease in *Portrait and Biographical Album of Stephenson County, Illinois* (Chicago, 1888), 412–413.

4. *Denison News,* January 13, 1877, August 31, 1878, and December 16, 1879; family followed more generally through *News* and *Denison Herald.*

5. Ruth Bordin, *Woman and Temperance: The Quest for Power and Liberty* (Philadelphia, Pa., 1981) and *Frances Willard* (Chapel Hill, N.C., 1986); on local movement, Graham Landrum, *Grayson County* (Fort Worth, Tex., 1960), 182; "Sarah C. Acheson" and "Mary Elizabeth Lease" in Elizabeth Brooks, *Prominent Women of Texas* (Akron, Ohio, 1896), 150–151, 202. Poems in, for example, *Wichita Eagle,* July 20, 27, and October 9, 1884.

6. *Kingman Republican,* for example January 17, 1884; *Kingman County Citizen,* e.g., January 24, February 7, and May 1, 1884. Reminiscence, *Star* clipping, Lease biographical file, KSHS.

7. Lease's Wichita activities noted almost weekly, 1885–1889, in *Wichita Eagle, Beacon,* and *New Republic;* campaign for office in *New Republic,* September 18 to October 15, 1886; suffrage convention in *Beacon,* October 20–22, 1886. On estrangement, see reminiscences (above) and Betty Lou Taylor, "Mary Elizabeth Lease: Kansas Populist" (master's thesis, Municipal University of Wichita, 1951), 3, n.5.

8. *Wichita Independent,* Lease announced as editor September 15, 1888, tours in *Labor News,* Larned, September 13, 1888, and *Plain-Dealer,* Pratt, October 26, 1888 (among others). On Coffeyville, James C. Malin, *A Concern about Humanity: Notes on Reform, 1872–1912, at the National and Kansas Levels of Thought* (Lawrence, Kans., 1964), 159–165; Harold Piehler, "Henry Vincent: Kansas Populist and Radical Reform Journalist," *Kansas History* 2 (Spring 1979): 14–25.

9. Robert McMath, *American Populism: A Social History, 1877–1898* (New York, 1993); Clanton, *Kansas Populism;* Elizabeth N. Barr, "The Populist Uprising," in *A Standard History of Kansas and Kansans,* ed. William E. Connelley (Chicago, 1918), 1113–1195; John D. Hicks, *The Populist Revolt: A History of the Farmers' Alliance and the Populist Party* (Minneapolis, Minn., 1931).

10. Richard Bensel, *The Political Economy of American Industrialization, 1877–1900* (Cambridge, 2000), statistics on 46; see also McMath, *American Populism;* Hicks, *The Populist Revolt.*

11. Mary E. Lease, "Do Kansas Women Want the Vote?" *Agora* 2 (1893): 197–198.

12. Lease's 1890 speeches were traced in dozens of Kansas newspapers. Particularly good examples (including quotations here and in final paragraph) are *Harper Sentinel,* June 6; *Topeka Advocate,* July 30 and August 20; *Alliance Gazette,* Hutchinson, September 26; *Lane Leader,* October 9 and 16. Later reminiscences in *New York Sun,* February 3, 1918; *Western Spirit,* Paola, Kans., November 3, 1933; *Kansas City Times,* February 25, 1935; Victor Murdock, *"Folks"* (New York, 1921), 97–101; *Wichita Eagle,* October 31 and November 5, 1933; see also Goldberg, *An Army of Women;* Blumberg, "Mary Elizabeth Lease."

13. *American Nonconformist and American Industrial Liberator,* Winfield, Kans., throughout summer and fall 1890 (e.g., July 25, August 13).

14. Goldberg, *An Army of Women;* Walter T. K. Nugent, "How the Populists Lost in 1894," *Kansas Historical Quarterly* 31 (Autumn 1965): 245–255; O. Gene Clanton, *Kansas Populism: Ideas and Men* (Lawrence, Kans., 1969); Clanton, "Intolerant Populist? The Disaffection of Mary Elizabeth Lease," *Kansas Historical Quarterly* 24 (Summer 1968): 189–200.

15. Mary E. Lease, *The Problem of Civilization Solved* (Chicago, 1895), 235–236.

16. *Representative,* Minneapolis, June 3, 1896, and on through the campaign; Blumberg, "Mary Elizabeth Lease."

17. *Kansas City Star,* October 25, 1912; *New York Sun,* March 6, 1912.

18. Omaha Platform in Hicks, *The Populist Revolt,* 440–441; Michael Kazin, *The Populist Persuasion: An American History* (New York, 1995), chaps. 1–2; Elizabeth Sanders, *Roots of Reform: Farmers, Workers, and the American State, 1877–1917* (Chicago, 1999).

Chapter 11. Charles M. Sheldon: Pastor, Author, and Passionate Social Reformer

1. C. Howard Hopkins, *The Rise of the Social Gospel in American Protestantism, 1865–1915* (New Haven, Conn., 1940); Ronald C. White Jr. and C. Howard Hopkins, *The Social Gospel: Religion and Reform in Changing America* (Philadelphia, Pa., 1976); James Dombrowski, *The Early Days of Christian Socialism in America* (New

York, 1977); Henry F. May, *Protestant Churches and Industrial America* (New York, 1949).

2. See Charles M. Sheldon, "Practical Sociological Studies," *Andover Review* 14:82 (October 1890): 369–377. This episode and most of the other events discussed herein are presented in more detail in Timothy Miller, *Following in His Steps: A Biography of Charles M. Sheldon* (Knoxville, Tenn., 1987).

3. Timothy Miller, "Charles M. Sheldon and the Uplift of Tennesseetown," *Kansas History: A Journal of the Central Plains* 9 (Autumn 1986): 125–137; Richard Kluger, *Simple Justice: The History of* Brown v. Board of Education *and Black America's Struggle for Equality* (New York, 1976), 383–388.

4. Quoted in Glenn Clark, *The Man Who Walked in His Steps* (St. Paul, Minn., 1946), 9. A useful contemporary survey of the Tennesseetown work is Leroy A. Halbert, *Across the Way: A History of the Work of Central Church, Topeka, Kansas, in Tennesseetown* (n.p., 1900).

5. Charles M. Sheldon, *In His Steps: "What Would Jesus Do?"* (Chicago, 1896).

6. "Many Join in Tribute to Noted Topeka Minister-Author," *Topeka Daily Capital,* May 4, 1935.

7. For a comprehensive look at the phenomenon of *In His Steps,* see John W. Ripley, "The Strange Story of Charles M. Sheldon's *In His Steps,*" *Kansas Historical Quarterly* 34 (Autumn 1968): 241–265.

8. Charles M. Sheldon, *Jesus Is Here! Continuing the Story of* In His Steps (New York, 1914); Sheldon, ed., *The Everyday Bible* (New York, 1924); Sheldon, *Howard Chase, Red Hill, Kansas* (New York, 1918).

9. An excellent and comprehensive overview of the Sheldon Edition experiment is John W. Ripley, "Another Look at the Rev. Mr. Charles M. Sheldon's Christian Daily Newspaper," *Kansas Historical Quarterly* 31 (Spring 1965): 1–40; for the opposition's take on the first issue, see "IT IS OUT," *Topeka State Journal,* March 13, 1900.

10. See, for example, Charles M. Sheldon, "When Carrie Nation Came to Kansas," *Christian Herald* 53 (January 4, 1930): 18.

11. Charles M. Sheldon, "The Common Task," *Christian Herald* 44 (May 8, 1921): 387.

12. Charles M. Sheldon, "Of Such Is the Kingdom," *Heart Stories* (New York, 1920), 89–124.

13. Charles M. Sheldon, "The Missionary Policeman," *Independent* 76 (November 6, 1913): 259–260.

14. "Dr. Sheldon Secretly 'in Prison' 40 Years Ago," undated newspaper clipping in the Sheldon archives at Central Congregational Church, Topeka. Sheldon's prison experience apparently did not become common knowledge for some years after the fact, and it is therefore impossible to date with precision; it probably occurred about 1901.

15. For a representative survey of institutional church activities at thirty leading locations, see William D. P. Bliss, *The New Encyclopedia of Social Reform* (New York, 1908), 630.

16. Charles M. Sheldon, "If Jesus Came Back Today," *Christian Century* 51 (June 27, 1934): 863; second quotation in L. H. Robbins, "Militant Pacifist," *New York Times Magazine,* December 3, 1939.

17. Charles M. Sheldon, "Can Religion Be Taught?" *Atlantic Monthly* 136 (October 1925): 467–468.

Chapter 12. William Allen White: The Voice of Middle America

1. "William Allen White of Emporia: An American Institution Is 70," *Life* 4 (February 28, 1938): 9–13.

2. William Allen White, *The Autobiography of William Allen White* (New York, 1946), 257–258.

3. John Higham, "Hanging Together: Divergent Unities in American History," in *Hanging Together: Unity and Diversity in American Culture* (New Haven, Conn., 2001), 3–21.

4. White, *Autobiography,* 61.

5. Ibid., 26, 44, 39.

6. Details here and throughout are drawn from Sally F. Griffith, *Home Town News: William Allen White and the* Emporia Gazette (New York, 1989).

7. White, *Autobiography,* 230.

8. Griffith, *Home Town News,* 32–34.

9. Ibid., 45–50; White, *Autobiography,* 273, 279, 287.

10. White, *Autobiography,* 297.

11. Griffith, *Home Town News,* 111.

12. Robert H. Wiebe, *The Search for Order: 1877–1920* (New York, 1967).

13. Higham, "Hanging Together," 18.

14. Griffith, *Home Town News,* 147–151, 157.

15. Ibid., 155–156.

16. White, *Autobiography,* 606–609.

17. Walter Johnson, *William Allen White's America* (New York, 1947), 354–355; White, *Autobiography,* 605.

18. White, *Autobiography,* 613–614.

19. Johnson, *White's America,* 503–507.

20. Ibid., 508–516.

21. Ibid., 522–524.

22. Edward Gale Agran, *"Too Good a Town": William Allen White, Community, and the Emerging Rhetoric Autobiography of Middle America* (Fayetteville, Ark., 1998).

Chapter 13. Samuel J. Crumbine: Individualizing the Standard for Twentieth-Century Public Health

1. Samuel J. Crumbine, *Frontier Doctor: The Autobiography of a Pioneer on the Frontier of Public Health* (Philadelphia, Pa., 1948).

2. Ibid., 112.

3. See, for example, Crumbine to G. H. Hoxie, MD, Lawrence, Kans., December 9, 1904, and Crumbine to Governor E. W. Hoch, November 28, 1904, letterpress books, 1885–1906, 348, 325 (58-06-01-08), Kansas State Board of Health Correspondence, KSHS (hereafter Crumbine Papers).

4. Crumbine, *Frontier Doctor,* 125–131.

5. See, for example, Naomi Rogers, "Germs with Legs: Flies, Disease, and the New Public Health," *Bulletin of the History of Medicine* 63 (Winter 1989): 599–617; Thomas Bonner, *The Kansas Doctor: A Century of Pioneering* (Lawrence, Kans., 1959), 120–171.

6. W. F. Bynum and Caroline Overy, eds., *The Beast in the Mosquito: The Correspondence of Ronald Ross and Patrick Manson* (Amsterdam, Netherlands, 1998); William Bean, *Walter Reed: A Biography* (Charlottesville, Va., 1982), 87–101. For a discussion of the relations between filth and disease, see Nancy Tomes, *The Gospel of Germs: Men, Women, and the Microbe in American Life* (Cambridge, Mass., 1998); Naomi Rogers, *Dirt and Disease, Polio before FDR* (New Brunswick, N.J., 1992); Naomi Rogers, "Dirt, Flies, and Immigrants: Explaining the Epidemiology of Poliomyelitis," *Journal of the History of Medicine and Allied Sciences* 44 (October 1989): 486.

7. See State Board of Health Correspondence, especially Crumbine to C. F. Menninger, MD, January 5, 1905, letterpress book, 386, Crumbine Papers, KSHS. He mentioned flies in this letter to Menninger, the president of the Topeka Board of Health and a generalist physician who, with his sons, Drs. Karl and Will Menninger, would later found the Menninger psychiatric clinic. See, for examples of Crumbine's publications, *Bulletin of the Kansas State Board of Health* 1, no. 1 (July 1905); *Bulletin* 1, no. 2 (August 1905).

8. L. O. Howard, *The House Fly: Disease Carrier* (New York, 1911), 108.

9. Letterpress books, 1885–1906, Crumbine Papers. See specifically Crumbine to Walter Wyman, Surgeon General, MHS, Washington, February 20, 1905; Crumbine to J. B. Carver, MD, Fort Scott, Kansas, December 16, 1904, letterpress book, 454, 362.

10. *Bulletin of the Kansas State Board of Health* 1, no. 2 (August 1905): 4–8; 2, no. 6 (June 1906): 141; 2, no. 8 (August 1906): 215–216; 2, no. 10 (October 1906): 262–263; 2, no. 11 (November 1906): 283.

11. Ibid., 3, no. 6 (June 1907): 129.

12. Crumbine, *Frontier Doctor,* 158.

13. *Bulletin of the Kansas State Board of Health* 3, no. 4 (April 1907): 87, 84–86; Crumbine, *Frontier Doctor,* 160.

14. William Riley and Oskar Johannsen, *Medical Entomology: A Survey of Insects and Allied Forms Which Affect the Health of Man and Animals* (New York, 1938), 336–344; Charles V. Chapin, *The Sources and Modes of Infection* (New York, 1916), 362–365; "Flies and Typhoid Fever," *Journal of the American Medical Association* 55 (November 19, 1910): 1812; "Conference on Infantile Paralysis Held at the Office of the Rockefeller Foundation, Saturday, August 5th, 1916, 10 o'clock A.M.," 55–56, Record Group 1.1, series 200, box 25, folder 283, Rockefeller Archives Center, Tarrytown, N.Y.

15. Allan Brandt, *No Magic Bullet: A Social History of Venereal Disease in the United States since 1880* (New York, 1987), 20; see also Raymond B. Fosdick and Edward Frank Allen, *Keeping Our Fighters Fit for War and After* (Washington, D.C., 1918); Tomes, *The Gospel of Germs,* 10–12.

16. Lee K. Frankel, "Social Hygiene and Public Health," *Journal of Social Hygiene* 11 (April 1925): 210–214; see also C. C. Pierce, "Venereal Disease Control: Methods, Obstacles, and Results," *American Journal of Public Health* 10 (February 1920): 132–136; *Journal of the American Medical Association* 71 (December 21, 1918): 2101; Edward H. Beardsley, "Allied against Sin: American and British Responses to Venereal Disease in World War I," *Medical History* 20 (April 1976): 189–202. The federal government did not allocate money for venereal disease control until the Chamberlain-Kahn Act of July 1918, which gave states matching funds up to $1 million a year to coordinate programs and quarantine the diseased.

17. Martin Pernick, *The Black Stork: Eugenics and the Death of "Defective" Babies in American Medicine and Motion Pictures since 1915* (New York, 1996), 29–30; Howard Markel, *Quarantine! East European Jewish Immigrants and the New York City Epidemics of 1892* (Baltimore, Md., 1997), 7–9; see also Barron Lerner, *Contagion and Confinement: Controlling Tuberculosis along the Skid Road* (Baltimore, Md., 1998), 117.

18. An example of what the CTCA involved itself with as of 1917 can be found in C. C. McCulloch, "Field Sanitary Orders," *Journal of the American Medical Association* 69 (October 20, 1917): 1345–1349. See also Brandt, *No Magic Bullet,* 53–56; W. C. Gorgas, "Venereal Diseases and the War," *American Journal of Public Health* 8 (February 1918): 107–111; Crumbine, *Frontier Doctor,* 234–237.

19. Crumbine, *Frontier Doctor,* 222–233. Eventually, with the help of social workers and the farm superintendent, "courses in typewriting, shorthand, domestic science—including both sewing and cooking—are being offered." Darlene Doubleday Newby, "A Study of the Causes of Delinquency of Women Quarantined for Disease at the State Industrial Farm for Women," draft report, Crumbine Archives, Clendening Library, University of Kansas Medical Center, Kansas City, Kans.

20. Newby, "A Study of the Causes of Delinquency." See also Crumbine, *Frontier Doctor,* 222–233.

21. Paula S. Fass, *The Damned and the Beautiful: American Youth in the 1920s* (New York, 1977), 18–19.

22. Crumbine, *Frontier Doctor,* 222–233. See also Kansas State Supreme Court, *Ex Parte Mcgee,* Case No. 22,691, opinion filed November 18, 1919, KSHS.

23. Superintendent's Report, *Third Biennial Report of the Women's Industrial Farm, 1922* (Topeka, Kans., 1922), 3–4; see also Mary Scott Rowland, "Social Services in Kansas, 1916–1930," *Kansas History* 7 (Autumn 1984): 212–225.

24. David J. Pivar, "Cleansing the Nation: The War on Prostitution, 1917–1921," *Prologue* 12 (Spring 1980): 29–40. See also Maude Miner, "The Policewoman and the Girl Problem," *Proceedings of the National Conference of Social Work, 1918* (Chicago, 1919), 134–143; Rachelle S. Yarros, "The Prostitute as a Health and Social Problem," *Proceedings of the National Conference of Social Work, 1918* (Chicago, 1919), 220–224; Mary Macey Dietzler, *The Campaign of the United States Government against Venereal Diseases* (Washington, D.C., 1922).

25. For discussions of germ control and venereal disease, see Brandt, *No Magic Bullet,* 7–17; Elizabeth Fee, "Sin vs. Science: Venereal Disease in Baltimore in the 20th-Century," *Journal of the History of Medicine* 43 (April 1988): 141–164; Pernick, *The Black Stork,* 97–99.

26. For discussions of germ theory–informed legislative action, see Tomes, *The Gospel of Germs,* 46–47; see also Elizabeth Fee and Dorothy Porter, "Public Health, Preventive Medicine, and Professionalization: Britain and the United States in the 19th-Century," in *A History of Education in Public Health: Health That Mocks the Doctors' Rules,* ed. Elizabeth Fee and Roy M. Acheson (New York, 1991), 33–38; *Bulletin of the Kansas State Board of Health* 10, no. 1 (January 1914): 4–8.

Chapter 14: Kate Richards O'Hare: A Life of Dissent

1. *New York Times* quotation in Scott G. McNall, *The Road to Rebellion: Class Formation and Kansas Populism, 1865–1900* (Chicago, 1988), 67; "laboratory for experiments" quotation in John C. Carey, "People, Problems, Prohibition, Politicos and Politics—1870–1890," in *Kansas: The First Century, Vol. I,* ed. John D. Bright (New York, 1956), 385. See also Kenneth S. Davis, *Kansas: A Bicentennial History* (New York, 1976), 128–159; and Hal D. Sears, *The Sex Radicals: Free Love in High Victorian America* (Lawrence, Kans., 1977).

2. James R. Green, *Grass-Roots Socialism: Radical Movements of the Southwest, 1905–1943* (Baton Rouge, La., 1978), 15; William Frank Zornow, *A History of the Jayhawk State* (Norman, Okla., 1957), 175–188; Elliott Shore, *Talkin' Socialism: J. A. Wayland and the Role of the Press in American Radicalism, 1890–1912* (Lawrence, Kans., 1988), 75–94, 219; Sally M. Miller, *From Prairie to Prison: The Life of Social Activist Kate Richards O'Hare* (Columbia, Mo., 1993), 8–10.

3. Kate O'Hare to Family, Jefferson City, Missouri, December 21, 1919, Prison Letters, 1919–1920, State Historical Society of Missouri, St. Louis, Missouri; Kate Richards O'Hare, "How I Became a Socialist Agitator," *Socialist Woman* 2 (October 1908): 4; Miller, *From Prairie to Prison,* 3–8; Neil K. Basen, "Kate Richards O'Hare: The 'First Lady' of American Socialism," *Labor History* 21 (Spring 1980): 169. Scott G. McNall and Sally Allen McNall, *Plains Farmers: Exploring Sociology through Social History* (New York, 1983), 23, 39–49, 67–71, 100.

4. Kate O'Hare to Family, May 25, 1919, May 31, 1919, June 22, 1919, July 26, 1919, Prison Letters. See, among others, O. Gene Clanton, *Kansas Populism: Ideas and Men* (Lawrence, Kans., 1969).

5. O'Hare, "How I Became a Socialist Agitator," 4–5; O'Hare to Family, April 17, 1920, Prison Letters; Henry C. Haskell Jr. and Richards B. Fowler, *City of the Future: A Narrative History of Kansas City, 1850–1950* (Kansas City, Mo., 1950), 61–68; *Seventh Biennial Report of the Secretary of State of the State of Kansas, 1909–1910* (Topeka, Kans., 1910), 110, 140.

6. Katherine Gertrude Aiken, "The National Florence Crittenton Missions, 1883–1925: A Case Study in Progressive Reform" (Ph.D. diss., Washington State University, 1980), 11–50; Theodore Brown and Lyle W. Dorsett, *Kansas City: A History of Kansas City, Missouri* (Boulder, Colo., 1978), 75–90; Miller, *From Prairie to Prison,* 16–17.

7. Rebecca J. Mead, *How the West Was Won: Woman Suffrage in the Western United States, 1868–1914* (New York, 2004), 9.

8. O'Hare, "How I Became a Socialist Agitator," 4–5; "The International School of Social Economy," *Comrade* 1 (July 1902): 217–219; Miller, *From Prairie to Prison,* 21–28; Peter Buckingham, *Rebel against Injustice: The Life of Frank P. O'Hare* (Columbia, Mo., 1996), 22–26; John Graham, ed., *"Yours for the Revolution": The Appeal to Reason, 1895–1922* (Lincoln, Nebr., 1990), 173–213; Shore, *Talkin' Socialism,* 123.

9. O'Hare, "How I Became a Socialist Agitator," 5.

10. Miller, *From Prairie to Prison,* 32–33, 40–43, 47–50, 52–55, 74–78, 86; Green, *Grass-Roots Socialism,* 50; Buckingham, *Rebel against Injustice,* 47; McNall and McNall, *Plains Farmers,* 186–188.

11. Kate O'Hare, "The Wages of Women," *National Rip-Saw* (July 1913): 2, 6; Kate O'Hare, "Priscilla at Her Loom," *Socialist Woman* 2 (July 1908): 8.

12. Miller, *From Prairie to Prison,* 101–104.

13. Sally M. Miller, "Other Socialists: Native-Born and Immigrant Woman in the Socialist Party of America, 1901–17," *Labor History* 24 (Winter 1983): 88–90; Basen, "Kate Richards O'Hare," 169.

14. Kate O'Hare, "Over the Sea and Back Again," *National Rip-Saw* (March 1914): 26–27.

15. Victor L. Berger to Morris Hillquit, October 12, 1913, and Morris Hillquit to Victor L. Berger, October 16, 1913, Victor L. Berger Collection, Milwaukee County Historical Society, Milwaukee, Wis.; Victor L. Berger to Morris Hillquit, February 13, 1914, Hillquit Collection, State Historical Society of Wisconsin, Madison, Wis.; Miller, *From Prairie to Prison,* 95–96; Buckingham, *Rebel against Injustice,* 74–75.

16. Kate O'Hare, "Good Morning! Mr. American Citizen," *Social Revolution* (June 1917): 5.

17. Kate O'Hare, "Shall Red Hell Rage?" *National Rip-Saw* (June 1915): 6–7.

18. Kate O'Hare, "My Country," *Social Revolution* (April 1917): 5.

19. Kate O'Hare, "Speech Delivered in Court by Kate Richards O'Hare before Being Sentenced by Judge Wade," *Social Revolution* (February 1918): 6–7; Kate O'Hare, *Socialism and the World War* (St. Louis, Mo., ca. 1919); W. E. Zuech, *The Truth About the O'Hare Case* (St. Louis, Mo., ca. 1918); Erling N. Sannes, "'Queen of the Lecture Platform': Kate Richards O'Hare and North Dakota Politics, 1917–1921," *North Dakota History* 58 (Fall 1991): 2–19; Miller, *From Prairie to Prison,* 142–154.

20. Miller, *From Prairie to Prison,* 163–169; 173, 176–180.

21. O'Hare to Family, December 7, 1919, Prison Letters.

22. Kate O'Hare to Otto Branstetter, Socialist Party, February 8, 1920, February 25, 1920, Prison Letters; Miller, *From Prairie to Prison,* 185–191.

23. Miller, *From Prairie to Prison,* 204–207, 216–217, 221–223, 226–228; Buckingham, *Rebel against Injustice,* 134, 165–168. The explicit reason that the local St. Louis chapter of the Socialist Party dropped the O'Hares was their failure to pay dues, but that fact is against a background of festering hostility and resentment of Kate O'Hare's prominence.

Chapter 15. Emanuel and Marcet Haldeman-Julius: An Innovative Partnership in Publishing

1. The best sources for Haldeman-Julius's life are Emanuel Haldeman-Julius, *My First Twenty-five Years: Instead of a Footnote, an Autobiography,* Big Blue Book (hereafter BBB) No. 788 (Girard, Kans., 1949); Emanuel Haldeman-Julius, *My Second Twenty-five Years: Instead of a Footnote, an Autobiography,* BBB No. 814 (Girard, Kans., 1949); Albert Mordell, *Trailing E. Haldeman-Julius in Philadelphia and Other Places,* BBB No. 834 (Girard, Kans., 1949); John W. Gunn, *E. Haldeman-Julius—The Man and His Work,* Little Blue Book (hereafter LBB) No. 678 (Girard, Kans., 1924).

2. Information in print about Marcet Haldeman-Julius is less easily available than writings about Emanuel Haldeman-Julius. See Marcet Haldeman-Julius, *What the Editor's Wife Is Thinking About,* LBB No. 809 (Girard, Kans., n.d.); see also Mark Scott,

"The Little Blue Books in the War on Bigotry and Bunk," *Kansas History* 1 (Autumn 1978): 159–160.

3. Tim Davenport, "*The Appeal to Reason:* Forerunner of Haldeman-Julius Publications," *Big Blue Newsletter* 3 (2004): 6–21; David Paul Nord, "The *Appeal to Reason* and American Socialism, 1901–1920," *Kansas History* 1 (Summer 1978): 75–89.

4. Haldeman-Julius, *My First Twenty-five Years,* 16–19, 22–29; Haldeman-Julius, *My Second Twenty-five Years,* 90–91; Albert Mordell, *Haldeman-Julius and Upton Sinclair: The Amazing Record of a Long Collaboration,* BBB No. 850 (Girard, Kans., 1950).

5. Haldeman-Julius, *My Second Twenty-five Years,* 53–57; Elliot Shore, *Talkin' Socialism: J. A. Wayland and the Role of the Press in American Radicalism, 1890–1912* (Lawrence, Kans., 1988).

6. Nord, "The *Appeal to Reason,*" 77.

7. Haldeman-Julius, *My First Twenty-five Years,* 13.

8. Ibid.

9. One could argue that the two activities were so closely intertwined that they were inseparable. Haldeman-Julius used his periodicals to advertise his book publishing activities and vice versa. Also, a number of the original works he published as books began life as articles in one of his periodicals.

10. Emanuel Haldeman-Julius, *The First Hundred Million* (New York, 1928), 117–137.

11. "Companionate marriage" is marriage in which the parties do not contemplate having children, that is, marriage for companionship and sex.

12. A useful reference is Tim Davenport, ed., "Little Blue Book Handlist," *Big Blue Book Newsletter* 1 (2004).

13. See ibid.; Haldeman-Julius, *First Hundred Million,* 99.

14. Haldeman-Julius, *First Hundred Million,* 13–35, other statistics at 17–21.

15. Mordell, *Haldeman-Julius and Upton Sinclair;* Haldeman-Julius, *My Second Twenty-five Years,* 80–84, 91. Harris did not like Kansas, and the feeling was mutual; see, for instance, Kate Stephens, *Lies and Libels of Frank Harris,* ed. C. Caldwell Smith (New York, 1929).

16. For Darrow's works, see Davenport, "Little Blue Book Handlist"; see also Marcet Haldeman-Julius, *Clarence Darrow's Two Great Trials: Report of the Scopes Anti-Evolution Case and the Dr. Sweet Negro Trial,* ed. Emanuel Haldeman-Julius, BBB No. 29 (Girard, Kans., 1927).

17. Emanuel Haldeman-Julius, *How the World's Greatest Scholar Can Help You* (Girard, Kans., 1931); Haldeman-Julius, *My Second Twenty-five Years,* 19–21, 91–99.

18. See Haldeman-Julius, *My Second Twenty-five Years,* 102–103, 118–199, especially end-page advertisements.

19. Among Marcet Haldeman-Julius's most important volumes were her reports of Darrow's trials, *Clarence Darrow's Two Great Trials;* Marcet Haldeman-Julius, *Great Court Trials of History* (Girard, Kans., 1937); M. Haldeman-Julius, *The Lindbergh-Hauptmann Kidnap-Murder Case* (Girard, Kans., 1937).

20. Haldeman-Julius, *My First Twenty-five Years,* 9–11, 13–14.

21. Haldeman-Julius, *First Hundred Million,* 263–322, 265–266, 282.

22. Haldeman-Julius, *My First Twenty-five Years,* 11; advertisements are reproduced with commentary in Tim Davenport, "Three Haldeman-Julius Ads," *Big Blue Newsletter* 2 (2004): 12–17.

23. Haldeman-Julius, *My First Twenty-five Years,* 11.

24. Ibid., 7. Edwardian periodicals are filled with advertisements for various products for sale by mail order.

25. Ibid., 11–12.

26. Scott, "The Little Blue Books in the War on Bigotry and Bunk," 168–169, 173–174.

27. Emanuel Haldeman-Julius, *The World of Haldeman-Julius,* ed. Albert Mordell (New York, 1960); Scott, "The Little Blue Books in the War on Bigotry and Bunk," 155.

Chapter 16. Alfred M. Landon: Budget Balancer

1. Donald R. McCoy, *Landon of Kansas* (Lincoln, Nebr., 1966); Homer E. Socolofsky, *Kansas Governors* (Lawrence, Kans., 1990), 172–179.

2. McCoy, *Landon of Kansas,* 67–90; Donald R. McCoy, "Alfred Mossman Landon," in *American National Biography,* ed. John A. Garraty and Mark C. Carnes, vol. 13 (New York, 1999), 110–112.

3. Apart from state government, there were more than eleven thousand political units that had the power to levy taxes or incur debt. U.S. Department of Commerce, Bureau of the Census, *Financial Statistics of State and Local Governments: 1932* (Washington, D.C., 1935), 604. See also *Estimated Direct Governmental Cost in Kansas by Governing Units* (Research Department, Kansas Legislative Council Publication No. 48, 1937); Glenn W. Fisher, *The Worst Tax? A History of the Property Tax in America* (Lawrence, Kans., 1996), 147–165; Kansas Legislative Council, *Summary History of Kansas Finance* (Research Report No. 60, October 1937), 25, 34–35; James T. McDonald, *State Finance: Expenditures of the State of Kansas, 1915–1953* (Fiscal Information Series No. 5, Governmental Research Center, Lawrence, Kans., n.d.), 7–13, tables passim.

4. *Message of Governor Woodring to the Legislature of 1931* (Topeka, Kans., 1931); Earle K. Shaw, "An Analysis of the Legal Limitations on the Borrowing Powers of State Governments," *Monthly Report of the FERA* (June 1936), 121–123, 126–127; Harold Howe, "Tax Delinquency on Farm Real Estate in Kansas, 1928 to 1933," *Agricultural Experiment Station Circular 186* (Manhattan, Kans., October 1937), 1–12. As a result of tax delinquency, the amount of revenue raised is always less than the amount levied.

5. *Public Welfare Service in Kansas: A Ten Year Report* (Kansas Emergency Relief Bulletin No. 127, December 1934), 46–49; *Topeka Daily Capital,* February 10, 1933.

6. *Kansas City Times,* September 27, 1932; *Message of Governor Alf M. Landon to the Legislature of 1933* (Topeka, Kans., 1933) 4–5; *Special Message of Alf M. Landon, Governor of Kansas, To the Legislature of 1933* (Topeka, Kans., 1933) 1, 4–6.

7. *Message of Governor Alf M. Landon . . . 1933,* 10–11.

8. "Budget-Balancer Landon," *New Republic* (January 15, 1936): 273; Alfred Mossman Landon, *America at the Crossroads* (1936; reprint, Port Washington, N.Y., 1971), 61–63.

9. *Message of Governor Alf M. Landon to the Special Session of the Kansas Legislature of 1933* (Topeka, Kans., 1933), 2–3.

10. Kansas Emergency Relief Committee, "Cost of Social Welfare Service in Kansas," 58, John G. Stutz Papers, box 3, file 39, Spencer Research Library, University of

Kansas; *Final Statistical Report of the Federal Emergency Relief Administration* (Washington, D.C., 1942), table XVIII, 307. The figure does not include $12.2 million from the federal government to fund the Civil Works Administration in 1934.

11. *Topeka Daily Capital,* June 12, 1935. The per capita cost figures are from *Estimated Direct Governmental Cost.* It should be noted that incomes in Kansas were higher in 1936 than they had been during the desperately bad years of 1932 and 1933.

12. *New York Times,* July 2, 7, and 8, 1935; *Time* magazine (May 18, 1936): 18.

13. *Topeka Daily Capital,* November 1, 1935.

14. Ibid., November 3, 1935; *New York Times,* November 6, 8, and 10, 1935.

15. Peter Fearon, "Kansas Poor Relief: The Influence of the Great Depression," *Mid-America: An Historical Review* 78 (Summer 1996): 175–179; *Kansas Relief News Bulletin* 5 (May 21, 1934): 3–4.

16. For example, "Budget-Balancer Gov. 'Alf.' Landon of Kansas," *Literary Digest* (October 12, 1935): 30–31; "Budget-Balancer Landon," 272–273; *New York Times,* October 5, 1936.

17. *Economist* (September 5, 1936): 429.

18. *New York Times,* July 24, September 24, and October 13, 1936.

19. Landon, *America at the Crossroads,* 47.

20. *Final Statistical Report of the Federal Emergency Relief Administration,* table XV, 263; *Analysis of Civil Works Program Statistics* (Washington, D.C., 1939), table 17, 30; *Public Welfare Service in Kansas, 1935* (Kansas Emergency Relief Committee Bulletin No. 355, July 1, 1936), 290–291.

21. Peter Fearon, *War, Prosperity and Depression: The US Economy, 1917–45* (Lawrence, Kans., 1987), 230–234.

Chapter 17. Walter A. Huxman: Leading by Example

1. Gov. Walter A. Huxman to Chancellor E. H. Lindley, July 11, 1938, Correspondence—Subject file, "Negroes, 1938," Box 26.5, and Board of Regents, Minutes, Topeka, August 6, 1938, box 26.3, Papers of the Governor, Walter A. Huxman, KSHS.

2. *Oliver Brown, et al., Plaintiffs, v. Board of Education of Topeka, Shawnee County, Kansas, et al., Defendants,* U.S. District Court for the District of Kansas, Civil Action No. T-316, Opinion of the Court (Huxman), August 3, 1951, KSHS; "In Memory of the Honorable Walter A. Huxman, Judge of the United States Court of Appeals, Tenth Circuit, 1939–1972," U.S. Court of Appeals, Tenth Circuit, Wichita, Kans., January 10, 1973; *Plessy v. Ferguson* 163 U.S. 537 (1896); *Gong Lum v. Rice* 275 U.S. 78 (1927).

3. Mary L. Dudziak, "The Limits of Good Faith: Desegregation in Topeka, Kansas, 1950–1956," *Law and History Review* 5 (Fall 1987): 351–391; Richard Kluger, *Simple Justice: The History of* Brown v. Board of Education *and Black America's Struggle for Equality* (New York, 1976); Robert J. Cottrol, Raymond T. Diamond, and Leland B. Ware, Brown v. Board of Education: *Caste, Culture, and the Constitution* (Lawrence, Kans., 2004); James T. Patterson, Brown v. Board of Education: *A Civil Rights Milestone and Its Troubled Legacy* (New York, 2001).

4. Walter M. Markley, *Builders of Topeka, 1956: Who's Who in the Kansas Capital* (Topeka, Kans., 1956), 121; Homer E. Socolofsky, *Kansas Governors* (Lawrence, Kans., 1990), 180–182; Jennie Small Owen, "Kansas Folks Worth Knowing: Walter A. Huxman,"

Kansas Teacher 15 (October 1937): 70–71; *Topeka Daily Capitol,* May 26, 1953, and June 26, 1972; *Topeka State Journal,* March 21, 1957; *Kansas City Star,* November 8, 1936; U.S. Census, 1900, Troy Twp., Reno County, Kansas; Kansas State Census, 1895, Reno County, Albion Twp.; Kansas State Census, 1905, Reno County, Troy Twp.; *Atlas and Platt Book, 1912,* Troy Township, Reno County, Kansas.

5. *Hutchinson Daily Gazette,* October 18, 1914 and November 3 and 4, 1914; *Topeka Daily Capitol,* May 26, 1953, and June 26, 1972; *Topeka State Journal,* March 21, 1957; *Wichita Eagle,* August 9, 1936; *Kansas City Star,* November 8, 1936.

6. Shane N. Galentine, "Huxman versus West: The Gubernatorial Race of 1936," *Kansas History* 11 (Summer 1988): 108–122; "Democratic Candidate for Governor Is Native Kansan," *Wichita Eagle,* August 9, 1936; Walter A. Huxman, Collection No. 2, scrapbooks, 1936–1939, 2 volumes, KSHS.

7. *Wichita Eagle,* August 9, 1936; *Kansas City Times,* November 5, 1936; *Topeka Journal,* January 11, 1937; *Kansas City Star,* November 8, 1936.

8. "Inaugural Address of Walter A. Huxman Governor of Kansas, January 11, 1937," Kansas State Governor, Messages, vol. 4, 1925–1943, bound pamphlets, KSHS.

9. "Message of Governor . . . to the Kansas Legislature, January 13, 1937," Kansas State Governor, Messages, vol. 4, 1925–1943, bound pamphlets, KSHS.

10. *Plaindealer,* July 22, 1938; Nancy J. Hulston, "'Our Schools Must Be Open to All Classes of Citizens': The Desegregation of the University of Kansas School of Medicine, 1938," *Kansas History* 19 (Summer 1996): 88–97.

11. *Emporia Gazette,* November 9, 1938; *Topeka Daily Capital,* January 9, 1939; A. L. Shultz, *Topeka State Journal,* to Walter A. Huxman, January 6, 1939, and Ben S. Paulen, former Kansas governor, to Gov. Huxman, November 29, 1939, Miscellaneous Walter A. Huxman Collection, KSHS; see also James L. Swank, "Walter A. Huxman's Gubernatorial Administration: A Partial Investigation of the Executive-Legislative Relations" (master's thesis, Kansas State Teachers College, 1968); *Topeka State Journal,* November 3 and 10, 1938.

12. *Kansas City Times,* April 24, 1939; A. L. Shultz, "Huxman to Get New Judge Job," *Topeka State Journal,* November 10, 1938.

13. *Topeka State Journal,* April 24, 1939; *Topeka Capital,* May 18, 1939; *Kansas City Star,* May 19, 1939; Huxman quoted in Justice Robert H. Kaul's Memoriam remarks, "In Memory of the Honorable Walter A. Huxman, Judge of the United States Court of Appeals, Tenth Circuit, 1939–1972," U.S. Court of Appeals, Tenth Circuit, Wichita, Kans., January 10, 1973.

14. *Pittsburgh Courier,* n.d.; "The Kansas Anomaly," quoted in *Plaindealer,* July 6, 1951; see also H. H. Robinson, superintendent, Augusta, Kansas, to Governor Arn, December 10, 1953, Papers of the Governor, Edward F. Arn, Correspondence, Subject File, "Segregation, 1952–1954," box 27-15-04-02, KSHS.

15. *Brown v. Board of Education,* August 3, 1951; Kluger, *Simple Justice,* 398–424; Paul E. Wilson, *A Time to Lose: Representing Kansas in* Brown v. Board of Education (Lawrence, Kans., 1995), 72–98.

16. Raymond Wolters, *The Burden of* Brown: *Thirty Years of School Desegregation* (Knoxville, Tenn., 1984); four cases ultimately linked to Brown were *Belton v. Gebhart* and *Bulah v. Gebhart* (Delaware), *Bolling, et al. v. C. Melvin Sharpe, et al.* (District of Columbia), *Briggs v. Elliott* (South Carolina), and *Davis, et al. v. Prince Edwards County Board of Supervisors* (Virginia).

17. *Plaindealer,* July 6 and 13, 1951; see also *Topeka State Journal,* June 25, 1951.

18. *Brown v. Board of Education,* August 3, 1951; "Finding of Fact," *Brown v. Board of Education,* August 3, 1951; *Topeka State Journal,* August 3, 1951; see also W. A. Huxman to Hon. Arthur J. Mellott and Hon. Delmas C. Hill, July 12, 1951, *Brown v. Board of Education* (and related cases), Correspondence, Notes, Draft Opinions, Memoranda, box 6, envelope 2, Gift of Prof. Richard J. Pierce, University of Kansas Law Library (hereafter Pierce Collection), for a preliminary draft of the critical finding.

19. *Briggs, et al. v. Elliott, et al.,* Civil Action No. 2657, U.S. District Court, Eastern District of South Carolina, Charleston Division, June 23, 1951, 98 F. Supp. 529, 538–548; Waldo E. Martin Jr., ed., Brown v. Board of Education: *A Brief History in Documents* (Boston, 1998), 110, 131–137; Tinsley E. Yarbrough, "Julius Waties Waring," in *American National Biography,* ed. John A. Garraty and Mark C. Carnes, vol. 22 (New York, 1999), 680–681.

20. *Briggs, et al. v. Elliott, et al.,* 548; Judge Arthur J. Mellott to Judge John J. Parker, Chief Judge, Court of Appeals, Charlotte, N.C., May 31, 1951; Parker to Mellott, June 4, 1951; Dissenting Opinion re. Civil Action No. 2657, *Briggs v. Elliott,* 21 pages, *Brown v. Board of Education* (and related cases), Correspondence, Notes, Draft Opinions, Memoranda, box 6, envelope 1, Pierce Collection.

21. "In Memory of the Honorable Walter A. Huxman," 10–11; *Topeka Daily Capital,* June 26, 1972; Kluger, *Simple Justice,* 424.

22. "In Memory of the Honorable Walter A. Huxman," 13–14; *Brown v. Board of Education,* 347 U.S. 483 (1954).

23. Yarbrough, "Julius Waties Waring," 681; Tinsley E. Yarbrough, *A Passion for Justice: J. Waties Waring and Civil Rights* (New York, 1987).

24. "In Memory of the Honorable Walter A. Huxman," 8; *Topeka State Journal,* March 21, 1957; W. A. Huxman to Hon. Jean S. Breitenstein, Denver, Colorado, May 10, 1962; Barton E. Griffith, president, Topeka Bar Association, to Huxman, October 30, 1957, Miscellaneous Walter A. Huxman Collection, KSHS.

25. Hon. James K. Logan, Overland Park, Kansas, interview by author, May 28, 2004; Logan, "Walter A. Huxman," 1991, unpublished manuscript, available in Library of the U.S. Court of Appeals for the Tenth Circuit, Denver, Colorado; Harry F. Tepker Jr., "Walter A. Huxman," in *The Federal Courts of the Tenth Circuit: A History,* ed. Hon. James K. Logan (Denver, Colo., 1992), 358–368.

Chapter 18. Gerald B. Winrod: From Fundamentalist Preacher to "Jayhawk Hitler"

1. For more detailed accounts of Winrod's life, see Leo P. Ribuffo, *The Old Christian Right: The Protestant Far Right from the Great Depression to the Cold War* (Philadelphia, Pa., 1983); Gail Ann Sindell, "Gerald B. Winrod and the 'Defender': A Case Study of the Radical Right" (Ph.D. diss., Case Western Reserve University, 1973). Also useful despite the pro-Winrod bias are G. H. Montgomery, *Gerald Burton Winrod: Christian Soldier, Crusading Patriot, Defender of the Faith* (Wichita, Kans., 1965); *Defender*'s editorial staff, *Fire by Night and Cloud by Day: A History of the Defenders of the Christian Faith* (Wichita, Kans., 1966).

2. For a learned yet accessible discussion of the developments within Protestantism discussed in this article, see D. G. Hart, *That Old-Time Religion in Modern America: Evangelical Protestantism in the Twentieth Century* (Chicago, 2002), chaps. 1–3.

3. For the most systematic statement of Winrod's faith, see his *Christ Within* (New York, 1932).

4. For dispensationalism, see Hart, *Old-Time Religion;* Ernest R. Sandeen, *The Roots of Fundamentalism: British and American Millenarianism, 1800–1930* (Chicago, 1970).

5. See, especially, Gerald B. Winrod, *Mussolini's Place in Prophecy* (Wichita, Kans., 1933).

6. Gerald B. Winrod, "The Highway Massacre," *Revealer* 2 (September 15, 1935): 2.

7. For example, see Gerald B. Winrod, *The NRA in Prophecy and a Discussion of Beast Worship* (Wichita, Kans., 1933).

8. Gerald B. Winrod, *The Hidden Hand*—The Protocols *and the Coming Superman* (Wichita, Kans., 1932), 19.

9. Mrs. Jim Craig to Representative Sol Bloom, March 25, 1941, and J. Edgar Hoover to Wendell Berge, April 20, 1943, Winrod file, FBI Reading Room, Washington, D.C. (hereafter FBI Winrod file). Most of the 20,000 pages in this file consist of copies of Winrod's publications. There are a few informative items, most of which I have cited in this piece. As is typical of FBI files, there are also many unsubstantiated rumors and factual errors. For instance, Director J. Edgar Hoover seems to have been informed that the Defenders of the Christian Faith was founded in 1936. "Re: Gerald B. Winrod" (n.d. but from early 1943), FBI file.

10. Gerald B. Winrod, *Hitler in Prophecy* (Wichita, Kans., 1933); J. Edgar Hoover to [redacted], July 19, 1943, FBI Winrod file.

11. Wendell Berge, memorandum for J. Edgar Hoover, April 15, 1943; Hoover to [redacted], July 19, 1943, FBI Winrod file.

12. Franklin D. Roosevelt to William Allen White, June 8, 1938, PSF 194, Franklin D. Roosevelt Library, Hyde Park, N.Y.

13. Kansas Friends of Democracy, *What's Wrong with Winrod?* (Kansas City, Kans., [1938]).

14. J. Edgar Hoover to L. M. C. Smith, March 27, 1941; Melvin Purvis to J. Edgar Hoover, September 18, 1940, FBI Winrod file.

15. Memorandum Laboratory Report, December 27, 1943, FBI Winrod file.

Chapter 19. John Steuart Curry: A Portrait of the Artist as a Kansan

1. "Curry of Kansas," *Life* (November 23, 1936): 28; "The Curry Murals," n.d., Paul Jones Papers, Coronado-Quivira Museum, Lyons, Kans.; *Kansas City Times,* December 7, 1931; Calder Pickett, "John Steuart Curry and the Topeka Murals Controversy," in *John Steuart Curry: A Retrospective Exhibition* (Lawrence, Kans., 1970), 37; *Kansas City Journal-Post,* December 13, 1931; *Kansas City Times,* December 7, 1931.

2. Kansas Senate Resolution 1809, January 24, 1992; Don Lambert, "Remembering John Steuart Curry," *Kansas!* no. 4 (1992): 6–7.

3. Laurence Schmeckebier, "Factual Romanticism and John Steuart Curry," in *An Exhibition of Work by John Steuart Curry* (Madison, Wis., 1937).

4. Jennie Small Owen, "Kansas Folks Worth Knowing: John Steuart Curry," *Kansas Teacher* 46 (March 1938): 34; Edward Alden Jewell, "Corcoran Gallery's 11th Exhibition," *New York Times,* November 4, 1928; Laurence Schmeckebier, *John Steuart Curry's Pageant of America* (New York, 1943), 61; Edward Alden Jewell, "Kansas Has Found Her Homer," *New York Times,* December 7, 1930.

5. Mrs. Henry J. Allen to William Allen White, December 16, 1931, microfilm roll 2743, John Steuart Curry Papers, Archives of American Art, Smithsonian Institution, Washington, D.C. (hereafter Curry Papers).

6. John Steuart Curry to Maynard Walker, August 1, [1932], Maynard Walker Papers, Garnett Public Library, Garnett, Kans. (hereafter Walker Papers); Thomas Hart Benton, quoted in M. Sue Kendall, *Rethinking Regionalism: John Steuart Curry and the Kansas Mural Controversy* (Washington, D.C., 1986), 26.

7. Kendall, *Rethinking Regionalism,* 37; "To John Curry," manuscript, roll 164, Curry Papers.

8. "Curry of Kansas," 28.

9. "Kansas Senators Take Potshots at Curry Murals in Statehouse," *Kansas City Times,* April 1, 1941.

10. Marguerite Stevenson to Maynard Walker, October 8, 1950, Walker Papers.

11. "An Interview with Mrs. John Steuart Curry," in *John Steuart Curry: A Retrospective Exhibition,* 10.

12. *Brooklyn Eagle,* December 7, 1930.

13. Schmeckebier, *John Steuart Curry's Pageant,* 10; Conwell Carlson, "Curry and Kansas," *Kansas City Star,* August 22, 1937 (on Curry's time in Arizona); "Interview with Mrs. John Steuart Curry," 8; Schmeckebier, "Factual Romanticism"; Margaret Curry to John Steuart Curry, February 3, 1938, reel 164, Curry Papers; "Address at the Agricultural College, February 24, 1937," typescript, roll 165, Curry Papers; "The Wisconsin Union Dining Service," roll 2748, Curry Papers; Jewell, "Kansas Has Found Her Homer."

14. *New York Herald Tribune,* November 23, 1930; John Steuart Curry to Margrit Varga, February 28, 1942, roll 166, Curry Papers; Jewell, "Corcoran Gallery's 11th Exhibition."

15. "Interview with Mrs. John Steuart Curry," 8; Margaret Curry to Clara Curry, May 2, [1930], roll 164, Curry Papers; Henry Adams, "Space, Weather, Myth, and Abstraction in the Art of John Steuart Curry," in *John Steuart Curry: Inventing the Middle West,* ed. Patricia Junker (New York, 1998), 122–123.

16. Benton, quoted in Kendall, *Rethinking Regionalism,* 26.

17. Thomas Craven, *Modern Art* (New York, 1940), 253; Robert Sanford, "Painter-Poet Who Became an Art Critic," *St. Louis Post-Dispatch,* n.d., Vertical File, KSHS.

18. Craven, *Modern Art,* 260; Thomas Craven, ed., *A Treasury of Art Masterpieces* (New York, 1939), 12; Craven, *Modern Art,* xx, 270–271; Craven, quoted in "Colored Litter," *Art Digest* (June 1, 1936): 42.

19. Review of Thomas Craven, *A Treasury of American Prints, Kansas City Star,* September 2, 1939; Craven, *Modern Art,* 329, 325; Thomas Craven, "John Steuart Curry," *A Loan Exhibition of Drawings and Paintings by John Steuart Curry* (Chicago, n.d.), 6, 8, 9.

20. Thomas Craven to John Steuart Curry, January 27, 1935, AAA, Roll 166, Curry Papers; Thomas Craven, "Kansas Refuses Curry," *Kansas Magazine* (1937): 86.

21. "Craven on the Moderns," *Time,* May 14, 1934: 52; Craven, "John Steuart Curry," 5.

22. Maynard Walker to John Steuart Curry, September 29, 1935, roll 2746, Curry Papers; Maynard Walker to Porter Butts, April 13, 1936, roll 167, Curry Papers; Maynard Walker, "John Steuart Curry," *Kansas Magazine* (1947): 73.

23. Maynard Walker to John Steuart Curry, November 1, 1937, roll 167, Curry Papers; Maynard Walker to Jack Harris, June 17, 1937, Curry Papers; Maynard Walker to Arthur Capper, March 14, 1931, roll 166, Curry Papers; James Dennis, *Renegade Regionalists* (Madison, Wis., 1998), 59; Maynard Walker, "Notes on John Steuart Curry," *A Selected Group of Work by John Steuart Curry* (College Art Association, 1937); Maynard Walker, quoted in "Mid-West is Producing an Indigenous Art," *Art Digest* (September 1, 1933): 10.

24. Walker, "John Steuart Curry," 72.

Chapter 20. R. H. Garvey: "Operations Are Interesting"

1. For Garvey's life, see Olive White Garvey, with Virgil Quinlisk, *The Obstacle Race: The Story of Ray Hugh Garvey* (San Antonio, Tex., 1970); Craig Miner, *Harvesting the High Plains: John Kriss & the Business of Wheat Farming, 1920–1930* (Lawrence, Kans., 1998); Miner, "The Wheat Empire of R. H. Garvey, 1930–1959," *Kansas History* 23 (Spring/Summer 2000): 88–99. The author probably met R. H. Garvey as a child and knew his wife, Olive, and son Willard long and well.

2. Olive Garvey interview by author, spring 1989; interviews with John Kriss when he was ninety were the documentation for the description of the trip in Miner, *Harvesting the High Plains,* 148–149; W. A. White to R. H. Garvey, December 8, 1941, box 14, Garvey Papers, KSHS (hereafter Garvey Papers).

3. *Kansas City Star,* February 1, 1959, clipping, box 36, Garvey Papers; R. H. Garvey to George Anderson, April 3, 1959, box 35, Garvey Papers.

4. Garvey, *Obstacle Race,* 34; C. Joseph Pusateri, *A History of American Business* (Arlington Heights, Ill., 1984), 5–16. Unless otherwise cited, the information on Garvey's early career comes from *Obstacle Race.* The author also had the benefit of interviews with Olive Garvey and access to her scrapbooks.

5. R. H. Garvey to W. D. Ferguson, March 20, 1930, box 1, Garvey Papers.

6. R. H. Garvey to W. D. Ferguson, January 5, 1934, box 6, Garvey Papers.

7. R. H. Garvey to W. D. Ferguson, March 25, 1930, box 1, Garvey Papers.

8. R. H. Garvey to Directors of Mutual Farming Company, December 6, 1931, box 3; R. H. Garvey to International Harvester, December 23, 1931, box 3; R. H. Garvey to Margaret Baker, June 2, 1931, box 2; R. H. Garvey to W. D. Ferguson, March 20, 1930, Garvey Papers. Miner, *Harvesting the High Plains,* 67; *Hays Daily News,* October 7, 1936.

9. R. H. Garvey to Stockholders and Directors, Mutual Farming, December 16, 1931, box 3; R. H. Garvey to Kenneth Crumly, April 19, 1930, box 1, Garvey Papers.

10. R. H. Garvey to W. D. Ferguson, March 11, 1932, box 4; R. H. Garvey to Service Oil agents, January 3, 1933, box 5, Garvey Papers. See also R. H. Garvey to Kenneth Crumly, December 5, 1930, and June 3, 1932, box 1, Garvey Papers.

11. R. H. Garvey to L. P. Harrison, January 15, 1931, box 3, Garvey Papers.

12. R. H. Garvey to Kenneth Crumly, June 14, 1930, box 1, Garvey Papers; Miner, *Harvesting the High Plains,* 76–78.

13. R. H. Garvey to Fred Seaton, May 21, 1937, box 32, Garvey Papers; Miner, *Harvesting the High Plains,* 79–94.

14. *Time,* June 8, 1959, clipping, box 36, and *Chicago Daily News,* February 11, 1954, clipping, box 27, Garvey Papers.

15. R. H. Garvey to Kenneth Crumly, March 8, 1930, April 19, 1930, June 24, November 5, and December 9, 1930, box 1; R. H. Garvey to Ralph Pivnoka, April 9, 1930, box 2; R. H. Garvey to Biggs & Harper, March 19, 1930, box 1; R. H. Garvey to W. D. Ferguson, February 20, 1931, box 2; W. D. Ferguson to R. H. Garvey, August 20, 1932, and R. H. Garvey to W. D. Ferguson, August 22, 1932, box 1, Garvey Papers.

16. For example, see R. H. Garvey to Kenneth Crumly, July 29, 1930, and June 27, 1930, box 1; R. H. Garvey to Kenneth Crumly, September 10, 1931, box 2; Kenneth Crumly to R. H. Garvey, October 12, 1937, box 7; R. H. Garvey to W. D. Ferguson, September 2, 1930, box 1, Garvey Papers.

17. R. H. Garvey to W. D. Ferguson, June 21, 1935, box 7, and June 22, 1937, box 9; W. D. Ferguson to R. H. Garvey, March 13, 1932, box 6; income tax returns, box 9; R. H. Garvey to W. D. Ferguson, July 14, 1937, box 9; R. H. Garvey to Kenneth Crumly, July 17, 1937, box 7, and April 25, 1935, box 6, Garvey Papers.

18. R. H. Garvey to Glenn Crumly, June 26, 1937, box 9; income tax return, 1938, box 11; R. H. Garvey to W. D. Ferguson, September 8, 1938, box 9; R. H. Garvey to O. S. Hitchner, January 28, 1939, box 10, Garvey Papers.

19. R. H. Garvey to Glenn Crumly, June 26, 1937, box 9; R. H. Garvey to Kenneth Crumly, September 13, 1935, box 6, and March 19, June 16, 17, 1937, box 7, Garvey Papers.

20. R. H. Garvey to W. D. Ferguson, June 5, 1940, box 12; R. H. Garvey to Ruth Hanna McCormick Simms, August 25, 1940, box 13; R. H. Garvey to Thomas Dewey, May 18, 1940, box 12; R. H. Garvey to John Kriss, October 30, 1941, box 14; R. H. Garvey to Charles Lindberg, December 11, 1941, box 14, Garvey Papers.

21. Miner, *Harvesting the High Plains,* 138–177. R. H. Garvey to H. C. Wear, May 1, 1943, box 18; Garvey Land Company to Harry Smith, October 26, 1935, box 7; Garvey Land Company to Van Vliet, October 30, 1935, box 7; R. H. Garvey to Gasoline Rationing Board, August 17, 1943, box 16, Garvey Papers.

22. Miner, *Harvesting the High Plains,* 158; R. H. Garvey to Elliott White, February 20, 1941, box 13, Garvey Papers.

23. W. D. Ferguson to R. H. Garvey, April 21, 1941, box 13; R. H. Garvey to W. D. Ferguson, April 19, 1941, box 13, Garvey Papers. Craig Miner, *Wichita: The Magic City: An Illustrated History* (Wichita, Kans., 1988), 183–198; Patrick O'Brien, "Kansas at War: The Home Front, 1941–1945," *Kansas History* 17 (Spring 1994): 6–25.

24. From interviews of Willard W. Garvey with author. R. H. Garvey to W. D. Ferguson, April 25, 1941, box 13, Garvey Papers; for examples of Garvey's objections to government rules, see R. H. Garvey to Leon Henderson, March 7, 1942, box 15, and R. H. Garvey to G. P. Uttley, May 18, 1943, box 18, Garvey Papers. Garvey, *Obstacle Race,* 123–124.

25. Garvey, *Obstacle Race,* 173, 176; Wayne Broehl, *Cargill: Trading the World's Grain* (Hanover, N.H., 1992), 738, 832; R. H. Garvey to H. B. Fink, March 9, 1959, box 35; *Wichita Eagle,* September 14, 1958, clipping, box 33; *Southwestern Miller,*

December 9, 1959, clipping, box 34; H. Bernerd Fink to family, October 22, 1958, box 33; *Kansas City Star,* February 1, 1959, clipping, box 36, Garvey Papers.

26. R. H. Garvey to Mr. and Mrs. R. L. Cochener, May 6, 1947, box 22; a list of Garvey's business interests in 1951 is found in R. H. Garvey to Willard, James, Dick, et al., April 3, 1951, box 24, Garvey Papers. Interview, Willard Garvey with author, October 7, 1993. He listed seventeen major businesses in which the family was involved and about $10 million in debt.

27. Interviews, Willard Garvey with author, October 7, 1993, January 6 and February 24, 1994. Garvey, *Obstacle Race,* 125, 175.

28. *Topeka Capital Journal,* March 7, 1958, clipping, box 33; R. H. Garvey to Harold Brandoli, April 27, 1957, box 32; and R. H. Garvey to David Neiswanger, March 6, 1951, box 25, Garvey Papers. Garvey, *Obstacle Race,* 137.

29. *Southwestern Miller,* December 9, 1959, copy, box 34; R. H. Garvey to Marvin McLain, March 31, 1954, box 27; R. H. Garvey to Wendell Beecraft, July 24, 1954, box 27, Garvey Papers.

30. R. H. Garvey to H. C. Wear, February 16, 1959, box 36, Garvey Papers.

31. R. H. Garvey to children and grandchildren, November 2, 1953, box 26; Muggs to James Garvey, July 1, 1953, box 26, Garvey Papers.

32. *Kansas City Star,* February 1, 1959, clipping, box 36; R. H. Garvey to family members, December 9, 1957, box 32, Garvey Papers.

Chapter 21. Esther Brown: In Pursuit of Human Rights and Social Justice

1. *Call,* Kansas City, Missouri, May 20, 1954; *Kansas City Star,* May 18, 1954; Hugh W. Speer, interview by author, September 15, 1990.

2. See Richard Kluger, *Simple Justice: The History of* Brown v. Board of Education *and Black America's Struggle for Equality* (New York, 1976); Hugh W. Speer, *The Case of the Century: A Historical and Social Perspective on* Brown v. Board of Education of Topeka (Kansas City, Mo., 1968); Milton S. Katz and Susan B. Tucker, "A Pioneer in Civil Rights: Esther Brown and the South Park Desegregation Case of 1948," *Kansas History* 18 (Winter 1995–1996): 235–247.

3. Esther Brown, interview by Susan B. Tucker, March 15, 1970; Ben Swirk, interview by Susan B. Tucker, August 13, 1974, Esther Brown Manuscript Collection, private collection, Susan B. Tucker, New York (hereafter Brown Collection).

4. Esther Brown interview; Paul Brown, interview by author, October 15, 1990; Federal Works Agency, Works Progress Administration, Division of Investigation, Chicago, January 14, 1941, Esther Elizabeth Swirk, case no. 2-MO-451, Brown Collection.

5. Barbara Rein, "The Black Community of South Park, Merriam, Kansas: A Part of the Whole," *Student Papers in Local History,* Johnson County Community College (1986), 147; "Hidden Histories: Cultural Diversity in Johnson County," *Johnson County Museums Album* 8 (Winter 1995): 1, 4; Franklin Williams and Earl Fultz, "The Merriam School Fight," *Crisis* 56 (May 1949): 140–141; Kluger, *Simple Justice,* 389.

6. Testimony of Alfonso Webb and Helen Swan, Transcript of Commissioner's Investigation, September 22–23, 1948, Kansas Supreme Court, *Webb v. School District No. 90,* case file 37,427, Records of the Kansas Supreme Court, KSHS; Esther Brown inter-

view; Esther Brown to Franklin Williams, August 30, 1948, and unsigned letter to Ted O. Thackeray, August 24, 1949, Brown Collection; Mildred B. Sharp to Glouster Current, January 9, 1948, and Edna Hill to Glouster Current, January 14, 1948, Merriam, Kansas, 1945–1955, Kansas NAACP Branch Office files (microfilm 1392), KSHS; Williams and Fultz, "The Merriam School Fight," *Crisis* (May 1949): 140, 141, 156.

7. Esther Brown interview; Brown to Williams and unsigned letter to Thackeray; Kluger, *Simple Justice,* 389; Williams and Fultz, "The Merriam School Fight," 141; Webb and Swan testimony; Motion for Writ of Mandamus, May 25, 1948, *Webb v. School District No. 90; Webb v. School District* 167 Kan. 395, 397 (1949).

8. "Motion to Advance Cause of Hearing," July 2, 1948, *Webb v. School District No. 90;* Esther Brown to Charles Howard, July 13, 1948, and Alfonso Webb and Mildred Sharp to William Towers, August 11, 1948, Brown Collection.

9. *Call,* September 24, 1948; *Plaindealer,* September 10, 1948.

10. Esther Brown interview; Alfonso and Mary Webb, interview by Susan B. Tucker, August 6, 1985; Hazel Weddington, interview by Susan B. Tucker, August 8, 1989, Brown Collection.

11. "Expenditures and Income in the South Park Case, Merriam, Kansas Branch NAACP, April 1948 until May 1949"; Esther Brown to Franklin Williams, December 16, 1948; Franklin Williams to Esther Brown, December 22, 1948, Brown Collection.

12. Edna Patterson to Esther Brown, May 26, 1949; H. C. Burnpass to Esther Brown, June 2, 1949; Esther Brown interview; Paul Brown interview; Federal Bureau of Investigation file on Mrs. Esther Elizabeth Brown, Kansas City, February 21, 1949, July 13, 1949, April 28, 1950, and February 8, 1951, file no. 100-1372, and Little Rock, April 7, 1949, file no. 100-2434, Brown Collection; Kluger, *Simple Justice,* 390; *Call,* April 29, 1949.

13. *Webb v. School District No. 90,* 167 Kan. 395, 397 (1949).

14. *Plaindealer,* June 17, 1949; *Call,* June 17, 1949.

15. Alfonso and Mary Webb interview; *Kansas City Star,* May 13, 1970; Franklin Williams, "Merriam, Kansas: Since the Parents Fought," *Crisis* (December 1949): 370–371, 423, 425; *Call,* September 16, 1949; Esther Brown to Charles Rutherford, September 30, 1949, Brown Collection.

16. Lucinda Todd, interview by Susan B. Tucker, August 15, 1990; Esther Brown interview; Robert Carter, interview by Susan B. Tucker, May 13, 1982; Jack Greenberg, interview by Susan B. Tucker, May 17, 1982, Brown Collection.

17. Esther Brown interview; Sidney Lawrence, "Eulogy for Esther Brown," May 26, 1970, Brown Collection.

18. *Kansas Commission against Discrimination in Employment,* House Joint Resolution No. 1, 1949; *Kansas Commission against Discrimination in Employment, Report,* 2 (1951). "Kansas Groups Form Organization on Civil Rights," *Topeka Capitol,* April 25, 1949; Joseph P. Doherty, *Civil Rights in Kansas: Past, Present and Future* (Topeka, Kans., 1972), 12–14.

19. HB No. 259 (1951 Sess.). Esther Brown to Walter White, April 3, 1951, Brown Collection; HB No. 388 (1953 Sess.).

20. "Panel of Americans Reaps Harvest of Understanding," *Kansas City Jewish Chronicle,* January 15, 1965; Ann Jacobson, interview by Susan B. Tucker, April 15, 1977, Brown Collection; Shirley Morantz, interview by the author, April 12, 1991; Esther Brown interview.

21. Corinne M. Bessmer, "The Panel of American Women: A Study of Social-Psychological Conflict," unpublished manuscript, 1970, 2, 3.

22. Samm Sinclair Baker, "Panel of American Women," *Ladies' Home Journal* (January 1965): reprint, 1, 2; Lois Mark Salvey, "The Panel of American Women," Part 1, *Woman's Day* (March 1968): reprint, 1–4, and Part 2 (June 1969): reprint, 1–6; "Panel of American Women Fights Prejudice in 75 Cities," *Kansas City Star,* May 10, 1970.

23. Esther Brown to Participants of Panels of American Women, April 19, 1968, Brown Collection; Bessmer, "The Panel of American Women," 3.

24. Baker, "Panel of American Women," 2; Esther Brown interview.

25. "Introduction to the first Esther Brown Memorial Lecture," 1970; Louise Bryant, interview by Susan B. Tucker, October 15, 1985; Homer Wadsworth, interview by Susan B. Tucker, November 16, 1978, Brown Collection.

26. Thorpe Menn, *Kansas City Times,* May 26, 1970; *Call,* May 28, 1970.

27. *Kansas City Star,* August 24, 1975; *Washington Post,* August 17, 1976.

Chapter 22. Dwight D. Eisenhower: His Legacy in World Affairs

1. Strobe Talbott, "Shutting the Cold War Down," review of Jack F. Matlock Jr., *Reagan and Gorbachev: How the Cold War Ended, New York Times Book Review* (August 1, 2004): 7; National Commission on Terrorist Attacks upon the United States, *The 9/11 Commission Report: Final Report of the National Commission on Terrorist Attacks upon the United States* (New York, 2004), 361–398. Historian Fareed Zakaria, in commenting on the report, praised the Eisenhower administration's long-term and multifaceted, fiscally sustainable approach. Fareed Zakaria, "It's More Than a War," *Newsweek* (August 2, 2004): 2.

2. William B. Pickett, *Dwight David Eisenhower and American Power* (Wheeling, Ill., 1995), 136–138, 170; George F. Kennan, *At a Century's Ending: Reflections, 1982–1995* (New York, 1996), 185; William B. Pickett, "New Look or Containment? George F. Kennan and the Making of Republican National Security Strategy," paper presented at the Kennan Centennial Conference, February 20, 2004, Princeton University, Princeton, N.J.

3. Pickett, *Dwight David Eisenhower,* 1–2; Geoffrey Perret, *Eisenhower* (New York, 1999), 9, 10, 16. Ike's mother called him by his middle name, Dwight, to avoid confusion with his father (a practice that stuck until it became Dwight David Eisenhower).

4. Transcript of interview, Dwight D. Eisenhower and A. Ross Wollen, November 27, 1964, DDE Post-Presidential Papers, 1965 Signature File, box 7, file: PR3 Interview; Ann Whitman diary of conversation with DDE, box 2, file: Eisenhower Writings, 1952 (3); Bela Kornitzer interview, December 1, 1953, box 2, Documents (1), Whitman Papers, Eisenhower Library, Abilene, Kansas; Perret, *Eisenhower,* 17.

5. Whitman diary of conversation with DDE, Whitman Papers; Pickett, *Dwight David Eisenhower,* 3, 5; Perret, *Eisenhower,* 11.

6. Ann Whitman to Mr. Allen, September 23, 1959, box 1, file: correspondence, A–D, Eisenhower Library, pp. 8–8A; Ann Whitman memorandum, July 5, 1955, box 1, correspondence, Eisenhower, DD (2), Whitman Papers; Pickett, *Dwight David Eisenhower,* 6.

7. Pickett, *Dwight David Eisenhower*, 15–16, 24–27, 30.

8. Rick Atkinson, *An Army at Dawn: The War in North Africa, 1942–1943* (New York, 2002), 3–4; Williamson Murray and Allan R. Millet, *A War to Be Won: Fighting the Second World War* (Cambridge, Mass., 2000), 443–445. Eisenhower's response to the critics is contained in Dwight D. Eisenhower to Lord Ismay, December 3, 1960, box 2, file: Eisenhower Writings, Letters (1), Whitman Papers.

9. Eisenhower to Ismay, December 3, 1960; Stephen E. Ambrose, *Eisenhower*, vol. I: *Soldier, General of the Army, President-Elect 1890–1952* (New York, 1983), 382.

10. Dwight D. Eisenhower, "Crusade for Peace," DDE Post-Presidential Papers, 1965 Principal File, box 16, file: PU-1 Publications Accepted, Eisenhower Library; Ambrose, *Eisenhower*, vol. 1, 309; Murray and Millet, *A War to Be Won*, 444–445.

11. Transcript of interview, Eisenhower and Wollen; Fred I. Greenstein and Richard H. Immerman, "Effective National Security Advising: Recovering the Eisenhower Legacy," *Political Science Quarterly* 115 (November 3, 2000): 342; James Surowiecki, *The Wisdom of Crowds: Why the Many Are Smarter Than the Few and How Collective Wisdom Shapes Business, Economies, Societies, and Nations* (New York, 2004), 32; Pickett, "New Look or Containment?," 11.

12. Ambrose, *Eisenhower*, vol. 1, 333; Murray and Millet, *A War to Be Won*, 444–445.

13. Pickett, *Dwight David Eisenhower*, 75; William B. Pickett, *Eisenhower Decides to Run: Presidential Politics and Cold War Strategy* (Chicago, 2000), 67–68.

14. Pickett, *Eisenhower Decides to Run*, 96–97, 118, 194–209.

15. Dwight D. Eisenhower conversation with Merriman Smith, 11-23-54, box 2, documents (2), pp. 1–3, Whitman Papers.

16. William B. Pickett, ed., *George F. Kennan and the Origins of Eisenhower's New Look: An Oral History of Project Solarium* (Princeton, N.J., 2004), 1–10.

17. Pickett, *Dwight David Eisenhower*, 106–107; John Lewis Gaddis, *We Now Know: Rethinking Cold War History* (New York, 1997), 108–109; Derek Leebaert, *The Fifty Year Wound: The True Price of America's Cold War Victory* (Boston, 2002), 147–148.

18. Howard Jones, *Crucible of Power: A History of American Foreign Relations from 1897* (Wilmington, Del., 2001), 288; Leebaert, *The Fifty Year Wound*, 148; Pickett, *Dwight David Eisenhower*, 121; Perret, *Eisenhower*, 454–455; *Reader's Companion to Military History*, "Korean War," http://college.hmco.com/history//readerscomp/mil/html/ml_027800_koreanwar2.htm.

19. Pickett, *Dwight David Eisenhower*, 111; Pickett, "General Andrew Jackson Goodpaster: Managing National Security," in *The Human Tradition in America since 1945*, ed. David L. Anderson (Wilmington, Del., 2003), 29, 32.

20. Perret, *Eisenhower*, 526–528; Joseph Persico, *Roosevelt's Secret War: FDR and World War II Espionage* (New York, 2001), 346, 364–365, 384–385, 405; William Taubman, *Khrushchev: The Man and His Era* (New York, 2003), 352; Pickett, *Dwight David Eisenhower*, 112.

21. Richard Rhodes, *Dark Sun: The Making of the Hydrogen Bomb* (New York, 1995), 563–565; Pickett, *Dwight David Eisenhower*, 136; Leebaert, *The Fifty Year Wound*, 244–245; Taubman, *Khrushchev*, 536. Any evaluation of Eisenhower's decision to undertake such a program at the risk of worsening U.S.-USSR relations must consider the extent to which the Soviets spied on the United States during and after World War II. See, for example, Arthur Herman, *Joseph McCarthy: Re-examining the Life and Legacy*

of America's Most Hated Senator (New York, 2000), 105–107; Perret, *Eisenhower,* 584; Christopher Andrew, *The Sword and the Shield: The Mitrokhin Archive and the Secret History of the KGB* (New York, 1999), 146–149, 164–165, 172, 177–178.

22. Perret, *Eisenhower,* 573; Campbell Craig, *Destroying the Village: Eisenhower and Thermonuclear War* (New York, 1998), 102–107; Taubman, *Khrushchev,* 439.

23. Memorandum of conversation: Dwight D. Eisenhower and Robert E. Matteson, November 24, 1964, Appendix A, DDE Post-Presidential Papers, 1965 Principal File, box 38, file: MAT, Eisenhower Library, 7; Taubman, *Khrushchev,* 454–457, 468.

24. Taubman, *Khrushchev,* 416, 352, 535; Craig, *Destroying the Village,* 105, 161–162.

25. Pickett, *Dwight David Eisenhower,* 120–121, 136, 171; Leebaert, *The Fifty Year Wound,* 227, 663, 241–243.

26. Stephen E. Ambrose, *Eisenhower,* vol. 2: *The President* (New York, 1983), 621.

Chapter 23. Gordon Parks and the Unending Quest for Self-fulfillment

1. Gordon Parks, *The Learning Tree* (New York, 1963).

2. Ibid., 20, 29, 60.

3. Ibid., 62; Gordon Parks, *A Choice of Weapons* (New York, 1966).

4. Parks, *Choice of Weapons,* xii.

5. Ibid., 194, 195.

6. Gordon Parks, *To Smile in Autumn* (New York, 1979), 24.

7. Parks, *Choice of Weapons,* 226, 227.

8. Parks, *To Smile in Autumn,* 24; Parks, *Choice of Weapons,* 231.

9. Parks, *Choice of Weapons,* 272.

10. Parks, *To Smile in Autumn,* 92; see also Gordon Parks, *Born Black* (Philadelphia, Pa., 1971).

11. Parks, *To Smile in Autumn,* 93.

12. Martin H. Bush, "A Conversation with Gordon Parks," in *The Photographs of Gordon Parks* (Wichita, Kans., 1983), 120.

13. Parks, *To Smile in Autumn,* 149.

14. Ibid., 216.

15. Stephen Spender, "Preface," Gordon Parks, *Gordon Parks: A Poet and His Camera* (New York, 1968).

16. Gordon Parks, *Arias in Silence* (Boston, 1994), foreword.

17. Philip B. Kunhardt Jr., "Introduction," Parks, *Gordon Parks.*

18. Gordon Parks, *Half-Past Autumn* (Boston, 1997), 13.

19. Ibid., 8.

Chapter 24. Vern Miller: Kansas' Supercop

1. Background information from Vern Miller, interview by author, February 5, 2004, and newspaper clippings (some unidentified) file, Vern Miller private collection, Wichita, Kans. (hereafter Miller clippings). Miller's unusual middle name was his grandmother's maiden name.

2. Bernie Ward, "National Police Officer of the Month, Sheriff Vern Miller, Sedgwick County, Kansas," *Master Detective,* October 1970.

3. "Here Comes Supercop," *Midway: The Sunday Magazine of Topeka Capital-Journal,* January 9, 1972.

4. "Wedding Bells May Not Ring," *Wichita Evening Eagle and Beacon,* September 7, 1961; "Marshal of Wichita Likes to Play Hood to Get Evidence," *Daily Oklahoman,* May 8, 1962; "Unpaid Fines Prove Costly," January 30, 1961; "Miller Rode in Trunk as Theft of Meat Set Up," July 25, 1970, Miller clippings.

5. "Here Comes Supercop"; "10 Arraigned on Liquor Charges Following Raids," *Wichita Evening Eagle and Beacon,* January 13, 1962; "Liquor Raid Tactics Hit by Sheriff," August 1, 1962, Miller clippings.

6. Ward, "National Police Officer of the Month."

7. "It's Almost Ballet as Sheriff Directs Traffic," January 27, 1967, Miller clippings; Ward, "National Police Officer of the Month."

8. Ward, "National Police Officer of the Month."

9. "McCarther Shot in Chase before Capture in Omaha," *Wichita Eagle,* July 28, 1965; "Paper Work to Delay Return of McCarther," *Wichita Beacon,* July 28, 1965; Miller clippings.

10. Ibid.

11. "A Bus Ticket to Limbo," *Front Page Detective,* October 1968.

12. "Attorney General's Race Eyed by Miller," *Wichita Beacon,* April 23, 1970; Miller interview.

13. Technically Kansas had never elected a Democrat; two Populist-Democrat fusion candidates were elected attorney general in the 1890s. "Lawman or Lawyer—Voters Must Decide," October 6, 1970; "Racial Tension at Heights High School Riot," September 18, 1970, Miller clippings.

14. *The Squire's Johnson County* 1, no. 1 (April 1972); "Seaton Baffled by Undecided Element," *Hutchinson News,* October 26, 1970; Richard Seaton, interview by author, April 14, 2004; Secretary of State, *State of Kansas Election Statistics, 1970* (Topeka, Kans., 1970), 30, 85.

15. "Here Comes Supercop"; "Lawrence Area Hit by Officers in Series of Early Raids," *Wichita Beacon,* February 26, 1971; "Drug Raiders Arrest 51 in Kansas Cities," June 2, 1971, Miller clippings.

16. "Vern's Objective 'To enforce all laws,'" *Kansas State Collegian,* March 19, 1991.

17. "Town's Not Wide Open Now: Miller," *Topeka State Journal,* October 4, 1971; Miller interview.

18. Miller interview.

19. John Frieden (longtime friend and adviser to Miller), interview by author, March 17, 2004; Secretary of State, *State of Kansas Election Statistics, 1972* (Topeka, Kans., 1972), 98.

20. "Malloy, Dick Docking Implicated," October 15, 1975, Miller clippings; Miller interview; "More Against D. Docking," *Wichita Beacon,* October 15, 1975.

21. Miller interview; Frieden interview.

22. Secretary of State, *State of Kansas Election Statistics, 1974* (Topeka, Kans., 1974), 78–79.

23. "Miller Predicted Defeat," *Wichita Eagle,* November 19, 1974; "Miller Ends His Public Career," *University Daily Kansan,* September 21, 1980.

24. "Miller Aims at Crime in D.A.'s Race," June 14, 1976, Miller clippings; "Miller Takes Aim at Sex Movies, Drugs," *Wichita Sun,* December 22, 1976.

25. "Miller Won Friends, Made Enemies with First-Year Campaign," *Wichita Eagle-Beacon,* January 22, 1978.

26. Ibid.; "Century II Rally on Obscenity Draws 2000," *Wichita Eagle,* March 1, 1977.

Chapter 25. Wes Jackson: Kansas Ecostar

1. "The View from 2090," *Life* 13 (Fall 1990): 114–115.

2. Wes Jackson, "The Age of the Ecostar," file "Biographical Information on Wes Jackson, founder and director of the Land Institute," box 1, Collection 777, Land Institute Collection, KSHS (hereafter Land Institute Collection); Wes Jackson, interview by author, Land Institute, Salina, Kansas, September 2, 2004.

3. "Biographical Sketch," file "Biographical Information," Land Institute Collection.

4. Wes Jackson to Ron Ellermeier, September 3, 1987, file 64, box 1, Land Institute Collection.

5. William G. Clugston, "Kansas the Essence of Typical America," *Current History* 25 (October 1926): 14–20.

6. Jackson interview.

7. Ibid.; Shawnee County, Soldier Township, Statistical Rolls, Kansas, 1936, Vol. 107, Kansas State Board of Agriculture, KSHS; Kansas Statistical Roll for 1946, R No. 5 N. Topeka, Kansas State Board of Agriculture, KSHS; "Why I Am an Environmentalist," file "Biographical Information," Land Institute Collection.

8. Jackson interview.

9. Ibid; "Biographical Sketch."

10. Mary Smith to Wes Jackson, n.d.; Wes Jackson to Mrs. Ben W. Smith, July 29, 1987, file 61, box 1, Land Institute Collection.

11. Jackson interview; "Biographical Sketch."

12. Wes Jackson, *Man and the Environment,* with foreword by Paul Ehrlich (Dubuque, Iowa, 1971), xv–xvi.

13. Jackson interview; "Biographical Sketch."

14. Ibid.; Wes Jackson, *New Roots for Agriculture,* new ed. with foreword by Wendell Berry (San Francisco, 1980; reprint, Lincoln, Nebr., 1985), vii–xv.

15. Jackson interview; Wes Jackson, *Becoming Native to This Place* (Lexington, Ky., 1994), 5.

16. Jackson, *New Roots for Agriculture,* 104–105, 133–135; "The Gospel According to Wes Jackson," *High Country News* (May 1, 1995): 13–14; Laura Jackson and C. L. Dewald, "Predicting Evolutionary Consequences of Greater Reproductive Effort in *Tripsacum dactyloides,* a Perennial Grass," *Ecology* 75 (1994): 627–641.

17. Jackson detailed his vision in chapter 9, titled "Outside the Solar Village: One Utopian Farm," in *New Roots for Agriculture,* 118–132.

18. See Jackson, *New Roots for Agriculture;* Jackson interview; "The Gospel According to Wes Jackson"; Robert Jensen, "Sustainability and Politics: An Interview with Wes Jackson," *Counterpunch* (July 10, 2003), http://www.counterpunch.org/jensen 07102003.html; Wes Jackson to Nick Brown, October 5, 1987, file 65, box 1, Land Institute Collection.

19. Wes Jackson, "Matfield Green," in *Rooted in the Land: Essays on Community and Place,* ed. William Vitek and Wes Jackson (New Haven, Conn., 1996), 95–103; already cited are *Man and the Environment; New Roots for Agriculture; Becoming Native to This Place;* and *Rooted in the Land.* For his criticism of modern thought, see his *Altars of Unhewn Stone: Science and the Earth* (San Francisco, 1987), especially 61–76. The sixth book, coedited with Wendell Berry and Bruce Colman, is *Meeting the Expectations of the Land: Essays in Sustainable Agriculture and Stewardship* (San Francisco, 1984).

20. Jackson interview; Wes Jackson, "The Land Institute: Summary Proposal to the Levison Foundation," file "Biographical Information," Land Institute Collection.

21. Jackson interview; Dana Jackson and Laura Jackson, *The Farm as Natural: Reconnecting Food Systems with Ecosystems* (Covelo, Calif., 2002).

22. Jackson interview; "The Gospel According to Wes Jackson"; Jim Hightower, *Hard Tomatoes, Hard Times: A Report of the Agribusiness Accountability Project on the Failure of America's Land Grant College Complex* (Rochester, Vt., 1978).

23. Wes Jackson to Wendell Berry, January 4, 1980, file 1; Wes Jackson to Wendell Berry, January 2, 1981, file 2; Wes Jackson to Nick Brown, October 5, 1987, file 65, box 1, Land Institute Collection.

24. Jackson to Berry, January 4, 1980.

Chapter 26. Robert J. Dole: Driven to Perform, Destined to Motivate

1. David Rogers, "Running Hard: Dole Senate Role Shapes His Presidential Campaign," *Wall Street Journal,* August 15, 1986, 1.

2. Richard Ben Cramer, *What It Takes* (New York, 1993), 132. Italics in original.

3. Rodgers, "Running Hard," 1.

4. Jake H. Thompson, *Bob Dole: The Republicans' Man for All Seasons* (New York, 1994), 45.

5. Some version of this story appears in all accounts of the Dole narrative; see, for example, Cramer, *What It Takes,* 238.

6. Thompson, *Bob Dole,* 45.

7. Bob and Elizabeth Dole, *Unlimited Partners* (New York, 1996), 103.

8. Secretary of State, *State of Kansas Election Statistics, 1960: Primary and General Elections* (Topeka, Kans., n.d.), 22, 66; ibid., *1962,* 18, 56; ibid., *1964,* 14, 60; ibid., *1966,* 18, 74; ibid., *1968,* 14, 79.

9. Thompson, *Bob Dole,* 115.

10. The Pew Research Center, "New Hampshire Voters Fault Candidates, Media, and TV Ads," February 2, 1996, http://people-press.org/reports/display.php3?Report ID=131. Thompson, *Bob Dole,* 100–103, has a fair-minded assessment of the campaign, Dole's impact, and the "Democrat wars" remark.

11. Thompson, *Bob Dole,* 88.

12. Dole and Dole, *Unlimited Partners,* 193.

13. Ibid., 195–196.

14. Gramm initially won election to the House as a Democrat (1978), later resigned and ran for the same seat as a Republican (1983), and ultimately won a Texas Senate seat as a Republican (1984). See *Biographical Dictionary of the United States Congress,* http://bioguide.congress.gov/.

15. Paul Light, *Still Artful Work: The Continuing Politics of Social Security Reform* (New York, 1995), 130.

16. Jeffrey H. Birnbaum and Alan S. Murray, *Showdown at Gucci Gulch* (New York, 1988), 223.

17. Address by Bob Dole, Leader's Lecture Series, Old Senate Chamber, U.S. Senate, March 28, 2000.

18. See Barbara Sinclair, *The Transformation of the U.S. Senate* (Baltimore, Md., 1989), along with numerous articles.

19. John J. Miller, "The Yuckster: Bob Dole, After Politics," *National Review,* April 30, 2001, 31.

20. See Thomas Mallon, "The Good Loser," *New York Times Magazine,* September 7, 1997, 50–53.

21. Dole memos, March 9, 1998, and undated (Oracle), Dole Institute archives, University of Kansas, Lawrence.

The Contributors

VIRGIL W. DEAN, a native Kansan who earned his Ph.D. in U.S. history at the University of Kansas, has been the editor of *Kansas History: A Journal of the Central Plains* at the Kansas State Historical Society since 1991. He has taught Kansas and U.S. history at the high school and college levels and has published numerous journal articles, book reviews, and encyclopedia entries. The University of Missouri Press published his book, *An Opportunity Lost: The Truman Administration and the Farm Policy Debate*, in 2006.

JONATHAN EARLE is associate professor of history at the University of Kansas and associate director for programming at the Robert J. Dole Institute of Politics. He earned his Ph.D. at Princeton and is the author of *Jacksonian Democracy and the Politics of Free Soil, 1824–1854* (University of North Carolina Press, 2004) and *John Brown's Raid: A Brief History in Documents* (Bedford/St. Martin's Press, 2008), among many other books and articles. Earle writes and lectures widely about the politics and culture of the antebellum United States.

REBECCA EDWARDS is associate professor of history at Vassar College, where she teaches nineteenth-century U.S. history. She is the author of *Angels in the Machinery: Gender in American Party Politics from the Civil War to the Progressive Era* and a narrative history of the late-nineteenth-century United States entitled *New Spirits: Americans and the World, 1865–1905* (Oxford University Press, 2006). She is now working on a biography of Mary Elizabeth Lease.

NICOLE ETCHESON is Alexander M. Bracken Professor of American History at Ball State University. She is the author of *The Emerging Midwest: Upland Southerners and the Political Culture of the Old Northwest, 1787–1861* (Indiana University Press, 1996) and *Bleeding Kansas: Contested Liberty in the*

Civil War Era (University Press of Kansas, 2004). She has written numerous articles on the political culture of the Midwest, as well as on the controversy in Kansas Territory, and is now at work on a book about the Union home front in Indiana during the Civil War.

PETER FEARON is professor of modern economic and social history at the University of Leicester. His academic field is U.S. history, with a special emphasis on the Great Depression and the New Deal. Fearon's main publications include *War, Prosperity and Depression: The U.S. Economy 1917–45* (University Press of Kansas, 1987); *Kansas in the Great Depression: Work Relief, the Dole, and Rehabilitation* (University of Missouri Press, 2008); and several articles on the impact of the Depression on the state of Kansas.

H. ROGER GRANT, who was recognized as Clemson University's Centennial Professor (2004–2006), is author of more than two dozen books, mostly in the field of transportation history. His latest books are *"Follow the Flag": A History of the Wabash Railroad Company* (Northern Illinois University Press, 2004); *The Railroad: The Life Story of a Technology* (Greenwood Press, 2005); *Rails Through the Wiregrass: A History of the Georgia and Florida Railroad* (Northern Illinois University Press, 2006); and *Visionary Railroader: Jervis Langdon, Jr. and the Transportation Revolution* (Indiana University Press, 2008). *Grant's Twilight Rails: The Final Era of Railroad Building in the Midwest* will be published by the University of Minnesota Press in the spring of 2010. He is presently writing a book-length study of the Georgia & Florida Railroad.

K. ALLEN GREINER, MD, MPH, is assistant professor of family medicine, preventive medicine and public health, and history and philosophy of medicine at the University of Kansas Medical Center. He is a practicing family physician, the Wyandotte County Health Department medical director, and the director of the Rural Primary Care Practice and Research Program and linked Kansas Physicians Engaged in Prevention Research Network. His research interests include the history of public health, the social determinants of health, and primary care health promotion.

SALLY F. GRIFFITH is a native of Lusk, Wyoming, where her father and grandfather published the local newspaper. She graduated from Radcliffe College and then returned to her roots when, as a graduate student at Johns Hopkins

University, she wrote her doctoral dissertation on William Allen White's journalistic career, published as *Home Town News: William Allen White and the Emporia Gazette* (Oxford University Press, 1989). After teaching at Grinnell, Vassar, and Villanova, Griffith published a history of the Historical Society of Pennsylvania and has recently completed a history of Franklin and Marshall College.

M. H. HOEFLICH, John H. & John M. Kane Professor of Law and former dean of the University of Kansas School of Law, holds degrees from Haverford College, Cambridge University, and Yale Law School. An internationally recognized authority on legal history, Roman law, and the history of the legal profession, Hoeflich is the author or editor of seven books, including *Roman and Civil Law and the Development of Anglo-American Jurisprudence in the Nineteenth Century* (University of Georgia Press, 1997), and more than seventy articles.

JIM HOY, professor of English and director of the Center for Great Plains Studies at Emporia State University, has studied and written about ranching folklife in the American West and in various other horse and cattle cultures. His numerous articles and books include *The Cattle Guard: Its History and Lore* (University Press of Kansas, 1982); *Cowboys and Kansas: Stories from the Tallgrass Prairie* (University of Oklahoma Press, 1995); with Lawrence Clayton and Jerald Underwood, *Vaqueros, Cowboys, and Buckaroos* (University of Texas Press, 2001); and *Flint Hills Cowboys: Tales of the Tallgrass Prairie* (University Press of Kansas, 2006).

THOMAS D. ISERN, a native Kansan who received his Ph.D. at Oklahoma State University, is professor of history at North Dakota State University, specializing in the history and folklore of the North American plains and the history of agriculture. His numerous articles and books include *Custom Combining on the Great Plains: A History* (University of Oklahoma Press, 1981); *Bull Threshers and Bindlestiffs: Harvesting and Threshing on the North American Plains* (University Press of Kansas, 1990); and *Dakota Circle: Excursions on the True Plains* (NDSU Institute for Regional Studies, 2000).

BRUCE R. KAHLER, who received his Ph.D. in history and American studies from Purdue University, is professor of history at Bethany College in Lindsborg, Kansas, where he has taught U.S. history and art history since 1988. He is the author of numerous articles, book reviews, encyclopedia entries, and op-ed columns for the *Salina Journal,* and he has served on the board of directors of the Kansas Humanities Council. His current project is a history of Civil War veterans in Kansas.

MILTON S. KATZ earned his Ph.D. at St. Louis University and is a professor of humanities and former chair of the Liberal Arts Department at the Kansas City Art Institute, where he has taught for over thirty years. He is the author of *Ban the Bomb: A History of SANE, the Committee for a Sane Nuclear Policy,* and over two dozen book chapters, articles, and reviews on peace and justice movements in contemporary American history.

BURDETT A. LOOMIS is professor of political science at the University of Kansas. From 1997 through 2001 he served as the interim director of the Robert J. Dole Institute for Public Service and Public Policy, and in 2005 he was Director of Communications for Governor Kathleen Sebelius. Loomis has written or edited more than twenty-five books in various editions, including *Time, Politics, and Policy: A Legislative Year,* which was set in the Kansas legislature, and *Kansas Pastoral: The Politics of Change, 1960–1975,* forthcoming from the University Press of Kansas.

SALLY M. MILLER earned a Ph.D. at the University of Toronto and is now professor emerita of history at the University of the Pacific, where she taught courses on the Progressive Era, labor history, and women's and immigration history. She is the author or editor of many papers and a dozen books, including *From Prairie to Prison: The Life of Social Activist Kate Richard O'Hare* (University of Missouri Press, 1993). Her honors and awards include Fulbright appointments to Finland and New Zealand and a one-year teaching appointment at the University of Warwick in England.

TIMOTHY MILLER, who received his Ph.D. in American Studies, is professor of religious studies at the University of Kansas and the author of *Following in His Steps: A Biography of Charles M. Sheldon* (University of Tennessee Press, 1987). Among his other books are *The Quest for Utopia in Twentieth-Century America, The 60s Communes,* and the edited volume *America's Alternative Religions.*

CRAIG MINER is Garvey Distinguished Professor of History at Wichita State University and the author of numerous books and articles, including *Harvesting the High Plains: John Kriss and the Business of Wheat Farming, 1920–1950* and *Kansas: The History of the Sunflower State, 1854–2000*. Among his most recent publications are *Seeding Civil War: Kansas in the National News, 1854–1858* and *Next Year Country: Dust to Dust in Western Kansas, 1890–1940*, a sequel to his 1986 book *West of Wichita: Settling the High Plains of Kansas, 1865–1890*.

BRIAN J. MOLINE, who chaired the three-member Kansas Corporation Commission from 2003 to 2007, received a juris doctor from Washburn University and a master's in public administration from the University of Kansas. He was an adjunct professor at Kansas University and Washburn Law School; the author of numerous articles on the history of law and lawyers and of *Regulation in Transition: Evolution of the State Corporation Commission*, a monograph about the KCC; and a member of the *Journal of the Kansas Bar Association*'s board of editors. Moline died unexpectedly in Topeka, Kansas, on September 29, 2008.

RITA G. NAPIER, associate professor of history at the University of Kansas, received her Ph.D. at American University; has authored studies in frontier history; and received several teaching honors, including H. Bernerd Fink Distinguished Teaching Award. She is the co-editor of *Kansas History*'s award-winning review essay series, the editor of *Kansas and the West: New Perspectives* (University Press of Kansas, 2004), and completing a book-length study of territorial Kansas.

KRISTEN TEGTMEIER OERTEL, assistant professor of history at Millsaps College in Jackson, Mississippi, earned her Ph.D. at the University of Texas at Austin. Her research has examined various aspects of Kansas Territory, and her book *Bleeding Borders: Gender, Race, and Violence in Pre–Civil War Kansas* was published by Louisiana State University Press in 2009. She is currently co-authoring a biography of Clarina I. H. Nichols, which is to be published by the University Press of Kansas in 2011.

WILLIAM B. PICKETT, professor of history at Rose-Hulman Institute of Technology, earned his doctorate at Indiana University and is the author of *Homer*

E. Capehart: A Senator's Life, Dwight David Eisenhower and American Power, and *Eisenhower's Decision to Run: Presidential Politics and Cold War Strategy.* He was an invited speaker at the George F. Kennan Centennial Conference at Princeton University in February 2004 and edited the conference monograph, *George F. Kennan and the Origins of Eisenhower's New Look: An Oral History of Project Solarium.*

LEO RIBUFFO, Society of the Cincinnati George Washington Distinguished Professor of History at George Washington University, is the author of *Right Center Left: Essays in American History* and *The Old Christian Right: The Protestant Far Right from the Great Depression to the Cold War,* which won the Organization of American History's Merle Curti Prize in 1985. His current project is a book titled *The Limits of Moderation: Jimmy Carter and the Ironies of American Liberalism,* which will interpret Jimmy Carter's presidency in broad social and cultural context.

NORMAN E. SAUL, professor of history and of Russian and East European Studies at the University of Kansas, specializes in Russian-American relations. In addition to several articles on the Volga Germans and Mennonites from the Russian Empire who settled in Kansas, his publications include *War and Revolution: The United States and Russia, 1914–1921; Concord and Conflict: The United States and Russia, 1867–1914; Distant Friends: The United States and Russia, 1763–1867; Friends or Foes? The United States and Soviet Russia, 1921–1941;* and *Historical Dictionary of United States–Russian/Soviet Relations.*

JAMES E. SHEROW is a native Kansan and professor of history at Kansas State University. He took his Ph.D. at the University of Colorado. Sherow's published work, which centers on environmental and Kansas history, includes *Watering the Valley: Development along the High Plains Arkansas River* (University Press of Kansas, 1990); *A Sense of the American West: An Anthology of Environmental History* (University of New Mexico Press, 1998); and *The Grasslands of the United States: An Environmental History* (ABC-Clio, 2007).

MARJORIE SWANN, Conger-Gabel Teaching Professor in the Department of English and director of the Museum Studies Program at the University of Kansas, studied at Oxford University and in 2002 won a W. T. Kemper Fellowship for Teaching Excellence. She is the author of articles on seventeenth-century English literature and material culture, as well as, with William Tsutsui, essays about art and artists in Kansas and the Great Plains. The University of Pennsylvania Press published Swann's book, *Curiosities and Texts: The Culture of Collecting in Early Modern England*, in 2001.

JOHN EDGAR TIDWELL, a native Kansan who received his Ph.D. at the University of Minnesota, is professor of English at the University of Kansas. He has published and lectured widely on aspects of African American literature. In 2007 his *Sterling A. Brown's A Negro Looks at the South; Writings of Frank Marshall Davis: A Voice of the Black Press*; and *Montage of Dream: The Art and Life of Langston Hughes* all appeared, in advance of *After Winter: The Art and Life of Sterling A. Brown* (2009).

WILLIAM M. TSUTSUI, professor of history and associate dean for international studies in the College of Liberal Arts and Sciences at the University of Kansas, is the author of *Manufacturing Ideology: Scientific Management in Twentieth-Century Japan; Banking Policy in Japan: American Efforts at Reform During the Occupation*; and *Godzilla on My Mind: Fifty Years of the King of Monsters* as well as numerous articles on Japanese economic and business history. His current projects include studies of the environmental impact of World War II on Japan and the globalization of Japanese popular culture.

Index